⌐

The Mind Is Mightier than the Sword

New Dharma Talks

MB

THE MIND IS MIGHTIER THAN THE SWORD

Enlightening the Mind, Opening the Heart

New Dharma Talks by

LAMA SURYA DAS

DOUBLEDAY

New York   London   Toronto   Sydney   Auckland

DD

DOUBLEDAY

Grateful acknowledgment is made to the following for permission to reprint
previously published material:

Alfred A. Knopf: Excerpt from "The Snow Man" from *The Collected Poems of
Wallace Stevens* by Wallace Stevens, copyright © 1954 by Wallace Stevens and
renewed 1982 by Holly Stevens. Reprinted by permission of Alfred A. Knopf,
a division of Random House, Inc.

Harvard University Press: "Some keep the Sabbath going to church" from
The Poems of Emily Dickinson: Reading Edition, edited by Ralph W. Franklin
(Cambridge, Mass: The Belknap Press of Harvard University Press),
copyright © 1998, 1999 by the President and the Fellows of Harvard College,
copyright © 1951, 1955, 1979, 1983 by the President and Fellows of Harvard
College. Reprinted by permission of the publishers and the Trustees of
Amherst College.

University of Illinois Press: "Lost" from *Traveling Light: Collected and
New Poems* by David Wagoner, copyright © 1999 by David Wagoner.
Reprinted by permission of the poet and the University of Illinois Press.

Library of Congress Cataloging-in-Publication Data is available upon request.

ISBN 978-0-7679-1864-0

Printed in the United States of America

Design by Elizabeth Rendfleisch

10   9   8   7   6   5   4   3   2   1

First Edition

CONTENTS

ACKNOWLEDGMENTS

It takes a sangha community to produce a Dharma talk, especially when using modern technology. I want to gratefully acknowledge the help of those who have generously contributed their time, energy, and expertise to this process over the last few years.

Thank you to Bob Hildebrand, the original editor of some early Dharma talks published privately by our Dzogchen Foundation ten years ago, and to Roz Stark for untiringly transcribing many talks. Much gratitude to Susan Burgraff and Julie Barker for research and edits; Ron Goldman for tape recording; Paul Crafts, Christopher Coriat, and Leah Weiss Eckstrom for many vital suggestions; and Joseph Goldstein, Sharon Salzberg, and Lew Richmond for friendship and advice. Hal Ross did a wonderful job early on in editing these Dharma talks, and Leslie McClain and Jill Stockwell did major work on the final version. And many thanks to my publisher, Random House, and to my editor there, Trace Murphy, and assistant editor Darya Porat for their enthusiasm about this book. My ever-helpful literary agent, Susan Lee Cohen, helped bring it out of the filing cabinet, and my Dharma teacher colleagues help remind me to just keep at it.

These new Dharma talks are dedicated to my students, who continue to ask great questions, make me rethink traditional concepts, and draw living Dharma out of me. May all their sterling prayers and aspirations be fulfilled!

the mind is mightier than the sword

new dharma talks

LIVING DHARMA

OLD WINE IN NEW BOTTLES

buddhist wisdom or teaching is called Dharma. *Dharma* means truth, cosmic law, religion, spirituality, as well as morality, duty, and reality. Etymologically, it is derived from a word meaning "that which carries or upholds," bears up, and sustains us, embracing us like the earth. Dharma is our very ground, the ground of being and existence. Dharma also means good medicine: that which heals what ails us, relieving suffering and confusion. How we need such healing during these violent, troubled times! To benefit others and help alleviate spiritual hunger today, in conjunction with the requests of my students, these new Dharma talks from the last decade have been transcribed, lightly edited, and offered here in print.

To me, the Dharma is like a splendid spiritual jewel, radiant with wisdom, love, peace, joy, meaning, and a multitude of other blessings and benefits. There are many kinds of Dharma—or spirituality and religion—in the world. And there is worldly wisdom and knowledge, which is a kind of Dharma, too, because it helps us live better and flourish. Buddha Dharma is what we Buddhists call noble Dharma, sublime Dharma, liberating Dharma—for it emancipates and frees us from illusion, suffering, and confusion. And it brings about inner freedom and total enlightenment, the ultimate accomplishment of our deepest, truest aspirations and greatest possibilities. Noble Dharma is the panacean, elixir-like gift that keeps on giving, not unlike that wish-fulfilling secret water Jesus offered that is said to slake thirst eternally.

There is a great spiritual hunger today amid the fears, uncertainties, and dangers of our time. Traditional religions, with their various limitations and often inflexible, anachronistic doctrines, seem incapable of genuinely addressing it. As Patrul Rinpoche, the enlightened vagabond of Kham, eastern Tibet, sang more than one hundred years ago in his renowned *Advice to Myself*: "For ages now you've been beguiled, entranced, and fooled by appearances. Are you aware of that? Are you? Right this very instant, when you're under the spell of mistaken perception, you've got to watch out. Don't let yourself get carried away by this fake and empty life." It is liberation from the illusions, confusion, dissatisfaction, and suffering of this inauthentic life that Dharma delivers to us. Would you like to know the true secret of spiritual living? *You are.* It is your authentic life which can save you, would you only find and genuinely live it.

Many of us are looking deeper for satisfaction, fulfillment, and well-being, for authenticity and meaningful spiritual connection after discovering the defects and limitations of worldliness, the fleeting nature of sense pleasure and material success, and the disappointing fact that selfish egotism, materialism, and scientific and technological progress still leave us wanting. For such reasons, Tibet's great yogi Milarepa went alone into the Himalayan wilderness long ago, becoming fully enlightened through assiduous meditation, yoga, and faithful devotion. It is said that his unshakable resolve and diligence is part of the powerful current still turning the life-giving waterwheel that is the spirit of living Dharma. Following in the footsteps of the masters of old, the siddhas (enlightened adepts) of ancient India—such as Saraha, Nagarjuna, Tilopa, and Naropa—Mila sang hundreds and thousands of extemporaneous enlightenment songs (dohas) outside his Himalayan cave, delighting the dakinis, angels, local gods and goddesses, nature sprites, and animals with his wise and melodious teachings. Later, these spontaneous songs of yogi delight were memorized by his disciples, and eventually written down, comprising one of the world's literary classics, *The Hundred Thousand Songs of Milarepa.*

In ancient China, the hermitlike vagabond Han Shan inscribed his Zen poems on the rocks and trees of Cold Mountain; other crazy-wise and carefree mystics folded their spontaneous songs of awakening into the shape of paper boats and set them to sail on river waters. Zen masters produced innumerable songs and even death poems (parting words) redolent of inconceivable wisdom. The wandering Zen-man Basho simplified his joy of authentic being in the world's shortest verse form, the seventeen-syllable haiku, which became the preeminent form of Zen artistry in Japan. All these activities outside Buddhist academia and monasteries helped renew and revitalize the Buddha Dharma in different times and places for new generations—fresh songs and spontaneous utterances intended to ignite blazing wakefulness in the minds and hearts of those who hear them, bringing to fruition all the good karmic seeds within us.

Dharma, like true higher education, edifies and awakens us. It brings out the best in us and helps us become our truest, most noble selves. Dharma teachings unveil a new way of being and seeing, a new world available through the enlightened life—a sane, good, and beautiful life, rich with meaning and connection, compassionate love, understanding, harmony, wisdom, and peace of heart and soul. I was once asked to write a book called *Dharma for Dummies* for that popular series of introductory manuals, but I respectfully declined. (My title would have been *Dharma for Dummies Like Me.*) Fortunately, Dharma is for smarties and dummies both, benefiting us individually and collectively, both in this life and afterward. I believe there is something valuable here for everyone. True Dharma is ageless; it knows no national boundaries, language barriers, isms and schisms, or gender limitations. Dharma is pure spiritual wisdom combined with the skillful means and practical methods to achieve it within oneself. Anyone, male or female, old or young, educated or illiterate, devout or skeptical, Buddhist or otherwise, can become as enlightened as Buddha himself did. How? We pursue the path of awakening; we cultivate formal Dharma practices such as meditation and self-observation; we integrate wise, loving, and selfless Dharma principles including attentive, moment-to-moment mindfulness into daily life. Buddhists today will notice, echoing the original teacher's words, that when we ourselves get clearer, everything becomes clearer. This recognition forms the basis of our inclusive, universal enlightened intention.

Today we have the shallows of bookstore Buddhism and the Internet to wade in, linking and aligning us as a far-flung but closely connected spiritual community of seekers and finders, awakeners all—as well as more deeper, face-to-face opportunities for the transmission of profound spiritual realization to occur. Dharma community and teachings are spread wide—like Indra's cosmic net, where each sparkling interstice reflects and contains the others. There are deeper opportunities to receive liberating teachings, such as intensive retreats, meditation centers, monasteries, experienced and accomplished teachers, and other established courses of study and training. We can learn Buddhism in modern academia, too, in many cases from learned and wise scholar-practitioners. Contemporary Dharma talks are live, freeform teachings in process, an art form not unlike spontaneous free verse or jazz played by those deeply rooted in classical forms. Live Dharma talks—including lively question-and-answer periods—depend in part on those who are present to hear them according to their wishes, needs, aspirations, questions, language, and inclinations. You get what you pray for.

The sole purpose of Buddhism is spiritual enlightenment, self-realization, total awakening from delusion's somnolence, and inner freedom and serenity, regardless of the school, country, or lineage tradition. Enlightenment, or nirvana, is said to be a blissful spiritual transformation beyond the vagaries of birth and death—rich with harmony, equanimity, and joyous fulfillment as well as freedom from anxiety, delusion, doubt, and suffering.

Through this incandescent awakening we can learn to protect this world and edify all—and I believe we must. In this agitated era of conflict, dissension, dislocation, alienation, and fragmentation, rife with extreme dogmatic views and intolerance, in which religion is too often part of the problem rather than offering viable social solutions, we can become wisdom elders, enlightened leaders, peacemakers, light-bringers, and beacons. We can help bring mutual understanding, sanity, and well-being to our world through secular as well as religious forms of enlightened living. Nonviolent Buddhist peacemaking and mediation through mindful listening and anger management are one example of what Dharma has to offer in this area of human need.

The impeccable path of attentive mindfulness and daily meditation awakens us to our innate Buddha nature, our Buddhaness, pure and transparent Presence—or whatever we label it. With direct experience of that serene center and fundamental spiritual meaning, a profound understanding and acceptance of *what is* and the realization that we are interconnected with *whatever we experience* arises, leading naturally to empathy, compassion, unselfishness, and altruism. We come to befriend ourselves and accept the world as it is, even as we might discover ways to help change it for the better. Anyone can achieve spiritual realization by following the practice path laid out by the unbroken lineage of master teachers, beginning with the Buddha and continuing through the centuries to us today. This timeless legacy transcends distance and time, offering us effective instruction and guidance, encouragement, inspiration, and interior illumination. It is directly accessible, wherever we are, whenever we are sufficiently motivated and aware. One moment can make all the difference. Spiritually speaking—it's now or never, as always. As the Tibetan tradition teaches, "One moment of total awareness is one moment of perfect freedom and enlightenment."

That is why we rely on experienced spiritual teachers, well-established spiritual teachings and practices, and wise spiritual friends and community to reach that goal. In Buddhism these are traditionally called the Three Jewels: Buddha, Dharma, and Sangha—enlightened teacher, liberating teachings and practice, and spiritual community—kindred spirits on the way. This triple gem is the refuge and sanctuary, the reliance of all Buddhists, regardless of nationality or sect. Some of the rich outer and inner dimensions of these Three Jewels will be unfolded in these Dharma talks, to help us better assimilate these ancient, timeless wisdom teachings on enlightened living, find them latent within ourselves, and integrate them into daily life.

It is traditional in Buddhist retreats to hear at least one inspirational and instructional Dharma talk each day from the resident teacher or leader. This custom reaches back into antiquity, when oral culture ruled, and is carried on today in Buddhist monasteries and meditation centers throughout the world. A Dharma talk helps inspire, exhort, and encourage us along the path while further informing our study, reflection, investigation, and actual practice. I have long been a learner and a listener. Today, although I still have elder teachers, I very much listen to my students—their doubts, questions, and heartfelt longings. This book contains a representative sample of new Dharma talks given since I first began teaching Buddhist meditation and practice in 1989 at the request of my Buddhist friends in Switzerland. Included are talks given in Europe and North America, as well as at our seasonal intensive meditation retreats and weekly sangha community gatherings in my Dzogchen centers in various cities. Material from the lively, highly interactive question-and-answer period that typically ends each Dharma talk has been folded into the body of the talk.

Here I have included those Dharma topics that seem most useful to Buddhist practitioners and meditators in general in the Western world, as well as to spiritual seekers regardless of tradition. As the Dragon Master, His Holiness the Twelfth Gyalwang Drukpa, says: "Dharma lectures and public teachings should be an effort to convey the essence of Buddhist philosophy and spiritual practices in the simplest terms, without any literary pretensions. I hope that these works will help you understand the basic meaning and true path of Buddhist practice." It is due to the auspicious coincidence of the sincere aspirations and requests of these students and the blessings and inspiration of my own lineage gurus and masters that these talks have come into being; any mistakes and misunderstandings are entirely my own.

My Tibetan lamas taught me to reaffirm daily the Bodhisattva's altruistic vow of selfless service and altruism, in order to uphold the Dharma and help others as part of my own path to enlightenment. I have tried to live up to their shining example by helping to bring the practical values and contemplative benefits of Buddhist Dharma to the West—including presenting masterful teachers and their most direct teachings—and making BuddhaDharma both accessible and practicable for people today.

For more than thirty-eight years I have dedicated myself fulltime to the Dharma, including twenty years in the Himalayas, two three-year monastic meditation retreats, apprenticeship with my venerable Tibetan masters, and Tibetan study. I have found that the joyous wisdom of Dharma best explains and makes sense of the central fact and ultimate mystery of being alive. It is often said that the lion's roar of BuddhaDharma is proclaimed for all beings seen and unseen, now and later, here and elsewhere. When the lion roars, all the jungle creatures awaken and become more aware. This is the practice of lions, which are also enlivened by doing so.

Truth is ever fresh, and speaks for itself. This is Dharma— naked truth, reality, gnosis in action. There should be little or no personal bias or distortion in its teaching and transmission. Of course this is all but impossible, given human nature, yet the ideal remains, to guide us. My own late teacher Dilgo Khyentse Rinpoche, a lama of lamas, in giving permission and blessings for me to begin teaching in 1988, said: "Go wherever you are invited; do whatever is wanted and needed; and want and need nothing yourself. Remember why you are there, to benefit others. Remember what you have been given." This is a high ideal to live up to, but an ideal the master himself embodied. He remains a polestar to guide us, to guide me. As for me, I feel more like Henry James's artist in his story "The Middle Years," who says: "We work in the dark—we do what we can—we give what we have."

Dharma is about what is happening *now*, reality just as it is. Still, there is nothing new under the sun. New Dharma talks are like old wine in new bottles. May these talks bring blessings and auspiciousness, provoke deeper reflection and inquiry, and help illumine the Way for those who feel compelled to seek and to find. Wisdom is the essence of Buddhism. Awareness meditation is its most essential practice. Love, service, and selfless compassion in action are its ultimate expression.

Truths are many, but Truth, reality, is one. May all realize it and live up to it.

Sarva mangalam.
May peace and harmony prevail.

Lama Surya Das
Dzogchen Center,
Cambridge, Massachusetts, 2008

PART I

---

sustaining the essence

you must be present to win

CHAPTER I

NATURAL MEDITATION

THE POWER OF NOWNESS

This morning, I went for a walk in the gentle rain. Mist partially hid everything—trees, pond, and houses—in a soft cloud, reminiscent of dreams. There was absolutely nowhere else I could have preferred to be. This is the place! I felt like the right person in the right place at the right time, the right moment. Suddenly I realized: It is now, or never—as always. For an incandescent, transparent moment, I was totally awake, attuned, fully present. Heart warm, eyes bright, senses wide awake, and breathing freely. I have rarely felt more alive. Eventually, after becoming soaking wet, I returned to my cabin, changed clothes, and sat on the porch rocking chair, blissfully feeling as I'd retired to the blessed Buddha fields—just hearing the rain and listening to its pattering on the foliage melodiously washing everything away while savoring the indescribable feeling of just *being*. It was a spontaneous, natural meditation. I could not have fabricated it myself.

Natural meditation means fully inhabiting the present moment. Meditation is finding yourself in that natural state of wakeful pure presence or lucid contemplation where you discover your authentic condition, and where everything is part of meditative awareness. This is the essence of nowness, beyond past and future, and even a little outside or beyond the present. In Tibetan we call it the fourth time, the transcendent, timeless moment of nowness, the atemporal eternal instant—the essence of beingness. We are naturally present and accounted for, although we so often overlook that fact. Like sleepwalkers, we stumble through life, wondering why there are stumbling blocks in our path and who put them there, why we keep stubbing our toes and having other so-called accidents. Mindfulness and awareness practice help us wake up, smell the roses, see through everything, remain calm and clear, and be free. When I teach natural meditation through a brief guided process, it involves three simple things: natural body, natural breath/energy, and natural mind. We can learn to rely on these three inner meditator's jewels. We learn to breathe and smile inwardly, to center and relax, and to focus while letting go into letting be. Furthermore, as we develop these practices just slightly further, we learn to settle, intensify, and then release into allowing—the three phases of basic meditation practice.

First, we have to let ourselves arrive, relax, and just settle down. Relaxing, stilling and settling the body, is the first step. Natural body is Buddha's body, *nirmanakaya*, perfect embodiment, just sitting. Second is breathing naturally, and just letting the energy go, come, and go in natural flow. Natural breath and energy is Buddha's breath, *sambhogakaya*—pure energy, just breathing. The third step is just being. Natural heart and mind is Buddha's mind, *Dharmakaya*, ultimate reality—just being, and aware of it: aware of physical sensations in the body; aware of emotional feelings and energetic movements; and aware of whatever momentarily bubbles up and presents itself in the mind or field of consciousness. This is the sole focus of natural meditation; present awareness, alert presence of mind—attentive moment-to-moment mindfulness, rather than mindlessness and distraction. Nothing more need be done. As we learn to relax more and more into the simplicity and depth of this natural awareness, letting things come and go as they will in the panoramic, transparent expanse of total awareness, we become free of clinging and grasping, reacting to and against whatever arises, and simply appreciate the sublime view of things just as they are. There is nothing more to do than remain in this view: enjoy the view, open and inclusive, nonjudgmental, appreciating the majestic, expansive totality as it is. There is nirvanic peace in things left just as they are. This is natural meditation, homegrown natural Buddha.

The essence of meditation is the intentional use of attention in the present moment, the heart-mind transparent to itself. One of the best natural ways for most of us to painlessly effect this change in consciousness is by connecting with nature. I myself love to sit by any body of water, alongside the ocean waves, a river or waterfall, or even a swimming pool. I love looking out my window over the still, placid face of the lake near my house, in which I see reflected—or perhaps sense intuitively—the fact that everything is at peace and perfectly in place. I like losing my solid sense of time and place and personhood in the gently coursing ripples. My favorite place is near the ocean, where I can just listen to the waves and let them meditate me, washing everything out of my mind while the ocean itself just breathes in and breathes out—long, deep, rhythmically—relaxing and freeing me of all mental preoccupations and physical tension. To try to meditate and concentrate by the ocean seems like extra busywork; why not simply let the waves spontaneously meditate you? This is the essence of natural meditation, when it just happens. Knowing how to place oneself in the right time and place helps. I am totally at ease and at home as self-appointed Surveyor of Waves.

Sitting before a blazing hearth is also helpful for this purpose. We might think, "This natural meditation is not for me," or "I don't know how to do this, it's too unstructured," or "I need further instruction." Further instruction can certainly be given, and we will feed that habit, for now. However, further instruction in the direct-access Dzogchen style is to point out what we already know. For instance, who doesn't remember as a child lying outside in the grass looking at the sky—not falling asleep, as we would do now—but just innocently lying out in the grass, looking at the clouds, seeing the faces in the clouds, and gradually forgetting ourselves, becoming the grass and the earth, dissolving yet remaining awake and in subtle delight, naturally part of and one with all of life. At that point in our young lives, we certainly had never heard the words *contemplative skygazing* or *Dzogchen meditation,* but this is genuine natural meditation. So right here is the delicious principle: we already know how to do this. Dropping our body, relaxing totally, just being there without falling asleep. Not even thinking we're doing something special, getting enlightened, or accumulating spiritual merits and good karma out of it. It's not homework that we're supposed to do. It's not church or synagogue we are obliged to go to on the weekend or schoolroom classes we have to attend during the week; and yet, for some strange and inexplicable reason, we find ourselves just doing it. Lying there like the grass itself, absorbed in this timeless, primordial, natural meditation, we find ourSelves. It is part of us, part of our natural spirituality. This is natural meditation, spontaneous meditation. Who doesn't know how to do it?

I wouldn't want to overidealize this by saying, "It's part of the natural spirituality of children. Aren't they cute, blessed, fantastic!" Of course they are, sometimes—often, even; but more important, this natural ease and relaxation is an inherent part of *our* natural spirituality. That untrammeled, childlike, innately pure and complete little Buddha or inner spiritual child is still in us, in all of us, underneath it all, regardless of and deep beneath our personas, our defense mechanisms, self-concepts, beliefs, and hang-ups. So of course we already know how to do this natural meditation. Maybe we could find ourselves in that way on a lawn chair or a beach chair in our yard, or on our tenement's fire escape, or at the beach or swimming pool, lying in the sun like a lizard while the kids are swimming or playing. We don't even have to make a big deal about it. No, we don't have to cross our legs and look like a freakish Buddha statue sitting cross-legged at the public swimming pool. But we could be doing this natural meditation; it might even come to us if we let it. Yes, you can wear sunglasses. You can wear a hat, sunscreen. Yes, it will still work for you, if it does—if it fits for you, this natural meditation. Try it and see. Posture doesn't matter much; it's all about present awareness.

Perfectly suited natural meditation is like your own personal mantra, like your own breath, your own inner tide or heartbeat. It could take the supportive form of the sound of the ocean's waves just washing everything away, or lovely music, or whatever moves and transports you beyond your habitual consciousness and out of your ordinary, dualistic, self-referential and preoccupied, reactive state of mind. We could hear wind as music, as mantra—mantra wind, breath mantra, all and everything as what we call in India *shabda,* sacred sound, celestial mantra. I'm sure we all experience that at some time or another. Connecting with beauty is and can be a transformative natural meditation—seeing a flower, a painting, a gorgeous sunset, sitting in our fragrant garden at night, or some other natural outdoor scene that so moves and transports us that we unexpectedly experience a sharp intake of sudden pleasure, and we are no longer pedestrian, but uplifted on wings of delight, and all else temporarily falls away. Nature often does that to me. However, I don't want to overemphasize the nature part of natural meditation, because it doesn't have to be something outdoorsy in nature per se. Everything in the world is a part of nature, actually, including the skyscrapers and bridges. Who doesn't feel a sharp intake of breath when you see an infinite number of lights spread out twinkling below as you come over a city in an airplane at night, perhaps for the first time, or when driving over a rise and spotting the gorgeous span of the Golden Gate Bridge or some other human-made wonder? It is all radiant—God's creation, to talk in English. Beauty is another way that transports us beyond our finite egoic self to another, more transpersonal kind of love and oneness, an inexpressible otherworldly dimension of authentic connection, belonging, and truth hidden right here within the ordinary here and now. This is the secret magic and the grace-full blessing of nowness, which opens up into a more reverential and cherishing sacred outlook on life.

Fourth Time

When we talk about this kind of direct, unmediated, experiential contact with the immediacy of isness, this moment is all there is. It is beyond space and time, and it is who we are, eternally. Here is the inexpressible union of oneness and noneness, the incandescence of pure being as yet unmediated by conceptual frameworks and interpretations.

Much of the Dzogchen teachings and introduction to the nature of the mind is taking place in this particular orientation or dimension, which is seemingly related to time as we ordinarily perceive it. The direct experience of the innate or natural great perfection pointed out by the advanced Dzogchen teachings does not particularly occur in the ordinary space and time of the past, present, and future. Thus there's not a lot of discussion in the nondual direct-access teachings of the Great Perfection about how long it's going to take to get to enlightenment, or how long you should meditate each day, as there is in some other scriptures and systems that you may be familiar with: how many lifetimes it takes, or how many years it takes, or how many things you have to do to purify and uproot all the many obscuring kleshas and hindrances until you get totally there. The uncompromisingly nondualistic Dzogchen orientation is not exactly in that common sequential notion of time: past, present, and future. It takes place in a different time, the atemporal dimension of nowness, the fourth time. It involves the mystery I like to call "being there while getting there," every single step of the way. Being right here, now.

Physicists today say there are ten or eleven dimensions, and some of them are related mainly to time. The three-dimensional world we live in is seemingly progressing from past to present to future in horizontal linear time. We don't usually get confused about this. For example, we don't think the future comes before yesterday. Yet in another dimension of circular time, it may, such as in curved time or warped space or some variation of Einsteinian inconceivability! Past, present, and future are linear time, conventional time. Most of us don't think that time goes any direction except forward, even if we may occasionally have déjà vu experiences that may momentarily confuse us before we get right back to our usual linear way of thinking.

Dzogchen practice—*rigpa* (naked-awareness) practice, to be more technical—takes place in what Tibetan masters call the fourth time, the timeless time. This is a special Dzogchen teaching rarely found in other traditions. The fourth time is the eternal instant, the holy now, the hidden context embracing the three times (past, present, and future). If linear time is horizontal, moving forward on a graph from left to right in horizontal fashion, then the fourth time is the atemporal ascendant dimension that intersects each and every moment of the three times. It represents the transcendent immanent immensity—groundless and boundless, indescribable, inconceivable, yet definitely experiencable and livable. Where is the fourth time on our theoretical chart, from the linear viewpoint of time's progressive movement from left to right? Envision a line right down the middle of our mental chart, from top to bottom: this represents the fourth time, the now, the holy now, the wholly now. It's always now, right? We can understand this. I don't think this is too rarefied or obscure. You all know that today it's the now, and tomorrow will also be the now when we get there. That's why we say, "Tomorrow never comes." It's always today. Kindly excuse the mumbo jumbo, but I'm just trying to teach poor old Dzogchen here. Be patient! Time doesn't really matter that much, anyway. We'll get there when we're there, as my late dad used to tell us rambunctious little backseat drivers. "We're going wherever the car goes," he liked to joke. And he was right.

The fourth time, the moment of Dzogchen—the nowness, the

timeless dimension, Buddha's golden age—is not the same as linear time—past, present, and future—what we often call in Buddhism "the three times." In prayers, we pray to the Buddhas of all the three times—meaning past, present, and future Buddhas, meaning all the enlightened ones of all possible dimensions of time, space, and existence. Or we chant and affirm: "May we liberate all the beings of the three times and the ten directions, all the beings of past, present, and future in the ten directions: north, east, south, west, and intermediate northeast, southeast, and so on, and the zenith and the nadir." Ten directions means the whole, three-dimensional, all-inclusive kit and caboodle. The fourth time means the eternal now, the eternal instant, timeless time; it's beyond that time notion contained within time past, present, and future. This is what mystic poet and artist William Blake meant in his splendid stanza,

> To see a world in a grain of sand,
> And a heaven in a wild flower,
> Hold infinity in the palm of your hand,
> And eternity in an hour.

Like my own dad, Blake was really on to something.

It is always the now, the timeless time, the golden eternity—the eternal if you want to talk in English, in Judeo-Christian terms. We don't think much in Buddhism about the eternal, but we do call nirvana, enlightened reality, "the timeless and the deathless." Even Buddha used the term *deathless*. "Deathless nirvana" is the term Buddha used for his own great peace, bliss, oneness, and spiritual enlightenment. That's the timeless dimension, the eternal now, the holy now. That's the moment of Dzogchen. That's the moment of rigpa; that is the heaven, the nirvana, the transcendent immanence that is *within*. That's our own birthright, our personal acre of nirvana, here and now, our secret inner pure land or paradise. That's the dawn of creation, in every moment, the Garden of Eden. That's the moment of rigpa practice, the golden age when Buddha lives: now, now, now. That's called the sacred fourth (in Tibetan the *shicha,* the fourth fraction). *Shicha* is the fourth time, the timeless time, the eternal now—which we can access in any moment through penetrating awareness, clear vision, profoundly insightful and far-seeing wisdom. Dharma friends, that's the secret. It's not that eternity is after we die, or heaven is elsewhere, as explained in some religions and in general exoteric thought—for instance, that after we die, we reach heaven if we're good and are abundantly rewarded in our own materialistic human terms.

Through an authentic enlightenment or a mystical experience, we break through, and we're out of time for a moment. Unfortunately, we usually don't get to abide there but just visit and are soon returned to our habitual karmic world of ordinary human experience. Maybe we all have experienced that timeless dimension in which we forget about reference points because we're so totally present or transported beyond our usual dualistic framework. This could be said to be the moment of Dzogchen, the timeless time, the nowness in which this practice is meant to take place—the time of rigpa, the fourth time, nowness, the eternal instant. That's why in Tibetan, we have the same word for an instant and a *kalpa,* an aeon; the same word for an instant and an aeon, the word *kaychik.* The snap of a finger is a kaychik, and also an aeon is a kaychik, because time is telescopic and insubstantial, unreal even, in that sense. Ask a learned physicist or a mystic.

There seems to be quite a lot of misunderstanding when we read some Tibetan text and it says something about, for example, "this golden kalpa, this golden age or aeon." It doesn't necessarily refer way back to when the compassionate enlightened Gotama Buddha of India walked this earth and fortunate beings met him in person and experienced his teachings in person. In a deeper sense, the true golden age is now; this is the time of Buddha, of enlightenment, of awakefulness—the golden age of rigpa awareness, the holy now. You, too, can know and directly experience Buddha's teaching right now. Buddha's sitting there right now radiating, teaching, beneath the Bodhi Tree and on Vulture's Peak and in Deer Park—and also Central Park, by the way—in the timeless dimension, right now and forever always—for those with eyes to see and ears to hear. Most of us are generally afflicted with obscured vision, spiritually speaking. We are all short-sighted, time bound.

Of course, we know that everything that's born dies and that Buddha was a historical teacher, and thus his physical body died eventually, at the age of eighty beneath a tree in Kushinigar in northern India, and was afterward cremated. That's the historical perspective. But the primordial Buddha, Samantabhadra—the All-Good, the all-complete, a personification of formless and bodyless rigpa—is just a personification of enlightenment, or an archetype representing the unborn and undying, innate Buddha nature immanent in us all. This is the meaning of the Buddha within, our own innate Buddha nature that I lovingly call Buddha-ness. The inner Bodhi Tree is and can be blossoming within our own spirituality, right here and now; we can find refuge and sanctuary in its shade. Like Jerusalem and the Holy Land, or Mecca and Medina, Tibet and the Himalayas may represent the high ground in much of the romantic modern imagination; however, forgive me for belaboring the obvious point that the inner high ground is not abroad or across the world but resides deep within. Even if we're not intrepid mountain climbers or world travelers, we all can ascend and cleave to it.

Doesn't that put a different perspective on the teaching about how long it takes to get enlightened, the bodhisattva's great vow of renouncing individual nirvana until all likewise attain it, and so forth? Are you really waiting for all beings to get enlightened? Wise bodhisattvas aren't waiting for anything, through the magic of being there while getting there—having realized the emptiness of all such concepts as time and space; past, present, and future;

here and there; oneself and others; good and bad; bondage and freedom. Freedom and blessedness is in every moment, in any moment, ever accessible; it's beyond time or waiting and postponing. Freedom's just another word for unified oneness with all and everything, beyond attachment, resistance, misinterpretation, dualism, fixation, or preoccupation.

Truth is always resonant now, in the now. It's up to us to catch up. It's kind of high speed, breathtaking actually. We have to catch up to that by slowing down enough to be present and attentive enough to sink our roots, take our Buddha seat, and be fully present in the now, not always a couple of steps ahead of ourselves, as we usually are—leaning forward, reaching toward the next step, staggering forward on the treadmill of karmic doings under the momentum of events. Although being is within and prior to doing and remains unaffected and unadulterated by actions, we tend to lose ourselves in doing, thus losing touch with our pure intrinsic being. If we can slow down enough and pay sufficient objective attention, becoming consciously awake enough to fully inhabit the present moment, we can catch up with that speed-of-light dimension. You all know the relativity theory saying "At the speed of light, mass is infinite." There's actually a felt kind of unifying oneness there, in that awesome dimension, inexplicably enough. I have felt it. You can, too.

Our Karma, Our Dharma

The point is that we each have to pursue our own path, making our karma into our Dharma by giving ourselves to something greater than oneself and learning to play more skillfully the hand we've been dealt so that we develop and share our true gift and find our true vocation here in this tenuous, dramatic yet dreamlike world. As we find our true selves, why we're here and what we're meant to be doing, a transformative and liberating spiritual ripening takes place. This true work happens in the moment, moment by moment, no matter how long it might feel that we have been trying to find ourselves. It happens in the moment. That's why there's been an ongoing and amusing debate for more than a thousand years in Buddhism between the two schools of sudden and gradual enlightenment, trying to bridge the apparent gap in or contradiction between the union of the relative and the ultimate levels of reality and of actual practice. Probably the truth is that it's both, not just one or the other. It's as if you're hitting a large stone with a hammer to make gravel, and, after you've hit it many times, all of a sudden it breaks to pieces. It seems sudden enough, but you can't intelligently claim that it just happened from one whack. So it seems obvious to my way of thinking that practice has to take place in some particular form or way over a period of time, and even through some lifetimes, for us to ripen. I like the Buddhist saying "Sudden enlightenment, followed by gradual cultivation."

Yet, it all comes back to this very moment, which is actually the only moment—and that's the moment of Dzogchen. This moment is the fresh, gleaming, ever-dawning sunrise of innate spirit or clear light, not when the world was created back before the biblical reckoning began. This moment is the first moment, the moment of creation—the only one under consideration right now. This moment and every moment is that transcendant and timeless dimension that's immanent, that freshly intersects with each moment of linear time. The sacred intersects with each moment of mundane existence; this is the union of the sacred and profane dimensions of our everyday life. There's nowhere else to find it except here in each moment of mundane existence. That's why Trungpa Rinpoche called his collection of poetry *First Thought, Best Thought,* which is a Mahamudra slogan. Actually, a better translation would be "this moment, only moment," because it's not really about thought alone. This fresh, vivid, new moment of thought or feeling, physical sensation or perception, or whatever is experienced: this moment, first moment, the only moment. Once these moments start to build up into a chain—once we connect the moments with the crazy glue of concepts—then we get ordinary linear, discursive thinking and become entangled in chains of thought, like a spider entangled in its own sticky, self-spun web, and lose ourselves.

Just being in the present moment, moment by moment, every nanosecond—each momentary flash of awareness—that is the time of Dzogchen, the moment of Dzogchen, both the golden eternity and the holy now. That is the nowness of naked-awareness practice, stripped of all supports, forms, accoutrements, goals, and even enlightenment projects. So, for example, when we start to sit to meditate, and we think about trying to discipline ourselves to sit longer—that's fabrication, that's building up a chain that can entangle us. That's not being in the moment of Dzogchen. When we're waiting for things to develop, that's again being in time, linear time, not recognizing the ever-present and transparent yet luminous moment of Dzogchen. Gradually progressive developmental training is indubitably necessary and important in the beginning and middle of our practice life. We can eventually outgrow that tendency that need, and realize spontaneous meditation anywhere, anytime.

Autobiography of the Primordial Buddha, or the Five Auspicious Certainties

In this fourth dimension or this notion of timeless time, then, we can talk about the autobiography of the primordial Buddha Samantabhadra (All-Good) and his famous twelve vajra laughs mentioned in the esoteric Dzogchen tradition. Why is he laughing? I'll leave that to you. You have to find your own inner giggle, the cosmic absurdity or whatever it is, so that you have the laughs yourself, just as you have to get a joke yourself—having the punch line just ruins it. As the seminal master Longchenpa sang,

"Since everything is deceptively simple, dreamlike, subjective, and not really what it seems to be, I feel like bursting out laughing." And yet we can still empathize with the difficulties and travails of those caught up in the nightmare of confusion, suffering, and misery, and be moved to help.

The primordial Buddha was not a historical figure, like Gotama Buddha, but a transhistorical iconic figure, a meaningful archetypal personification of our own timeless, divine, compassionate Buddha nature, birthless and deathless, outside time and space—symbolizing the innate Dharmakaya, or luminous dimension of cosmic enlightened mind within us all. The autobiography of the primordial or Adi Buddha called All-Goodness relates to what we call in Tibetan the Five Perfections or the Five Certainties. These bring us to full conviction, pure vision, and authentic mystical experience, giving birth to the awakened and primordially enlightened heart-mind within us. It is how we are taught to arrange and prepare ourselves as we begin to listen to Buddhist teachings. My own Vajrayana (Secret Diamond Path) teachers have often mentioned these five auspicious endowments or glorious assets in the beginning of their tantric teachings, to set the joyous, gratefully appreciative, and attentive mood or framework and orientation for those participating in initiatory transmission. These five certainties help reframe how we see ourselves and what we're engaged in, purify our perceptions, and render us more suitable as vessels for the most profound mystic teachings—an antidote to the defects of unsuitable vessels, including being closed, turned away, inattentive, distracted, faithless, overly skeptical and cynical, polluted, dull, leaky, unteachable, and so forth. Cultivating these five certainties or purified perceptions helps enhance our openness and devotion, trust, gratitude, and confidence in the teachers and teachings as well as in ourselves; exponentially empowers the learning process on all levels, conscious and unconscious; facilitates the efficacy of the transmission taking place; and ensures the intended transformative, healing, and enlightening results.

The classic Five Perfections or auspicious, certain endowments of Vajrayana are the perfect time, the perfect place, the perfect teaching, the perfect teacher, and the perfect student.

1. **Perfect time.** This very moment is the *perfect moment*. This very moment is the very first, fresh and pure, virginal, dreamlike instant: the Dzogchen Buddha field, the highest heaven—*Ogmin*, as they say in Tibetan, which literally means "none higher." This moment is the perfect moment, the perfect time, the golden age.

2. **Perfect place.** This place where we are is the perfect Buddha field. This very location is the *perfect place,* the Buddha field, a radiant and stainless mandala or spiritual gathering. It's not just that after we die we'll go to the Buddha field of great bliss in the West, or somewhere else.

3. **Perfect teaching.** This is the timeless teaching, the ultimate, naked, absolutely true and candid, direct-access, spontaneous enlightenment, nowness teaching, perfectly liberating and freeing. This teaching is not comparative, particularly; it simply asserts that *this* is the perfect teaching for here and now, for those who are listening and receiving it. This, what is, right now—not necessarily our doctrine or tradition, but the facticity right now is it. THIS is the perfect teaching.

Get it? This moment's teaching, whatever you're getting, is the perfect teaching. If it's silence, this is the perfect teaching. If it's birdsong or traffic noise—this is it. If it's a harsh lesson or somewhat confusing, this, too, is it. None other to seek or long for; utmost reality is encoded in it, right here and now. The noble Dharma is being eloquently expressed right here and now, for those with unobscured ears to hear and eyes of pure vision to see.

4. **Perfect teacher.** The primordial Buddha is the ultimate teacher who is coming through here and now in various forms and guises. All-Goodness is "doing" all this, presenting this, ex-

pressing this. It is all "his" dancing expressions and Buddha activity, a skillful, magical display, not just ordinary concepts and appearances from human teachers with their limitations and foibles but radiantly shining sutralike emanations, clear as a ringing bell or alarm clock.

5. **Perfect student.** This auspicious certainty is probably the hardest, the most challenging, for most of us to get. "What?" the inner defendant screams. "Who, me? I ain't perfect, far from it!" Yes, you can be the right vessel for this elixir-like divine snow lion's milk of truly timeless wisdom teachings. This fifth certainty is also termed "the perfect entourage," recontextualizing the teacher-student situation as the Buddha and his closest disciples.

Yes. This is the autobiography of primordial Buddha in the Five Perfections, complete with the certainty of the perfect student as vessel and receptacle. This is the genetic root or womb or enlightenment experience. Treat yourself to it. Help yourself!

Once upon a time, in a Nyingma three-year retreat, one of the American monks, said to our guru, Khyentse Rinpoche, in a group question session in front of all: "Rinpoche, I get this; what could be better than this? This is obviously the perfect place. This is definitely the right place! This is the right moment! This is the right teaching! This is the perfect teacher! But I don't feel like I'm the right person!" How honest, how human and how true. Can't we relate to all of that? Even if we might have little questions with the first of the four Perfect Certainties, isn't that fifth one the really tough one, at least for most of us? Who is ready to step up this kind of perfect certainty right now? Any volunteers?

This is the autobiography of the primordial Buddha, Samantabhadra: the Five Perfections, the diamondlike vajra pride of inner certainty—confidence in innate Buddha nature, leading directly from here to right here and now. We ourselves are like his twelve diamondlike vajra laughs, his twelve disciples—like spontaneous poems, sung to the lovely tune of the power of nowness.

Just laughing aloud is the moment of Dzogchen, the great natural perfection, the dawning of clear light. Let's appreciate this. Why miss out?

Meditation Anatomy

Detachment is the root of meditation
And devotion its head, as 'tis said.
Bodhicitta (loving compassion) is its soul.
Penetrating wisdom is the transparent eye of meditation.
Mindfulness is the breath,
Vigilance the skin.
Nondistraction is the essence.
Self-discipline—the very bones of Buddha.
Present-moment awareness—the heart of it all.
Balance and harmony—the seat of meditation.
Nowness is the time,
This is the place.

CHAPTER 2

ENLIGHTENED LIVING

THE HEART OF AWAKENING

meditation is the heart of the path of awakening, the essence or active ingredient of the liberating Buddha-Dharma. This is the way of awakening to one's fullest potential, in Western terms—of finding out who and what you are, what you're doing here, and why. Meditation familiarizes us with our inner, spiritual consciousness as well as the essence, nature, and potential of our own hearts and minds, bodies and souls. It involves mental and spiritual training in clear seeing, direct knowing and experiencing, and the ultimate realization and actualization of transparent, unobscured being. The way of spiritual awakening universally known as the path of enlightenment requires a combination of large outlook, actual practice(s), and way of life: view, meditation, and action, in Tibetan Buddhist terminology. Just meditating, praying, or doing yoga is not sufficient, if we don't know how or why—view, outlook—nor integrate and embody it in daily life through the wise art of mindful living and some form of the transformative exercises and ethical disciplines that go with it.

"Awakening from what?" you might ask. Awakening from the confused sleep of semiconsciousness, the dream of delusion. Awakening to enlightenment, illumination, freedom, nirvanic peace, inner peace as well as outer peace. This is a path that we travel, not a dogma or belief system that we need to accept. Many say Buddhism isn't a religion, but a psychological, ethical philosophy of awakening, because it doesn't dogmatically believe in anything or require creeds or conversions. Ultimately, even the notion of Buddha or enlightenment is recognized as just another concept, definitively not what we think it is. That is where the special Buddhist notion of emptiness (*sunyata*) or subjectivity comes in as a very useful balance to our tendency to reify things and ideas. The notion of sunyata, or voidness, undermines that concretizing tendency and opens space for other possibilities. When we meditate, we really are becoming more sensitized to how things actually *are* in the present moment. We become like Emerson's "transparent eyeball," the spiritual mind knowing itself. We discover that we *are* what we experience, and there is no separation.

In Buddhism we generally say it doesn't matter what we experience, but it matters how mindful, wise, and aware of it that we are. The outer and inner—both the phenomenal and noumenal worlds—are totally inseparably interwoven, interconnected, interdependent. It is what we *are* that counts, even as that *is* what we do. Our inner state shows up in our behavior, doesn't it? My own guru lama used to say he could see and feel exactly where people were at on the path from the very moment they walked in the door. Buddhist Dharma is the way of developing transcendental wisdom and loving compassion within oneself and eventually overflowing to others, too, showing up in life in innumerable ways, great and small. Spiritual living coupled with transformative contemplative practices can help us become better people and significantly contribute to a better, safer, and saner world.

Excuse me if I am being too abstract. I'll start again. It only matters what we do on this path, for wisdom is as wisdom does—to coin a saying. So there is actually nothing to believe; there is everything to *discover*, to uncover, to recover. This is a path to travel, a journey to be undertaken—a new way of life to be lived and a whole new world to be loved. As the Buddha said, "I only point the way. I am not a God. I am not a special avatar sent from above. I am simply awakened. I point the way of awakening. You yourself must walk it, as I have, if you choose to." In that sense, it only matters what we do and how we do and understand it. If we practice this path, we, too, can and will experience its fruits, the munificently beneficial results. It's scientific, in a way: if and when we reproduce Buddha's experimental procedure, we can replicate the results—in ourselves, to our immense benefit.

Each of us innately has Buddha potential or Buddha nature, enlightened perfect nature, the essence of being. Not just in us, like a needle in a haystack, so hard to find; rather, it *is* us, through and through, just waiting to be realized fully, to be recognized and consciously *actualized*. So this path of meditative practice, of self-inquiry—of the cultivation of daily, moment-to-moment, mindful awareness—is a practice path that we travel ourselves.

We always think that *It* is somewhere else, and certainly not here. As they say, the grass of enlightenment always seems greener on the other side. Actually, it is *here* or nowhere. This meditative practice is like a mirror to help us see ourselves, to better know ourselves, thoroughly—our true selves, not just our superficial personalities and conditioned social selves, our persona and defense mechanisms, our habitual conditioning and propensities, but our true nature, our *true* selves. To develop, unfold, and fully realize that this is possible is what we call awakening the Buddha within. The authentic Buddha has no material form or shape and can be imaged in so many ways. So the Buddha within would be . . . Who else would it be? Look like? Where would we find it? But I am just like a plagiarist, a jukebox, a ventriloquist's dummy; so many have said these things before. Rabbi Hillel of ancient Palestine said, "If not you, then who? And if not now, when?" If you are not the bodhisattva, an awakener, wisdom warrior, altruistic spiritual activist, and everyday hero serving the welfare of beings, who will be? And if not now, when? This is a call to action—not just worldly, compulsive, busybody-like activity, but a call to selfless Buddha activity, beneficial enlightened activity through enlightened living. Many are called, but few choose to show up, I've noticed. We can change that, voting with our feet and our good hearts. Not just wishing for peace and praying for it, but working for peace.

This is a path of enactment, of embodiment, of self-realization and self-actualization. Not just living wisdom from the eyebrows up, totally cerebral and intellectual, but rather actually embodying truth and love and living those sterling qualities—loving our way all the way to enlightenment. We are all seeking truth in one way or another, one form or another, however various our efforts appear to be. Even the most worldly or difficult among us are seeking true happiness, true love, true meaning, true God, or whatever it is called or conceived as. But I should take this step-by-step. As spiritual seekers, as Buddhists and bodhisattvas, we are seeking truth even while we are also living truth: living truly, speaking truth, being honest, being genuine and straightforward. Being ourSelves, not just pretending. Buddha's not pretending!

But how to authentically be ourSelf—our true Self, not merely some faint, semiconscious shadow of it—without knowing who and what we are? I do not think that we have to find truth as if it's a golden key somewhere that will unlock the universe. Of course, it does, it would, it can—truth, also known as wisdom, is a universal panacea—but things are more exquisite, subtle, and deliciously mysterious than that. Truly living does unlock the universe. But it is not like a golden key that we can get for Christmas or order from some mail order catalog; nor can the pope or anyone else just present it to us, like the key to a divine mansion or city. Living truth is what counts—actually realizing it and embodying it. This is an entire way of life, not just something that we do one hour on Sunday mornings or Monday nights. Sabbath must come every day, for each day is the main event and each moment is our life in a nutshell. Buddhist practitioners gradually learn to cultivate mindful awareness in every moment throughout each day, as much as we can, while the realization slowly but surely dawns that *this is it,* right now, this very moment— nowhere else! What it comes down to is a sane and centered way of life that is joyous, wholesome, and loving, intuitively honoring the connectedness of us all; and not just we humans, but all creatures everywhere. For everything is sacred, everything is equally part of the mandala of suchness, of isness. As my own lamas teach, truth or wisdom pervades all forms of consciousness. There is nothing that need be excluded from our path.

Contemplative practice is not just a selfish activity, simply meditating for ourselves or praying for our own welfare. We may be alone for the moment, meditating or praying or studying *by* ourselves, but it not just *for* ourselves. Raising consciousness is for one and all, since we are all inseparably connected, even if we don't always realize that or even if we don't always want to know that. A hermit is also part of society, in an unusual way, just as the hermit crab exists in relation to other creatures and the Hermit is just another card in the entire tarot deck. In the Himalayas I once heard a story about a hermit who lived in a cave high on the mountainside above a small riverside village. When a great flood wiped out the village and no one returned to rebuild it, the hermit had to move to another cave at some distance, yet still in relation to a village. He was not really as absolutely independent as an immature teenager might dream of being.

During World War I, a very difficult time in Europe, the Jesuit anthropologist Pierre Teilhard de Chardin said: "I feel it is only the prayers of the hermits in the caves that are keeping the world afloat, sustaining the world." I hear this as a very radical statement of the far-reaching power of interbeing and the depth of possibilities within the individual heart and mind in the invisible spiritual realm. Whether we call it prayer or meditation, or service, love, or truth, they are all more or less the same, just various scintillating facets of the same precious jewel. Prayer is like talking to God; meditation is like listening. I like to think that the prayers and meditations of the great hermits keep the world afloat in our volatile times today. Teilhard's statement is a prayer, in a way, and a recognition of the power of the heart. Not just the power of the mind, not just of the body, not just of the might of armies or force of economic power, not just of information, but the power of the heart, the power of spirit, the dynamic energy and efficacy of pure *intention*.

Spirituality is a path of heart. It is not always possible to see it all with our visible, physical eyes. Nor do we have to see the entire staircase before making a step or two on it. I am not just talking about rainbows or auras or angels here, but remembering that there is actually a lot going on, much more than meets the eye and much that we don't understand. There is never nothing going on, as the Peaceful Warrior's guru once said. There are so many dimensions, so many levels of reality; universes within universes within universes! Who hasn't been amazed just to look through a microscope or telescope, for example? So let's not be too overly rational, too materialistic, too narrow minded and opinionated. When we practice in a truly open-minded and true-hearted manner, all are included. Contemplative practice is extraordinarily profound and enlivening; enlivening to ourselves and to all. That's why this is called the path of enlivenment. May all beings be enlivened together!

Meditation is the opposite of killing time, which would just be deadening ourselves. When I am on my annual two- or three-week solitary meditation retreat at my retreat center outside Austin, I feel that every day, every hour, and even almost every minute is meaningful, rich, and blessed in ways I can hardly begin to understand or articulate. Moreover, who needs such prolonged formal, silent meditation? How about just delighting in joy and rejoicing, when reverence, gratitude, and bliss sometimes just well up by themselves for seemingly no good reason? Nobody can object to that, right? Let's cultivate joy in our lives, following our joy path toward the inconceivable joy of being. We have all come here for some purpose, which we have barely begun to realize and fulfill.

You don't necessarily have to formally meditate or pray and contemplate, but it is hard to not *be*. The joy of being is enlivening; let's celebrate and delight in that. BuddhaDharma is more than a path or a religion; it is a psychophilosophy and ethical self-discipline, an inner science of investigation, and a meaningful way of life. That's why we say Buddhism isn't really a religion. It is a way, a great highway, a high way, and also a low-to-the-ground way; and it courses every way, all ways, in every possible dimension, without going anywhere in particular. The Great Way is all-inclusive, ever-present, pervasive; it is that from which one can never stray. There are said to be many gateways to Dharma, but in truth, the gateless gate is everywhere and open, and there is neither inside nor out. When you feel outside looking in, you have to penetrate the gate; from inside, there's no within and without, no walls, no gates, nowhere to go or remain or hide. It is all right here, in great completeness, forever and always.

Now, in meditation, we are just sitting, just breathing. As in that Zen cartoon, you might turn to your friend and say, "Is this all? What happens?" Nothing. This is it. If you knew it fully, you would not be disappointed—I promise you. When we know it fully, it is not disappointing—quite the opposite—because nothing really *happens*. It's not nuttin'; it's really somethin'! However, the truth of the matter is, the most important things in life often require patience and perseverance. We come to our meditation seat to get down, to let our hair down and turn inward, to get real for once, to see how simple, clear, and transparent we can actually get. Can we ever just let go and let be—authentically, uncompromisingly—and just for a moment or two, just *be*? Do we always have to be doing something, learning something, improving ourselves and our existence, accumulating or achieving? Are we human beings, or human *doings*? We can say we are meditating, that we are learning about ourselves, and, of course, this is part of it. Contemplation, analysis, reflection, and investigative self-inquiry are often included in various stages of different meditative practices. But, more profoundly, we are learning just to *be*. To be with ourselves, to be comfortable, to be relaxed, open, natural, at ease—to be totally present. To befriend ourselves. To be one with what we are, which we can't know but can just be. And that's a lot!

They don't usually have classes like that in school, do they? At least not in the American schools I went to. I had to go to the Himalayas in the early seventies and eighties. This process can be extraordinarily growthful, in many unusual directions and dimensions. You never know what you may find out and discover when you undertake a fabled journey; and the journey within, looking more deeply into everything, outer and inner, is the most incredibly surprising and fruitful voyage of all.

Spiritual Journeying

Spiritual journeying involves inquiring honestly into the nature of God and man, the very nature of reality as well as oneself. Of course, we must recognize that each of us, in the conventional sense, is somewhat different. This is the conventional, healthy adult, individuated self. But deep Dharma reveals something more—that in the ultimate nature of things, there is no permanent, independently existing self-entity even while there does seem to be some underlying animating principle, spirit, or luminous essential nature. During the guided part of the meditation, I often say something like, "Now look at who and what is looking; perceive the perceiver." If you really go into Buddhist terminology, you have to make everything sort of inside out, open ended rather than concretized. You have to say "groundless ground" and "the perceiverless perceiver." But you can't speak in that kind of somewhat annoying Zen-like doubletalk all the time. "Settle in the groundless ground of being and nonbeing" . . . it's too much! I just try to talk simple English here today. It works.

Concepts of identity, being, self, and reality are definitely grounded in groundlessness, in openness and the mystery of transcendence and immanence. All these words and concepts are just pointing to deeper reality, beyond thought and concept. *Anatta,* or the Buddhist concept of no-separate-self or no-owner, means that each of us is a *process* rather than a fixed, independently existent, solid entity, soul, or thing. Our Dzogchen practice tradition is a Buddhist lineage, a Buddhist teaching. Therefore, it is based in the fundamental teachings of impermanence, dissatisfactoriness, nonattachment, and no-separate-permanent-self. What do you experience when you trace back to the source of your perceptions, memories, thoughts, feelings, and sensations? Can you trace back to the source of all this radiance, all the scintillating brilliance of phenomena and noumena? Who or what is experiencing? Try to see and understand more precisely. What is yourSelf? Look at the looker, and see who/what is seeing and being. Who or what is experiencing the experience? What is it? Are there thoughts? Is there a thinker somewhere behind, or in, the thoughts? Who or what is thinking? Who is wondering, "Who am I?" "What shall I do?" "Where does it all come from, and return to?" Trace back to the source of all this cognizance or radiance.

"Don't know" is good enough as a genuine answer enough for now—because it is true! But we are not satisfied with that, are we? We have to make more stories about it. We reify ourselves and speculate about our experience, superimposing conceptual interpretations on the open and mysterious ground of being. Try to notice that. We don't know all that much, in truth, but we go through life as if we do. Based on that illusory knowledge, we think we know what we can do and can't do and should do and shouldn't do, and act as if we know who and what we are. But we are not who we think we are! Just try to recognize and comprehend that, nakedly, deeply. Recognize your illusions, imaginations, self-made story—all the "mind-forged manacles," as William Blake insightfully called our self-imposed limitations. Notice the whole world that evolves out of that, like a sticky spider's web entangling the spider itself. . . . "I can't do that. I'm a woman." Wait a minute. I thought you didn't know who you were—yet now you suddenly pretend to know something, and problems begin. This kind of turning the mind back on itself can prove exquisitely liberating. It cuts through and sees through all such egocentric concepts and reifications; all these separations, these illusions, our assumed and mostly unexamined identity. This investigative self-inquiry leads to self-knowledge and wisdom of understanding ourSelves.

That's the process. Can you get it down to everything that comes? Whatever arises *is* your path, the Way; there is no other way. We are what we experience. The truly awakened awareness of innate wakefulness unmediated by conceptual bias or distortion is directly knowing that we are what we experience, in this very moment, every moment—no separation. Which makes me at least wonder, "Am I that? What is that? Who is experiencing this?" Apply that laserlike questioning to each momentary perception, sensation, thought, and feeling, moment after moment, and observe whatever comes up. Who is personalizing it? Who is the subject of our own personal subjectivity and self-referential bias? That's why I always say, "Who or what?" It's really transpersonal. It is in us, but is not ours. That doesn't mean to keep intellectually analyzing. Just keep sensing it directly. Turn toward the perceiver, the experiencer, again and again, and see what is actually occurring.

That is the peeling process itself, which needs to take place. It is important to begin, and to keep going. This ruthlessly honest, self-scrutinizing unmasking and self-peeling process makes it more difficult to identify so much with each passing emotion, like anger, for example. It makes it more difficult to say, "I am an angry person. I shouldn't be angry." It's more, "Oh. I am not that, either. It's just another bubble. It's just that old familiar tune, that old tape loop playing itself out again—I don't have to go there." In this way, through this process of unpeeling and unmasking ourselves, things gradually do get more clarified and freed up. We start to have more space to choose our actions and self-expression. Rather than just reacting blindly, we find more choice points and more intentional, creative, productive avenues of expression through widening the mindful space between stimuli and responses. We find more space to breathe, to be *aware,* to center and recognize and recondition our habitual reactions and unthinking reflexive patterns, and to restrain blind, knee-jerk reactions we may afterward regret in the cool, dispassionate, 20/20 vision of hindsight. When we have enough mindfulness and clarity to exploit and extend the sacred pause between stimulus and response, we experience freedom far beyond belief and mere concepts. This moment between stimulus and response—between immediate experience and reaction—is precisely where we can intercede and manage our difficult reactive emotions, choosing more intentional, conscious, desirable responses and proactive initiatives rather than simple habitual knee-jerk reactions.

I have a lot of faith in this way of practicing mindful awakefulness, moment by moment, day to day. I think it is very illumining. Why even call it Buddhist? It is truth itself, I find. Socrates was into it; study his entire dialectic, summed up in his famous exhortation as "Know thyself." This is finding truth through introspective awareness. A lot of people of all kinds all over the world are evolving in this way; this is not just somebody's dogma or fanatical brainwashing cult or untested superstition. All the religious and congregational trappings are just secondary practices, compared to that direct path of self-knowledge through personal truth seeking, self-observation, and awareness cultivation. Direct inquiry and experiencing the experiencer leads to infinite certainty and unshakable inner conviction. This is how we can find ourSelves, our true Selves. Finding the groundless ground is a process, an ongoing journey of exploration; there is no wizard here behind the screen. Yet that is something you have to experience. Therefore I exhort you in that direction. See if you can stand in that "I don't know" and strive to find out—for yourSelf . . . for the good of one and all.

As Wallace Stevens once wrote, in his poem *The Snow Man:*

For the listener, who listens in the snow,
And, nothing himself, beholds
Nothing that is not there and the nothing that is.

How to Get Here

The conundrum is, How to learn to be—when we already *are*? How to to get there when all the mystics agree that it is all right here? This is a koan, a Zen-like existential riddle—which I summed up in my book *Buddha Is as Buddha Does* on the bodhisattva's ten panaceaic virtues in the phrase "Being there while getting there, every step of the way." Famed Catholic monk Thomas Merton, who was starting to study Dzogchen in Darjeeling when he met his untimely death in Bangkok in 1968, wrote: "We are already one and we imagine we are not. And what we have to recover is our original purity. Whatever we have to be is what we are."

Even if we are just sitting and watching our breath, following our breathing—just sitting, just breathing, aware—that's already a lot . . . a lot more than doin' nothin', daydreaming, killing time, dozing, or spacing out. In fact, just sitting is *zazen*, or traditional Zen sitting meditation. In some places it's like a whole religion, enfolded entirely within that simple, meaningful contemplative act. In this manner, we come to be living the enlightened life, not just aspiring to it. Not just trying to reach for and catch hold of the legendary pot of gold at the end of the rainbow, always in the far distance; in actual fact, all is magically revealed as a form of light. And not just the rainbow, but also the shadow, the cloudy rainstorm, and even inert wood and stone, for those with eyes to see and ears to hear. It's a golden rainbow every step of the way, not just in some mirage-like pot at the radiant arc's supposed end. The wise and enlightening life does not always imply or require smiling; it also includes appreciating the tears, concerns, sadness, loss, and so on. Everything is part of it. "God is found even amid the ashes." Let's not just be simplistic New Age love-and-lighters but learn to appreciate the entire spectrum of dreamlike, magical experiences, just as they are. Every step of the way to heaven is heaven, as the saints and mystics say. What we must be and become is what we are.

Just sitting in awareness is the main meditation practice; not chanting, not praying; not analytical questions, koans, or splendid visualizations; not memorizing and reciting. What we're exploring right here is the renowned Tibetan form of meditation called Dzogchen or Mahamudra, which is usually related to the tantric Vajrayana (Diamond Path) teachings. Namkhai Norbu Rinpoche has said, "Tantra is action." When Buddhists say "sitting" or "meditation," it should be understood to mean mindfulness through alert presence of mind and cultivation of intentional awareness, not just crossing the legs or closing the eyes and remaining silent in one and only one still position. Meditation is not about getting away from it all, avoiding anything, numbing out, or stopping out. Without trying to be rid of pesky thoughts, feelings, perceptions, and sensations, we learn how to practice being mindfully aware of them in the immediacy of the very moment in which they fleetingly present themselves. Everything is grist for the mill, even those things we find terribly unpleasant. This is the heart of the nondualistic, tantric principle of transmutation through fearless inclusion. Yoga and tai chi are also effective forms of meditation in movement, powerful and profound contemplative practices. *Tantra* actually means integration, interwovenness—oneness, if you like. "Just sitting" actually means just *being*. Enlightened living implies authentic presence, *genuine embodiment*. It means impeccable living, not mere sitting down, trying not to think, nor mere quietism or piety. Bodhisattva warriorhood includes inquiring deeply into things, facing the truth, truth telling, achieving self-mastery and selflessness, as well as seeing everything we do as like a ritual, as spiritual in nature—as inherently valid and valuable just for its own sake, without ulterior motive or expectation of outcome. This is one reason why virtue is its own reward.

The deeper implication of letting go and letting be—famously called nonattachment or cling-free equanimity by Buddhists—is that it leaves room for disinterested objectivity and unbiased clarity to reveal itself. Nonattachment doesn't just mean getting rid of everything; genuine renunciation implies that besides prioritizing and simplifying our lives, we must learn to let go of holding back, fearlessly meeting life all along the length of her gorgeous, undulating, shape-shifting magical body. This implies total engagement, openness, intimacy with every moment, with nothing left in us to protect, wall off, hide, or control. It's pretty advanced, actually—simple, straightforward, but not always easy.

The much-discussed similarities and differences between nondual Dzogchen and Zen Buddhism are sort of a rarefied topic, much discussed since early debates in Tibet over one thousand years ago between Chinese and Indian masters about sudden and gradual enlightenment. "Sudden enlightenment, gradual cultivation," my Korean Zen master liked to say, attempting to resolve the age-old debate and help us to just get on with our daily spiritual practices. As for myself, I try to keep it simple and workable, guiding students a bit during the meditation while they are sitting there, kind of like a sports coach. In Zen, someone usually goes around with a lovely carved antique stick to keep people on their toes, or the edge of their buttocks at least—the Kyoto cattle prod, we used to call it. I try to prod, too, but gently, midwifing the birth of something fresh and genuine. Tibetan meditation masters teach from the sutras spoken by the historical Buddha but especially like to emphasize the boiled-down, essentialized pith instructions—potent experiential instructions intent on hitting the nail of present wakefulness right on the head with a ringing sound. Our outlook is very similar to Zen's: that we are all Buddha, and our only task is to awaken. That Buddha nature is human nature and when we become genuine and authentic, Buddhist practice does, too. In fact, from the point of the absolute truth of innate Buddha nature, we don't even have to awaken, for we are already Buddhas by nature, albeit some sleeping Buddhas and some awakened ones. But that absolute and ultimate viewpoint is a very steep cliff, a slippery slope, without steps, gradual stages, milestones, handrails, or crutches for support; it is all too easy to misunderstand or use as a rationalization for spiritual paralysis and what I have called "premature immaculation." It's probably safer and more useful at this point to see that our human ego or self is but the tip of the iceberg of divinity or the totality of innate Buddha nature, our own inherent Buddha-ness. Yes, in the ultimate perspective, it is true that all is perfect, just as it is, and that we are all perfect just as we are; and yet, amusingly enough, we could still use just a little tweaking. It is probably too soon for you to say that everything is IT, as the mystics say. My teacher and friend the Twelfth Drukpa Lama always says, "Everything must be meditated. There is nothing outside the path, no obstacles or hindrances, for those who can practice this." This is the essence of the highest, deepest tantra, or nondualism.

In Dzogchen, some of those gradual steps are skillfully unpacked, clearly delineated, as part of the Tibetan Buddhist approach to tailor-made personal instruction and individual guidance. In Tibetan Vajrayana Buddhism, there is usually more of an emphasis on supportive practices, such as devotion, prayer, yoga, ways of moving your energy and so on, than in the Zen tradition. In Tibetan Buddhism, we are provided with some steps and handrails to climb the spiritual cliff. We don't usually try to just jump to the top of the sheer cliff, or start "climbing up from the top of the flagpole," as one Zen master succinctly put it. It is usually too simplistic to say, "Just be!" Or, "Everything is Dharma, we are all Buddhas." Who knows and lives that way, through and through? One of my students once asked, "Okay, it sounds good; but if I'm a Buddha, why do I feel so crummy and tangled up most of the time?"

In Dzogchen and in tantric meditation, we do more than just sit and just be. Zen and Dzogchen-Mahumudra are similarly rooted in nonduality, in using the fruit (innate awakefulness,

Buddha-ness) as the path, rather than always trying to grow the tree from the seed of Buddha potential to get fruits later. The vajra shortcut of the Secret Diamond Path (Vajrayana) is renowned as the path of skillful means, and offers us a multitude of other ways of working with energy—with mind, body, spirit, emotions, sexual energy, attitudes, conditioning, dreams, and death. By balancing and enhancing your sitting practice with psychological work, visualization, walking, bowing, devotional practice, breathing, and chanting, you bridge some of those differences between schools and sects, especially between yourSelf and others, bridging the gulf between yourSelf and the world. Just sitting hour after hour can become like a pressure cooker, especially if you are having problems with mental disturbances. Some forms of meditation and yoga practice are contraindicated for certain individuals, depending on their constitution, pathology, and conditioning. That is one reason why it is very important to have a teacher, or at least some structured, skillful, methodical instructions to follow. Of course, we are all experimenting and improvising all the time, but it can be helpful in certain times to get feedback from those who have been there before, who have traversed the same territory, who have climbed the mountain and have experienced the path and its possible twists and turns, dangers, and pitfalls. For example, once you know the rules of grammar, you can play more freely with language. Wise and experienced teachers can be very helpful in clarifying and facilitating the way, especially in the beginning and middle of the journey.

In Japan, during walking meditation, the Soto Zen groups walk around like zombies, slowly, and the Rinzai groups run around the zendos like maniacs. It's fascinating and refreshing to notice the different styles of walking meditation practice! There are so many different ways to train in mindful awareness practice; thus there are different schools and traditions, different lineages and traditions, each with their different emphases. I used to think that walking meditation must be done very slowly and mindfully to be effective, to be authentic; but I now can laughingly remember from my Kyoto days in the seventies how it takes tremendous awareness to run around like a maniac in a beautiful Zen temple with five-hundred-year-old paper painted screens without tripping and falling over, pushing an errant elbow through the thin wall, or knocking over an ancient museumpiece statue! It is always the same principle: Pay attention! Focus. Be aware. While practicing walking meditation in that doubletime fashion, you have no time to think about anything else, such as, Why am I doing this? One learns to just do what one is doing, single-mindedly, wholeheartedly, attentively, one-pointedly; this is the point.

One Korean master has his students jog backward through the fields for a half hour every morning at dawn as a meditation. It takes a lot of ultrapresent attention to do that. Pay attention. All that is meditation in motion, not unlike yoga, meditation in action, tai chi, or other martial arts and ritual ceremonies, including the artful Zen ways of tea, flower arrangement, and so forth. In Vajrayana Buddhism, we, too, employ a lot of traditional bows, mudras (hand gestures), rituals, ritual instruments, visualizations, chants, and litanies as part of Tibetan meditative awareness cultivation through devotional practice. These contemplative practices help intelligently channel, balance, and harmonize our energy so we don't just get tense or rigid, dull or explosive. Chanting is a great way to let off steam. It vibrates the chakras, and includes sacred words and redolent concepts. Sacred chant is a form of meditation I love dearly and do daily. We also use visualizations while chanting, to further concentrate and refine conscious awareness.

If you look at modern scientific research, you'll see that creative visualization and breathing exercises lengthen and smooth out the brain waves, bring up the serene alpha rhythms, and reduce all the stress factors that can presently be measured. Meditation masters have long known that these practices change our body and mind, heart and soul; modern research has confirmed that cultivating certain states of consciousness can even help restructure the brain and its functioning, definitively effecting consciousness, a recent discovery called neuroplasticity. Using certain shapes and colors also has a similar effect. There are many tools, methods, and skillful means in our Dharma tool chest. A spiritual practitioner as well as a teacher needs to be flexible and resourceful in adapting and effectively decanting the old wine of Buddhist Dharma into today's new bottles, preserving and maintaining the essence without clinging rigidly to the outer forms. If the practice fits, we can wear it.

When we come together to meditate, I feel that it is a very significant gathering of spiritual energy—awakening and enlivening, beautifying and edifying us all. Let's not overlook it, perhaps being deceived by the simplicity of this practice; there is a lot of ancient, timeless Buddhist wisdom behind it, of which the books, texts, and commentaries are just a small part. Milarepa, the peerless Tibetan yogi and song master, said, "Nature is the only book I need to read." We can also study and contemplate our true nature—the nature of our own hearts and minds. This is called the womb of all the Buddhas, the womb or source of enlightenment *tathagatagarbha,* to use an expensive Sanskrit word. The womb of the Buddhas. *Sunyata:* a fertile void, not merely a sterile, empty vacuum. Creative openness, delightful and joyous. Totally engaged, one with everything. Not withdrawn, not hiding. The sacred feminine—integrated with and attuned to whatever is, just as it is: the groundless and boundless, radiant ground of being.

The historical teacher named the Buddha, age eighty, died lying prone under a tree in Kushinagar, India, with his most enlightened disciples around him. His last words were, "Everything is impermanent. Work out your own enlightenment with diligence." It is up to each of you, to each of us, to work out our own spiritual practice and ultimate deliverance and salvation. It is not something that somebody drops on your head or puts into your hands as a gift. That's the bad news, but it's also the good news. It is sometimes called "the Buddha in the palm of our hand" in our Tibetan tradition. The miracle of total awareness, the potential of Buddha nature, is in ourselves, in our hands. How we use it is up to each of us. It is not even a matter of if we use this inherent freedom of being; we are all using it all the time. It depends upon *how* we use it, what we get out of it, how it becomes us, and so forth. And by "we," I don't mean just Buddhists. All beings are using it all the time. It is what we are. It is up to us to use it however we like. We can be as enlightened or as miserable as we choose to be. So make the choice: Will the dog wag the tail, or vice versa? Are we masters of awareness, or servants and slaves of mere thought? Don't fall prey forever to identity theft, or a simple case of mistaken identity through misknowing ourselves.

My root guru, the late Sixteenth Karmapa, said, "If you have one hundred percent dedication and confidence in the teachings, then every living situation can be part of spiritual practice. You can be living the practice instead of just doing it."

From the Karmapa's Karma Kagyu meditation tradition, sixteenth-century master Dakpo Tashi Namgyal sang, in his "Clarifying the Natural State":

Five Ways of Sustaining the Essence
Elevate your experience and remain wide open like the sky.
Expand your mindfulness and remain pervasive like the earth.
Steady your attention and remain unshakable like a mountain.
Brighten your awareness and remain shining like a flame.
Clear your thought-free wakefulness and remain lucid like a crystal.

CHAPTER 3

SWOOPING DOWN FROM ABOVE WHILE CLIMBING UP FROM BELOW

ABSOLUTE OUTLOOK AND RELATIVE PRACTICE

The Third Karmapa Lama, renowned as Rangjung Dorje, the self-arisen diamond, was a greatly enlightened Dzogchen master, and the Dharma brother of Longchenpa, the preeminent Dzogchen lineage ancestor (1308–1364). This nonsectarian Karmapa gave us "The Single Word of Heart-Advice," the important secret, oral pith-instruction lineage of the Mahamudra and Dzogchen tradition. This is one of my favorite dohas, or songs of enlightenment:

The Single Word of Heart-Advice
Homage to all the sacred masters.
The heart-mind of all the Buddhas of the past, the present, and the future, widely renowned as Dharmakaya, as enlightened mind, is precisely your own mind, which thinks of this and that.

What kind of Buddhist teaching is this? Even with all the inner obscurations and defilements, today's mind is inseparable from Buddha mind? This is what the Karmapa Lama says! But let's find out for ourselves if that actually is true, if it's possible.

When my root teacher Lama Kalu Rinpoche used to say this

to me decades ago, it didn't seem to make much sense. Not possible! I thought, in my ignorance. It must be something else: self-improvement, enlightenment or bust, get better, purify and transform, find something, understand something, learn something special, become different. I wanted the Enlightenment Project, to be a seeker joining other seekers in seeking the holy grail of Buddhahood, enlightenment with all my heart. We think like that, don't we? But what about the other side? Seekers must one day become finders, to make this path meaningful. What about pure *being,* not our self-centered and limited doings? Where we are coming *from,* not just where we think we are going *toward* on this highly touted express train to enlightenment. It seems too good to be true, but it *is* true. It's too obvious and too evident, so we don't notice it. It's too transparent, too close, and too marvelous.

The Karmapa says that the essential nature of your own mind, which thinks of this and that, *is* the Buddha mind, *is* Dharmakaya, absolute truth, Dzogchen—the natural Great Perfection. All the phenomena of samsara and nirvana appear within this unique awareness, your awareness. Samsara is not downtown somewhere while nirvana is uptown, or in the higher realms, the sylvan countryside, or on the other shore. Karmapa says all the phenomena of samsara and nirvana fit perfectly within this unique awareness. This incandescent innate awareness is the heart-essence of all the sutra teachings, the tantra teachings, and all the commentaries and pith instructions. It is both the ground and the goal of practice and is employed along the path, too.

Yet, when you apply it in contemplative practice, there is nothing whatsoever to be meditated on. It is an empty, luminous, spacious, unobstructed void.

Simply allow this unique awareness to rest vividly awake and present in its natural way.

This is Karmapa's teaching. That's what you have to do. There's nothing to meditate on. Just allow innate awareness to rest totally present and awake in its naked state of freshness and immediacy. That's why it's called mirrorlike awareness, skylike awareness, natural awareness—natural meditation and nonmeditation. Not doing anything. Everything happens as if in that skylike mirror of mind. The sky and the mirror don't do anything of their own volition, but simply accommodate transitory reflections without essentially changing.

> You don't need to worry or think, "Is this really it?" Don't bother yourself with these doubts and questions. Don't hope for improvement or be afraid of degeneration.

But how can we progress and develop spiritually if we don't hope for improvement? How can we both be there and also be *getting* there, undertaking the spiritual journey summed up in the traditional Buddhist path to enlightenment. What kind of Dharma path is this Dzogchen-Mahamudra teaching? Karmapa says: "Don't hope for improvement and don't fear ruin; don't chase transient concepts like improvement and degeneration. Just rest nakedly at home in this vividly awake present awareness. Relax loosely and rest. Besides this, you don't need anything to meditate on." So let that be the object of your meditation, of nonmeditation—the nonmeditation called sustaining present wakefulness, which is the inner essence of any meditation practice.

> By practicing in this extraordinarily simple way, again and again, you will definitely recognize the groundless, rootless open essence of all thoughts, appearances, and phenomena. When that happens, realization blooms naturally. All attachments, all habitual patterns, all conditioning is spontaneously liberated and released in this blossoming of realization.

This is called Buddhahood. This is what is meant when Manjusri says, "One moment makes all the difference. One moment of total awareness is one moment of perfect freedom and enlightenment." That's why this practice is so profound. One moment is enough. Some old-fashioned people say you can't become a Buddha if you're a woman, that you can only become an *arhat*, a liberated saint. Some people say you can't become a Buddha without developing through the ten *bhumis* (bodhisattva levels) for three endless aeons. People say all kinds of things, but, based upon the tantras—the nondual teachings of Vajrayana Buddhism—our nonsectarian practice lineage teachers say we are all Buddhas by nature; we only have to awaken to that fact. And that happens in the present moment, through total awareness, penetrating insight, a total moment of illuminated yet transparent *presence*. One eternal instant—the holy now. You don't have to build it up like an investment portfolio until it ripens. One moment includes it all. Why not *this* moment? What are we waiting for? It's now or never—as always. We are all far more Buddha-like than we think. See for yourself if this isn't true.

The Dalai Lama gets up at four every morning and meditates, studies, and does his practices. That can be said to be an expression of enlightenment itself; but I shouldn't use the word *enlightenment,* for it has too many imprecise interpretations. Dogen Zenji said, "Meditation is enlightenment." Not that you meditate to get enlightened, but rather that meditation *is* Buddha, is freedom. That's the other side of the seeker's notion of spiritual quest, the climbing and ascending to the heights of holiness. But if you can practice from that primordially whole and complete Buddha-ness place, rather than from an impoverished mentality of incompleteness, it's much more vast. Let Buddha do your sitting through you. If you don't conceive that it's "me" and "mine," "my distractions" and "my accented voice" and "my weariness," then it all takes on a very different character. It's not just meditation in action, it's freedom in action. It's the view in action. Spiritual practice is a way of life, not just a means to an end. It's like living sanely or healthily. It's not necessarily to get some other goal; it is to be fully present here and now. It is to be totally one with all and everything, totally present here and now. That is why St. Catherine of Siena said, "Every step of the way to heaven is heaven." Every step of the way is the Great Way; which we can never really fall from. This Way is all encompassing.

I have a lot of faith in this practice. I've found, after many years—and much to my surprise—that it is all true. When my beloved teacher Kalu Rinpoche used to tell us this thirty years ago, I couldn't believe it. My head was too thick. It seemed too good to be true! He said, "Your very mind, thinking of this and that, is not apart from the Buddha mind." It's not *your* mind, *your* problem. It's Buddha's problem; give it back to Buddha. Buddha already "got enlightened for your sins" is my funny way of thinking of it. You can relax; it's not your problem. It's Buddha nature expressing itself as a rainy day, as a storm, or as a sunny day. It is Buddha nature expressing itself as winter and also as summer. Also as fall, when we are dying, and as spring, when we are being born. Everything is an expression of Buddha nature or suchness, tathagatagarbha. Everything is it. Nothing isn't. In this light, everything is sacred, all are equal, and nothing special is holy— not holier than thou nor holier than anything else. And yet everything has its own intrinsic magic.

The View

There is nothing else happening out there. Naked awareness or pure transparent (selfless) presence is the beginning and the end: the alpha and omega, as we say in our Western wisdom tradition. We are alpha and omega both. Nowhere to go and nothing missing. That's why Karmapa says that "this very heart-mind" is it; don't overlook it! It is too close, so we overlook it. It is innate, so we can't obtain it. No one can give it to us, or has to, and no one can keep us from it or take it away.

Mount Analogue, a novel by René Daumal, is a spiritual allegory about many seekers seeking something special, the crystal mountain or the mystical jewels—the transparent diamonds of enlightenment. Actually it's an unfinished story, because the Frenchman Daumal died before finishing his book. Nonetheless, in the story the seekers are walking on the transparent mountain, and every rock is the transparent jewel they seek, but they can't recognize it because it really is so clear, pure, and perfectly transparent. You see, it's not just one jewel-like thing that they have to find; it's actually everything. And in the ultimate sense, it's the climbers, too. Often the best place to look for what you're seeking is right beneath your feet, under your nose, or within your current situation or relationship. I remember reading that the legendary teacher and groundbreaking nineteenth-century scientist Louis Agassiz taught his students: "If you want to know all about the science of icthyology, look at the fish right before you." When a student did so and reported what he saw, Agassiz said, "Okay, look at your fish!" "Look, look, look!" was the repeated injunction.

So how to find something that's not separate from you? Moreover, how to become what we *are*? In the eighteenth century, Longchenpa's greatest disciple, the fearless master Jigme Lingpa, sang that we are living on a continent of jewels but still feel impoverished because of our delusions about reality. All we have to do is awaken and recognize where and what we are already. A friend of mine once aptly designated this immanent natural state of jewel-like perfection we unknowingly participate in and are endowed with as pre-enlightenment, or enlightenment before enlightenment. This refers to our own primordial spiritual nature.

It's very subtle, this mystical truth of transcendent immanence; therefore, it's hard to recognize. But we might start to look in this direction, toward the view, the primordial outlook or bigger picture that encompasses the groundless ground of being. Toward where we are coming from, not just where we think we are going. Toward the goal, not just the present means or meditation technique. Then we can experience this incredibleness, what we might call in English "perfection" or completeness, illumination, realization, great peace, unconditional love, and openness. Freedom. When we have no more illusions about enlightenment and nirvana and when we have no more illusions about ourselves; then we're free of illusion, free of everything—free! Not just getting into the right concrete castle or blissful, peaceful meditation state. Not just teenage freedom. Genuine freedom is much bigger and deeper than that, more inclusive, and genuinely proactive rather than reactive.

Any constructed state of mind, mood, or feeling is temporary, fabricated, conditioned, and therefore impermanent and unreliable; we can fall from it, lose it, miss it. Any seat, throne, or pedestal, we can fall off of. But the ground we can't fall off of. Like gravity and reality, wisdom awareness is the good earth, the ground of being. The Dharma, reality, is upholding us; even if we jump up, there's nowhere to go. We don't need to stand on tiptoe to get higher; we just exhaust ourselves in that way. We can just stand up as ourselves.

It looks as if we keep trying to tie knots in the vast, trackless, open sky so we'll have something to hold on to. We keep trying to jump up, to get higher, or to get out of our familiar ruts. We stand on tiptoes trying to get above it all, and keep reaching up to erect a ladder or climb a tower or Himalayan peak; but, still, we can never leave the groundless ground. Even if we fly or are in orbit like an astronaut, it is the groundless ground of being that we are all based in. This is what we are looking into. And this is what we are using and living and breathing every day, while hardly even knowing it because it takes so many different forms. We are lost in the myriad forms without recognizing the oneness in diversity, the underlying continuum.

I love the vital teaching in the Wisdom Heart Sutra that says: "Form is emptiness, and emptiness is form." Not just that all forms are empty, but also that emptiness takes form. Recognize the shapes of emptiness also so we know what we are doing here. This is what we call in Tibetan coemergent wisdom, or wisdom arising simultaneously with illusions—for example, seeing dreams and knowing you are dreaming, or watching a movie while enjoying the drama, yet remembering it's just a play of light and sound, mere illusions on the silver screen and not serious matters of life and death. One should be able to see *through* the transparent window (of awareness) without forgetting the window is there. Otherwise, you just break it, or crash into it like a bird. Did you ever see a bird flying into a window because it wasn't seen? That's an example of merely seeing the emptiness of things, the empty and transparent side, without simultaneously recognizing the forms and functioning of the infinite manifestations and expressions of emptiness—the karma, the interconnectedness, the interdependent origination, the endless dance of emptiness. This is why spiritual high-divers sometimes have crash landings. If we are unaware of the mental projector, the projections, and their inextricable interrelationship, we crash into them again and again, entangled in the illusion of their permanent substantiality and concrete reality. Sage Nagarjuna said, "It's a pity that some people believe in concrete reality, but much more pitiful are those who believe in emptiness." It's easier to get stuck in emptiness than in materialism, for there's no way to get out, and no steps, no footholds. No exit, as Sartre famously and succinctly said. No enlightenment. No handholds, no helping hands. No *anything*.

Wisdom sees the transparent nothingness of things while recognizing the form and functional practicalities of this relative world we live in and love and strive to understand. As we say in the Mahayana Middle Way teachings, "See how things *appear* to be, as well as how they actually are." Appearances aren't everything, as every teenager must eventually learn; yet appearances are not nothing, either. If you are having a dream or a nightmare, you could know that. You don't just say, "No, there's no dream." It is a dream. It's a nightmare or perhaps a good dream, yet it's just a dream. Recognize the various appearances to be what they are, through discernment and discrimination, as well as intuiting their underlying essential nature. And as for ourselves: learn to understand our own appearance and manifestation in this world—how we are and what we seem to need and how we work—as well as who we essentially *are* and can be. This twofold wisdom understanding is called the two levels or aspects of truth: absolute and relative, or ultimate and conventional, essence and function. So, everything may be perfect, as the Great Perfection tantras proclaim, but it is probably too soon for us to say that. Everyone may be perfect as they are, and acceptance can go a long way in this prejudiced and intolerant world, yet we could still each use a little tweaking.

Meticulous Actions

Let's try to be very conscientious, committed, and diligent about our spiritual work, which is ultimately meaningful and can also be joyous and satisfying in the short term, too. Imagine how much progress we'd make if we practiced Dharma as much as Olympic athletes and professional musicians practice their skills. As we say in the Dzogchen tradition: *Swoop down from above, with the vast view of everything perfect, as it is—absolute truth, emptiness—while at the same time climbing up from below according to our capacity through relative practices, relative truth.* Swooping down while climbing up from below. Padmasambhava, the lotus-born guru who brought Buddhism to Tibet in the seventh century, said, "Though my view is higher than the sky, my actions regarding cause and effect (karma and conditioning) are as meticulous as finely ground barley flour."

Let's broaden our minds a bit, so we're not stuck with just one perspective. Can we hold both at the same time? Can we see the forest while we are down amid the trees? It is very important to be sensible and balanced in our spiritual work so we don't just space out, swooping down from above—which might sound great, exciting, delightful—but then suddenly being startled by a crash landing. Skiing straight down the mountain is a good example of too much hubris. You can get out of control and crash right into the parking lot at the bottom of the slope or go through a guard rail and over a cliff. On the other hand, we don't want to be totally bogged down with the Puritan mentality of grimly schlepping up from below with all our heavy baggage, being so deadly serious about how far it seems to be to the distant peak of enlightenment while missing all the joy and surprise discoveries of the journey. We need both the absolute picture—swooping down, with the effortless joy and the freedom of freefall flight—*and* the relative picture—carefully, meticulously taking care of all the details, climbing up from below according to our capacity through relative practices, including virtuous living, honesty, ethics, purification, and all the transcendental *paramitas* or panacean virtues of the bodhisattvas. Each of these limitless virtues is a practice: the perfection of patience, the perfection of generosity, the perfection of effort, skillful means, meditation, discriminating wisdom, and so on. All of these are practices to do. They don't just come because we read about them or believe in them. BuddhaDharma is mainly a do-it-yourself path. We have to actually walk the talk, not just verbalize it. Wisdom is as wisdom *does*. Buddha is as Buddha does. Let's learn to unconditionally love our way to enlightenment—loving to enlightenment sounds good, doesn't it?—and not just schlep, hurry, struggle, stress, memorize, study, and imitate, hoping and waiting for something to happen.

I find in my own life that although I'm often thinking about the highest mystical truths and am inspired when I read about these things—and I hope you read them, too, writings by poets like Longchenpa, Patrul Rinpoche, Shabkar, Rumi, Kabir, St. Francis, and Milarepa—I need to bring the mystical mountaintop spirituality down to where we live and, on a very practical level, to how we actually live. Do we always grab the best seat? Do we cut people off in traffic? Do we cut corners? Do we steal little things? Do we lie? (Just little white ones, right?) Are we selfish? Or are we kind and generous at the very least?

Maybe we keep the moral precepts. We don't hear much about the Buddhist precepts here because that's not really the emphasis of a Dzogchen teaching; but of course we understand that the training in virtue, restraint, nonharming, morality, and loving-kindness in action is very helpful. "Of course I don't kill," we might think or even assert aloud. Maybe we forget that our speeding car kills a lot of moths and other helpless little insects, but at least we try to cherish life and not to kill intentionally. For example, myself: I don't fish, hunt, swat mosquitoes, or step on ants and spiders. But maybe I eat meat, wear leather clothes, and have ivory on my mala beads and millions of silkworms' remains in my kimono cloth. Maybe you do, too. The entire precept is not simply about not killing; it is about cherishing life. We ought to really look into what it means to respect and cherish life in all its forms. Life is all we have, and it is a genuine gift, not to be squandered or misspent. Let's revere, appreciate, and cherish it.

Another moral precept is not stealing. Well, maybe I don't steal formally, but maybe I invest in companies that steal from other countries or that steal or destroy the environment or that support cruel and harmful policies (like apartheid or genocide, for example). It's not just that we shouldn't and can't afford to steal because of the consequences; it's that we shouldn't exploit. We don't need to take more than our share. You can apply this to any of the precepts. Maybe I don't lie (that's probably a lie), but what about slander, gossip, harsh words, and the little white lies we tell ourselves every day along with our internal story line? You get mad sometimes at somebody, and you say harsh things, don't you? They count, too; words can harm, like swords and knives. So that's the principle of the precepts: nonharming and conscientious caring, kindness and compassion, on the outer behavioral as well as the inner character and integrity levels. For the little lies and small deceptions, the mindless deaths in our wake, the well-covered and deeply denied, greedy exploitativeness of our modern American lifestyle—all these count karmically, too. Self-deception also counts. How straightforward, forthright, and honest are we, really?

You can say the same with the precepts regarding intoxication, sexual misconduct, and pride. It says in the Buddhist sutras things like "Don't sleep on a high bed." And you say, "I don't sleep on a high bed. I sleep on the floor—on my imported Japanese futon with silk sheets and duck feather–filled pillows." But who cares about inches and feet high and low? That's an old-fashioned manner of expression. The precept is about pride, about taking the higher place, about being above others. And it's about simplicity and contentment, rather than excess. How many ducks have died so I can use their comfortable feathers?

Mahatma Gandhi asked us to consider our relationship to both need and greed, and where we usually settle along that continuum. I find this a useful and informative practice. How many homes and cars do we own? How much excess do we have—at home, let's say? How many tape recorders, cameras, TVs, phone numbers, cell phones, credit cards, and computers do you have? Maybe you have one of each, but I know some of us have more than one of each, even in a single room of the multilevel houses we inhabit today. We have last year's and this year's gadgets of similar kind and are looking for next year's, too. Excess is wasteful and costly. I read the horrifying statistic that every year 15 million children die of hunger. Fully one-third of the world's population is starving according to the World Health Organization, and it is estimated that some 800 million people in the world suffer from hunger and malnutrition. Meanwhile, many of the First World countries are collecting the best from the developing countries, exploiting them, mining them, deforesting them. Of course, it's not just in Western countries; now new world power China is deforesting Tibet, mining all the border regions of its large new national boundary, and bringing all that natural wealth back to the central homeland, without even benefiting the local populace in the areas in which it was found.

If we realize the profound mystical truths that we are all Buddha, that everything is sacred, wouldn't we treat everybody the way we treat our own bodies, like we treat ourselves and our most beloved family members—acting as a responsible, affectionate, caring family and community guardian and earth steward rather than as a dominator and an exploiter? If these teachings don't filter down from the highest level right into all aspects of our lives and into our relations, where it really counts, what use are they? So let's examine and see how these spiritual views and insights change our life. Are we becoming better, less selfishly greedy people and contributing to a better world? Does our spiritual practice actually affect our life for the better? Do our beliefs positively change our life? Does the BuddhaDharma actually work for us? Because if it doesn't, who needs it?!

One of my Western Dharma teacher friends once said, "It doesn't matter what you believe. It only matters what you do." I thought that was very profound for somebody who had been a full-time Buddhist "believer" for more than thirty years. I then asked whether it helps to believe that the practice you are doing will help you, and what's the use of doing certain Buddhist practices if you don't believe in them? Or of praying if you don't believe in it? He answered that if you meditate or pray, it means you believe in it, whatever you may think you believe in. So if you meditate, you are already accomplishing something. It is the actualization of a deeper belief, deeper than our conscious mind.

Does it matter what we believe, or does it matter more what we *do*, how we live and *are*? That's why Gandhi said, when asked by a reporter what the heart of his teaching was, "My *life* is my teaching. How I live is my teaching." He tried to walk his talk, to practice what he preached. So look at how you live, and you'll know what your teaching is and what message you're passing on. And it's not just your teaching, but it's also indicative of your inner wisdom and spiritual realization. Look there; don't just look at the gilded antique Buddha statue on the altar here. Look in the mirror; have a good look every day. Reflect on what you perceive there. But please don't get too depressed! There's nothing to get too depressed about, actually, but there's also nothing to get too excited or elated about. Getting enlightened is just one more experience. The world will just keep turning. Not to worry! No one can do it all, yet no one is exempt from participating.

What is it that is most truly transformative? What is the actual transformative essence of Buddha's liberation teaching, and what is secondary, and even tertiary? I've been thinking about this a lot lately, in meetings with other teachers and in assessing and evaluating my own students' progress and development. Eating oranges is supposed to be good for a cold, but what is it that is good for the cold? (The vitamin C, the ascorbic acid, I suppose, although research results seem to vary.) So what is it in the various spiritual activities and practices and studies we Buddhist practitioners undertake that is essentially and most truly and positively transformative? Some people say mindfulness. Some people say devotion, love, compassion, mind training, or selfless good works. Some people say deep investigation and objective self-inquiry. Some people say meditation. There are many ideas; what is most truly transformative remains an open question. The Dalai Lama once answered, "Analysis and meditation." I have been thinking that most transformative for me is the longing, the aspiration, the passion for truth, reality, enlightenment—and keeping at it over a long time, in all parts of life, not just in religious settings, but all the time, wherever life leads me.

So what is it for you? Look at your own life. What is it that actually works, helps, and genuinely makes a difference in both the short and long term? Stay with it, and keep refining it like an art form or a life koan (Zen riddle). Delve more and more deeply into *that* question, gradually letting go of what is extra and heading more directly toward it—always asking, What is truly transformative? How shall I live my life, and toward what end?

the facts of life from a buddhist perspective

turn the searchlight,
the spotlight, inward

CHAPTER 4

BUDDHA'S ENLIGHTENMENT EXPERIENCE

recently I was in Austin, Texas, visiting my Dzogchen Center sangha, offering several evening talks at a church there and a weekend meditation retreat. The local Montessori school invited me to come during the day and talk with its seventy-five students between the ages of seven and eleven. I wondered just exactly what I was going to do, but no need; from the moment the children started trickling in the door, they came right up to me, climbed on me—I was sitting on the floor on a cushion at the front of the room—and began asking questions. There was no beginning and no end; it all just happened. Toward the end of our time together, we did a gong meditation—following the sound of the gong, seeing where it goes, and just being there for a moment or two.

That weekend, one of the women in the retreat came up to me at lunchtime and asked if she could speak with me. She told me a story about her eight-year-old son, Ryan, who came home from school during the week and told her that something very unusual had happened that day at school. She'd asked him, "Do you want to tell me about it?"

Ryan said, "Yes, a monk from Tibet, New York, came." (Sort of like Paris, Texas, I guess.) The boy said that the monk (me!) taught them about God and Buddha and the gong meditation. She asked what that was.

He said, "Well. He told us to watch where the sound came from and where the sound went, and to listen very carefully. I didn't know you could watch and listen to the same thing. It was very interesting. He said that if you followed and watched where the sound went, that you might get closer to God. And I did that."

His mother said, "Yes, and . . . ?"

And the boy said, "Well, when I watched and listened to where the sound went, I didn't get closer to God. I *was* God."

I thought, "Out of the mouths of babes," as the scripture says.

That gong meditation took only about thirty seconds. Sometimes God realization doesn't take very long, if you are young and innocent enough! When I asked the children, "So where did the sound go?" every hand went up! I couldn't believe it! Then I said, "Shh. Don't say anything." I didn't want to ruin it. But they all *knew*. Isn't it amazing? Some even had both hands raised! I was very touched by that, by the freshness of the youthful experience of just sensing. Not even wondering, "What is God?" or "Who am I to say I am God?" or "What if I'm wrong?" No such editing taking place at that age. Just, "Oh yeah, God. I know. I am that."

That is the whole teaching of Dzogchen, the innate Great Perfection: "I am That." But who can simply and clearly say it with certainty at this moment, as that little child did? So perhaps we have strayed a little bit from home plate; perhaps we are out somewhere in left field. We seem to have missed the bases while coming round. Or even worse, we're in the bleachers just watching the game, not even playing anymore. Still, we started at home and we can come home again. That child took only about ten seconds; for us—as adults, maybe it takes an hour. Remember Thomas Merton's insight: "We are already one and we imagine we are not. And what we have to recover is our original purity. Whatever we have to be is what we are." This is the mystic's secret of secrets. Don't start a day without recalling it. The ultimate is never afar.

As one of my Zen teachers used to say, "It's good to try to sit rocklike in zazen, but nobody gets enlightened after half an hour of zazen." So we shouldn't expect too much, too fast, too easily. Haste and instant gratification are banes of our society today—what I call Instant Coffee Mind. (Just add water, and poof! You'll have what you want.) Spiritual maturation and conscious evolution is a life's journey, not just an instant high of enlightenment experience or one deliciously sweet moment on the lips. But it is, I find, very available to us, this awake enlightenment experience. Actually, realization is now; it is now, or never—as always! One eternal moment is enough, and includes everything. Then we develop and stabilize it through continuous application in spiritual practice throughout our lives. First, take notice; then watch for it; then observe it, become familiar with it, and ultimately become it.

I should define terms a little bit. The only way to define enlightenment is to say that it is not what we think it is. That's the safest thing to say. As Kris Kristofferson sang, "Freedom's just another word for nothing left to lose." Freedom and enlightenment—nirvana, in Buddhist terms—are not exactly what we think they are. We have a lot of concepts about these things; those concepts are probably best left aside. That child in Austin, Texas, didn't have so many preconceived notions, and so he got right to the point quickly, which was very profound and gratifying to me. I hope and pray that moment is like a seed, informing his whole life. What is the point in a nutshell? That what we seek, we *are*. All we need can be found within, and within each other. Let's look deeply.

We are not exactly what we think we are, which, I think, is where it starts to get really interesting. If not, then, what are we? Who are we? Is life a joke? Are we nothing? Is there no purpose or meaning to our existence? We might do well to turn the searchlight inward at this point, and start to find out a little bit, come home, and make ourselves at home, here in this universe, instead of acting like disenfranchised aliens, orphans, strangers in a strange land—mere silent partners in this cosmic pageant.

In this section, I will introduce the basic, fundamental teachings of Buddhism, from the ground up—Buddhism 101, as I lovingly call it: Buddha's enlightenment experience, the basis of his renowned Middle Way to higher sanity, deathless peace, truth, wisdom, and love; the Four Noble Truths taught by the Buddha twenty-five hundred years ago, the basic facts of life according to enlightened vision; and the Eightfold Path to enlightenment. I have been thinking of these eight steps as eight principles of enlightened living that help us to better understand what is going on with us and around us, and how our spiritual practice relates to our personal life as well as to freedom and nirvanic peace, bliss, and ultimate fulfillment. Let's see if we can apply it to our lives, where it counts—on our authentic journey of awakened, enlightened living.

As explored in early chapters, meditation helps us realize these truths or facts of life, which are actually self-evident. The BuddhaDharma—the teachings of Buddha, or the truth of how things *are* (meaning the vision of reality according to awakened enlightenment)—is not something we have to believe, like creeds and dogma. In Buddhism, there is nothing to believe; there is everything to learn, to explore, to discover for ourselves, to recover, to come home to, and to inhabit at last. To fully inhabit our lives, our genuine being, and become who and what we really are and are meant to be, in the highest sense—our best, most true, and authentic Selves. How to do this? In short, by fully inhabiting the present moment—the only place we can ever be, in any case—and learning how to sink our roots more deeply into that fertile soil and imbibe its delectable essences. The path laid out twenty-five hundred years ago by the sage teacher known as Gotama Buddha is scientific, in a way. He tells us that if we reproduce the experiment that he made, we can replicate the results within our own experience. And many millions have.

Buddhism is descriptive: it says how things are. It is not prescriptive: it doesn't exactly tell us what to do. It describes how things are, how things are connected, what causes things to happen and how; then we get to choose. We are responsible and will experience things principally according to those choices, whether skillful or unskillful, wholesome or unwholesome, fulfilling or frustrating. That is both the good news and the bad news. The Buddha is in the palm of our hands; our life is our own, as it were. What we do with it makes all the difference.

Our True Nature

The basic, most fundamental thing about Buddhism is the so-called enlightenment experience, which is our birthright, our true nature. It is utterly possible and accessible. It's not just something Buddha experienced; many have realized enlightenment throughout the ages—many millions, probably, at least to some significant degree. That's what all of this business is about, whether you call it Buddhism, the wisdom traditions, the conscious evolution project, or the perennial philosophy. Enlightenment, spiritual awakening, illumination, self-realization, satori—these are all more or less synonyms. It means recognizing who and what we are, realizing the most profound wisdom and insight about existence for ourselves. Lao Tzu says that knowledge is knowing the world; wisdom is knowing oneSelf. Wisdom and self-awareness means discovering or realizing our true nature. It is coming home; it is not finding something that we never had before. It is right here, always; the problem is that *we* are usually elsewhere! It is here, even now. What we seek, we are. It is all within.

Out of such a personal breakthrough or epiphany-like peak experience, we perceive everything a little differently, which is exquisitely fulfilling, meaningful, and liberating. We don't just see different things—we see things differently. When I become clearer, everything becomes clearer. For example, we might notice that things are not exactly the way we thought they were. This can effect a radical transformation in our lives; it depends on what we do with that insight. We might realize that we are barking up the wrong tree or chasing our own tail, like mere dogs. We might realize that we have climbed the ladder of success in some way, but that the ladder is leaning on the wrong wall. We may realize we're always hurrying, but heading where and for what? We might have an identity crisis, even if we're forty or fifty years old, and wonder what we are doing and why? Why do we die, and what if anything happens afterward? Why are we suffering? Why are we so rarely satisfied? We might actually plumb life's big questions. Why am I here? How to live my life? What does it all mean? Why do bad things happen to good people? Who am I?

Buddha, out of his awakening—known as supreme enlightenment—gave his first talk about these matters in the Deer Park outside Benares, at a place now known as Sarnath, where the deer came out of the forest to listen. It is called the Fire Teaching, because he said, when asked why he was shining with nirvanic peace and bliss:

> Because I have realized a truth that is beyond suffering. All created, conditioned things are unreliable or ultimately dissatisfying; all are burning with conflicting desires and confusion. The eyes are burning, the ears are burning, the tongue is burning. I have realized something that is unfabricated, timeless, and unconditioned, far beyond this conditioning, this unreliable, impermanent, dissatisfying, fervid world. It is the nirvanic peace and deathless ease right in the midst of it, but it is not the things themselves.

Our true nature, our luminous core, our ineffable spiritual nature—our Buddha nature or innate Buddha-ness—is not a created, impermanent, corruptible thing. It is not dissatisfactory or unreliable, neither fragile nor corruptible. It is perfect, luminous, free, and complete from the beginningless beginning. It is not something in this world that we can shop for and obtain. Practicing meditation is a path to rediscovering that, to awakening the Buddha within, to recognizing that which is ultimately fulfilling, satisfying, meaningful, joyous, and even deathless.

That's what all this is about. It's not simply about religion, belief, dogma, or rituals. It's not the newest fad to get high. It's not merely about joining and belonging to a group. This path of truth, wisdom, and love concerns a very personal and intimate relationship with something beyond yet immanent in each of us, however one conceives of it—the divine, the higher self or soul, one's true self, our true nature—at the heart of which we are all interconnected. It is not selfish, nor is it merely impersonal; it is transpersonally related to each of us, yet beyond any one of us. These noble truths are something we should know. Then we can see if they are true, if they apply to our own experience, and how they can actually work for us, to provide the spiritual rewards this path promises to whoever chooses to follow it, male or female, young or old, regardless of race, creed, background, status, or even religion.

The Buddha taught his famous Four Noble Truths twenty-five hundred years ago, soon after becoming fully enlightened beneath the Bodhi Tree. The First Noble Truth or fact of life is *dukkha,* that suffering is universal because of the dissatisfactoriness inherent in all conditioned, created, dysfunctional things; that the unenlightened life is full of disappointment and suffering. How impermanent, hollow, short lived, unreliable, and uncertain fabricated things are, if carefully scrutinized. In short, this first verity is summed up in the simple statement that unenlightened life—worldly life as we usually know it—is chock-full of difficulties, confusion, conflicts, anxiety, maladjustment, and suffering. It is not that there aren't plenty of other positive, and even joyous and beautiful, aspects of life, but it is full of suffering and delusion. Yet there is a way beyond those universal problems, which the Buddha directly addressed in his original teachings.

The Second Noble Truth is the cause of that dissatisfaction. After all, the Dharma is interested in only one thing: the end of suffering, the alleviation of dissatisfaction and distress, and the realization of blissful nirvana. That's what the Buddha said. "Don't ask me whether God exists. Don't ask me where the world came from. That's not my business. My business is solely dissatisfactoriness and the end of it; suffering, misery, ignorance and bondage, and their end, the sure heart's release." Furthermore, he explained that overweening attachment, craving, self-clinging, and greed are the cause of *dukkha* (suffering and dissatisfaction); this ignorant attachment to what cannot ultimately satisfy and fulfill us, he explained as the second fact of life. Because everything is uncertain, unreliable, impermanent, flowing and passing, how can holding on to what is slipping through our fingers ever be ultimately satisfying, or give us anything but the irritating pain of rope burn? Even if we get what we want, how long can we hold on to it? Even if *it* stays around, *we* are or will soon be gone, since we—each of us—are just another impermanent thing. The cause of that dissatisfactoriness is our incessant holding on, resistance, grasping, and confused desire—acting out of our ignorance about the true nature of things. Let's look and see if this is not the case in our own lives.

The Third Noble Truth is that the end of this dukkha, the end of suffering and of fervid craving, is attainable by the cultivation of contentment through nonattachment, which is release, nirvana, total freedom, and the openness of emptiness. That's the end of suffering right there, the end of attachment. In the sutras it is called "the heart's sure release" or relief. Nirvanic peace is relief from confusion and suffering, change, dissatisfaction, confusion, weariness, and so on. Is it not true that when we kiss the joy as it flies, rather than cling to it, we live in eternal sunrise, as Blake sang? Aren't greed, desire, and clinging dissatisfying, even when we momentarily get what we want—for we so soon fear losing it, or even intuit its imminent passing away?

The Fourth Truth—perhaps the most important one—is the path to that release, the path by which we can actually experience that heart's sure relief from suffering, from dissatisfactoriness. That's traditionally called the Eightfold Noble Path, the eight principles of enlightened living, or the eight steps to enlightenment. The path is divided into three sections: *sila, samadhi,* and *prajna*—ethics, meditation, and discriminating wisdom.

The Four Noble Truths offer a complete description of how things are; how to solve our problem, our suffering; and what the result is. The first two truths, or verities, are the diagnosis; the second pair provide the cure. The first pair is like the theory regarding our true dilemma, which is to be known. The second pair is the practice, which is to be applied and realized.

Again, this is just a description. We get to decide if this is the path for us. For example, let's honestly ask ourselves, Is it even our problem? Perhaps we are totally content and satisfied with our lives and the world around us. Maybe we haven't noticed that there is any problem. That's fine, as far as it goes. We shouldn't be visiting a doctor's office if we're not sick. No need to be in the pharmacy looking at all the different medicines; it's not a mall or museum. We should be out enjoying life. The Dalai Lama himself has said that happiness is the purpose of life. So let's seek our highest, most long-lasting happiness and deepest fulfillment, not just cheap thrills. How to find what we seek? I believe it comes through conscientiously striving to look further, deeper. To become what we seek. Through the most powerful force in the world, the heart-mind, the inner spirit, this is what we can and must do.

We are all at different stages of conscious evolution. This is not a judgment. However, it is obvious that, to some extent at least, we each experience the same things somewhat differently. I go around the world saying we are all Buddhas, and people come out of the audience and say, "I love what you said, Surya, but why did you start your talk by saying we are all Buddhists? I'm a Christian." I say "Buddha," and she heard "Buddhists"; someone else hears I don't know what—"voodoo" maybe! Let us all become enlightened Buddhas, rather than mere Buddhist followers! Moreover, we want leaders, not followers. So, American Buddhas awaken! Throw off your chains, your neuroses, your concepts. Live up to your freethinking, spiritual inheritance.

It is never easy to genuinely see things as they are—which is the definition of wisdom in Buddhism. Seeing things as *they* are, not as *we* are, with all our interpretations, prejudices, preconceptions, and biases. Seeing things as they actually are, not as they ain't. It seems that people can only take so much reality at one time, as some philosopher once cracked. It is difficult, if not impossible, to perceive and understand anything objectively when we are conflicted and afflicted by attitudes and opinions, preconceptions, biases, beliefs, and other concepts, just as it is difficult to really listen and hear what someone is saying when we are impatiently waiting to get our words into the conversation. Active, open-minded listening is one of the conscious skills learned and cultivated through mindful living. It seems to take extraordinary imagination to face truth nakedly.

We are all flowers in a universal garden, in different stages, going in different directions, with different shapes, backgrounds, interests, and psychological conditioning. Yet we all have an intrinsic spiritual tropism: just as flowers and most other growing things instinctively reach toward the sunlight, so do we grow toward the inner, divine light. We are all dealing with different things, and often in different ways, but for more or less the same ultimate purposes—survival, evolution, happiness, love, belongingness, and security.

Did you ever notice that sometimes you don't notice or feel anything, yet the next person feels or perceives something? Maybe one simply is not tuned in to or interested in that partic-

ular level of feeling or is not receptive to that level of environmental vibration. Each of us has different realities going on, as it
were, different perceptions and interpretations—not to mention
varying goals, intentions, and foci. For example, I'll bet that water looks very different to you and me than to a fish, doesn't it?
Since you are reading this book, you are probably looking for
something—perhaps seeking something deeper out of life. Perhaps we've found out that we have so much, almost everything,
but that having, even having everything materially, is never quite
enough. That's the problem, isn't it? Never quite enough *for us.* So
we are seeking something deeper, truer, more meaningful and
even long lasting.

We can all find fulfillment and free ourselves from the incessant, gnawing inner feeling of dissatisfaction and lack at the heart
of so much of our travails. That is the hope in this joyful message
of the Dharma path: that there is always such a tremendous possibility, without necessarily altering outer circumstances and
conditions. Nothing is eternally fixed or ruined or hopeless;
everything is changing, and is not exactly what we think it is. So
every situation, wherever we find ourselves, is somewhat workable. Even ourselves—workable! There is always hope. Yet work
still must be done. This work is the true work—the conscious
and intentional wisdom work we do on ourselves and for the
benefit of all. Buddhism is an inside job, and we are all capable of
undertaking it.

Engaged Wisdom

Enlightenment is such a vast concept, the ultimate spiritual
awakening—the flowering and actualization of all that we are
and can be. It is very hard to reconcile that with life down here
on earth amidst the hurly-burly, the dog poop, and the daily
news. Yet, I think the real important question is, How does spir-

itual enlightenment relate to us? What can such do for me, for each of us? That can only be realized through your own practice, your own inner work, your own conscientious investigation—your own continuous engagement in a meaningful form of spiritual life.

Are you wondering whether enlightenment is enough, or if it is somehow selfish, narcissistic even? Rest assured that the serenity and calm of enlightened wisdom naturally manifests as loving-kindness and compassion in action. Before jumping to quick conclusions, we need to recognize that there are some selfish practitioners even in the so-called helping professions—doctors, nurses, therapists, social workers, schoolteachers, and priests—who exploit their patients, clients, students and parishioners in different ways. When we are talking about the awakened heart, *bodhicitta,* and selfless altruism, selfish exploitation has no room in that. Let's not use the word *enlightened* here. What is *enlightened* supposed to be, anyway? It is what in the West we would call an illumined saint or sage, a truly wise spiritual elder. Regarding such individuals, we must examine the behavior, not just the beliefs and the ideas. What fits and what doesn't fit? What are the results, at least those we can see? Does it actually serve to help anyone? Actually, there are no perfectly enlightened individuals; there is only enlightened activity. Let's not be too idealistic.

Wisdom and compassion are inseparable, like the two wings of a bird. Wisdom is the close companion to truth; compassion includes unconditional love and warmheartedness. Truth without love is sterile, and too often kills; love without truth is blind, directionless. Profound wisdom is not merely some kind of abstraction. For example, if you have an objective understanding of reality, then—in the best case—you treat others as you would be treated because you intuitively experience the inseparability of yourself and others. With deep insight naturally comes reduced selfishness and egotism; realizing the interrelatedness of all, and that others need and want more or less the same as oneself does, you automatically treat them accordingly. That is engaged wisdom; that is loving our way all the way to enlightenment. Its natural outflow is empathic compassion. Why would wisdom harm that which it is one with? Does your right hand harm, or work with, your left? This is a simple equation. As we develop the wisdom of self-knowledge through reflection, contemplation, integration, and honest self-scrutiny, we also understand others far better, and we learn to recognize ourselves in each other. If you realize the nature of your heart and mind, you realize the oneness with everything and everyone. Then, how can you harm or exploit anyone or anything?

A natural morality emerges from the insightful experience of unselfishness and interrelatedness. We realize our inherent kinship with others, and not just humans; that we need each other, to exist and to flourish and evolve; and that we are together for many significant reasons, not just randomly thrown together like flotsam and jetsam on the current of the ceaselessly flowing river of reality. So when you get to the level of doctrine, ethics is all laid out for our edification and guidance. In the teachings of Buddhism, we find ten precepts, not entirely unlike those in the Good Book. They are called the ten nonvirtues, including three of body, four of speech, and three of mind. These include proscriptions against killing, lying, stealing, slandering, jealousy, covetousness, and so forth. However, out of genuine enlightenment experience comes a natural morality based on genuine sanity and wisdom's realization of the universal nature of us all, seeing that we all need and want the same things and fear much the same terrors, anxieties, and insecurities—a morality concerning ourselves as well as our loved ones and communities.

Let's not be too idealistic. The moral activity we are describing takes place in the *relative* dimension, here where we live and breathe and inhabit corporeal bodies of flesh and blood. This is the dimension where we relate to each other as separate, where everything is connected yet there is still karmic cause and effect, conditioning, and what goes around comes around; that's all in the relative, horizontal, time-bound earthly plane where we live. The absolute or ultimate dimension is such a sheer, steep, vertical, formless plane that there is nothing to relate or compare it to; there is no good and bad, no karma, no self and other, neither time nor space in the absolute. In the absolute, nothing happens. In the relative, everything counts, and every small thing we do, say, intend, and think *matters* and has implications and karma. That's where everything happens. This is the Buddha's understanding: not veering toward one or the other extreme, such as nihilism or eternalism/materialism, nor both, nor simultaneously, either. The cross is a beautiful symbol for that, like a simple mandala: in the horizontal and the vertical we discern the relative and the absolute dimensions all at once, the true joining of heaven and earth, God and creation. It is at that great crossroads—in that wholeness, that critical, ever-present meeting, the nowness—where we live and transcend while simultaneously integrating all possible dimensions, a sublime synthesis that completes the whole picture—transient time and eternity; infinity amid the finite; all polarities, dichotomies, and dualities abolished; oneness and noneness conjoined, coemergent, integrated.

Therefore let's genuinely look into things and see what's wrong and bothering us, if anything. Let's see what the problems actually are in our lives and on this fragile green planet; let's look into the cause, its origins, patterns, and principles; and let's discern how to comprehend and transform, accept and transcend, integrate and be free. That's what the Buddha's powerful path of awakening offers. It remains up to us to confirm it for ourselves; otherwise it is just a rumor. It is up to us to keep it alive, and to us to truly live and evolve. We are the ancestors now, for the generations to come; what we do will affect all those who may follow. What shall we re-create together?

CHAPTER 5

SUFFERING AND THE CAUSE
OF SUFFERING

What is bugging us? Doesn't it sometimes seem like *every-thing* is bugging us? Buddha's First Noble Truth, or the first fact of life, is that all created or conditioned things are ultimately dissatisfying. The word in Sanskrit is *dukkha,* the root of English words like *darkness, discomfort, distress, dysfunction,* and *disease.* Sometimes *dukkha* is translated as suffering, but that is a weak translation. Etymologically, *dukkha* means hard to bear, off the mark, hollow. It means dissatisfactoriness—what Christianity might put as nothing in this world can satisfy us, or everything this side of the heaven-and-earth dichotomy is imperfect. Buddha meant that all forms of unenlightened life are laced with difficulty, suffering, and dissatisfaction in the ultimate analysis. Everything that is conditioned falls apart, is uncertain, unreliable, and unsatisfying in the long run. The more we are invested in created things, the more we suffer. Can you think of anything that is ultimately satisfying? Anything? True satisfaction and everlasting fulfillment are hard to find; they are heaven, the shining pearl beyond price, the Holy Grail.

We do have moments of satisfaction. But what is beyond this roller coaster ride, this yo-yo of ups and downs, highs and lows? Through enlightened vision, through awakening, through spiritual realization, we realize a nirvanic peace, which is not a mere fabricated, composite, or conditioned thing. It is not a particular state of mind that can change and deteriorate. It is the natural state, the original fundamental, underlying nature. This untrammeled, innate spiritual nature is not unreliable and uncertain. It is not dissatisfying or subject to change or corruption. So that's the first fact of life: dukkha, the dissatisfactory nature of all conditioned, fabricated things; that suffering and difficulty are a fact of mortal life.

I personally have found that this is true. It is very simple when you finally get down to it: that ignorant greed, overweening attachment, and resistance *are* dissatisfying. Look at our relationships. Selfishness, egotism, and ignorantly clinging to what isn't ultimately good for us doesn't work very well, even as it is difficult to reform our deluded habits and desires. On the other hand, intelligently letting go and being more accepting, spacious, and gracious—open hands, open arms, open heart and mind—actually works. This kind of more equanimous, generous, collaborative win-win approach goes a long way toward relieving a lot of the tension, stress, and friction generating all this energy of conflict and confusion. It can help alleviate certain forms of illness, too, that stem from energy imbalances and stress. Look at your own closest relationships and see if this is not true. If we don't apply the Dharma teaching to our own lives and our own personal way of thinking, it's not transformative and liberating BuddhaDharma at all; it's just a sham, a shell—a husk without essential heart.

This First Noble Truth about the fundamental dissatisfactoriness of unenlightened life is profoundly informative. It does sometimes seem like everything irritates or at least disappoints us, later if not sooner. This is the truth of dukkha. Everything is off the mark, fraught, cracked. What is the cause of that? It's this ignorant attachment and clinging to things; craving for something; holding on to that which dissipates, which falls apart, which is impermanent and ungovernable; identifying with things that are not ultimately true, illusions like our separatist self-concept, which is also just a fleeting, hollow fabrication. And yet we resist. We are stuck with our self-image, our ego clinging, invested in our time-worn persona and identity, our personal act and role in life—all of which conspire to severely limit our own possibilities. You might think your name is "Alison" or "Henry," and you probably have some other concepts and even delusions—like that you're a woman or a man, you're American, you're Canadian, good or bad, and so on—but are you *just* that? Are you not possibly also Buddha, a god or a goddess, a global citizen, and male/female energy embodied in human form? As long as you think you are just so and so—a lawyer or graduate student or whatever—who has no power over what you do and what happens to you, you limit your true possibilities. One of the main differences between our current consciousness and the awakened mind of enlightenment is the scope of outlook.

Take Mother Teresa, for example. She was about four and a half feet tall and hailed originally from Albania. She was an obscure, impoverished nun in a Roman Catholic order. Where did she get the idea that she could just go and save the world, that she could transform Calcutta and take on all the poverty and injustice of India? Instead of being a disempowered, Sunday school lesson–giving nun, she prayed for God's help and guidance, took action, and totally reinvented herself. Taking Jesus's mission to the poorest of the poor, the street people and lepers of Calcutta, she blossomed, eventually forming her own order of actively engaged charitable sisters. Experiencing some kind of spiritual rebirth with an entirely different and vastly more empowered image of what is possible, she must have altered her self-concept, or perhaps loosened her own self-concept and got out of her own way so that the inexhaustible energy of her Lord could flow through her into the world; thus she became something completely different, more like the Dalai Lama, Mahatma Gandhi, or Albert Schweitzer. Unlike the Dalai Lama or J. Krishnamurti, nobody found Mother Teresa when as a child and said, "You are special, an avatar sent from above. You should work to save the world." She reinvented herself. She took on that mantle, selflessly taking on the plight of all the poor street people in Calcutta. She didn't have much of anything to work with. She didn't have the Gates Foundation or any governmental agency behind her. She just went to Calcutta and started doing it. Her devoted heart provided more than enough strength and energy to get her going and to carry many along on such a remarkable journey. Once she said that the problem today is that we draw our circle too small, resulting in unequitable distribution of resources, loneliness, and separation.

The point I want to make here is that *your* self-image and personal identity are a hoax, not unlike identity theft. It is the original case of mistaken identity, stolen by ignorance and confusion. Of course, one has to function, so one must go through socialization and develop some sort of persona, personality, a mask to present to the world; however, one doesn't have to be totally invested in it, identified with it, stuck with it, and deceived by the mask one has assumed. When we see through ourselves and know our true, authentic, best selves, then we can don and doff any mask and any costume at will, as appropriate, as needed, for different occasions and roles in life. Self-knowledge as spiritual self-realization helps us realize that it is the hand inside the Muppet that makes it stand up, move, and function, and we remain undeluded. We no longer forget who and what we really are and why we are here.

That's the point of spiritual evolution and liberation. You don't have to be stuck with anything, anywhere. We all inherited our genetic makeup from our parents, but that doesn't mean we have to be particularly stuck with that or overly identify with it. Maybe our parents weren't very healthy, but that doesn't mean we can't be reasonably healthy. When we take responsibility for ourselves—which is an important part of growing up, both physically and spiritually—we can actually develop better character, more integrity, and even total self-mastery. It is not the cards we're dealt, but how we play them that determines the game's outcome. Here is one of life's most powerful secrets.

Most of us, due to misknowing and simple ignorance, fall prey to the hollow illusion of a permanent self-image. We are attached to our selfish identity because it is familiar, and all that we know—our cozy, familiar-smelling, rag-lined nest. Perhaps that is why we think often of Mother Teresa's myth. Maybe she is actually like Santa Claus and doesn't really do anything good; I don't know. (She did seem saintly.) But we all, for the most part, need to have somebody like her to hang our hopes on: Santa Claus for the children, others for us—Mother Teresa or the Dalai Lama, Jesus Christ, Princess Diana, the Messiah, or whoever is your favorite bodhisattva. As long as we need to have hopes, we need to hang them somewhere. But let us not fall prey to too much idealization and give in to our immature tendency to totalize things as either black or white. For we are usually disappointed in the end if we place anyone or anything on a high pedestal. We ourselves have to be the bodhisattvas who are the actively awakening Buddhas-to-be, the ushers to help bring into this world the kingdom of heaven, rather than simply waiting and praying for a messiah or future Buddha to come and do it for us.

The Cause of Dissatisfaction

Knowing the bare fact that things are dissatisfying won't free us from dissatisfaction. The crucial part is knowing and addressing the Second Noble Truth, which is the cause of that dissatisfaction—not the things themselves, since the things themselves neither suffer nor have true power over us; it is *we* who suffer and who have the power of autonomy and choice. The cause of that suffering is selfish clinging, deluded attachment, greed, desire, fixation—whatever you want to call it. It is often called craving. The word in Pali is *tanha,* which suggests overweaning thirst. Because we crave, continually desire, and thirst for various experiences and things—and because the pursuit and enjoyment of created things cannot prove ultimately satisfying—we suffer. That's where the chain of suffering can be addressed: whether or not we cling to things and crave for experience. It's not that we have to get rid of the things themselves. Things are not the problem. It is the attachment, the identification with things that causes suffering. Tilopa, a yogic master of ancient India, once sang to his disciple, "It is not outer objects which entangle us, Naropa. It is inner clinging which entangles us."

This grasping and ignorant clinging takes many different forms, as we all know. We might well examine our own lives and see what forms attachment and fixation actually take. Traditionally, attachment is laid out as taking three different aspects: The first is craving for pleasurable experiences, what we want. The second aspect is craving to get rid of what we don't want, which is also a desire, although in the form of aversion. This is interesting, because here we see how attachment (or desire) and aversion (or anger, aggression) are actually the very same movement, a craving for something other than what is—both based on egoic ignorance and delusion involving feelings of insufficiency and separateness.

The third aspect is also very interesting as we go a little deeper into it: craving or desire to *become* something or someone—that is, egotism itself. It fuels the whole process of rebirth, of wanting something, reifying that notion, and gradually becoming that. There is a great deal of dissatisfaction in this aspect, since whatever we can become, however we can seem, whatever we get or achieve, doesn't last forever. Yet we exhaust ourselves and absorb ourselves in getting it; we are invested in our goals and identify with achieving them. That's why clinging or attachment can also be called identification or reification. If we identify with things—if we identify with our body, if we identify with our mind, if we identify with our self-concept—since they are not ultimately permanent or satisfying, it is very trying; if we reify things as being more substantial, real, and solid than they actually are, it's like investing in fool's gold. We never quite get what we need out of this incessant clinging and demanding.

Tanha is thirst: thirsting for pleasure, thirsting to be rid of pain, and thirsting to be or become something or someone, or for things to be other than they are. Like drinking salt water, tanha never alleviates our inner thirst. The more we drink, the thirstier we become, ultimately to sicken and die of thirst. Let's explore and see for ourselves whether we are really getting what we want out of it, or not. That could be quite revealing. I think that if we ask ourselves honestly, we might be surprised to see how deep this goes. How hard it is to really know how addicted, semiconscious, and conditioned we are! Can we acknowledge how ill at ease, how dis-eased, we actually are? What is this incessant irritation gnawing at us? That is why we are always gnawing—sort of like Pac-Man gobbling—always gnawing at things, always seeking, always shopping and traveling, desiring and consuming, because this ignorant dissatisfaction is in us, gnawing at us like a hungry ghost within our psyche, like the inner addict. This incessant gnawing is the truth of dukkha. Maybe that's a good translation of *dukkha:* gnawing dissatisfaction. The cause of it is ignorantly desiring and craving things that aren't very satisfying.

Therefore, I feel that if we really look into the most basic teaching of the Dharma, the First and Second Noble Truths— suffering or dissatisfaction, and the real cause, ignorant craving—we might actually find, even in our own simple life, that our good old boringly familiar sitting meditation practice is still, after all these centuries and lifetimes, the panacea, the antidote, the ultimate answer to those questions that all of the eighty-four thousand Dharma teachings are built upon. We don't even have to study those many teachings and commentaries, thank God! We can actually practice them in essence and realize their essence, even right here, even without using the word *Buddhism,* without converting to anything, without believing any dogma or received teachings, but directly through inquiring honestly into our own personal experience. We can cut through the tangled knot of conditioning, of becoming, of craving, clinging, and aversion, thus reconnecting deeply and rediscovering our pure beingness in whatever form it takes. If we really look into our daily lives and examine how much this tanha, this thirst, drives us, I think we would be amazed at how little peace we have, how we are always plugged in, driven, compulsive, leaning or even rushing forward, dependent, and ill at ease in ourselves. We are often multitasking like a cartoon figure, plugged in through every sense: ear plugs, nose plugs, something in the mouth, watching something, listening, feeling, the seat vibrating while we're watching television and talking on the phone with the computer humming and text messages coming in, and radio or stereo as background music. Whatever we can get, we try to experience, rubbing our feet on the foot roller while the beer rumbles in our stomachs with the TV on, and so on. We can't just *be*, without being a little high, without having our charger on, and on and on and on. You know how it is. None of us is an exception. All of this stimulation and incessant searching for sensual gratification is like drinking salt water. The more we drink, the more we seem to need and want, till it becomes an addiction. The sane and immaculate enlightened vision that the Buddha offers us is something else entirely. Buddhism's attention training and attitude transformation alone are worth the small price of admission.

That blind drive to have and to become, that deep habitual physical and psychological conditioning, perpetuates itself and proliferates into all of our activities: always trying to make something happen, become something or someone, get something, get rid of something and find satisfaction. It's endless, isn't it? We seem to be more human doings than human beings. Marathoning, working, doing yoga for health, walking slowly, and even meditating—still we are on the treadmill trying to get somewhere. Idealizing the Buddha and the way to Buddhahood while postponing awakefulness is another treadmill when understood in that way—the great effort to be or become Buddha. Yet in terms of trying to be or become something, that should probably be one of the last aspirations to go! We can raise our sights a little bit, but still it is the treadmill of becoming; there is desire or craving there. There is suffering in that. Who today knows the timeless yet timely spiritual secret of being there while getting there, every step of the way?

If we can stop mistaking movement for meaning and momentarily step off the treadmill of conditioning, cease staggering forward under the momentum of our conditioning with a big out-breath, a Dzogchen sky-breath, one now-breath in, we might find that in truth nothing is missing in this precise moment. As the mystics say—though it still remains for us to confirm—nothing is missing and nothing is in excess. We don't have to try to become Buddha, desiring something higher, trying to get rid of something lesser, while striving blindly to *become*. We can afford to actually *be* as we are, since we already are, anyway. It is not so far. That's why the direct-access Dzogchen teachings talk about the ground or basis, and the fruit or result. It is really a rainbow bridge. The ground and the result are not far at all, so the path joining them isn't very long. It is much more a matter of recognizing who and what we are than of desiring something else, for that thirst and expectant future orientation continuously perpetuates our dissatisfaction. There is no pot of gold at the end of the illusory rainbow; every step of the entire spherical arc is golden, all the way round from beginning to end.

Spiritual Detachment

I see it as a progression from unhealthy attachments like addictions onward to attachment to positive things, like health, sensible eating habits, stress-reducing exercises, good works, prayer, meditation, and all forms of spirituality. Yet it has to get more and more subtle, or else we get stuck even in those relatively positive places. As our enlightened mind blossoms and evolves, it also gets more subtle. A Zen teacher calls it "the stink of enlightenment," when the last thing you get attached to is the freedom and bliss of enlightenment. That would be like having golden shackles rather than rusty iron ones. Maybe you can just raise your sights and get attached to higher and deeper things, and trust that this sort of teaching leads beyond even itself. As Buddha said, "Dharma is like a raft, to cross the raging river of suffering. Don't carry it on your back afterward." All rafts may be left behind when we reach the other shore.

What would be worthy of great attachment? You tell me. If you want to say God, or something very high and ultimate, then I'll say, "Good. Be totally attached to that. But what is that? It is not a thing." The great medieval Christian mystic Meister Eckhart prayed to God to be free of God. Our aspirations can get higher and higher, deeper and deeper, more and more subtle. That would be helpful. Attachment is really a pernicious cycle of demandingness, resistance, clinging, holding on. It is hard to believe that these are very helpful, yet we continually act as if we do believe just that.

Of course we are attached to our children and other family members. Of course we are attached to sanity and to health, and we should be. Let's use our common sense. That's why when I say the word *attachment,* I try to define it so we understand what we are talking about—greed, rigidity, grasping and fixation, resistance, preoccupation, self-clinging. Ignorant clinging doesn't sound great, does it? We've talked about relinquishing attachment. Let's talk about it in the positive sense: cultivating openness, spiritual detachment, equanimity, and objective clarity and transferring our internal attachment to higher, deeper, more meaningful and enduring values, goals, and purposes. Spiritual detachment doesn't mean mere indifference; it implies disinterested objectivity, like an impartial judge who can make clear dis-

tinctions and fair decisions. It means being more even-handed
and centered, and seeing the big picture, having more perspective. Since we all like some things and don't like others, we could
benefit by cultivating more detachment so as to be less invested
in such personal preferences, leaving room for inner equanimity and balance. You may still have subjective preferences, but
don't necessarily have a drama-queen tantrum if things don't
always work out as you would have liked. That's the positive side
of detachment. It doesn't mean you are complacent and indifferent, that if you see a kid running out in the street, you wouldn't
even bother to stop him. That's insanity. This discussion about
nonattachment is not about indifference or complacency. It's
about equanimity and balance, clarity, and objectivity, a bigger
perspective—about learning to appreciate all things and experiences, good and bad, pleasurable and painful, light and dark,
each in its own way.

This is the nature of the Second Noble Truth, the cause of dissatisfaction, which is ignorant clinging to and craving for things
that don't fulfill us. I will reiterate that the cause of the dissatisfaction is holding on to our habitual framework and way of doing things. When you start to see how that works, then you start
to see how letting go, allowing, being more flexible and generous
with yourself and others, tolerance, acceptance, and so on can be
very, very satisfying. It is a great relief. It just simply *works*. Every
day, every moment, it works. This is not some big abstraction,
some mere theological dogma. It's not like promising that at the
end of your life you hit the jackpot of enlightenment and you get
airlifted up to some paradise. This way of life works every moment. Even here in meditation, we are replicating the whole
macrocosm of our life and lifetimes in the microcosm of this moment. When we can relax totally and just be, accepting and allowing everything without having to strain to do or accomplish
or put together anything—isn't it a relief? Isn't it restful, relaxing,
on every level satisfying? There's no force or willfulness, so it's

not tiring. There is no will and no striving. Spontaneous joy and peace naturally bubble up. It is inconceivable. There is no good reason for it to be so satisfying, but it is. Incessant attachment and greed erode our inner peace of mind. Better offer yourself to everything. Surrender. Dance with life without resistance or inhibition, no matter what tune is being played. Why be a wallflower? Dance with life; you'll love it.

We'll discover that the Dharma teaching is about inner peace, harmony, and ease, revealing the superknowledge that everything is available within our natural being, our spiritual ground, the Buddha nature—as it says in the nondualistic, direct-access Dzogchen (innate Great Perfection) teachings. This message, this truth, this radical possibility is so liberating. We don't have to just change our desires over to "now we want to become Buddha" and spend countless lifetimes craving for something different called "Buddha" and trying to reach the so-called other shore—which seems never here, always somewhere else—that fabled place called nirvana. That's just more becoming and craving to become something different. How to become just what we *are*? That is the conundrum, the koan of spiritual life, how to get from here to totally here.

When we look with the Dharma eye of spiritual practice, we see that if we settle back into the beingness of Buddha, which we participate in even now, we can experience and delight in, celebrate and affirm this beingness of Buddha. Ultimately, peace and serenity are deep within. We can see through this incessant chain of craving and clinging, of wanting and not wanting, the multifarious afflictions of this thirst that brings so much dissatisfaction and pain and, even worse, creates suffering in the world and in ourselves. We can really ease back and reconnect with the inner component of luminous being, rather than being lost so much in doing, achieving, and becoming and staying disconnected from our inner spiritual selves. We can ease back and experience a little more balance with complete and innate being, in which there is nothing missing—just as we are, even while striving to develop and become better people so as to contribute to a better, more beautiful, safe, and sane world. From that natural state of harmony and ease, everything can and will spontaneously proceed. There is no need to try to do anything or to be a quietist, either. All the doings, all the achievements, take on an entirely different meaning. They become the *art* of living instead of the drudgery of reactivity and conditioning, creative and proactive rather than reactive. This art of enlightened living is the spontaneous Buddha activity and beneficial, resourceful creativity delightful to all concerned, rather than mere reactive, ego-centric, habitual karmic activity, and it spontaneously brings unimaginable, unspeakable delights.

CHAPTER 6

THE END OF SUFFERING

We have been talking about Buddhism from the ground up, Buddha's enlightenment experience, and the first teachings he gave: the four facts of life, the Four Noble Truths. The first one is dissatisfactoriness or dukkha—that all conditioned or created things are off the mark and ultimately dissatisfying. The second truth is the cause of this dukkha: foolishly clinging to those ephemeral things, investing in that fool's gold, greed for those illusory, dreamlike, impermanent objects of desire. The cause of that suffering is attachment, greed, craving—in Pali, *tanha,* holding on to things that can never really satisfy and fulfill us and mistakenly identifying with fleeting things as *me* and *mine.*

Now we finally arrive at the third truth: nirvana, deathless peace. Ahh, finally! Enough of all this suffering already; let's get on to nirvana. We've been running for so many miles . . . when are we going to get there? Nirvana, cessation of suffering and confusion, is the Third Noble Truth. First there is the fact we all face dissatisfaction, then its cause, attachment; these first two truths are the diagnosis of our condition. Then, as part of the cure, comes the fact that suffering and dissatisfaction do have an end—that the fire of ignorant craving and self-clinging, the roiling ocean of the passionate, conflicting emotions, do have an end. The end is in nirvana, the relinquishment and cessation of craving and deluded clinging, the heart's sure release, the great peace of nirvanic bliss—everlasting fulfillment, enlightenment itself. The great letting go, spiritual freedom, and completeness, and the profound wisdom and acceptance and oneness with things as they are that arise naturally through releasing our tight-fisted grasping and craving into the harmonious simplicity of *letting be.* Here is true openness and natural purity of heart, which doesn't need anything anymore: contentment, the ultimate form of wealth and abundance, natural comfort, and ease. *Sems nyi ngalso* in Tibetan, as Master Longchenpa advises: "Rest your weary heart-mind at home and at ease in the immediacy of nowness, the natural state of Innate Great Perfection." This is the phrase my late Dzogchen master Nyoshul Khenpo Rinpoche always used in his teaching on naturalness, simplicity, extraordinary ordinariness, and the radiant Great Perfection. "Relax, let go, and let be, leave it as it is—just as it is." There is tremendous justness and rightness in the karmically lawful unfolding of things just as they are, whether or not we happen to like or comprehend it at present. You can take this statement to the bank and invest in it, I assure you.

At the risk of repeating myself—this cannot be overstated—the cause of our gnawing dissatisfaction and anxiety is incessant greed and demandingness, which generates reactivity, disappointment, conflicts external and internal, and the continuous friction and malcontent that continuously irritate us. Although Buddhism has filled up many, many shelves with books and teachings over the more than two millennia of its existence, according to the Buddha himself, it all comes down to the fact of our confused dissatisfaction with things, the cause of it and the end of it—which means the real relinquishment or burning out of the fire of wrongheaded craving, the irritating friction of wanting, of clinging, of holding on to that which cannot be held for long nor produce the lasting satisfaction and fulfillment we ardently long for. For everything changes, nothing remains, not even the mountains and the seas. Sun lovers, even this solar system will someday die and be gone. Keep in mind the larger picture, the cosmic perspective: all that is born dies, and all those who gather together are eventually separated. True wealth and nirvana is within; it is all available and ever accessible to those with eyes to see and hearts to know. Only inner peace, fulfillment, and contentment are true wealth. This is the Buddhist outlook in a nutshell. Why get lost wandering in the thicket of isms and schisms, doctrines and opinions? What we seek is right beneath our noses, so don't overlook it.

Nirvanic freedom and peace are ever present, just on the other side of the tight knot of our clinging. We can actually experience it in a moment. It's not something that we have to build up with bricks and mortar over a long period of time. The crazy glue of our own attachments, ambitions, and preoccupations can only carry us so far. Awakened enlightenment is available through breakthrough, *ah-ha* experiences as well as gradual evolution and can be cultivated by simply letting go and letting be, an openness and *allowing*. The word *nirvana* originally meant extinction or annihilation of suffering. The ancient, etymologically based traditional example given to describe this state is when a fire goes out and even the embers are cooled—when the conflicting emotions are no longer burning us. This is the cessation of dissatisfaction and suffering, the end of the friction of duality rubbing against itself creating that fire, the friction of attachment. This friction is generated by "me," as subject, wanting "other," as object, and the interaction between the two; this friction that irritates us finally blazes up into a fire, the fire of suffering. Yet nirvanic peace and deathless bliss is a lot richer and more positive than simple extinction or oblivion. It is actually the alpha and omega of all existence.

I try to be careful with these words, so as not to further misunderstanding. I talk about the *conflicting* emotions and the afflictive obscurations. Of course, I am translating from a foreign word, a Sanskrit word, *kleshas,* which is defined as the inner defilements or obscurations of greed, hatred, and delusion. For example, it is not pure unconditional love, but attached, greedy, self-oriented love that is the problem—the deluded defilement that ruins the genuine nourishment of intimate relations. Unconditional compassion based upon heartfelt empathy is not dualistic pity, as if looking down on others, feeling sorry for and superior to them. There is a significant difference between such noble love and selfish love. The conflicting emotions, the defiled passions, the selfish emotions themselves are full of suffering from the outset, while boundless virtues like unconditional loving-kindness and compassion approach divine qualities and can be developed through panacean practices. Pure love, unconditional love is a positive emotion, as the Dalai Lama calls it, and not a conflicting emotion, an obscuring klesha. It is warm, caring, empathic, supportive, and nurturing—not indifferent or complacent, but full of equanimity, clarity, and selfless spiritual detachment. Of course, most of us are afraid, unwilling, and even momentarily unable to let go of our self-oriented conflicting emotions, because they form our habitual, comfortable nest, and our little ego—our small, tenuous, separate self—is insecure, fearful, and anxious, as it surely must be. Yet that's where we live and come from, so much of the time—this constricted egoic state. Obviously it is frightening to shake that up, isn't it? "What will I do without my familiar comfort zone?" one wonders, however uncomfortable that zone may actually be, day to day. "Who will care for me if I don't make it my own lifelong priority? Let's look into that zone, our habitual rut, and see what we get out of it. Maybe we *want* to continue in that way; who says we shouldn't? Let's be very honest with ourselves. Then we can change if and when we choose to. We may even leave our rut all together and find a new life, rather than merely pouring some sweet spiritual icing atop our cozy rut's smelly nest.

Discovering Equanimity

Detachment doesn't imply complacence, passivity, or indifference. It is more like equanimity or impartial evenness. It's like when mature, disinterested, yet caring elders are disinterestedly supervising, enjoying the grandchildren's games, sometimes even participating in the childlike charades without being totally taken in by them or attached to their pretend outcomes. If you're young, maybe detachment and renunciation seem a little scary. Maybe you need to explore desire and attachment a little more and learn the lessons. Get a little more intensely attached and involved, committed, and experienced, and see how it goes—the up and down sides of that passion play—discovering for yourself what it brings. Investigation, reflection, and discovery are the essence of conscious living, authentic spiritual seeking, and eventual finding. We don't have to give up anything really, except deluded attachment and expectation. You don't have to give up your job or family or credit cards or house, necessarily, but we can all observe—if and when we investigate and analyze carefully—that it is overattachment to family and loved ones that makes us unhappy. A good example is when we as parents fall into smothering rather than mothering. If you have children, maybe you feel that they aren't doing what they should and could be doing, or simply that they don't appreciate or visit you enough. You don't have to give up the children, but you can experiment with trying to give up such expectation, because it is that very expectation or wish that makes you unhappy, not the kids per se. You can still, of course, feel the wish that they would visit you, but hold it more lightly, with less fixation and preoccupation, less attachment. We all have feelings and desires, but we don't all respond equally intelligently to those outer stimuli, invariably arising impulses, and diverse energies.

Every day we are very involved in our lives, working hard toward desired outcomes of all kinds—personal, social, communal, and professional, which is perfectly natural. But what happens if we go on vacation for a few weeks? Travel for a few months or take a year off, and look back from afar at our daily travails? Don't we inevitably discover that most things we obsess about aren't as important as we thought they were in the heat of the moment? Even if you just go to the beach or skiing for an extended weekend, look back and see what being detached from all of the day-to-day hustle and bustle means to you. Maybe there is room for something else to come out, to come up, whoever you are, wherever you may be. Maybe you find your authentic inner self a little more since you are not so absorbed in all the things you are daily attached to here—jobs, roles, cares, responsibilities, and obligations. Consider vacuum cleaners. They have a lot of attachments stuck to them. Our accumulated stuff—outer and inner, material and emotional—is too often merely excessive baggage. It's hard to navigate when you have all those attachments stuck to you all the time; meanwhile, you have to pay for every extra pound you're carrying. A Buddhist vacuum cleaner comes with no attachments. As a cartoon Dalai Lama once exclaimed happily when unwrapping and opening a big empty gift box on his birthday: "Nothing! Just what I need and have always wanted."

The question of attachment and desire is one of the most mis-understood things in the spiritual realm. Spiritual detachment means equanimity and impartial evenness or objective disinter-est, a clarity including unconditional openness and appreciation for everything just as it is and presents itself. We all want to give up pain, but we don't want to give up pleasure. But here's the problem: since these two actually go together, like heat and cold, or light and dark, we can't really have one without the other. It is desire either way: we want what we want, and we want not to have what we don't want. Attraction and aversion are two sides of the same hand. Both are equally wanting, demanding, craving, and ultimately dissatisfying—based on the delusion of lack and separateness. This lack is most often coming from mere feelings of insufficiency, illusion, and misunderstanding. We run through our whole lives by pushing and pulling on this lack like an auto-matic door, in the throes of the fervid pleasure/pain principle: "I want. I don't want. Gimme! Get away!" Isn't it exhausting? No wonder we so rarely experience true peace and ease.

One of the interesting things in the Third Noble Truth is the notion of the *cooling* of the burning, conflicting emotions, the loosening up of those defiled, virulent, selfish, obscuring pas-sions. This truth is tied up very much with the ancient Indian concept of *sila*, moral self-discipline, which literally means cool-ing. The more we simplify and clarify our lives, the more honest and straightforward we are, the less there is to worry about. Things become more focused, cool, and calm, because we are more clear. Because we are truthful, there's less to try to remem-ber and no need for paranoia or keeping our stories straight. There's less friction and conflict. How can we call ourselves seek-ers of truth if we're dishonest in our day-to-day dealings and in-authentically ourselves? Moral virtue or self-discipline, character development, and integrity *are* very important and conducive to this cooling of the fire of suffering. They help things get clear, straightened out, simplified. Then we're just like an unencumbered vacuum cleaner that simply does its job without complaint, without inner critics or external enemies. We don't have all these extra, crooked attachments stuck to us. We can just know that everything is available. If you need something, you can just pick it up and use it any time, then put it back down. That's detachment. You can use everything, but you're not stuck with anything, including your ego, your personal history and clan background, or body or mind. You have your possessions, but they don't have you. This is the proper kind of balance taught in the Middle Way. Not too much and not too little, neither too tight nor too loose; everything in its appropriate proportion.

Obscuring Emotions and Letting Go

We have been talking about deluded attachment to things, to ourselves, and so forth. Now let's apply it to the obscuring emotions as a practical matter. Let's look at the most dangerous negative emotions, anger and hatred, which so easily morph into aggression and violence. As the peace master Shantideva of ancient India said in his classic Mahayana text *The Way of the Bodhisattva*: "Anger is the greatest evil. Patient forbearance is the hardest spiritual practice. . . . A single sudden spark of anger can burn down an entire forest of accumulated good deeds."

As a klesha, an obscuring emotion or fervid passion, anger, before it becomes aggressive or destructive, is just an energy. You might try to see if you can release and liberate this energy rather than simply lashing out or turning if inward at yourself by constricting around it and identifying with it as "my anger" or telling yourself, "I'm a bad person." Because you just get more angry with yourself for being angry, it's a vicious cycle. The definition of samsara, or conditioning, is "vicious cycle" or endless wandering around. Loosening our tightfisted grip on things—what we mistakenly call "reality"—includes the pain-relieving letting go and letting be that can profoundly undo that vicious cycle of conditioning, stimulus-reaction pattern that drives us like a tightly coiled spring of thoughtless reactivity. Then all the emotions become the display of wisdom, like the wrathful deities in tantric iconography, surrounded by flames—anger transmuted or realized as pure energy, not as aggression. It can be very sharp, brilliant, wakeful. Anger can manifest as discriminating awareness. The immediacy and potency of anger has the sharp cutting edge that can clearly see what's wrong. It need not manifest as aggression; it is very pointed, sharp, and clear seeing; helpful, not harmful. In such a way, anger can be an adornment rather than a hindrance. It is a tool useful for troubleshooters, auditors, activists, analysts, and so forth, who need to see what's wrong in order to help rectify a situation.

The place to feel the energy is *before* you see somebody as deserving angry retaliation. Instead, we train ourselves to pay attention through mindful emotional management in the present moment, the moment of an emotional energy's arising; we learn to mindfully feel anger, experience the heat of the energy arising, and leave some room or inner space for it just to be there, momentarily, without instant reactivity. Perhaps you need not *do* anything about it, but rather simply notice and experience it as energy, heat, a sensation in your chest or stomach, or whatever form it takes. Cradle it rather than rejecting it out of hand, and get to know yourself and your inner workings better.

We feel anger because there is anger inside all of us, along with seedlike imprints of all the other passions and emotions. There are seeds of anger, just seeking objects as provocative stimuli to focus on and be expressed. The habitually conditioned, subtle internal imprint of grasping seeks to find objects to grasp on to. Without an imprint, there is just all this stuff floating around in the substratum of consciousness, as it were, like water on a plain without any riverbed, ditch, or rut to channel it. The imprint is looking for expression, looking for a means to release itself. This is all just energy's inevitable creative display. The ego is looking for a way to fortify and perpetuate itself, so it is accumulating all those bubbles and trying to build them into a bastion as if they can shore up and help confirm ego's territory and ego's illusory existence. The alleviation and creative release of that process is up to us, should we choose to work at doing so. We're the ones who keep rubbing the two sticks together, the subject-object pair encompassed in the term *duality,* implicit to all polarities. We're the fire starters, the troublemakers, like sneaky, unconscious arsonists seeking excitement. It's all in our two hands, the hands of the duality of subject and object, grasper and grasped. That's why the nondualistic Dzogchen meditation teaching of resting in the natural state is so significantly freeing and deconditioning, through the simple and direct experiential contemplative process we call "seeing, recognizing, releasing" (whatever arises) through incandescent present awareness denuded of conceptual framework. This kind of simple yet profound naked-awareness practice cuts deeply into the heart of the matter. When there is nothing wanting, there is nothing working against anything; there is no grasping at anything. There is just the unimpeded, free experiencing—beyond pushing or pulling, beyond attraction or aversion, beyond self-centered reactivity.

As Buddha said, "In seeing, there is just seeing. No seer and nothing seen. In hearing, there is just hearing. No hearer and nothing heard." This suggests thoughts without a thinker, as a fine book about Buddhist psychology by psychiatrist Mark Epstein is called. Buddha said that in hearing there is just hearing; no one hearing and nothing heard. Can we be that empty, open, objective, and clear? The answer is that we choose not to be, mostly unconsciously. Guess who chooses? Who's responsible? It's scary, so we'd rather not face up to it. We are responsible for our experience as well as our actions. Thoughts without a thinker is too scary. We'd rather write down all those precious thoughts for posterity, catch and bottle those thought bubbles and make them into haikulike poems, or To Do lists and projects—trying to bottle all those infinite mind-moment flashes going by in the flickering thought stream and possibly make some kind of profit out of them. We mistakenly identify with thoughts and reify a solid thinker out of that mere shimmering luminescence. We think so much but accurately know and understand so little.

Letting go is like the exit leading to the suburbs of nirvanic peace and deathless ease. That release point is like the suburbs themselves. Nirvana is the end of suffering, so releasing is an approach to it; however, since the spring recoils every moment, it has to keep being released until it doesn't recoil, contract, and constrict—until the knot is released, or the curl is straightened out. Only stone or wooden Buddha statues can sit there with no pain, no wants, no nothing! Human beings, like all creatures, are more dynamic, complex, and in process. Enlightenment or nirvana is the end of the habituation, the clinging, the contraction and constriction of a separate egoic entity. Releasing is fine, but what happens in the next moment? Conditioning reappears. Continuous practice can recondition and ultimately decondition even the worst of us, the most entrenched and recalcitrant. Nirvana is the end of all those confused complexes and habitually conditioned states, and is full of freedom and delight.

About twenty years ago, when celebrated poet Allen Ginsberg, a disciple of the late Chogyam Trungpa Rinpoche, was going on a solitary one-month retreat on the Vajrayana foundational practices in Colorado, he told Trungpa Rinpoche that he was going to bring many little pads to keep by his meditation cushion so he could write down those beautiful haiku that would flash after many hours of meditation. Trungpa said, "Can I see your pads and pens?" Then the lama snatched them away and threw them out the window into a stream, saying that one reason for going on solitary retreat and meditating is to *stop* collecting, reifying, and cherishing all those fabricated thought bubbles. Ginsberg loved to tell this story with irony, because he was still—

like all of us—so attached to his lifelong habit of assembling beautiful mind bubbles. The more we meditate, the more good ideas we seem to get, don't we? We can't wait to go back home and tell somebody, write about them, paint them, whatever! Bottle them, market them. Nirvana perfume. Nirvana T-shirts. Nirvana Café. Enlightenment glasses! Come to the nirvana store; have plastic, will get enlightened. Nirvana Express: don't leave home without it.

Nirvana, the end of all the world's woes—the extinction of this blazing fire of craving—is just on the other side of each moment of craving, of holding on. That's where the great Letting Go comes in and must take place. Then the great peace is there; total fulfillment, wholeness, the end of all thirst and incompleteness. Tibetan tradition tells us that nirvana is radiantly luminous; simple, uncomplicated, yet utterly profound; delightful, joyful; unknowable, unfathomable, bottomless, yet inexhaustibly rich; unfabricated and uncorruptible. Not like those odd little thought bubbles that we are always trying to collect, so that at the end of one month in a cabin in the Rocky Mountains we have something to show for ourselves: a whole pile of little bubbles on a pad. Big deal!

Even the inimitable Allen Ginsberg's precious poetic verbiage was better left on the compost heap of present awareness, at least from the point of view of the Dharma. Of course, we enjoy poetry, we very much appreciate and miss Allen Ginsberg, and we love everything that is original and fresh, whether it is formally viewed as art or nature. And yet these fabricated egocentric productions that we collect and show off are somewhat canned and stale compared to simply experiencing the startling, poetic, dewy freshness of the infinitely fertile and creative present moment without having to bottle or accumulate anything as if saving it up for use on a rainy day when nothing's happening. The secret is that it's always happening, this great nothingness and dreamlike magic show referred to by Buddhists as "not what you think it is."

In the fresh immediacy of this ever-present timeless moment, the holy now, every single moment bespeaks truth, with or without literary musings. It's so clear and transparent that we see right through it without noticing, most of the time.

If you wonder what good is spiritual life, which to some seems airy-fairy or mere superstition, I will up the ante: What good is music? Of what value is poetry? We intuitively believe and know that these fine arts are important. Our muse is calling us. We can't necessarily figure out the connection between music and the alleviation of suffering, and yet we feel summoned, inspired, called. Many are called, but few choose to actually awaken.

Shifting Our Perspective

To talk of nirvana and enlightenment is like speculation about heaven, for the most part. Actually, we have to consider ushering in the kingdom of heaven here on this earth, as Jesus intended. We have to find access to peace and harmony, at some level hopefully nirvanic bliss, even here and now. It is not enough just to clean up one's own act here—although to save one soul is to save the world, as the Jewish Talmud says—but we must also notice that we are all in the same boat and that we all rise or fall, sink or swim, together. We must wisely address the social ills and injustices—political, economic, systemic—as well as individual morality and delusion if we are truly committed to skillfully integrating enlightened vision and values into this benighted world of ours. Unjust social systems continue to breed woe and wreak havoc among us, both at home and abroad.

There is obviously enormous suffering and iniquity in our shrinking world. We could volunteer and go to help in Bosnia or Darfur, in Jerusalem or Sri Lanka, or perhaps help out in New York City or New Orleans. Just don't forget, in New York City and throughout the country, churches of all denominations are having prayer vigils and asking for heartfelt prayers as well as other forms of cohesion and support from all over the world. That is because people actually draw solace from this kind of community action, too. There is a built-in support system in spiritual community; we're all meaningfully connected, aren't we? Buddhism is an inside job, and our own inner, mostly invisible work on ourselves also helps in a more visible outer sense, sooner or later, since we are all mutually interconnected. Even with terrible things dominating the general news media today, let's continue to examine what part of that blatantly visible greed, aggression, deception, fear, and alienation is still in our own hearts and minds, and root it out. We can and must honestly address those parts of ourselves that may be somewhat racist, fanatic, dogmatic, aggressive, deceitful, downright stupid, angry, or bitter. We can all feel helpless before the enormity of such evil as terrorist bombings, world hunger, or the AIDS pandemic, but we are not helpless to find evil and prejudice in ourselves and pacify it there. We are not helpless or hopeless in that sense. War begins with the greed, meanness, and conflict in the human heart. Both warfare and aggression begin and end within.

We all have our place in the universe. I think it is very important to settle more into that. Our place might very well be going into relief work. Or it might be being a musician or a poet. Look at all that Allen Ginsberg did, through his acute sensitivity, sociopolitical conscience, and decades-long activist commitment to truth, both outer and inner. Consider rocker Bono's marvelous charitable works. Spiritual work doesn't just refer to inner or quietist activity. It also can and even must eventually include altruism, service, community building, giving back, paying it forward, and so on. Compassion means genuine empathy and love, being moved to help, support, encourage, protect, and nurture. It is not just that you feel others' pain—you feel their joy also. You feel what others feel, which opens and expands the narrow aperture around which we are constricted. By doing so, we don't just feel more pain—we also have more joy. What we really have is less selfish preoccupation; we are taken beyond ourselves and our petty preoccupations into a world we hardly knew before. It's like when you have children around—sometimes they seem to drive you crazy, but what they really do is drive you beyond yourself. You can't just stay with your ordinary preoccupations. They lift you out of that somehow. They naturally pull the best out of you, through your own instinctive love and good-heartedness. That is why we hear about the sacred arts: sacred music and dance, sacred art and architecture, sacred lovemaking. Music or pottery making or nature hiking also can awaken and educe our higher angels within, as the indefinable muses course through our being, opening us up to the greater life around and within us.

Needless to say, enlightenment, nirvana, inner freedom coupled with primordial wisdom is not exactly what we think it is in our somewhat obscured state of mind. But still, let's not be too mystified by all of those highfalutin words. According to Buddha himself, awakened enlightenment is simply the relinquishment of craving, of clinging, of selfish attachment. This is not a small thing. However, the more our spiritual practice, our awareness meditation, and our altruistic activity in life is congruent with that; the less rigid, inflexible, demanding, deluded, and greedy we are, the more nirvana starts to creep in—quietly, since it is there all along, and it is we ourselves who are holding it away from us. It is always right here; the problem is that *we* are always elsewhere! It's not just like the guy with his thumb in the dike. We *are* the dike, and there's a tiny hole where it is trying to creep in. Let's widen that inner aperture a little bit by relinquishing some of our barricades, our persona, our holding on, our fixated, repetitive, fear-based, dissatisfying habitual behavior—in short, our conditioning. Get off the treadmill of conditioning for a moment and let the light in—or, for that matter, let it out. We are that dike. It won't be there forever, but we are doing our very best to keep it together. Think of all the tremendous energy tied up in holding together our entire act, our ego fortress, the dike that keeps us from the liquid light. Can we let go? Or is it simply too frightening to contemplate? As inconceivable amounts of nuclear energy were released when the secret of splitting the atom was discovered, our infinite positive energy is released when our egotistic shell is cracked open and the radiant core of splendid authentic being is unveiled. I have seen that.

This kind of genuine breakthrough requires a shift in perspective. Do we currently think that holding on and accumulating, collecting, and protecting ephemeral things and experiences will solve our problems? Don't we realize yet that everything is slipping through our fingers anyway, so there is no need to exhaust ourselves by trying to hold on forever? If we can honestly delve into this and develop a certain amount of world-weariness, we'll discover to what extent we are invested in the fool's gold of our own self-concepts and the pleasure-pain dichotomy, our possessions, activities, roles, and status—always being busy, being who we think we are while mistaking movement for meaning. No wonder we are exhausted! It's a full-time job, keeping all that together, like a lifelong juggling act or charade we constantly maintain. It is in our higher self-interest to let go and let things fall where they may. Perhaps instead of constantly trying to get it all together and make things fall into the right place, perhaps *wherever* they fall can possibly, for now at least, be the right place. Try it at least, just as a thought experiment. For there is nirvanic peace in things left just as they are.

When we really do let go and get used to letting go, that inner fire, that irritation, that friction heat of suffering actually does die down, and we can experience more and more of the inner peace and harmony that nirvana epitomizes. We become less dependent, less demanding, less complicated; less speedy, needy, and greedy, and far more content, fulfilled, secure and serene, centered, at home and at ease wherever we are.

Good energy is more subtle than negative energy, but it is also perhaps more significant. It might seem that the negative energy is more dramatic, so it gets more news coverage! No news helicopters are racing to some county or state where everything is peaceful. (News flash! No crime at all in Calaveras County this month.) I think it is incumbent on us to foster the good, to engender the best in others as well as in ourselves, and to just keep showing up—whatever happens, keep showing up as a witness to the basic goodness and truth we believe in. We must keep showing up, through living a principled life and being true to our own sense of integrity—and not let the forces of darkness overwhelm us. We must remember that agreeing and going along with things and following is a choice. Who empowers the leader? Who enables the current system to continue in the ways it does, except us? I don't think we should engender followership; we should and must foster character and engender awakened leadership. We have to take responsibility for our choices, find out for ourselves.

This is the Third Noble Truth, the end of suffering at the hands of delusion and confusion through the realization of nirvana, enlightenment. The fourth truth, the final one, is in a way the most important. Although the first one is the most important to *know,* for it is the diagnosis, the Fourth Noble Truth is the path to the end of suffering, the path that is to be practiced—the cure that is to be undertaken. This is the Buddha's famous Noble Eightfold Path: in short, the three liberating trainings in ethics, meditation, and wisdom. It is this well-worn Eightfold Path that actually leads to and actualizes the way to the end of suffering, nirvana, the burning *out* of the fire of deluded craving—the evaporation of the ocean of suffering. If you can find anything that isn't ultimately dissatisfying, please let me know so I can go out and buy some! I'm still looking, as I'm sure you are, too—although I must admit, this shopping around and disappointing bait-and-switch involved with many worldy allures is starting to really wear out. J. R. R. Tolkien said, in his popular Lord of the Rings trilogy: "All that glitters is not gold; all who wander are not lost."

CHAPTER 7

THE THREE TRAININGS

What are virtue, contemplation, and wisdom—the three liberating trainings? When you unpack them, for practical purposes these three become the Eightfold Path. *Sila*, virtue, becomes right or impeccable action, impeccable speech, impeccable effort, and impeccable livelihood. *Samadhi*, focused contemplation, is impeccable concentration and mindful meditation. And *prajna*, wisdom, is impeccable vision and penetrating understanding. We actually practice those with body and soul, heart and mind—what we call in Tibetan body, speech (or energy), and mind. That's enlightened living, compassionate living, wisdom, and love in action—the very secret of joyous and productive, wise and loving life.

Everyone knows the age-old adage that virtue is its own reward. We don't necessarily have to be good and do good now to reap rewards later, perhaps in heaven or some other form of the afterlife. It is simply good to be good and do good, here and now, where we live and breathe. I believe we all want to be better people and contribute to a better world, for ourselves and for our children and grandchildren. Moral virtue, ethical self-discipline, compassion, and kindness—all part of the cultivation of virtue—are not merely things we have to do now so we get the jackpot later, in other lifetimes. Virtue itself *is* the jackpot, here and now:

heaven on earth, in the form of an unselfishly warm and good-hearted, enlightened life. This is the secret to enlightened life: loving our way all the way to the end. And there really is no end nor limit to love; thus the saying "Love is greater than death." Amen.

I have found that these timeless spiritual practices are extraordinarily helpful in purifying and detoxifying us both mentally and physically, integrating and eventually dissolving our neurotic tendencies, and restoring us to inner peace and serenity, clarity, mental health, emotional balance, and wholeness. Then a sane, carefree, effective, and joyful life becomes possible. Sacred living is not just a dream, a myth, or an aspiration. It's not just for somebody else, somewhere else, who has different possibilities than we do—the Dalai Lama, perhaps, or your wonderful yoga teacher. Wise, unselfish living actually becomes realistically possible for each of us. That's the whole notion of the spiritual path in BuddhaDharma. It's a path, a journey that we can undertake daily. It's a spiritual life, not a temporary epiphany or breakthrough, a mere spiritual experience that fades into memory and is then gone. It's not something we merely have to believe. It's not something that somebody else gives to us. It's something we live and apply ourselves, something we do—a beautiful, fulfilling, and wholesome way of life. It is our path. It is right beneath our feet. Don't overlook it or mistakenly seek it elsewhere.

So the big question is, How to relinquish and let go of these addictive patterns, all this craving, self-clinging, greed, anxiety, and aversion? How to give up that which causes suffering, and how to experience the deathless peace and fulfillment of nirvana, which is the end of fervid craving, clinging, conditioning, karma, and all forms of dissatisfaction and dis-ease? The know-how concerning this kind of *how-to* is Buddha's main Dharma teaching. It is a kind of operating manual for enlightened living—a do-it-yourself operating manual with very clear instructions that anybody can do and benefit from. This is the Fourth Noble

Truth, the truth of the path. It's called the Eightfold Path, or the eight principles of enlightened living. Eight steps to enlightenment, a great highway of awakening. An eightfold recovery program, for recovering our true selves, our higher selves, and our true life—a far better one than most of us currently experience.

This is a big subject. I will discuss the eightfold way of looking at it. But first I'll discuss how those eight were originally taught, as the three liberating trainings, the three facets of enlightened living that mutually support each other; sila, samadhi, and prajna—that is, virtue or ethics, meditative mindfulness and concentration, and wisdom awareness.

Sila

Socrates considered virtue—*arete* in Greek—a combination of justice, moderation, goodness, courage, and piety. He said that you can only improve your soul by a combination of right thinking and right action, and that you can't have one without the other. The Navajos call virtue *hozho,* which means harmony and goodness, that which brings everything into harmony and beauty.

In Buddhism it's often taught that first we have to develop moral self-discipline (sila) to control ourselves enough to settle down, to pacify our nature and cool down our blazing passions sufficiently to practice samadhi (meditation and contemplation). Then, when we practice that mindful, contemplative mediation, we gradually develop insight, discernment, and inner clarity and wisdom. Yet all three of these higher trainings—ethics, meditation, and wisdom—are actually mutually supportive and interrelated. It is wise and kind to be ethical and straightforward, isn't it? It's not that morality comes first and then comes wisdom; they are all inseparably intertwined. We must look into ourselves and see, first of all; we can start by looking into which of the three is most out of balance for us. For example, after some time, we might become very concentrated meditators, while at the same time we might still by lying, manipulating, and cheating or being addicts, alcoholics, or even drug dealers. It is really in our higher self-interest to take stock and conscientiously scrutinize ourselves so that we might be able to clean up our act. It's not sufficient just to try to meditate and quiet our mind so we won't think about how paranoid we are that someone might be tapping our phones and searching our house. If we're paranoid, we are always looking around corners and over our shoulders. It's very hard then to develop the straightforward simplicity of concentrated meditative awareness that can bring the wisdom and unselfish mindful living; hard to just be present with and aware of things just as they are, moment by moment, when we are morally compromised and energetically unbalanced. Our body, energy, consciousness, conscience, and mind are far too interdependent to mature in a healthy way in one of those dimensions while leaving other aspects of our entire being far behind.

The first principle of enlightened living, sila, is very important and helpful. Moral virtue is not just like a Buddhist form of God's commandments imposed on us from the outside. It's sensible and eminently practical. It's a natural morality to be helpful, unselfish, open, and honest with our loved ones, is it not? Who wants to be lied to or cheated? How can we pursue wisdom and truth if we are lying, if we are excessively manipulating and scheming, deceiving ourselves and others, stealing, cheating, exploiting, and abusing? Traditionally, theft is described as taking what's not given. Yet, it's a little subtler than mere stealing. It's also using things that aren't ours, exploiting others, and hoarding or squandering resources that belong to everyone. One could widen the circle of our conscientious self-inquiry and ethical virtue to conscientiously consider the great gap between rich and poor and the gross inequalities in this world, which are mainly the result of immorality and greed, and notice that societal problems, including war, violence, and poverty, are matters of moral values that we have hardly as a society begun to effectively address. Thus ethical virtue and moral self-discipline could expand to include social conscience, impartial justice, and systemic change as well as spiritual purification and interpersonal honesty.

The point of developing some kind of ethical ground or self-discipline is very helpful when we enter into meditation and mindful concentration, the second training. If we have a life that is straight, we don't have to worry about telling different lies to different people and whether they will find out. We don't have to be paranoid. It's much more clear and sane to just be honest and straightforward, isn't it? If we deceive ourselves, don't we harm ourselves in the end? What are we getting away with? In the non-theistic Tibetan Buddhist teachings, it is always said that the wheel of karma grinds exceedingly fine; this means we could and even should be meticulous if we strive for humane decency and, ultimately, impeccability. In the theistic teachings of other world religions it is said that God sees and judges everything, which implies the same kind of inexorable moral law, as in the well-known biblical teaching that we reap what we have sown. In Buddhism, we don't talk much about theology, a creator, and God's activities; we prefer to say that cause and effect, known as karmic law, is very tightly fitting, and incontrovertible. Sweeping the dirt under the rug may sometimes prove fine, but how long before the rug starts to lift up at the corners or hidden rot sets in? Bury radioactive waste in the ocean, and perhaps we'll never have to face it again; but what about our children and grandchildren? They might face an unpleasant surprise, not to mention the effect on the fish and the rest of the entire environment!

Therefore, it seems obvious to me that it is incumbent on us to act responsibly, and even impeccably, without undue perfectionism or giving in to the harsh critical voice of the inner tyrant. What does it mean to be impeccable? It means to be what my late father called a mensch, a mature and decent person.

China's great philosopher Confucius called it the Superior Person: not superior to others, but becoming the best self that we can be. I believe that we all know when we fall short of even approaching that mark. I think practicing the ideals of sila daily, living a righteous and virtuous life, including giving of ourselves to the greater good, is for our own betterment as well as for the benefit of society. If we cannot be role models for coming generations, who will be?

Living a morally unimpeachable life will greatly help to develop our samadhi, our focus, our pure powers of concentration and meditation. We won't be distracted by anxiety every time we hear a sound: Who's that? Are they coming to get me? We won't be susceptible to inner voices that wonder what others are saying or thinking. Therefore it is always explained that, when we enter into meditation and introspection, if we're not straight with ourselves, if our character is weak and our lives riddled with hypocrisy, then how can we be simple and at ease with ourselves and others and really find truth and wisdom within?

Samadhi

I find that through meditating every morning, a lot of things just fall into place, and one doesn't necessarily have to try and figure them all out. Not that we should become anti-intellectual and simpletons or stop questioning, investigating, seeking, planning, or studying. But sometimes forcing problem solving to occur is similar to getting a knot in your shoelace—the more you fight with it, the more you can't open it but just pull it tighter. Sometimes if you just stop and take a breath, relax, take a break, and then start again—then the knot just opens. With meditation— with a single moment of incandescent awareness—things can fall into place, as if magically, when we stop battering our head against the wall of concepts and intellectual fabrications. We might even suddenly discover, much to our amazement, that there is an open window or door next to the wall that we'd overlooked in our pigheaded frenzy. As long as we are battering our head, it's unlikely that we'll find this opening even if someone is calling to us from the open door.

If and when you look into this time-tested path of enlightenment, you'll find that it is not just about meditation. Westerners often just extract the meditation component from the entire Dharma teaching, try to practice meditation alone—without the other Buddhist trainings and virtues—and then wonder why their lives remain much the same. If you just suppress your thoughts for a half hour every morning, and naively try to control your mind, then you may well wonder why your life still seems to be such a mess. Well, I guess you didn't suppress all life; you just suppressed thoughts for half an hour. If you could delete the whole program, everything might possibly be fine, but a mere half hour won't do that. To really master and transform your life, which means yourself, there is the Eightfold Path—the triple training path of action, introspection, and wisdom: complete, impeccable effort; impeccable livelihood; impeccable action; impeccable speech; impeccable thought; impeccable vision; impeccable meditation; impeccable mindfulness. So the path is not just quiet meditation alone. It includes impeccable, mindful livelihood, or finding our true vocation. Thus this is not a quietist or life-denying path, but an engaged way of life that can accommodate all sorts of different individual styles, like an eight-step recovery program to recover our true selfless Selves and our authentic, free, and delightful life.

Impeccable speech is very interesting: When you do a silent, intensive retreat, you find that actually you really don't have to talk that much. There is enough inner chatter to keep us occupied all day anyway, but in hermitage retreat you realize that you spend your whole life dissipating energy and distracting yourself through the speech gate, although it isn't actually necessary to talk constantly. You might find yourself entirely being with a flower or the sound of rain instead of looking for somebody else to tell about it or turning on the radio or TV. If absolutely necessary, you can always write a poem or song about it for posterity. But why try to bottle little drops of the river, which is endlessly flowing?

Silence, focused introspection, and self-inquiry are a significant part of the traditional monastic vocation, and are timeless spiritual disciplines we can each explore and apply in our own lives to become more aware of what we usually give our time and mental energy to. Then we can consciously retool ourselves and channel our energy into more explicitly constructive, fulfilling, and enlightening pursuits and priorities. We get to choose, of course; nobody's telling us that's what we have to do. We might find it sensible to more intelligently, intentionally, and masterfully direct ourselves rather than just blowing along like a dead leaf in life's winds, totally subject to external circumstances and conditions.

Prajna

Out of that inner wholeness and integral focus grows wisdom, common sense, discrimination, and total integrity. Our inner gyroscope starts to guide us more and more reliably in principled ways congruent with reality. Inner wisdom, spiritual understanding, helpfulness, unselfishness, and personal power grow. That's the relation between sila, samadhi, and prajna—morality, meditation, and wisdom. Each develops from and enhances the other. It's wise to be ethical, just, and caring, is it not? No one wants to be harmed or have their loved ones harmed. It's wise to be focused and aware rather than scattered and dissipated, isn't it? It's not that we have to meditate all day, but conscious living does imply being attentive and focused—examining our own life, not just fragmenting ourselves. Plato famously said, "The unexamined life is not worth living." That is one of the main points of his famous cave allegory: not to settle for the shadowy reflections on our dark cave's walls, but to explore and seek the sunlight of reality outside of our habitual containment.

It is extremely important and relevant to be practical and commonsensical, which is the beginning of wisdom. Let's not be so foolish as to overmystify the spiritual life; it transpires right here in our daily activities and relationships—or not at all. Discriminating wisdom is philosophical and existential as well as practical, including an uncommon common sense. Sagacity includes insight into the true nature of things; discernment, discrimination, sound judgment; the knowledge of right and wrong, helpful and harmful; knowledge of the world and how things work, as well as self-knowledge, self-realization. If we find ourselves having serious problems, we can reflect on this threefold scheme of ethical self-discipline, meditative mindfulness, and selfless wisdom and see where we are with it. Is our life so complex and riddled with contradictions that we can't just show up and be at ease, dealing with each situation as it happens? Perhaps we are out of integrity with ourselves, or out of balance in other ways, outer or inner. Do we feel as if we need a higher-octane teaching—some powerful beneficent presence or savior to give us a shot of kundalini energy or marvelous blessing or healing—to change our mind because it is riddled with all kinds of superstitions, confusion, fear, and doubt? We must be lights unto ourselves, as Buddha exhorted. It is our life, after all. We must learn to *see* and to authentically *be*. Clear vision, seeing things as they are—not as they ain't, not as we'd like them to be—is the beginning of wisdom. Clear vision is the first step to wisdom on Buddha's noble Eightfold Path to enlightenment.

If we live a morally unimpeachable life, we will feel much more serene and content, balanced, healthy, harmonious, and at ease. There is unimaginable spiritual wisdom and inner peaceful contentment in realizing that you can just *be,* regardless of what you're doing or where you find yourself. Actually, we don't have to do very much to just *be.* It is more a question of letting go and letting be, and of undoing the tangled skein of our compulsive habit of overdoing. Radical acceptance goes a long way to help transform things. Spiritual freedom and liberation helps us be free from outer circumstances and conditions, feeling centered and complete regardless of what we may be experiencing.

We don't always have to undergo all kinds of intensive Dharma chemotherapy to cure the spiritual rot within. Often just a little genuine sunlight is enough to open the lotuslike inner lightbulb. Just a moment of that spiritual sunlight or one breath of that fragrant fresh breeze from sunnier, deeper climes can be enough to aerate a claustrophobic day. Virtuous living, mindful contemplation, and discriminating wisdom are not so mysterious. These three transformative virtues or values were taught by Buddha as his way of life, not as dogma to be believed, but as skillful and intelligent training steps to be taken on the highway to enlightenment, laid out with his own footprints as stepping stones. Buddha was interested in engendering enlightened leadership, not mere followership. We too can become far more Buddha-like than we may think by cultivating this enlightened and enlightening way of life. The Zen haiku poet Basho of Japan said: "I do not seek to follow exactly in the footsteps of the wise men of old; I seek what they sought."

These principles of enlightened living are extraordinarily practical tools that create a joyous, impeccable, wise life. You won't have gorgeous light rays pouring out of the bump on top of your head as in medieval religious paintings—rather, your whole being becomes a beacon light in the world, illumining the way for yourself and others. We become lighter and become the light—lightening up while enlightening up, without taking it all, or ourselves, so damn seriously! In summation, the three liberating trainings are sila, samadhi, and prajna, which are unpacked as the Eightfold Path of impeccable view (seeing things as they are); impeccable thought (helpful and wholesome, rather than harmful, deluded, and negative); impeccable speech; impeccable action; impeccable effort; impeccable vocation; impeccable meditation; and impeccable mindfulness. You can study this in the traditional sutras (Buddhist scriptures). It's actually a very rich and interesting subject. My book *Awakening the Buddha Within: Eight Steps to Enlightenment* explains all this in detail.

This path is not just about virtue, self-discipline, and morality. It develops character and integrity, compassion, kindness, altruism, and a sense of fair play. It's not just "right view," like subscribing to the Buddhist dogma. It's seeing things as they are; the impeccable, mindful outlook; the enlightened, wise perspective—Buddha vision, which is both aligned with and one with reality. This objective, pure perception is obscured because of delusion, selfishness, and egotism, all of which are merely adventitious, conditioned obscurations covering our radiant, innate, enlightened mind. That's why it's not enough just to say "impeccable speech" or "thou shalt not lie." *How* to purify our afflictive obscurations and genuinely actualize the possibility of living the good and true life?—this is the question. How to love and treat your neighbor as you would be treated? I believe each of us must look into this more—both the know-how and the how-to. This is the specialty of transformative spiritual practices and inner work such as Buddhist practice. What would it mean not to criticize, not to put others down, not to gossip or slander or cheat, even in small ways—noticing that karmic cause and effect is inexorable, and there's no sweeping it under the rug? If we carp or snipe at others, it could be helpful to scrutinize ourselves and try to see why we are putting ourselves up, why are we so critical. Maybe we're self-critical, so it spills out in others, whether they deserve it or not; it's just our critical nature looking for expression. The more we can learn to love and accept ourselves, the better we'll love and accept others, and the more they'll return that to us. In terms of action and reaction and karmic causation, everything depends on motivation, intention, and our inner state of heart and mind.

As the Buddha said, twenty-five-hundred years ago: "When I was enlightened, everybody was; everything was totally clear and awake." What a world-shattering, radical, visionary statement! Such splendid, immaculate, enlightened vision is pretty steep, rarefied, and difficult to understand. Maybe he means outside of time: for instance, in the eyes of God, everyone is God, but in the eyes of man, everyone is screwed up. Which side of the two-sided mirror-window do you want to use? Can you access both? Can you see the problem while also holding the bigger perspective, at one and the same time? Can you perceive unity in diversity and appreciate and enjoy the dance of the one and the many? Let me retranslate Buddha's Zen saying as, "When I became clear, everything became clear." Isn't this clearer? When I am clear, everything is much clearer.

It is very challenging to say that when you awaken, everything is perfect. That's steep, nondual, and ultimately absolutely true. But to transform the high frequency of that profound insight down to something we can relate to, we have to return to the basic teaching verse of Buddha: To give up what is harmful, adopt what is wholesome and helpful, and purify the heart and mind— this is the essence of the sacred Dharma. If and when we give up what is negative and adopt what is positive and purify ourselves, things certainly improve. The more positive we are, the more positive feedback we get. This is karma, the ineluctable law of cause and effect. Wouldn't you say that's true, usually? The more negative we are, and the more we project anger, the more everybody seems against us. But on a good day, the same things seem utterly different. I like to say it's not what life gives us, but what we make of it that makes all the difference. We can't control the winds, but we can learn how to sail and navigate better instead of just being blown away in whichever direction the wind happens to be going. So let's smarten up and take hold of the rudder of our own life, individually and collectively—which is owning karmic responsibility for our own decisions, reactions, and karmic conditioning—and learn how to work skillfully with it. Otherwise, we're just continuing to look for happiness, satisfaction, and fulfillment in all the wrong places.

CHAPTER 8

THE EIGHTFOLD PATH TO ENLIGHTENMENT

I t says in the Lankavatara Sutra that things are not what they seem to be, nor are they otherwise. I like to say that you just can't believe whatever you think.

We are not what we think we are; so who and what are we? This is a deep question, a koan or conundrum that one might chew on for a long time. Who are we? What are we? Where are we? Who am I? Have you ever directly asked yourself this provocative and compelling laserlike self-inquiry question—the fundamental question concerning our true identity? Some make this their entire spiritual path, and practice it throughout their lives. Who is experiencing our experience? Where is that experiencer? Is it in our head? Is it in our brain? Is it in our heart? Is it in our body? What is it? Is it mind? Is it ego or self? Is it soul, spirit, psyche? Male or female? Our profession, our role in life? American or otherwise? What is it? Who do we think you think you are, anyway? If and when we honestly look into this—if we lift the lid off of this particular Pandora's box—all kinds of interesting things might fly out. So maybe we'd better stop there.

I'd like to talk about the Noble Eightfold Path and the law

of karma or cause and effect, reactivity and conditioning. We've been going through the basic teachings of the Dharma, beginning with the enlightenment experience of the Buddha. That enlightenment experience is the crucial experience that we ourselves could have on the Buddhist path. In fact, Buddha's enlightenment experience is the root of all Buddhism, and our guiding polestar. From that pivotal experience and the discovery of supreme spiritual enlightenment or inner nirvana evolved the first teachings given by the Buddha regarding the dissatisfactoriness of all conditioned things and the difficulties of unenlightened existence as we know it: dukkha—that there is no life without suffering—the First Noble Truth, or first fact of life. And the Second Noble Truth, the cause of suffering: ignorant clinging and greedy attachment to that which can never really satisfy us. These first two truths are like the diagnosis by our wise and knowing doctor: suffering, and the cause of suffering (ignorance craving).

The second pair of truths, or facts of life, are like the cure, the therapy. The Third Noble Truth is the end of suffering—nirvana, the enlightened life, the relinquishment of ignorant craving, attachment, fervid thirst, and greed. The Fourth Noble Truth is the Noble Eightfold Path, the eight-faceted way of enlightened living, the eight principles of enlightened living—an eight-step recovery program for samsaraholics to recover and rediscover our truly meaningful life of freedom and well-being. It is the way to the end of suffering and the heart's sure release, which is blissful, peaceful, radiant nirvana, deathless ease, divine bliss. The eight-limbed practice path is the way to gain objectivity and realize reality. We begin to see how subjective we usually are, and how relinquishing attachment, greed, egocentric partiality, and delusion leads directly to the alleviation of our insatiable thirst for freedom and lasting peace, love, and meaning; the end of suffering, the end of anxiety, confusion, doubt, and despair.

The Eightfold Path of awakening is divided into the three liberating trainings, as we've already explored: sila, samadhi, and prajna—morality and ethical self-discipline; meditation or mindful reflection; and wisdom awareness. These three trainings are further explained in eight steps, so we can actually apply these principles in life. This is the tried-and-true way of attaining enlightenment as well as a way of enlightened living. These eight steps are: impeccable vision and understanding; impeccable attitude; impeccable speech; impeccable action; impeccable livelihood; impeccable effort; impeccable concentration or focus; and impeccable mindful awareness.

Wisdom

Buddhism posits that it is not money or sex, the devil or destiny that are the root of all evil: rather it is ignorance and misknowing, ignorant craving and deluded attachment that are the root of all suffering and confusion. Thus, since ignorance is at the root of it all, insightful penetrating wisdom is the antidote, the necessary cure, to cut the root of the proliferating tree of dissatisfaction and suffering, confusion, conflict, and anxiety.

The first two steps on the Eightfold Path thus pertain to wisdom, since wisdom appears front and center in Buddhism as a wisdom tradition rather than merely a faith, creed, therapy, or philosophy. We strive to live life according to penetrating wisdom, so wisdom comes first and remains foremost. We don't just live life to *develop* wisdom; we also embody it through wise and intentional actions and discover it within as we go along. We love our way all the way to the wisdom of complete, perfect enlightenment. Wisdom or prajna is explained in two steps:

1. **Impeccable vision and understanding:** Seeing things as they are in the present moment, not as they ain't, clear seeing, objectively and without coloration, free from distortion and self-

deception, without projections and subjective interpretations. Seeing karma at work, seeing that as we sow so shall we reap. Seeing that we are responsible for the kind of experiences we experience. Virtue brings its own reward. Wholesomeness and positivity furthers itself, and negativity brings back negativity to us. Deeply perceiving and intuiting this, moment by moment, we become more and more at one with this process and this reality, rather than out of tune with it, misaligned, unbalanced, and disharmonious.

2. **Impeccable attitude:** Impeccable thought and understanding, free from aversion and desire, enmity, illusion, and ignorance. This step must become very practical. As Trungpa Rinpoche would say, it's all about being cheerful, friendly, and positive. Maitri (loving-kindness) actually means friendliness—positive, buoyant, fresh. "Always maintain a joyous and open mind," as Pandit Atisha said long ago in his renowned Mahayana mind training–attitude transformation *lojong* teachings. Not just as an ideal that we should be like this, but actually cultivating these things—and why not? Unleashing our spontaneity and buoyancy, our innocent and wondrous, childlike nature. Accessing the deepest recesses of our original good-heartedness through the practice of seeing others in oneself and oneself in others and warmly wishing the best for one and all. Unselfishness and altruism is the heart of it all. Being good and doing good.

I remember that when I was a kid, I wanted everybody to be happy. By everybody, I meant the people in my world—principally, the five or six in my immediate family. I really wanted that. Didn't we all, when we were little children? But then what happened? Is that how we go through life today, wishing well to all we're with, and even to whoever we happen to pass or meet in the street—which is the heart of maitri, metta, the Buddhist virtue of loving-kindness? We might pray it or say the wishful words "May all beings be happy and well," but it is not really in the forefront of our consciousness much of the time, as it was in-stinctively and quite naturally back in early childhood. I re-member how much it would upset me if any member of our little suburban nuclear family circle wasn't happy, if something was bothering them. In that protective cocoon of our 1950s American household, I genuinely thought and assumed that everybody should, could, and would be happy. But as time pro-gressed, my life became more complex, and that purity of heart was socialized out of me while I became a competitor and self-centered striver like everybody else I knew. Our childhood pu-rity of heart is something we can reconnect with: impeccable thought, impeccable attitude, unselfish intentions—the second part of the eight principles of enlightened living. Warmhearted-ness is the essence of spiritual life.

From the wisdom of seeing things clearly, just as they are, when we cultivate this impeccable, altruistic attitude regarding others and the world itself, we see that everyone more or less wants and needs what we do and is simply pursuing similar if not identical goals in a myriad of different ways. When I think of compassion, I think of this warm and heartfelt sense of empathy and connectedness. Compassion has become a mere buzzword today. However, when you feel what others feel, or if you put yourself in their shoes, then you can treat them as you would like to be treated—and you will more naturally feel warm toward them, inclusive, connected, spontaneously helpful, com-passionate, and kind, rather than exclusive, abusive, exploitative, manipulative, or aggressive. The more we cultivate compassion, loving-kindness, and well-wishing prayers and the more we practice continuously in daily life the virtues of charity, service, and altruism, the more we warm up the whole environment and the more we accumulate meritorious good karma and progress spiritually. Compassion and altruism really are a tremendous force; there is nothing weak or fragile about it. We don't neces-sarily radiate visible light rays of inner strength, warmhearted love, and compassion, but out of that attitude comes natural action, compassion in action through caring, assisting, and helping. Compassion also resonates with others in a way that can help generate consensus and model a fruitful and meaningful way of being, especially for the younger generations who look to us, consciously and unconsciously, as examples, role models, and mentors.

Ethical Self-Discipline

So from impeccable view or impeccable understanding and impeccable attitude—comes the second ethical self-discipline training group of three character virtues or integrity principles and practices on the Eightfold Path: impeccable speech, impeccable action, and impeccable livelihood.

3. **Impeccable speech:** Not lying, manipulating, gossiping, slandering, speaking harsh words, putting people down, and so on. Also being true to ourselves. Not talking about others all the time. When pioneering Buddhist meditation teacher Joseph Goldstein vowed not to talk about others for an entire day, he was surprised to discover that he almost didn't have anything to say to anyone anymore. Not that he's a big gossip or critic, but aren't we all somewhat like that? Impeccable speech implies saying what is helpful and wholesome, appropriate and necessary. Buddha said that one word that produces peace is better than a thousand meaningless ones. Let's refrain from squandering our energy in endless verbal static for no sensible reason, just chattering, twittering like parakeets while defusing our energy and scattering our attention, rather than intentionally channeling and focusing it toward positive purposes. That's why this kind of self-discipline, impeccable speech, is helpful for developing meditative mindfulness and for maturing our

spiritual experience into wisdom—containing, focusing, and directing our energy, rather than just dispersing it, frittering it away, distracting ourselves with verbal doodles and endless internal monologues.

4. **Impeccable action:** Not harmful, but helpful, wholesome, sane. Refraining from killing and stealing and all that regrettable negativity. Refraining from sexual misconduct, including violence and adultery as well as obsessive, exploitative, or even merely inappropriate behavior. And not harming our own bodies and energies through negative actions and compulsive or addictive behavior.

5. **Impeccable livelihood:** Following our own true work and genuine calling and living positively and helpfully. Doing what we love, so we can do it fully and passionately—finding work that grows us rather than stunting us—and not just trying to get the job over with so that we can live our so-called real life on the weekend or after 5:00 p.m. on weekdays. Rather, creating and pursuing a livelihood in tune with the higher interests of both ourselves and others. Not being harmful, such as by pimping, drug dealing, arms selling, false advertising, or unethical and exploitative business practices such as selling out-of-date pharmaceuticals in developing countries; watering down gasoline, paint, or olive oil before sale; or degrading the environment as many companies have done. We have to look at our own responsibility in these things, in terms of our own vocation or our own investments. Impeccable vocation is very helpful in living the enlightened life and achieving clarity in our dealings with the world while making a life and not just a living—so that we can find meaningful work in a way that develops and shares our greatest inner gifts with the world. Isn't it interesting that Buddha himself, who was a monk, included right livelihood as one of his eight steps on the path of enlightenment?

Awareness

First we discussed impeccable vision and understanding and impeccable attitude, then impeccable speech, action, and livelihood. Now comes the last triad in the eight steps to enlightenment— the three trainings called the meditation section: impeccable effort, impeccable concentration, and impeccable mindfulness or awareness.

6. Impeccable effort: There are different kinds of effort. One kind gets you started—sometimes translated as launching effort—and another, slightly different kind sustains you, called persevering effort—patient and heroic effort, which keeps you going in the long run. Not just enthusiastically launching and jumping in, but also keeping going after the honeymoon phase of any new endeavor wears off, after the delight wears off and you get into the boredom and, worse, the madness and chaos of your own mental imaginings, projections, resistances, vacillation, and other interpersonal reactions. Remember Buddha's famous Middle Way, neither too tight nor too loose—neither too much nor too little. Impeccable effort is balanced and appropriate effort, not merely compulsive effort or unmitigated hard work. Learning to work smarter and not just harder is a good example of right effort and wise perseverance. It implies continuous, joyous effort and energetic endeavor as well as a certain relaxation and moderate pacing as time goes on—for continuity is the secret of success, as my first Indian meditation instructor U Goenka always used to say. The genuine virtue of effort seems to require sufficient delight in what we're doing to sustain constant inner motivation, such as when we're passionately engaged or while following our own true calling. If and when we are passionate about what we are doing, interest runs high, so we don't have to force or strain ourselves. We are naturally motivated, so it's an effortless effort—

not just a grim chore, hoping to get it over with already, so we can enjoy vegging out somewhere, perhaps even on the other shore of nirvana. Rather, impeccable effort means finding the serene fruits of meaningful activity even while still doing it, in the very midst of every part of daily life.

7. **Impeccable concentration** or focus, contemplation: Having balanced attention—stable, attentive, intense, and yet open. Focused and alert, yet lucid and free; incandescently luminous yet simultaneously relaxed, receptive, and attuned. One with what we are doing and being. Centered, not distracted. Really doing what we are doing, 100 percent. That is the way of straightforward naturalness and ordinariness, a significant spiritual virtue and important part of the humility and simplicity inherent in enlightened living. Not always doing things for some other ulterior reasons or rationalizations. Since we're doing it anyway, whatever it is that we have chosen to do, we might as well *really* be doing it. Why wish we were elsewhere? If we wish we were elsewhere, we should go elsewhere. No one's keeping us here. This isn't compulsory public school. We must own our own projections and subjective interpretations. We are all responsible, autonomous adults; let's not mindlessly abdicate that responsibility. Let's focus on the task at hand, doing what genuinely needs to be done, neither too much nor too little.

8. **Impeccable mindful awareness** is the last part of the concentration samadhi triad of the meditation training portion of the eightfold path: Simply being aware with total presence of mind, rather than being absent-minded. Lucidly mindful, rather than mindless; attentive rather than inattentive to what we're doing and who we are. There's nothing very mysterious about this. In the ultimate sense, life is utterly mysterious, of course, but we don't have to mystify it and make it into something we cannot understand, like theological concepts of hosts of angels dancing on the head of a pin, speculative arguments about God's existence, or any kind of exotic Oriental mumbo-jumbo. We must

endeavor to be conscious, rather than unconscious; present, rather than absent. The more we empty ourselves of our preoccupations and selfishness, the more present and understanding we may become, curiously enough. The less full of ourselves we are, the more truth—or God, for that matter, and even true love—might show up. Those who lose themselves will find them-Selves, as the mystics say. There's actually a little mysticism everywhere, if you look.

Regarding this impeccable awareness or mindfulness, the historical teacher Gotama Buddha said in his original teachings: "In hearing there is just hearing. No one hearing and nothing heard. In seeing there is just seeing, nothing to look at and no one seeing it." There is just the incandescent, iridescently shimmering, indescribable moment, inconceivable and yet undeniable—like the gorgeous beauty of a desert sunset or the immediacy of a starry night sky. And yet, so soon we feel the need to try to make it into something: "Oh, it's a beautiful night, I think I'll write a poem about it." Or, "Ugh, traffic noise—it sucks!" That's the second and third and fourth moment of discursive chains of thought, not the vivid freshness of momentary, spontaneous awareness itself, the natural state, the immanent Buddha mind. In the first fresh instant there's just hearing, just seeing—long before conceptual imputation and subjective, karmically conditioned likes and dislikes enter the picture and start driving us hither and yon. In seeing, there is just seeing; no one seeing, and nothing seen. (I'm condensing here: the Buddha went through all the five senses.) In thinking, there is just thinking. No one thinking and nothing thought. "Me and mine" is just a thought, just a concept; of course, it's actually a bunch of thoughts, feelings, identities, and so forth. When we have a lot of thoughts bundled and woven together, it becomes like a whole ball of wax—dense, heavy, unwieldy, important seeming—and we start living too much in our head and through our concepts. But it all just begins with that first, single, unbound, fresh thought. If only we could

just stay with that first moment, just the thought or feeling, physical sensation or perception, trying to be present before getting
swept away by the proliferating popcorn stream of "Who's thinking?" or "Why am I always thinking?" or "Damn thoughts. When
are they going to stop so I can concentrate?" Before those concepts, upstream from all that mentation, there's just a flashing,
incandescent, indescribably delicious, and freshly wakeful moment. That's the dawn of creation, in every moment—in this very
moment, too. Nothing has happened yet. Samsara has not yet se-
ceded from nirvana. The war of dualism has not yet begun. You
are there! This is the secret of being there while getting there,
every single step of the way. Being right here. An open secret.
Seeing clearly, understanding, and acting appropriately—even
while accepting, letting go, and letting be.

Impeccable awareness, total presence, is as imperturbable as a
mountain, unchanging as the ocean amid all its different, superficial changes, for it never leaves its broad and inclusive bed. Un-
moved, yet totally reflecting clearly whatever appears in it, like a
mirror: whether it's faced with a lovely jewel or steaming feces, or
a wet paintbrush even, reflections simply don't stick. Totally at
ease, at home in every situation, one with all and everything
without clinging or misconception—that's impeccable awareness, with a little Dzogchen nondualism to spice it up. That's
view, meditation, action, and fruition, according to the Vajrayana
pith-instruction tradition. Like a mountain, like an ocean, like a
mirror, like the spacious sky, and at home, ever-always.

As we go into these steps in more detail, we see that the whole
Dharma teaching is explained through these eight principles of
enlightened living originally taught by Lord Buddha in his
renowned Noble Eightfold Path. These are not simply divine in-
junctions or Eight Commandments: you should do this, then
you'll get to heaven later. Rather, these principles are simply basic sanity for intelligent living. Isn't it sane to be helpful rather
than harmful, and unselfish rather than selfish? We don't need

other glorious or complicated ulterior motives. It is sane to be present and accounted for, attentive, rather than to be distracted and absent-minded, which just leads to all kinds of misunderstandings and so-called accidents. It is sane to be pursuing one's true vocation, rather than compromising and selling short one's precious, evanescent life, isn't it? It is sane to be energetic and buoyant and doing one's best to keep on in a consciously chosen direction, to have courage, to keep going and make efforts toward that which is meaningful. These are simply principles of sanity and enlightened living.

Rather than calling this the Eightfold Path, I like to call it the eight principles of enlightened living or the eight steps to awakening. It's really eight facets of one jewel. If you look at that jewel—which can of course have infinite facets—these eight original practices and principles taught by Buddha long ago form the basis and backbone of Buddhism, regardless of school or country, and pretty much sum up everything he himself taught twenty-five-hundred years ago. However, I will go further and say there is a very important one that's not here. As the "ninth fold," the ninth inning, I say we should include *exercise*. If the Buddha had taught today, I'm sure he would have included exercise—exercising and developing our faculties for health and relaxation through yoga, martial arts, swimming, jogging, at whatever level you want to tap in to. Exercise is extraordinarily useful and healthy. The ninth inning on the path is wise exercise and healthy living. Why not? Don't we as bodhisattvas need and want to maintain our physical vehicle and keep it on the road as a useful and safe conveyance, and for as long as necessary?

Come to think of it, there should be another extra principle of enlightened living: humor—a tenth and extra inning. If we take ourselves too seriously, make religion into a grim and terrible chore and can't appreciate the lighter side of things, it just ain't very funny! So good humor is our sweet and delicious "tenth fold" on the path.

When I told this to one of my close friends, psychologist and

parent Janet Surrey, she insouciantly said that for her right relationships it is an important and necessary step on the Eightfold
Path, especially today for us lay folk. If we don't end here, we're
going to end up with our precious Eightfold Path becoming a
twelve-step program for recovering from samsara!

I find it's quite healthy to exercise our freedom to inquire, discuss, debate, and think creatively about things. We should exercise our speech as well as our intelligence, and not just swallow
the Dharma whole and undigested. You know the old Zen koan:
Does dogma have Buddha nature? So please take the opportunity
to think about these things under consideration here and try to
actually apply them in your life. I think you'll find it extraordinarily helpful. The main work is to apply these things in life, day
by day, hour by hour, minute by minute. Then we will lead an enlightened, sane, beautiful, and righteous life. And we won't have
to wait until we die or the future Messiah or Maitreya Buddha
comes down to help us go to heaven; we'll help usher that process
along, right here and now. We won't have to wait for anything. Instead, we are totally present at the moment of creation, right now,
at every moment: there is nothing missing and nothing extra to
get rid of. That's the joy of this jewel of the Dharma. Dharma as
truth, or things as they are. Thank God for the Dharma!

CHAPTER 9

THE FIVE SKANDHAS AND THE NATURE
OF INDIVIDUALITY

When we look inside—when we wonder who and what we
are and what's going on, when we ask who or what am I,
who is experiencing our experience—what do we find, if any-

thing? Who am I? What am I? Where is the experiencer? Is it in my head? My brain? My heart? My legs? My mind? What do we find? Do we really exist as we think we do? (I doubt it.) Are we who we are habitually used to thinking we are? Am I different from you, the same, both, and neither? That's the main subject of self-inquiry in Dharma—to know oneSelf; to know one's true nature; to realize who and what we all are; to recognize the Buddha nature, the transpersonal, innate nature, rather than merely identifying so strongly with our superficial, momentary, conditioned personality, which is just the tip of the iceberg.

The original teacher of Buddhism in this world (the enlightened Buddha, 563–483 BC, in India) gave us his idea about who and what we are. He described the individual as composed of five heaps, aggregates, or *skandhas*. We can use that as a framework, rather than just wandering around with, "Oh, I don't know who I am" or "Who could know?" or "Who knows," always passing the buck and continuing to drift along on the great river of denial. In truth, the buck stops here, in your own lap. That's the bad news. But that's also the good news: self-mastery is in one's hands. We can know ourselves, as Socrates (among others) exhorted us. And this self-knowledge will make us free. I myself have been worshipping at the shrine of this god my entire life—the shrine of inner knowledge. Inquiry is a spiritual practice.

We have, or we are, a form, but what else are we? Are we just a body? Are we just flesh and blood, from dust to dust, as is said? The Buddha said we are the five skandhas, or heaps of composite accumulations. The word *skandha* is a tough word to translate. It means group, aggregate, or component of individuality. We are these five whirling congeries of forces. Let's check these out and see what they mean, and what else there might be, if anything at all.

1. *Form.* Form comprises solidity, all matter, materiality; the physical elements of earth, water, fire, air, and space—all of which make up one human being.

2. *Feelings or sensations.* We all learned about the five senses in school: touch, taste, hearing, sight, and smell. To this group Buddhists add a sixth sense—mind.

3. *Perception.* This component combines feelings and sensations with recognition and judgment. This is where we get into thoughts of liking and not liking arising. This is where the whole problem, the whole duality, the whole push-and-shove starts, the entire, exhausting treadmill or roller coaster of ups and downs.

4. *Will.* Intending to do things. This is where karma comes in. Your will and intention direct your mind and the way you act and speak. Karmic reactions such as liking and not liking, for example, arise in perception, then devolve into reactions—reactions rather than the freedom that comes from enlightened, proactive Buddha activity. Our form feels things, perceives things this way or that way, liking or not liking them. Then actions or intentions push or pull, trying to get more, get less, ignore it, or get away from it. Avoidance, denial, greed, demandingness, attachment, and so on equal dissatisfaction and misery.

5. *Consciousness.* This element refers to states of mind and the consciousnesses associated with each of the six senses.

These five skandhas, then, are what we are, according to the Buddha's wise perspective. Has anybody found anything else they think we are that is not included in those five? So where is the soul? Where is the ego, the id, and the superego in that scheme? If you analyze your own essential makeup, maybe you feel guilty or depressed, or maybe you feel victimized, or maybe you feel powerful—which skandha does that fit in? In the skandhas, memory fits into consciousness. If you look into Buddhist psychology, known as Abhidharma, in consciousness there are fifty-two mental factors. You can unpack those fifty-two into more numbers of lists, groupings, and classifications. It's not just a question of a moment of anger or lust or covetousness or jealousy, but the past, present, and future moments of them. That's the point of all of this. Then you start to see what is actually happening, how it works. You get a little more space around, say, your anger, a little less identified with it as "mine." It's just a reaction to a cause, moment by moment. Just mind-moments popping and crackling. Enjoy that spectacle, and remain undeceived! We are not just what we think, feel, or perceive, but also our interpretations and reactions and habitual sense of identity, personal story, background, and so forth—all of which contribute to our contingent, protean self.

Memory is pernicious in a sense: It helps us link up or identify with notions like "It's mine" and "That's how I am," and "my story," "my history," "my drama." Thought is just a moment flashing, but then there are chains of discursive thought that are conducive to memory, connecting and strategizing, plans and agendas, and all of it. You end up reifying things until you feel solidly being, or even stuck, in a certain position, going in a certain direction through unconsciously and semiconsciously adopting regular habitual patterns. You put a lot of body English on the ball—it doesn't just go straight—and then, before you know it, either you are moving in that direction or at the very least giving rise to all sorts of unseen consequences. Our self-image is like self-memory; it conditions how we relate to every experience.

You can then see that all of the skandhas, these heaps, these piles, are bunches of stuff themselves. Like a pile of sand, a whirling composite of forces, yet there's no fixed entity anywhere. The body changes all the time, right? Do we look the same way we looked five or ten or twenty years ago? Every seven years, every cell in the body changes completely. Not to mention how our mind is changing all the time. And our feelings, sensations, and perceptions. So who or what are we? Who am I? Ask yourself that simple, utterly profound question. Who or what am I? Who is experiencing your own experience, right now, this very moment? Feel it, sense it; don't just think and analyze. Who is present, in yourself, right now?! What or where and *how* is my most basic ens, or core being?

Blake famously said that "exuberance is beauty." I like that. We can fantasize exuberantly about ourselves—we are an eternal soul; we are light, pure energy, spiritual essence, and so on. We can each make up our own notions, if we choose. But it's all equally made up, speculative—exuberantly, creatively made up. We create and reify and then experience our reality. All this comes out of our own psychological and karmic conditioning. Karma is the creator, in actuality—cause and effect; there is no eternal being behind pushing or determining it all. Check this out for yourself, conscientiously, objectively, in every way possible. Everything is subjective.

Each of these five skandhas is composite, like congeries, whirling groups of forces, just like the body is. Not a fixed thing. The feelings, sensations, perceptions, intentions, states of consciousness—where is that "What am I"? Where is your immortal soul? Where is your who you think you are? Check it out. That's the exercise. That's the direction you can look when you go more precisely into "Who or what am I, and what's happening here?" That's how to trace the source of all the radiance of our own undeniable experience. We might have heard that Eastern thought purports that life is like a dream, but what a dream it is! And why not have a good dream instead of a nightmare, if and when we can, for both ourselves and others? This is why we strive toward illusory enlightenment through illusory spiritual exercises and enjoy the illusory joy of freedom, bliss, and delight.

One's own name and form and self-concept are less solidly real and perceptible than we think and more like a constellation being named, with lines drawn in between the points of light to shape them into a form—a concept superimposed on reality, somewhat different than reality itself. This analysis leads to the realization of Buddha's famous three characteristic marks of existence: *anicca, anatta,* and *dukkha*—impermanence; therefore no-separate-permanent-self or owner; and dissatisfactoriness.

We can see that the body is anicca, impermanent, changeable. This is not dogma; this is just how it is, at least according to the enlightened vision of Buddha. Tell me—is it right? And the mortal, fleeting body is dukkha, ultimately dissatisfying. Who can get lasting, ultimate fulfillment from a body, from a mere momentary sensual experience? Even the highest, most exquisite body experiences are fleeting and ephemeral, leaving us thirsting for more. Of these three facts of life, the most tricky nut to crack is anatta—not-self, ungovernable, selfless. Is the body anatta? Is there a governor? Who's running the show? That's the meaning of anatta, not-self, which opens into great sunyata, or emptiness, openness—not just of the self, but of all created things. No independent existent entity anywhere. Not a solid thing, yet everything continues to appear.

You can call the bronze, round, bowl-shaped ritual antique from India that we use to begin meditation a "gong," but you could also call it metal. You could also call it brown. You could call it a musical instrument. Or you could call it an antique. It depends on how you relate to it, how you conceive of it and label it. Similarly, everything depends on conceptual imputation. Nothing is just a particular thing, in essence; it's all contingent, interrelated, subjective. Everything is relative. Things can be viewed from any number of different angles. Look deeply, explore reality in your own experience, moment by moment; genuinely try to find out for yourself. This can be incredibly rewarding. We are not who we think we are. One person says she's a woman. Someone else says about the same person, "There's a beautiful woman." Someone else says, "There's a young woman." Someone else might say, "There's an American." From the point of view of aliens from other planets or earthbound animals, what would they say? Who knows, but it would be quite different, right? It all depends on one's perspective, experience, karmic perceptions, and projections. So we are not just exactly who we think we are.

We all have these fantasies, almost like superstitions, about ourselves; but when you check, there's just form, feeling, perception, volition, and consciousness. *That's* what makes up our individual existence, according to the enlightened Buddha. This is a very interesting reduction of all of our sandcastles and fancies about ourselves. It's not meant to be depressing, but to introduce how things are, to introduce enlightened view or complete understanding to help us come to clear vision and objective, penetrating understanding of our true existential situation and fundamental nature, along with the unfortunate implications of misknowing the basic facts of our life. There is karma, conditioning, and causation through cause and effect; and just as there is a way to perpetrate ignorance and its concomitant confusion, delusion, and suffering, there is a way to end suffering, through insight and understanding how things actually work and who and what we are. It is not beyond our grasp when we apply ourselves to the spiritual work, the inner investigation. So turn the spotlight, the searchlight, inward; discover yourself. Awaken and realize who and what you truly are and how you fit in to the bigger picture. The innate spirit is magnificent in its natural state, as my Tibetan master used to say.

This kind of deconstructionist approach can be applied to anything, so we can understand that things are not exactly what they seem to be. We can relinquish some of our clinging and our concepts about things, including *mine* and *yours* and our incessant craving—*I want* and *I must have*—and that plaintiff common cry *What about me-me-me?* What is all this me and mine, my body? We can say "my body." No one is going to argue if I say this is "my" body. Except for the Lord of Death! And how can we really, seriously say "my mind," or "my thoughts and feelings"? I never have had an original thought in my whole life, and I'm supposed to be creative, a poet. *My* mind; it's a joke. *My* intentions. Somebody said about a political leader, "He's just like a pillow. He always shows the imprint of whatever head was just leaning on it." I'm a teacher, a leader, a poet, and a creative writer and thinker; and yet I'm just passing on what's been passed to me. My wife and my work and my group, my this and my that; it's illusion, like echoes and mirages in the desert, yet like everyone I remain so overly invested in it. It's fool's gold, but we invest our whole life and energy in it, with very small returns. Me, myself, and I: the Three Stooges! It's fun, it's fine, yet it's absurd. One might as well burst our laughing!

All that wrongheaded concretization and bullheaded reification falls apart gradually when you undermine it by, again and again, striving to see through the illusion that these fixed entities are real and that this fixed entity—one's self—is real, true, central, and lasting. Then selfish grasping loosens, our cocoon drops off, and our wings can open, inconceivable freedom dawns, and we are more naturally at ease with everyone and everything, with things just as they are. Do you think that nuclear power is the most powerful force in the world? I don't think so. The innate powers of the mind or inner spirit are far greater and, in the long run, more significant.

States of consciousness change all the time. There is no one state of consciousness that is lasting or fulfilling. So as Buddhist practitioners, well acquainted through study, reflection, and contemplation with the impermanence and unreliability of all created things and experiences, we stop taking refuge in or relying on any particular, temporary state of mind, not to mention on material objects of wealth and status. As we grow up and mature, we get less and less idealistic and more disillusioned about the pleasures of the senses as being ultimately fulfilling. We seek more deeply and see that it's not just the physical sensations that are fulfilling, that are the answer to our existential questions, to the crises we all face today and will have to face tomorrow, too. Pleasure and success alone are not enough, not what we really and truly want, need, and aspire to. It's not just beautiful perceptions or sights or sounds, or hearing beautiful music all day that's going to answer our quest, our doubts and anxieties and insecurities. It's not material possessions. It's not just having the right state of mind that's going to answer our deeper issues, for mind states are notoriously changeable. States of mind are always changing—no matter how high, no matter how ecstatic we become, no matter what new drug or new meditation comes around; it's just another trip. This path, this truth quest, this spiritual journey is not about getting high. This is about the inherent freedom and wholeness of being. Transformative Dharma practice eventually makes us wise, loving, serene, harmonious, and blissfully free.

So when we look into ourselves, it might be interesting to reflect on these five skandhas. You can read about them more deeply in different books, in the sutra texts as well as in modern books. As a touchstone, apply this analysis to yourself, which is where it really counts. That is where spiritual movement and meaningful growth actually occurs, in the crucible of one's interior experience, through regular spiritual practice.

A Basis for Letting Go

All this analysis and examination can actually help support the meditative process, which ultimately becomes far more intuitive, nonanalytical, and nonconceptual. It can help us have some basis for letting go and letting be, for relaxing and allowing—relinquishing a lot of the dualism and selfishness that drive all the incessant pushing and the pulling. (I want, I need. I'm happy, I'm sad. What about me and what I want and need?!) All our neuroses, psychoses, and pathology—basically, our dissatisfying behavior and thought patterns. According to Buddhist medicine—and there are Buddhist medical tantras and teachings—all the poisons, all the kleshas (conflicting emotions and inner obscurations), all the illnesses come from mental, spiritual, emotional, and energetic imbalances, which can be said to stem from the more basic levels of mind and spirit. It's not just saying that everything is psychosomatic; it's a little deeper than that. It means that it's all karmic, and that it is spiritually rooted. It's all effects of causes that we create through negative actions and intentions, unwholesome ways of being, causing our inner energies to become tied up and knotted. The diseases come from the imbalance of the energies and the humors, which are related to the movements of the spirit and the mind, all interconnected. And just as the causes of illness and suffering are within us, true health, happiness, and abundant well-being are within us, too.

We can heal many of these illnesses and imbalances from within, as it were, by working with the subtle energy, the *prana*, and through purifying the heart and mind, realigning our karma, skillfully rebalancing our karma and conditioning. Once we see that it is not just rigidly "me" and "mine," that's it's a process— everything is in process and interdependent—we can see where to skillfully adjust. Where to apply the lever, how to use the rudder. A little rudder can move the whole boat or aircraft. If the boat is going in the direction of madness or lack of health or unhappiness, a little steering is called for. It's not very mysterious, actually. We don't have to commit suicide and hope we get a better physical vehicle next time. There are other alternatives, and I think it is incumbent on us to find and adopt them, rather than to just give up and give in to despair, hopelessness, depression, addiction, and pain. We can heal and wholify ourselves; we can also transcend, go beyond; we can even heal our so-called souls, if not our bodies and minds. There is always hope.

I think this five-skandha scheme is a very interesting, very thorough one, in the sense that it can begin to raise some valid questions and help us dig deeper, rather than just having a vague, amorphous kind of understanding. We are individuals. We have to be individuated, mature adults and recognize both our separateness as well as our inextricable interrelatedness. We are each responsible for ourselves and our karma, and our relations. Our individuality is composed of these five aggregates. We can work practically with that. These are actually an expression of the innate Buddha nature, the authenticity or immediacy of being. Now, don't you want to say, "I didn't hear anything about Buddha nature in the five skandhas. Where's the Buddha nature? Who made that up?" That's the right question. What Buddha nature? Buddha never said anything about it. Who made that up? What enlightenment? What nirvana? Who made all that stuff up? Is it in us or elsewhere? How to get from "here" to "there"? Why are we here? What are we looking for, and what's the most direct route to it? The Dharma addresses these trenchant questions directly with, I think, a minimum of extra scaffolding, a minimum of assumptions, beliefs, and dogma. Investigation and questioning are a sacred art. This depends on us, on whether or not we can really get to the vital point and stay on it moment by moment. Really being with what *is*— *being* what is: that's Buddha nature. Are we ready, willing, and able to objectively address life's biggest, most deep and mysterious questions, free of received beliefs and underlying assumptions?

In the five skandhas, there's no Buddha nature, no special sixth skandha, a fancy feather or Buddhic aura sticking out the top. That is just a mental construct, a placeholder for those who need something positivistic to replace their current limited self-concept until all such conceptual scaffolding is no longer needed and dissolves. That's why emptiness (sunyata) is so fearsome, so awesome as a teaching. It's like infinite openness, synonymous with ultimate mystery. There's no final answer, no idealized totalization possible that answers everything automatically; and this open-endedness itself functions as a liberating answer. Just be observant, every moment. Dance in the sky, with no ground to stand on and no ground to fall to, either; that's emptiness, that's liberation, that's freedom from the barbed-wire concentration camp of concepts superimposed on reality. That is the natural Great Perfection, in which everything is just as it is, without need for further discussion or alteration.

We're all looking for something to hang our hopes on, but when we really get down to the present moment—to our own direct experience, to clear vision and direct intuition—we come to what Buddha said: "In hearing there is only hearing; no one hearing and nothing heard." There is just that moment, that bare hearing. You might think, "Oh, a beautiful bird." How do you know it's a bird? It might be a tape recorder. It might be a bird call by some prankster or the sound of distant bicycle brakes squeaking. Don't be sure of the validity of what you think you perceive, what you seem to know. In the very first moment of raw experience, there is just hearing; then we get busy, and our minds and conceptual imputations get involved. The Buddha went through all the five senses. "In seeing there is just seeing; no one seeing and nothing seen." And so on, with tasting, touching, smelling, and thinking. Thoughts without a thinker. In thinking there is just thinking. There is just that momentary process. There is no discrete, separate, solidly extant thinker. The notion of an inner thinker is just one more thought, a mere concept. We imagine that there is somebody thinking. It's like the Wizard of Oz. Dorothy and friends thought there was this glorious, all-powerful wizard, but it was just a lost little man back there behind the screen, behind the veil. That's how it is with the ego. We think there's a great big monkey inside working the five windows, the five senses. Or maybe five monkeys, one for each sense; a whole chattering monkey house, which it sometimes feels like. But is there really a concrete individual or permanent soul inside at all? It seems more like the lights are on, but no one is home.

Know Thyself

I think if we really look into ourselves, it will be very interesting and helpful. It will have a lot of implications, too many to even consider right now because it really affects everything. That's why Socrates, who is at the beginning of our Western knowledge lineage, said, "Know thyself." All philosophy can be unpacked from those two words. Know thyself and you'll know everything. You'll know everyone; everything is available there. We don't have to make up some fancy foreign words—tathagatagarbha or Buddha nature, sunyata emptiness, or some other Sanskrit word. Just know thyself. Even better, let's get rid of the archaic word *thy:* just know yourSelf. Then you'll know what's what. You'll know who's on first. Everything will start to make more sense. It's like having a cosmic key that unlocks all mysteries, or finding the fabled philosopher's stone. Knowing oneSelf unlocks all and everything. This is absolutely true.

The medieval Christian mystic Meister Eckhart (whom Zen master D. T. Suzuki studied in depth, and whose insight he endorsed as congruent with the Mahayana doctrine of sunyata, emptiness) said, "The eye through which I see God is the eye through which He sees me." There is just the seeing. There's no me and God in this mystic's construct, just the radiant, transparent eyeball. Maybe we can't understand God talk, so let's retranslate it: The eye through which I see Buddha is the eye through which Buddha sees me. The eye with which I recognize awareness (Buddha nature) is the eye with which awareness (Buddha nature) recognizes me. That's an introduction to nondualism, to the mind or spiritual awareness transparent to itself. In that way, we can really be totally present, not separate, not alienated, not scattered, undistracted. Totally present, whole, at home and at ease, coherent. It makes sense. Everything falls into place; everything fits from that perspective. There's room for everything. You don't have to get rid of anything. You see things as they are. That's wisdom. That's *prajna paramita,* transcendental knowledge. That's enlightenment. That's the direction that this practice follows. Seeing is freeing. Seeing things as they are; not adding on all of our fabulous fantasies. Of course, it's beautiful to add on as much as we want, but we should know that we are doing it, so we can also see through it and don't take it—or ourselves—so damn seriously. When we put on our rainbow-colored sunglasses, we factor that in when we look at things—until we forget! Then we get lost in a magic spell of our own making.

What is our existence? What is the force impelling this existence? Are we free to steer and master that, or do we just have to be blown forward by the karmic force, like dead leaves before the wind? Of course, you can "exist" if you want. We are all here existing. But are we exactly what we think we are? As we go on, if we feel depressed about who we are, are we stuck with that? If our lives feel claustrophobic, are we stuck with that? It would probably be just as false to say you don't exist as to say you do exist, because that would be another absolute, merely another mental construct—just one more attempt at a total answer in order to provide the security of a final solution. Things are not that manageable, that neatly packagable. Life remains just a little bit more messy, juicy, and marvelous than that.

There's a sane, healthy ego and grown-up adult individuality that one has to maintain, obviously. We must develop from the early stages of dependence to independence to eventually realize interdependence. But that's not the whole story. There's also a mature, transpersonal, unselfish engagement with the world we can maintain at the same time, so we're not so closed in, constricted, barricaded, self-preoccupied. It doesn't mean we don't know the meaning of "me" and "mine"—my shirt rather than your shirt. We still know which closet is our own and where to put our shirt. You put it on your body; you don't put it on your refrigerator or on the rosebush outside the door. Of course you understand and know about yourself in the conventional sense. This conventional self exists, temporarily—obviously! But there's also the not-mine. Do we know about that? Do we appreciate the beyond-ourselves level of being? It is as if there are two kinds of self to discuss here: the conventional self, which functions and exists, relatively speaking, and the nonexistent ultimate, eternal Self, which is actually what anatta (not-self or ownerlessness) refers to.

Let's make it very practical in terms of meditation practice. When we have a thought, of course we think it's our thought; but at the same time, do we also know that it's not our thought, that it just sort of popped up? You could say the thought comes out of emptiness, or you could say it is just the karmic ripening of previous thoughts, or you could say that thoughts arise from the mind. But where does the so-called mind arise from? Maybe we think it's a thought worth writing down, so we write it down. We catch it in the form of a poem, a haiku, or an epigram. But what does *my* mean? Like with "my body"? Who gave you this body? Where did you get the copyright on it from? Did you buy it? Did you build it? Did you fabricate and create it? Are you truly in total command of its doings, its processes, longevity, and so forth? What does "my mind" actually imply, as an idea? We can look at everything like that, and see how we are a little overly involved in holding on to those things as "me" and "mine"—when they are merely on loan, as it were. The Buddhist doctrine of no separate, solidly existent independent self implies no ownership, no governor, but rather mutual reciprocity, stewardship, humility, and responsibility.

A moment of anger comes, and instead of just experiencing the simple energy of the emotion, which might actually have some intelligent function, such as to know something's wrong—that there is injustice, for example—you identify with it: "I'm an angry person. What's wrong with me? I can never get rid of this anger." But each of the emotions has its own validity and logic before it devolves into the property of "me" and "mine," way before reaction and aggression—before it becomes judged and conceptualized and identified as, say, "my anger." The emotions have their own logic, their own intelligence, their own place and function. They can actually help us experience the world, not just bring us into conflict. We could train ourselves in emotional intelligence, and utilize the awakened aspect of these emotions to vividly perceive and discriminate. The emotions are like intelligence agents functioning on the frontiers and hidden realms of consciousness.

If and when we reflect on selflessness and contingency, the impermanence and tenuousness of everything, including ourselves—and on the five skandhas as comprising our individuality—it helps us identify less with momentary perceptions and habitual, mostly unconscious patterns, even while we become more conscious, wakeful, clear, intelligent, and aware. Then we have more autonomy and less reactivity. Then we develop deeper understanding and self-knowledge. This is the road of freedom and delight.

CHAPTER 10

THE SIX PRINCIPLES OF ENLIGHTENED LIVING

The Six Perfections (Sanskrit: *paramitas*) are six cardinal Buddhist virtues as well as principles of enlightened living and wise leadership. They make up the Mahayana manual for awakening, providing far-reaching, well-rounded guidelines for living the truly good life. The Six Perfections—generosity, ethics, patience, balanced effort, contemplation, and wisdom—are the peaceful, wise, and loving code of the bodhisattva, the selfless spiritual awakener and wisdom warrior. In the Mahayana teachings about universal enlightenment, it is always said that there are four ways to help spiritually mature and ripen others: through generously establishing a positive relationship with them; through discussing what is truly beneficial and harmful; through encouraging them to undertake and apply what they have understood; and by embodying those spiritual principles oneself. The Six Perfections are six Buddhist virtues that most potently express enlightened vision and powerful moral and spiritual leadership, for the bodhisattva is the ultimate social and spiritual activist and altruist—having dedicated this life and all his or her lives to the highest good for the greatest number.

These paramitas or transcendental virtues and transformative practices tell us how to integrate into daily life the outer, inner, and subtlest innate levels of enlightened living and how to carry all circumstances into the path—how to make a meaningful and productive life, not just a living—how to integrate everything as our path and assimilate everything into spiritual learning, inner growth and development, and conscious evolution. This involves illumining and awakening our minds as well as opening our warm, good hearts.

In one way, these paramita or virtuous and skilful bodhisattva practices are traditionally taught as training, going gradually, sequentially, through the six virtues from the more easy to the more difficult—from generosity up to wisdom—and from the gross to the subtle, from the outer behavioral to the inner attitudinal dimensions of sacred action and intent, and on to the ultimate innate or oneness level. More profoundly, seen from the bigger perspective, these six virtues are wisdom's expression and make up the enlightened way of living itself. They are not just steps leading up to awakening; they ARE it. This is the bodhisattva's secret magic of being there while getting there, every single step of the way; not merely waiting to get there after many lifetimes, or at least decades, of strenuous schlepping to enlightenment. Here in a nutshell is the joy of spiritual life: being fully *here* while getting there. "Every step of the way to heaven is heaven," as the mystics say.

Is it not sane, wise, enlightened, and liberating and freeing—perfect, in fact—to be moral, to be disciplined, to be inquiring or reflective and mindful, and so forth? All and each of these splendid bodhisattva virtues are included in each other, and each is guided—like active arms and legs—by the all-seeing eye of wisdom, the sixth paramita. Transcendental wisdom, or prajna paramita, is both an uncommon and a common sense; it can often seem so ordinary yet comes in quite handy as practical penetrating insight and deep-seeing far-sightedness along with its more mystical aspects, including higher knowledge; gnostic, intuitive knowing; and even what some call omniscience. When we talk in general about the six principles of enlightened living, they are a training, something we can apply in life and develop ourselves, thus becoming wiser and more compassionate; more sane, rather than more conflicted or disturbed; more balanced and whole; and more helpful rather than harmful. On the other hand, the six paramitas actually embody the way and express transcendental wisdom itself. Each of them *is* wise, is perfectly impeccable, is a path in and unto itself, and embodies enlightened living. And each supports the other like the six spokes of a radiant wheel or facets of one single radiant jewel.

Generosity

The first one of the six principles of enlightened living is called *dana paramita* in Sanskrit, or the virtue of perfect generosity. Dana paramita means openness—open hands, open heart, open mind. It's like Christian charity, caritas, which means self-giving as well as divine, unconditional love and openness. Externally, it means being generous with material goods, with helping others, with sharing one's resources, with feeding the poor, not being stingy and miserly. Internally, we can help others by providing protection and security, love and encouragement; by giving of ourselves—lending an ear or a shoulder; and by being generous with our energy and our emotions in a healthy way, rather than being stingy, withholding, reactive, or overly judgmental.

We can also be generous with love, and with the good-hearted warmth and natural caring that is in all of us. We have plenty of it to go around; we don't have to keep it for special people or save it like an investment. Being generous with our love means not only being nice to the ones who return it, who are nice to us; it means being much more generous and nonmanipulative, giving unstintingly—royal giving, noble generosity—without expectation of much in return. Giving and offering ourselves, we learn to yield, soften up, give in, give way, and let go. Practicing nonattachment and restraint and moderation is a way of cultivating generosity, by becoming less grasping and devouring. In actual fact, we can give ourselves totally to every single moment. That would be perfection; that would be enlightenment and freedom. We can be unconditionally engaged with everything that comes up in each moment, without ulterior motive. That would be dana paramita, transcendental generosity.

On the innate level, we have an inexhaustible fund of energy, spontaneity, love, and creativity. Inexhaustible sources of health, love, and healing powers are within us. Let's not squander them by letting them lie fallow. Let's exploit those natural inner resources for a change. Let's mine and refine that spiritual gold. It is innately there; let's not waste it. We each have unique gifts that need and want to be used. They are given to us to be used, to be shared and expressed. Contentment is the ultimate form of wealth. Practice nonattachment and equanimity, and see how much easier it is both to breathe in and to breathe out, to give and to receive. "Much is expected of those to whom much is given." At the level of pure be-ing, the perfection of generosity means being open minded and open hearted, content and fulfilled, detached yet not uncaring—with room for everything; being accepting, tolerant, and inclusive while letting go of judgments, opinions, and fixations. This is the meaning of transcendental generosity. Not even trying to hoard up our brilliant thoughts, our extraordinary meditation experiences, or our realizations. Using our innate pure and untrammeled Big Mind would be the ultimate generosity. Ultimately, there is nothing worth holding on to, nor can we—at least, not for very long.

Ethics

The second principle of enlightened living is *sila paramita*. Externally, it implies ethics, morality, doing what is wholesome and helpful rather than harmful, loving-kindness and compassion, and so on. Ethical discipline upholds purity and simplicity as a fulfilling standard of living, accomplishes good karma, and protects, inspires, and benefits others. It means being righteous and morally upright, steadfast, straightforward, and honest. We practice this through right living—right speech, right action, right intentions, right livelihood, and the rest—beyond merely adhering to legalistic codes or commandments handed down from above, but tuning into the natural laws of being and noticing that it is in our higher Self-interest to live in an impeccable manner. This means acting from our recognition that nobody wants to be harmed, any more than we do, and that we're all the same in that we all want and need more or less the same things—peace, love, safety, and happiness. So we can really treat others as we ourselves would be treated. It becomes a natural morality, coming from the recognition of our own interconnectedness and oneness with all—a recognition of the common ground that we all share.

Internally, sila shows up as integrity, as character. We strive to practice not fooling ourselves. So, internally, we need to have the character and integrity to live authentically and to be truly, genuinely ourselves, straightforward and natural, and not to pretend, not adulterate ourselves with pretense and always trying to keep up a persona, not lose touch with our true Selves. To live truly.

Most innately, sila paramita is to be ourselves, to know ourselves and be ourselves, without prevarication. Internally, sila is authenticity and trueness, as a self-discipline; but most innately, it is our innate purity and untrammeled, incorruptible pure spiritual nature. We can never be anything else than ourselves anyway; thus the ultimate behavioral training vow or ethical discipline is authenticity, to be true to the facticity of our own primordial being. Who else can we be? Children play all kinds of games, but they each play in their own way. They are so much themselves, whatever show they put on. We are not much different, are we? Buddha called everybody children. He saw that we are all still like children, whose wisdom and self-actualization has not yet fully matured. He talked to everybody as if he were an elder, and used forms of address for children even when he was talking to aged people. He knew that they were children in the sense of not being fully grown up in terms of wisdom. And he said that all these teachings and all these techniques are like toys. He said that children won't come out of the burning house of worldly delusion and confusion, so he put toys (Dharma practices and theory) in front of the house so they'll come out.

We're all like children, but it is possible to guide and liberate us. We're always true to ourselves, at the core, however much we may pretend, dissemble, or fool ourselves. The more we know how that is, the freer and the more skillful, wholesome, and uninhibitedly liberated we will be. We will be like beacons in the darkness of ignorance. So most innerly, there's sila that's beyond self-discipline. It's the authenticity of purity of our own true, original Buddha nature—of truly being ourSelves.

Patience

The third principle of enlightened living is *kshanti paramita*, which means patience, forbearance, and tolerance. It's sometimes translated as "peace," but that's a mistake, though peace is included. It means patience, tolerance, forbearance, acceptance, and forgiveness. Externally, it means being patient, tolerant, accepting, open, and so on, including being patient with enemies and adversaries; patient in the face of criticism and abuse; patient in the face of suffering, illness, and difficulties of all kinds; and patient also in the face of the harsh realities of Dharma truths. Practicing these kinds of patience helps develop our inner strength and fortitude, making our interior certainty and conviction like an inner fortress and sanctuary. Kshanti means being reticent to judge, discreet, moderate in all things—including moderation. We don't want to get too excessively moderate, like puritans, and fail to enjoy anything.

Internally, kshanti paramita means really accepting and trusting ourselves, forgiving ourselves, giving ourselves permission to be relaxed and unhurried. As a wise man once said, "I'm too busy to hurry." He meant too busy doing significant things to be hurried. So, internally, this peace, this patience, shows up as inner peace, serenity, assured centeredness—natural calm and focus. It means being in it for the long run, and enduring. Of course, patience spills over into the next paramita, *virya*, which is effort, heroic energy, and enthusiastic perseverance. Patience and forbearance help us to bear whatever comes and to see things through without hurrying them—for example, not trying to jump to conclusions or instantly be gratified. The Korean Zen master Soeng Soen always calls it "long-enduring mind" or indomitable attitude. In one of his famous poems, he sings: "Only go straight for ten thousand years." That's Zen practice. He always throws in his other famous teaching: "Just don't know." So the poem has two lines: "Just don't know. Only go straight for ten thousand years." So you don't have to know anything, but just go straight, forever. That does require some patience and inner fortitude and strength, doesn't it!

This kind of timeless wisdom relates to the innate side of the transcendental virtue of patience. Is there any other way we can go than straight ahead? There's a Zen poem that says, "Just keep your head on your shoulders and your nose facing forward." That's the teaching. It's not very hard, and yet for some strange reason this clear and simple injunction seems almost impossible—perhaps because we are so complicated, crooked, out of touch with our true Selves, bent out of shape. Innately, this great patience, or the great peace of nirvana, is always there. The eternal, underlying, ineffable fact of the immutable, natural peace is always accessible. Ultimately, transcendental patience is the timelessness of *being* itself, which we definitely participate in. We each have our share. The Dharmakaya is in each of us; it's our share of nirvana. "The mind is magnificent in its natural state," as Longchenpa says, "so leave it as it is. Don't bother yourself." That's kshanti paramita, the great peace of nirvana within ourselves, within our own experience. There is nirvanic peace in things left just as they are.

Balanced Effort

The fourth transcendental virtue is *virya paramita*—the perfection of energetic zeal, of courage, effort, perseverance, and diligence. There's something very interesting about virya that I found out one day while reading a Buddhist book about etymology. Virya is usually called effort, endeavor, or diligence and enthusiastic perseverance. Effort sounds dry, but this virtue includes enthusiastic courage, heroism, and fearlessness. Here we cultivate the courage to keep going on the path, with the passion for truth and enlightenment that keeps seekers going until they become finders and awakeners. It's not that the path is like some kind of drudgery, mere chore, or annoying task you have to complete. The secret is finding your own true path, and following it all the way, which morphs into the passion of true vocation and living truly—finding oneSelf and what one is ultimately here for.

Externally, virya shows up as enthusiastic effort—right effort, complete effort, balanced effort—not just compulsive effort. This includes effortless effort, arising within those inner qualities of one's true vocation and the passion for doing and accomplishing what one loves to do. Diligence is like armor, which protects us from laziness and indolence; it's an appetite for spiritual truth and continuous progress along the path. Externally, it's endurance, exuberance, boldness, perseverance, diligence, and energy. Exuberance and boldness have their own power and magic, including the outrageous boldness to dream, to envision, and to aspire to the highest. "Who am I to wish to be a Buddha?" little mousy me says. But the teaching is that each of us can undertake the bodhisattva aspiration to become an enlightened Buddha in order to liberate all from dissatisfaction and suffering. Therefore, virya paramita includes boldness, fearlessness, and courage, and the joyous energy and dynamism inherent in that.

Internally, there is joyous energy that functions like an updraft that carries one indomitably forward through everything, no matter what ups and downs come along the way. We feel strong and firm in inner certainty, and that we can go on forever in our selfless spiritual efforts, without becoming discouraged or giving up, even if we are the last bodhisattva on earth.

Innately, it is the courage to just *be,* and not to have to *do* anything. The subtle fearlessness that allows us just to be, as is, rather than always doing and forcing and controlling everything, takes some digging to reach down to, but it is definitely there; see if you can't find it yourself. Virya paramita sounds outwardly a little like too much doing, but let's not get caught in the doer. It's doing without doer-ship. Can we ever do anything without straying into the illusion of doer-ship? Innately, we are without doer-ship, and everything just happens. Great, joyous courage and passionate intensity spontaneously blaze up when we are freed of the burden of doer-ship, and free from the pride, egocentric agendas, and self-identification implicit in doer-ship. The great updraft of the aspiration for enlightenment, for universal liberation, can carry us all through the long process, so that we have the patience and endurance to continue in self-discipline and in giving ourselves to what is truly helpful and meaningful, no matter what. In Shantideva's wonderful classic book about the bodhisattva path, the *Bodhicharvavatara* (*Entering the Bodhisattva Path*), it says, "May my vow to liberate all continue, as long as there is any sentient being suffering in the entire universe. Until the ocean of suffering is dried up, may my vow continue." That's virya paramita, the fearless courage and boundless, inexhaustible joyful energy of the bodhisattvas.

Contemplation

The fifth principle of enlightened living is *dhyana paramita*, the perfection of meditation, or mindfulness and contemplation. Externally it refers to meditation, contemplation, calming the mind, and purifying the spirit. It also includes intentionally cultivating mindfulness and utilizing attention for purposes such as self-observation and self-inquiry, in order to know and understand ourselves better; dismantle reactive emotions and dissatisfying habitual patterns; and free our minds and hearts. Through meditative concentration and insightful awareness, we experience peace and bliss within our own mind and become freed from depending on or seeking it outside. This virtue of focus awareness and mindful meditation helps us attain spiritual realization and self-mastery. Of course, there are many forms and styles of meditation and the intentional use of attention in the Buddhist tradition. Externally, meditation and mindfulness can be understood as sitting with awareness or standing, eating, working, and walking mindfully—that is, meditation in action through mindful behavior and vigilant self-awareness.

Inwardly, dhyana implies spiritual curiosity more than any posture or speed of movement, and an exploring, inquiring, wholehearted, and self-reflective mind. Tibet's greatest Dzogchen master Longchenpa calls it wonderment combined with sheer lucency. This bodhisattva virtue includes both alert presence of mind, as in mindfulness practice, and also a certain degree of childlike openness and wonder, as when wondering, "What's going on here?" when seeing things for the first time. There are Zen koans in which one mulls over, "What is the sound of one hand clapping?" It's very hard to figure out, and there's an even more absurd koan, harder to figure out, which is "What is it?" What is it?—with a big question mark. My translation is, "What the hell is going on?" What is THIS? That's what it means. That's the koan to reflect on, to chew on your whole life till you break ultimately through and find out.

Internally, dhyana paramita, this meditative or contemplative life, shows up as wonder, as investigation into how things work and how things are, how we are, and into knowing ourselves better—and yet without any real purpose or goal consciously in mind. One of the greatest scientists once said: "My whole life has been like a child playing on the beach." Just looking at all the seashells and whatever else is on the beach all day, so that he doesn't even notice the sun's going down at the end of his life, because he's still playing on the beach, as it were—investigating everything on the beach, carefree and in the eternal moment like a little child. That's the inner side of dhyana paramita, beyond self-conscious efforts at quieting the mind or stilling the senses through formal meditation practice; rather, resting at ease by being in touch with innate natural peace of spirit. Then our meditations aren't just nodding and dozing while trying-to-get-through-the-early-hour morning meditations; they're wakeful, interested, and inquisitive, penetrating what-the-hell-is-going-on meditations every day of our lives, not just on Sunday or in the formal meditation period. And it's not just about thinking about it; it's even much deeper, into actually experiencing, and gnostic, direct, intuitive experiential knowing. Through minding the mind and turning the mind upon itself through meditative attention, we learn to experience the experiencer, not just praying and hoping for something to happen like throwing rocks in the dark and hoping to hit some target outside of ourselves. Internally, dhyana paramita is the ever-rising dawn of awareness, simply sustaining innate wakefulness.

Most innately, dhyana paramita is our incessantly interested and awake intelligence, our innate luminous natural mind or bodhicitta (awakened heart-mind). It's not just about one's IQ, or information, but our innate spiritual intelligence, responsiveness, purity of heart, and Buddha nature. True meditation includes moment-by-moment wonder at the sheer magnificence, beauty, and splendor within, marveling at the infinite spiritual mind, the infinite potential for knowledge, and even glimpsing the elusive answer to that maddening koan we all go through life asking, in one way or another—"What is it?" (Please don't ask me what IT is.) IT is everything. But what is everything? What is anything? What is it? What's going on? However you want to translate it in your own language, whatever resonates with you, just keep the koan alive, not just try to come up with an easy answer. It's not enough to say, "Everything is empty, I read it in a book." That won't help when you are approaching death or dealing with some kind of tragedy, loss, disappointment, or other crisis.

Wisdom

The sixth principle of enlightened living is *prajna paramita,* transcendental wisdom. In one way, all of the paramita virtues lead up to prajna paramita, transcendental wisdom, nonconceptual awareness, intuitive gnosis. In another way, each of the principles include and embody it. It is wise to live according to each of these transformative principles of enlightened living and selfless leadership.

Externally, wisdom shows up as great, boundless generosity and openness, and all that we talked about—integrity and character; natural restraint and self-discipline; pure ethics and morality; and patience, forgiveness and tolerance, enthusiastic energy, and insightful awareness. Of course it does! Have you ever met spiritual masters? They're like children in that they're so spontaneous; yet they are also supremely *knowing.*

Wisdom shows up as all the enlightened qualities we discussed in the other five enlightened principles. But what is wisdom? That's a very inconceivable, inexpressible thing to describe. Externally, it shows up as all these enlightened qualities. There is conceptual wisdom and practical, worldly wisdom—such as excellent judgment and discrimination—as well as existential wisdom, mystical wisdom, spiritual wisdom, discernment, and profound sagacity. In Tibetan Buddhism, we talk about the five wisdoms or the five forms of transcendental awareness: unifying wisdom, mirrorlike wisdom, discriminating/discerning wisdom, effective wisdom, and all-inclusive totality wisdom. We can develop and realize these wisdoms through the fourfold scheme essential for spiritual higher education: learning, analytical reflection, meditative introspection, and integration through application in life.

Internally, prajna shows up as a kind of intuitive knowing, penetrating insight, and luminous clarity. Centered and still in the midst of all movement, without deviating into quietism, this virtue includes a peaceful atmosphere that one carries with one-self wherever one goes, even in a busy downtown intersection.

Innately, it's just the ability to be as one and at ease with every-one and everything. There is an ineffable sense of completeness and fullness, beyond relying on any particular form of activity, religious or otherwise.

There's a story about Socrates. One day he was sitting in the bathtub in the sun, like an eccentric crazy-wise master. Alexander the Great came and stood next to him and said to Socrates, the wisest man in the world: "What can I do for you; what can I give you? What can I do for you? You're the wisest man in the world." While lazing in his bathtub, Socrates said, "Could you move out of the sun?" That's wisdom—direct and to the point. The master was in the sunlight; the Macedonian king was obscuring his sunlight. That is all. The wise man wanted and needed nothing more, neither from his king nor his gods. Wisdom shows up in funny ways, which is why it's sometimes called "crazy wisdom," which famously startles us into awakefulness through iconoclastic unexpectedness. Or, as I like to think of it in Dzogchen, "lazy wisdom." Even if God walks by, if the master is sunning himself, he might not even deign to raise an eyelid. Why? Because he never lost or lacked for divine connection, nor needed to seek it. Transcendental wisdom is inexpressible, of course, but it does show up, definitely, and we can recognize it. We all can become wiser and more awake and radiant. Wisdom is within the reach of ALL. We are all mystics, in one way or an-other; we're all living spirits.

Enlightened Principles as Natural Experience

All these enlightened principles are actually something to ex-press as part of our life, not just something we have to study, memorize, or aspire to. Probably if we just remember one word out of all them, and just reflect on it once in a while, then that would bring out the whole of all of them. It's like a hologram, in which each part contains the whole. We can work from the outside in, such as shaving our heads and taking training vows and precepts to become monks or nuns and following strict spiritual self-discipline externally, in order to train ourselves internally and eventually realize our innate completeness and purity; for an impeccable way of living can certainly help us to realize that. That is wise to undertake, and includes all the paramitas. Alternatively, we can start from the inside out, through the more mystical or nondualistic internal awareness teachings and practices centered around natural mind, innate perfection, and just being, for in one moment of total awareness, there is one moment of perfect freedom and enlightenment, as the Dzogchen scripture says. There is no self, no doer, no one in control; nor is there any separate *other* or them. From such a profound realization of inseparable oneness and interdependence, all the enlightened qualities and loving possibilities latent within us can emerge and surge forward. Then arise spontaneous expressions of natural, inexhaustible, appropriate responsiveness, unselfish helpfulness and caring. Anything that is needed can and will come forward, and since there's no holding back, there can be total generosity, natural morality, empathic compassion, profound recognition of interbeing, and so on.

More likely, we work on ourselves by walking a path in between those extremes, working from the outside in while also working from the inside out, step by step, according to the great Middle Way. We can take the bodhisattva vow, a vow for all our lifetimes to strive wholeheartedly, unselfishly toward universal enlightenment, liberation, and the end of suffering. That trains us both externally and internally. Externally, it trains us in impeccable acts and in enlightened living. Internally, it trains us in character, attitude, and integrity. And it helps us actualize and embody our innate perfection and wholeness, the innate Buddha nature, which is none other than our own innate goodness and wholeness. Each of us embodies the notion of deity. We are each like God's pseudopods, God's appendages. We each have our dance, our job, our mission that we work to fulfill. We are all Buddhas by nature—some sleeping Buddhas, some awakened Buddhas. We only have to awaken to who and what we truly are; that is transcendental wisdom. That is the goal of this path of awakening; that is enlightenment.

In terms of impeccable acts and enlightened living, I think our truest course is to find and fully live our true vocation. I think discovering and realizing our true work here in this life is our highest calling, which solves most if not all of our doubts and travails. This seems quite clear to me here and now in America, where most of us are lay practitioners and aspiring bodhisattvas. This is something we can all do; there's nothing keeping us from that. Let's not abdicate our responsibility toward our true Selves, to all, and to truth itself. The bodhisattva is the ultimate social atruist, like a spiritual altruist dedicating his or her life toward the greater good of all. I know of no higher, more inspiring spiritual ideal in this world. May we all be able to live by the bodhisattva code, and fulfill our vow of service and enlightenment, through practicing the six paramitas for the limitless benefit of all beings.

A bodhisattva prayer, from the original Tibetan

From now until enlightenment is reached, now and through all my lifetimes

I go for refuge in the Buddha, the Dharma and the Sangha community;

May I wholeheartedly practice the Six Perfections

For the boundless benefit of one and all,

Until we all together complete the spiritual journey.

practice is perfect

JUST DO IT

CHAPTER II

TAKING REFUGE

AWAKENING COMPASSION

What does it mean to take refuge, in the Buddhist sense? What does it mean to go for refuge in the Buddha, Dharma, and sangha; to find reliable refuge; and to think beyond oneself; to generate compassion or altruistic bodhicitta, the altruistic mind of enlightenment, the aspiration for enlightenment? This is a very basic, yet totally profound area of spiritual inquiry. It is not just going through some formalities, chanting some mumbo-jumbo that some high priests alone understand. If we really get down to it, what does it mean to say, "I take refuge in the Buddha, the teacher who embodies enlightenment." Does it mean I bow down to a piece of statuary from the antique shop? Or to a wise man who lived twenty-five-hundred years ago? What does it mean to take refuge in the Dharma, in the sangha? Naropa, Marpa's guru, sang: "My heart-mind is the perfect Buddha; my speech is the perfect Dharma; my body is the perfect sangha." To realize truth for one's Self, within one-Self, or to find refuge in the trikaya—the three kayas or Buddha bodies, Dharmakaya, sambhogakaya, and nirmanakaya—within the empty openness, the luminous clarity and the unobstructed compassionate responsiveness of your own true nature—these are the three innate jewels—the good, the true, and the beautiful: Buddha, Dharma, and sangha.

Stepping on the Path of Awakening

So, what *does* it mean to take refuge? It means to make a commitment to spiritual awakening. That's the Buddha—awakening; Buddhahood; Buddha nature; Buddha mind; enlightened mind; reality; realization. Buddhas and bodhisattvas have unveiled their minds so that their true Buddha nature shines forth—no more clouds, open and radiant. So when we take refuge, in the outward way it is in the Buddha—the beautiful Buddha statue or picture, representing on one level Shakyamuni Buddha, the historical enlightened teacher who is an example and inspiration for us all; but in an inner way it is taking refuge in knowing truth for ourselves. Knowing truth within, the genuine wisdom of intrinsic awareness itself. That is Buddha nature. That is the refuge. The ultimate Buddha is the realization of Buddha mind, pure and open. That alone is a sanctuary, an authentic reliance. That's what it means to take refuge in awareness itself, which is freedom and peace: an awakening each and every moment, through the immediacy of present awareness.

By taking refuge, we make a commitment to awakening. Not just to bow down to an idol, not just to subscribe to a dogma, but to make a commitment to knowing the truth. When you say, "I take refuge in Buddha, the enlightened teacher," it means that you take refuge in the Buddha within, to know how things really are. That's the ultimate refuge. That's the inner truth, the inner teacher, the absolute guru—to know the truth, to know reality just as it is. Not just knowing with the mental computer, the brain, but knowing with the intuitive heart-mind. Not just to knowing information with the conceptual mind, but knowing through direct experience, self-realization. That's finding refuge, something to rely on—inner freedom and enlightenment itself, within one's own experience.

Knowing the truth is the ultimate reliance, the ultimate

refuge, like a safe port in a storm. What does it mean to say, "I go for refuge in the Dharma"? The Dharma is the truth, the teaching, the practice of Buddhist doctrine; not just something to believe in, like dogma. It is the truth of how things actually are. We find refuge in expressing that truth, learning that truth, integrating that truth. That's the Dharma teaching. That's the way to find refuge in that way of life: speaking the truth, sharing in the truth of realization. When we truly take refuge, no obstacle can stagger us for long. As one great Tibetan master, prayed long ago:

> Bless and empower us that our hearts and minds turn towards the Dharma.
> Bless and empower us that our Dharma practice follows the authentic path of liberation.
> Bless and empower us that the path truly dispels suffering and confusion.
> Bless and empower us that confusion itself dawns in the light of primordial awareness.

That's the Dharma. The Dharma is what relieves suffering and confusion, alleviates pain, and heals what ails us in the deepest sense. It is something we can rely on, and find refuge in—the truth, not just Buddhist doctrine, but truth itself; being truthful and straightforward, having good character, integrity, and impeccability; in harmony with life as it is. It's where we can find refuge from all this confusion and madness that we see around us and within us. That's a refuge, a sanctuary, an oasis.

My late teacher Kalu Rinpoche said Buddha's speech, or Dharma, is "vast and deep as an ocean, joyous, and continuously benefits beings in this world and many other universes. Buddha's speech is the rare and sublime Dharma." We exert ourselves in both study and practice of the Dharma: awakening to that and living truly, speaking truth, expressing truth, not just studying the Dharma doctrines and teachings. Speaking it, sharing it, being honest, straightforward, impeccable, genuine. Even being ourselves is Dharma, our own homegrown Dharma. Being authentically true to ourselves; not just living someone else's life, doing something because we think we should. How about walking our own path? That's finding refuge in the truth, in Dharma, living truly. That is a reliable sanctuary or refuge. If we lie and so on, we can't really say we are seeking truth, because that's crooked, not straight.

And, finally, there is taking refuge in the sangha, in the community. Buddha is knowing the truth; Dharma is knowing the truth and speaking the truth; sangha is being the truth, living and embodying it. Of course, all these are very much connected: three facets of one single jewel. Buddha, Dharma, and sangha are traditionally called the Triple Gem, the Triple Jewel. Taking refuge in the sangha on the outward level is listening to the teachings with respect, and practicing to follow the example of the teachers. Sangha is embodying the truth, living the truth; it is those who live the truth and live truly. It's a great support, something we can all rely on in the midst of all the confusion and agitation, deception, distress, and alienation of these modern times. It is a commitment to living harmoniously with others, awakening together, and working to bring all beings along with us toward lesser suffering and greater freedom, peace, and clarity. That's refuge in sangha; not just taking refuge in people who have orange monastic robes. Not just taking refuge in Buddhist groups or being a mere member. Sangha implies true community, a beloved community of kindred spirits helping each other along the way of awakening.

It is taking refuge in true community itself; communion with others—collaboration, connectedness, engagement, responsibility, working together, in an organic way and not in an addicted manner. As the brilliant crazy wisdom master Trungpa Rinpoche said, "If you lean on somebody in a weak moment of your life, the person you lean on may seem strong, but he will also begin to

catch your weakness." So the principle is not for a whole community to be leaning on each other like a set of dominoes—for if
one falls, they all collapse. Rather it means a willingness to work
together and support and help each other while remaining autonomous. No one person should strive excessively to act as the
spokesperson for the whole group. The sangha can be like a caul-
dron, or a batch of barley—add yeast and each grain becomes
powerful as fermentation occurs. The sangha is the entire living
community, for all sentient beings are spiritual beings, living
spirit in essence. Let's affirm our connection with them; that's our
real community. Not to mention the Buddhist Dharma brothers
and sisters that we are consciously walking together with on the
path; that slippery, muddy, uphill-seeming path to enlightenment. Here we are, paving and making that beautiful path with
our awkward footsteps. Let's rejoice in that Way making. It's a lot
of fun and meaningful, too. This is a good time to be strong Buddhist bulldozers and icebreakers, pioneers, bridge builders between East and West, between past and future, too. Not just for
ourselves—always having to achieve something—but for the
community, being snowplows clearing and opening a wide and
safe path that all can walk on.

This refuge is not a small thing. Affirming it every day is a
very beautiful practice, done in all Buddhist countries, and now
in all the Western countries also. Whether you chant it or just
think it in your own language, go deeper, keep inquiring and exploring until finally finding refuge in clear awareness and discriminating wisdom itself, which is the real Triple Gem, the true
Buddha within. Recognize that, and see that there is really nothing else needed, nowhere else to go, nothing missing and nothing
extra to get rid of. We can just *be,* we can live like Buddhas. We
are far more Buddha-like than we think. Whether we are momentarily sleeping Buddhas or awakened Buddhas, still we can
live like Buddhas, sit like Buddhas, walk like Buddhas, eat like
Buddhas, talk like Buddhas, and act like Buddhas. We can self-

lessly awaken others, too, as Buddhas do. Recognize the Buddha nature shining in each person you meet and in all beings and every experience; then every part of our life can be Buddha-like. That's refuge in the Three Jewels: making every part of one's life Buddha-like. If you really want to know what Buddha-like is, don't think Buddha sat cross-legged and silent all day. He also had a life. For forty-five years after enlightenment, he was walking around with friends, eating, talking, teaching, and answering people's questions. Every part of life can be part of the Buddha Way. Not just sitting like a stiff wooden or bronze statue all day— better to be a living Buddha than an inert one. This is the refuge and altruistic bodhisattva resolve we chant three times daily:

In Buddha, Dharma and the Supreme Spiritual Community
I go for refuge until full enlightenment.
By the power of all six perfections,
From generosity to nondual wisdom,
May we realize Buddhahood for the sake of all beings.

I personally find a lot of joy in chanting the ancient prayers and refuge stanzas, and in reflecting on these things, thinking these things, and remembering and reaffirming these things daily as a practice. These practices are very helpful. It turns one more and more inward in the sense of being more centered, with less reaching for other refuges, other oases, other reliances, other commitments. With the commitment to awakening, everything becomes part of the way to realization, and opens the heart of sublime love and compassion.

Opening the Heart of Compassion

It says in the Mahayana scriptures that as soon as you make the bodhisattva vow to realize enlightenment, to relieve universal suffering, all the Buddhas, bodhisattvas, and devas applaud and rain down flowers. As poetical and metaphorical as that seems, I really feel that it is true. You can feel it yourself as you start to open a little more to the joy of the awakening spirit. The Mahayana scriptures also say that when the bodhisattva vow has taken root in your heart, then everything you do is beneficial, even turning over in your sleep. They say that even when a bodhisattva turns over in sleep, beings are awakened! So even if it's only poetic or metaphorical, the point remains that this awakening mind, this bodhicitta, this aspiration for enlightenment, this altruistic bodhisattva is absolutely indispensable.

Don't think that there is nothing to seek. It is ultimately true, but it's too soon to say it. Seek, and you'll find it. Don't paralyze yourself with nihilistic philosophy: "There's no one to seek, nothing to do, no practice. Or so I have heard. I'll just sit at home and follow my usual habits and drink, smoke, watch TV, or whatever. It doesn't matter!" In fact, these habitual activities are just a different practice, not spiritual in nature. Why do even those particular practices then, if there is nothing to do? Doing those world activities is also doing something. That is karma. So it is too soon to say there is nothing to do, nowhere to go, nothing to seek. Seeking with all of your heart *is* bodhicitta. Rumi calls it the passionate longing for the Beloved, for awakening, working on oneself and opening with passion and compassion—intensively, with heart and soul.

We have gotten into this spiritual journey as if by accident already. Bodhicitta means the enlightened heart-mind, the aspiration for relieving the suffering of all by becoming increasingly wise and enlightened. The whole Dzogchen teaching, and the whole Tibetan Vajrayana teaching, is based on the universal compassion and caring embodied in the Mahayana bodhisattva vow. Realizing suffering, we want to end it everywhere, not just in our knee or in our back or in ourselves temporarily. Wherever suffering is, may we release it! When we do this, we really dissolve the selfishness, egotism, the self-clinging that we have. It is often taught that the entire spiritual life depends on your motivation, not just what position your legs are in. It depends on your motivation, your intentions and aspirations. That's why many saints have said, "Be careful what you pray for. It may come true." Everything depends on what you're motivated toward. Oscar Wilde said, "There are two tragedies in life: One is not to get your heart's desire; the other is to get it!" In this way, we make this outrageous wish that we are going to liberate all beings without exception. It is beyond the scope of our conceptual mind, this boundless aspiration to never stop altruistic spiritual work until there is no more suffering left in the universe. That greatly enhances our spiritual power and possibilities.

Manufacturing the bodhisattva vow is the beginning of genuinely committing to it. That's the beginning. This is a path of self-cultivation and training. It includes an attitude transformation. It is a cultivation of bigger, more unselfish attitudes and concerns. Of course, it seems a bit much to take on freeing all beings when we can't even free ourselves from fighting with our wife and colleagues, or suffering at the hands of our inner conflicts and struggles. Still, we try; we try to cultivate unselfishness, mindful awareness, restraint, patience, tolerance, and lovingkindness. We ourselves individually are included in that wish to liberate all beings; it's not just thinking about all of them and excluding ourselves. But the bodhisattva vow takes away some of the selfishness. It is a way of broadening our scope, an undermining of ego clinging and narcissism. Of course, we are here for selfish reasons, because we are individuals seeking our own happiness. And that's fine; I'm not asking you to repent for that. This is a vow for the present moment to let go of selfishness, to raise our aspirations, elevate our gaze, awaken the bigger mind, open our loving heart, including all beings and the entire environment in our prayers and practices.

Unbiased compassion and altruism is the essence of spiritual life and is essential in our turbulent times. It is something we can cultivate and practice. It is not something we have to wait to come and land on us one day. We can train in transforming our attitudes to be more gentle, kind, unselfish, compassionate, and empathetic. Feel what others feel; that's the root of compassion. Then we treat them as we would like to be treated, as Jesus says. So this is a practice path. We can actually practice this and develop in this way. It is doable! It is very important to develop this genuine heart of compassion, this warm, basic goodness, a good, warm heart. We don't necessarily have to use fancy foreign words like *bodhicitta, karuna, maitri, metta*. Even in our own native language, we can say all this. How about *unselfish, compassionate, empathetic, tenderhearted, caring, kind*? If it doesn't show up in our life in that way, what kind of spiritual practice are we really doing? Are we just fooling ourselves, hiding in a corner in a dark meditation or yoga room or shrine where nobody will bother us? Trying to get away from it all. If you want to get away from it all, get drunk or take a good drug. That will get you away from it all for a brief time. But we've all tried that. How long does it last? Why hide in the corner like a cur that has been kicked too many times? Life is to be lived, fully, fearlessly.

Let's face it. We'll do almost anything to find what we are seeking. So let's really go for it wholeheartedly, not just sit around waiting for the meditation period or teaching hour to end. If you are just waiting for the gong to ring, it is better just to get up and go do something else. Killing time is just killing and deadening ourselves. If we don't really love this meaningful work of awakening, we had better do something else. Look for it somewhere else, wherever one may think it is. But do look for it wholeheartedly. That's also an aspect of bodhicitta. Wholeheartedly, thoroughly, passionately, put oneself into it completely. Not just hiding in the corner hoping that nobody will bother us until we die; that's just hiding and denying. That's not awakening. And that's irresponsible. We are the guardians of this gift of life. We should share it with all. We must bring forth the Dharma, our own Dharma, our own truth, through our lives—every day, every moment. We are constantly voting as to how this world will be through our actions—if we only knew that!

Compassion and love are the heart engine of enlightened activity. If we just think of Buddhism as wisdom, clarity, insight, and realization, we are just living from the neck up. What about the rest? The rest of our being: our body, our emotions, our feelings, our relationships, and our life? How does it show up in our life? Is spiritual practice helping us to be more sane, or not? This whole Dharma teaching is about sanity, not insanity. It is about wholeness and togetherness, not about being flaky. The spiritual way is responsibility, straightforwardness, impeccability, integrity—not crookedness, avoidance, denial. Not just trying to get by, but doing your best, wholeheartedly and thoroughly, and at the same time learning to accept and let things go—whatever happens, happens. As a Zen master said, "My life is just one mistake after another." But you keep trying. You fall on your face, but you just get up again and keep going. We have no choice anyway. Let's just keep on keeping on, in the great Way of awakening.

Recognizing the Power of Intention

Shantideva prayed, "As long as space endures, as long as beings remain, as long as there is any suffering anywhere—may I continue to strive toward universal enlightenment." That's where compassion, empathy, loving-kindness, and the other paramitas (bodhisattva virtues) come in—energy, effort, patience, fearless courage, ethical self-discipline, and so forth. It is a huge, boundless undertaking. But we are never going to give up until suffering and confusion are ended. That's the vast scope of our intention. Again, I want to reiterate: Everything depends on our intentions, So it is very important to check our motivation. Why did we come here? We must be looking for something. Let's not pretend that we are not looking for anything. What are we looking for, really? Can we ask ourselves? What are you looking for, each of you? Trying to get away from your wife, your husband, the crying baby at home? Trying to quiet your mind for a moment? Trying to meet a boyfriend or a girlfriend—Dharma dating? Why are we really here, what are we doing, and why? Here in this meditation group, here in this world, here in this life?

What are we looking for? The answer to all of our questions? The end of pain and dissatisfaction? What are we afraid of? Death? Confusion? Meaninglessness? Are we looking for the meaning of life? What are we looking for? That determines very much what happens. The motivation, the intention is very crucial. Are we coming here just to get in the right club, be part of the latest fad, or find the perfect answer that will solve all our problems? Maybe we're hoping we won't feel any discomfiting feelings or pain or confusion; just suppressing ourselves and not feeling anything, like staying in the closet where nobody will bother us. That may be fine, but it is a very limited motivation. And it brings very limited results, because when we go out of here we just get bothered again. No matter how quiet we make our minds, when we go out the volume is turned up again. The fast-forward button is on, and life speeds up. Only wisdom, realization, insight stay with us. Not the concentration and the peace, which is conditioned, fabricated here for however long it lasts. True peace is beyond the polarity of quiet and noise. Peace means inner fulfillment, wholeness and ease, knowing and being at one with ourselves; inner serenity and ease.

So what are we looking for? Are we just looking to get by until we die? To be part of Club Meditator? Or are we really looking for the inner freedom and eternal peace that the sublime Dharma promises? The perfect peace and innate wholeness at our true heart's core. The end of all suffering. I ask you to ask yourselves, because everything depends on intention: What drives you?

What truly moves and animates you, on all levels, outer and inner? That's the essential teaching of karma: not just what we do, but what we think, aspire toward, and intend. As it says in the first line in the *Dhammapada*, the sayings of Buddha, "As you think, so you become." The mind is the ruler. Like the cart following the horse, body follows mind. If you want to go somewhere, you don't prod or command the cart; you prod the horse. It is the intention, the heart-mind, the inner spirit that moves us; not just the cartlike body. Body is like a mere shadow of innate consciousness. One's motivation is crucial. That's why we make the indispensable bodhisattva vow to liberate all beings, transcend illusion, master the Dharma teaching, embody the truth, become enlightened, and so on. We are not just trying to stop our thoughts, to pacify our brains, which is only temporary. We can have a lobotomy if that's all we want, or take some drug or drink. Enlightenment in a bottle! But that is only very short term, stopping our thoughts. The mind will start again; it is an eternal-motion machine. Tarthang Tulku wrote, "Mind is not matter, but mind does matter. That is why looking into mind means investigating what seems to matter most of all." Mind rules over matter.

I think it is very important to look into these things and learn about egotism, the nature of Self, desire, selfishness, and the end of selfishness. People sometimes tell me they are not getting anywhere with their meditation. That doesn't bother me in the least bit. I really like to hear that, because I know that we need to reflect on this and keep trying. Who knows, maybe you have to be enlightened to see the results! So what's the point? Does meditation work? Buddha said, according to Zen teachings, "When I was enlightened, the whole universe was enlightened." Therefore, we can't very easily evaluate if we are getting anywhere or not; but if we are just complacent and satisfied, we are probably not getting anywhere. It's good to keep looking into our intention and motivation, to keep questioning and to live the question, as Rilke said. Not simply being satisfied with some easy, quick answer or someone else's ideas or beliefs. We all would prefer instant-coffee answers. Just add hot water and presto—there's the answer. Enlightenment powder: just add hot water. But the truth is subtler than that, far better than that. We must continually refine our spiritual pursuits, not become brain dead, if we would grow, transform, and evolve consciously.

In fact, forget about enlightenment. Go for what you *really* want. What do you want? Peace? A better job? Money? Can you be honest with yourself? Or do you have to say "love" or "enlightenment"? Many people are afraid of enlightenment and what it might mean. "Does enlightenment mean you become a monk or have no more fun, or disappear into nirvana?" people have asked. Enlightenment as we think of it is just a concept. That's why Trungpa Rinpoche sardonically said that enlightenment is the biggest disappointment of all: it's not what we think it is. But it's not really disappointing, of course; it's a great joy. It is our highest, ultimate, deathless happiness, peace, and blissful fulfillment.

Let's really look into ourselves, and see what it is that we crave and grasp. What are we seeking? What are we missing? What do we want? Let's put it very crassly. Not just what do we "aspire to," but what do we really *want*? And then try to go for that. Even if it is just money or a new car or a boyfriend or girlfriend. Because then when we have that, we might still find that we want more, something else. Then we must go on and go deeper and look deeper into the question and the intention until we find out what is truly satisfying in the long run. But if we are afraid to reach out, afraid to ask, to want or take anything for ourselves; if we pretend we don't want anything; if we deny all our impulses, desires, and needs, then we don't get anywhere. We drain all the passion and energy and juice out of our path with the puritanical pretense. Ask yourself what you are really seeking and want. Also, ask yourself what you are afraid of. What is holding you back? What is your greatest fear, and would you be willing to face it? What would make it safe for you to proceed, even in the face of that fear? Ask yourself what you believe and why? Is it really true?

Those fears and mostly unexamined beliefs are driving, motivating, and conditioning us. If you are afraid of being alone, then everything you do is fabricated, is unconsciously coordinated, so you won't be alone, in an attempt to protect you from discomfiting feelings of loneliness. If you are afraid of pain, then you are always seeking pleasure and avoiding painful situations, uncomfortable situations, difficulties, so you are never free to really follow your true vocation and find fulfillment, even if it is difficult at certain points—painful even—to pursue it. You are always limited by some unconscious fear or neurosis or habitual desire. The Dharma is the end of all desire. Not the end of passion, but the end of grasping desire and fervid craving. It is a transcendence, not a rejection, denial, suppression, or repression. A lot of pure, raw energy awaits us just below the surface of desire and passion. There is joyous bliss and harmony in attaining nonattachment and equanimity.

Tricycle magazine was interviewing a number of Buddhist teachers, asking us if we thought the Buddha had an emotional life. After Buddha was enlightened, did he have any emotions? There has always been, over the centuries, some kind of debate about this, but the real question is, Can *we* have emotions or not? Do we have to get rid of them all? From the tantric point of view, I had to say, of course Buddha had emotions. Maybe he didn't identify with them, but he had them. He also had thoughts. It says in the sutras that he had a headache one day. I don't know why it never says in the sutras or in the Bible that Buddha or Christ ever laughed. Do you really think they were that overly serious? I doubt it. Maybe the monks who followed were too serious to record frivolity of any kind. They didn't want anybody to think their master was just a comedian or an ordinary person, neither common nor superficial. But you know and I know that they must have laughed, so let's not be too rigid, grim, and earnest. Today in India, they even practice laughter meditation!

We too can allow ourselves to freely experience our authentic emotions and feelings, along with fantasies, imagination, passion, anything. What we do with them makes all the difference. What are we holding back for? What are we saving ourselves up for? The *real* thing? Saving ourselves for the real thing?! "Not this dance, I'm waiting for the big dance. The real dance. The real relationship. Then I'll give myself." Yet many never do and are just kidding and procrastinating. It's not outer things that entangle us. It's inner clinging and attachment that entangles us, as Tilopa once told Naropa. You become a mere wallflower in life's grand ballroom that way, and miss most of the meaning as well as the fun. Why be so stingy with yourself?

Master Atisha said ego clinging is to blame for all the different varieties of suffering. We are all afraid of our negative emotions. Aren't we also afraid of our positive ones? We are just quite conflicted, as if afraid of ourselves. Yet we don't really have to be, because it's actually no big deal. Everybody can see them anyway. We don't have to think we are hiding them and that nobody knows. Everybody knows! We can relax and be ourselves—it's fine. I love, accept, and honor you just as you are. But, do you? Let's learn how to relax and relinquish our tendency to always hold back. There are many skillful ways of working with our energies without just trying to deny and suppress them. We can't control our conditioning and karma, but we can learn how to be more skillful with them, how to channel them constructively rather than destructively, and how to be finally free of them. So let's look into our intentions and motivations and fearlessly go for it, really seeking what we are after.

Taking refuge leads us and guides us on our path to enlightenment; to seek refuge until we reach enlightenment for the benefit and well-being of all sentient beings provides the key to spiritual life and helps us enter the true path. When we take

refuge, we are born into the path of awakening—the refuge of innate awakefulness within each moment. Taking refuge is about
how we are going to lead our lives—in every moment, with the
heart of love and compassion for the boundless benefit of one
and all.

> Take now your refuge in the Buddha,
> The Dharma and all the Sangha,
> Who eradicate fear in the frightened
> And who protect the unprotected.
> They who take refuge in the Three Jewels
> Will gain fearlessness.
> —From Gampopa's *The Jewel Ornament of Liberation,* 12th Century, Tibet

CHAPTER 12

THE TEACHER: LEARNING FROM BOTH THE FOOLISH AND THE WISE

YOU HAVE ONLY THREE THINGS TO DO IN THIS LIFETIME:
HONOR YOUR GURU.
DEEPEN YOUR REALIZATION OF EMPTINESS.
DEEPEN YOUR COMPASSION.
—LAMA KALU RINPOCHE

People often ask, Do we need a teacher? Why do we need a
teacher? Who needs a teacher? Why is there so much discussion these days about gurus, teachers, swamis, masters, ava-
tars, tulkus, charismatic leaders, and so on? The word *teacher* has
many meanings. We have a kindergarten teacher; we have a driv-

ing teacher; we might have a language teacher, a martial arts teacher, a pottery instructor, a meditation teacher, a college teacher, or a professional mentor. Our parents teach us. We might have a religious teacher. We might even have a guru. But what is this all about? Don't the questions themselves, and how they are put as well as to whom they are put, reveal a lot about ourselves?

To talk traditionally at first: A guru functions like a mirror that reflects our highest nature or best self. In India it is taught that the guru or wise spiritual teacher is a door to the infinite, to the absolute, to realization, fulfillment, enlightenment. We don't need to collect those valued door frames; we need to go through them. We don't need to collect mirrors and have a different gilded and shaped one for every day of the year—we simply need to look in them and recognize our own nature. Gurus can, in the best instance, help us return home to our true Selves, to the inner guru, the Buddha-ness or divinity within.

A guru is supposed to be an accomplished spiritual master. I'm starting from the top here, or from the higher guru level of this broad discussion. There are so many traditions and different issues we could explore later. In the Tibetan Vajrayana tradition, for example, we are exhorted to perceive the guru as Buddha, for if we see the guru as a Buddha, we can get the blessings of Buddha, we can learn from the Buddha. The Buddha energy will course through us, and eventually to others through us. We can receive blessings and become Buddha. It says that if we regard the teacher as a bodhisattva, we'll at best receive the blessings of a bodhisattva. If we see the teacher as ordinary, we'll only get the blessings and good wishes of an ordinary person, and we don't become as spiritually realized as an enlightened Buddha or bodhisattva.

The tantric practice of sacred outlook or pure perception is called *daknang* in Tibetan. Recognizing the teacher as an embodiment of perfection is a very powerful one, if it suits us. If we are on the tantric Vajrayana path, if we actually have a teacher in our lives who inspires us so that we view him or her in that way, it can be highly transformative and liberating. Many people say to me, "I know a lot of lamas, but who is my root lama?" (In Tibetan Buddhism we say "root lama" or "root guru" as the term for principal spiritual teacher.) The answer is: the one to whom you are most grateful. That is your root lama. This doesn't mean the most famous one or the highest one in the hierarchy. It is the one to whom you are the most grateful. You can have a refuge lama—the teacher who gave you the refuge vow—you might have a bodhisattva preceptor or a monastic ordination teacher also. But the root guru is the one you genuinely feel closest to and most blessed and uplifted by, whether they are near or far, alive or dead.

One can have more than one guru. I have had several marvelous gurus. When you've seen one guru, you've seen them all—that's what I say! And that is very true and profound. It's funny, but don't take it too lightly. Therefore, one guru is enough, but you can have more than one also. My root lama, the wonderful Milarepa-like lama, Kalu Rinpoche, who passed on in 1989, always used to say, "See all teachers as emanations of your root guru."

There is no need to get confused. You can get teachings from anyone, actually, even from the foolish. Eventually, it is not just seeing your guru as Buddha and everybody else as chopped liver; you come to see the Buddha-ness, the clear light, the love in everyone. But at first, the question is, Can we see *anybody* as a Buddha? So let's start with the Buddha or honored guru. Then, perhaps we can extend it to the recognition of the Buddha in everyone and even in oneself. That would be radical! That is where the guru yoga and pure perception practice leads. Not just obsessing about your gurus and how great they are, carrying their pictures around all the time to show to everybody like a proud grandmother with baby pictures. There is no need to plaster the walls of your house and every flat surface with pictures of your gurus, although you certainly can, if you like. It's a free country. But we can go a little bit deeper than that. Strive to recognize everything as reflections of the guru energy or the magical Buddha nature. Seeing the guru as Buddha is part of the practice of daknang, as I've said—pure perception, sacred outlook—of which the *real* practice is recognizing everyone and everything as Buddha and Buddha fields, enjoying all and everything as the natural great perfection. That is too steep a path, like a sheer cliff, in fact. It is too hard just to jump into that, so we start with the person we look up to, or an archetype of Buddha, or Tara, or our guru. In the Buddhist context we use the term Buddha—as in the Christian context we use the term God—for the most highly positive value. Therefore, it seems to make sense to start with that, to start there, from where our sincere reverence and respect is. Similarly, in loving-kindness meditation, it is easy to start radiating love to somebody you love, then expand it to other people to whom you are related and sort of love, and then to other people who you are friendly with, until finally (with practice) you can also radiate love to your enemies. That's the progressive, developmental principle of practice.

Of course, it is all just a conceptual superimposition. It's a conceptual overlay or fabrication to see your teacher as a Buddha. But any formal practice is a construct, too. It is good to simultaneously keep in mind the absolute view. With the view of emptiness and the absolute view we can really let go and more fully enter into any form of practice, like seeing the guru as Buddha. That doesn't necessarily mean you have to literally see your teacher as Buddha, but regard the relationship in the highest possible way. This is about the relationship, not about the teacher-person. If you are in relation with Buddha, that's called getting the blessings of Buddha. "Waves of inspirational grace" is a literal translation of the Tibetan word for blessings, *chinlab,* for they just pour over you and through you.

There is an old Zen teaching tale in which the Zen master shouts out, "What are you all gawking at?" Everybody's looking up at him, so he shouts, "What are you all gawking at? The Dharma's about you. So gawk at yourself for a change." We are always outward turned, it seems, so we use contemplative practice to transform that tendency. We turn from worldly things toward spiritual things, until finally we are not so outward turned. Then, when we are truly integrated, there is really no impermeable separation between inner or outer. But for now, we turn to the Buddha, as if in an outer way, and see everyone as Buddha. We bow to Buddha, and so on. But that should have an inward-turning, integrated aspect also. The real transformative principle is the reverence, the gentling of heart, the devotion.

Devotion cuts through discursivity. The Third Karmapa says in the "Song of Mahamudra," which all the nonsectarian Rimé lamas teach, "In the moment of devotion, rigpa (nondual awareness) nakedly dawns." Isn't that interesting? It's not about the teacher. It is the luminosity of that total presence, that devotion when you are beyond yourself—as if you're lost in love, as Rumi would label it. In the moment of being lost in love, the clear light of reality naturally dawns. That's the point. It's not about the teacher. This is far deeper than any external object. It's about spirit, about deeper connection or relationship, like a homecoming. There are many things we could say about the guru. In this really wonderful old Tibetan classic, *The Jewel Ornament of Liberation*, Milarepa's disciple Gampopa gives a list of the qualities of the guru, including being well trained and wise, experienced, selfless, compassionate, generous, and so forth. This helps you in finding an authentic guru, not just somebody who is well advertised. You have to feel a heartfelt connection to ask someone to be your guru, or spiritual guide, and genuinely to get something out of it.

Different Forms of the Teacher

Spiritual teachers can be in different forms. You might meet your teacher as a human being in ordinary form, easy to overlook; or as a bodhisattva living on a high level of spirituality, a Dalai Lama–like person; or as a nirmanakaya, like the historical teacher we call the Buddha. In the sambhogakaya, in a vision perhaps, you might meet Tara or Avalokiteshvara in a numinous form—that might become your teacher. For example, some people say Christ is their teacher, and might even meet him. So there are different levels of bodies and dimensions (kayas, in Sanskrit) of the teacher.

Gampopa says that a teacher should have certain powers and abilities, including the power to benefit others, to overcome selfishness, to love and treat others equally, to generously share with everyone who needs, and to be wise and compassionate, patient and humble. Other, less indispensable powers could include the ability to see past lives and to be clairvoyant. There are a whole lot of these siddhis (powers) that are sort of optional: miracles, power over longevity, or intentional rebirth like bodhisattvas. Those are several of the qualifications of certain gurus. If the guru is a bodhisattva, he or she will normally possess self-discipline, moderation, virtue, a loving heart, and helpful, altruistic ways. He or she should be well versed in scriptures, the methods of life, and social morals. He or she should be full of compassion and love, fearless, indefatigable, gentle, graceful, and so on. Tibetan texts also say gurus should be very learned, able to dispel doubts and clarify questions, agreeable, and able to point out reality in various ways according to the different needs of various individuals. Moreover, these texts say that a real bodhisattva teacher would never, even for the sake of his or her life, give in to hatred or give up the altruistic intention to help others. These are easy ideals to espouse, but a challenge to live up to, aren't they?

In the Vajrayana, the guru is considered lord and master. The disciples are asked to do what the guru commands. Even if the disciples don't know *why* to do it, it's taught that the guru can just tell us to do it and save us a lot of trouble in having to learn everything about the whys and wherefores. Thus he or she can lead us over the vajra shortcut, like leading a blind man over a dangerous pass. Maybe we would be afraid to go over a dangerous pass, so the guru says, "Close your eyes and hold my hand." Otherwise we have to learn everything about the Dharma to guide ourselves. Of course, blindly following along can have some serious repercussions, too. So we must be very aware what we are doing, why, and with whom; check our motivation and intentions; and proceed with awareness.

In the Mahayana, the teacher—the *kalyanamitra,* meaning spiritual friend—is like an elder or more experienced brother or sister, or like a doctor who has special knowledge, who knows how to prescribe medicine. Again, we should do what he or she says, but we are a little more free at this level of relationship as to whether to do it or not. However, we still must have a certain amount of trust or faith, coming from confidence that he or she actually knows. Otherwise, we have to study organic chemistry and all kinds of things to know how and why that little pill will actually help us before we take it. It is a longer path than just having faith, trust, devotion, and conviction in our trustworthy guru. So if and when he or she says, "Take this pill," we don't have to research every little detail every time. We can just do it. Of course, we should have examined the guru beforehand so we know he or she is an authentic teacher who is appropriate for us, and who cares principally for our welfare, before we sign on to such an absolute relationship. But in the Mahayana, the guru is more like a doctor who is advanced in the altruistic bodhisattva way and who can guide us, rather than the more iron-clad, samaya-based, student-teacher relationship that the Vajrayana teachings describe.

In the basic Theravadan teachings, the teacher is more like a good friend who helps us along but doesn't necessarily have so much more experience or arcane knowledge that we ourselves don't have access to at this stage in the journey. Our level of commitment to a teacher-student relationship depends on what kind of apprenticeship or practice we are doing. If we are just visiting a sitting group and taking in information, that's fine; that's like the basic approach to Buddhism. We are not yet a member of the formal sangha. We are not a disciple of the teacher. We may not even know if we are a Buddhist. It doesn't matter. We are there to do something positive and to search and meditate and enjoy ourselves. That's the basic thing, the ground. That doesn't take much commitment. You're listening to me, so you are trusting at least that, since I am sitting in front here, I must have something to say. That's an assumption, but that's the basic ground of this momentary relationship we have. This is the basic Buddhist approach. As Lord Buddha himself used to say, "Come and see." Check it out.

As the historical Buddha Shakyamuni himself, said, "When I am gone, take the Dharma as your teacher; take the practice as your teacher." I always find that teacher's words enlightening and liberating. He has helped me practice through all these years, even when the going got tough within groups, institutions, and organizations. Those words helped me find refuge and solace within, through spiritual practice.

At the Mahayana level, you feel that the teacher knows because you have already had some experience of the practice, so you put yourself a little more into his or her hands like a patient in the hands of a physician. At the more risky and powerful Vajrayana level, you have come to the conclusion that the teacher is like a Buddha, or at least enlightened enough so that even if the teacher tells you—like Tilopa told Naropa—to jump off the roof, you do it. That story is a metaphor for extreme devotion to the order or command of the teaching master. And through his

twelve years of hard training and devotion to Tilopa, Naropa became fully enlightened.

But that raises some interesting questions, doesn't it, about
faith, about trust, about devotion. What is the place of those
things in our practice, if any? Devotion and faith are hard to fabricate. Also, questioning, doubting, and healthy skepticism can
be very valuable, too. I had a discussion recently with somebody
who is really well along in practice. I said to her, so what is it that
you think we've learned after all this time? Did we learn anything
from all those masters we knew in Asia? And she said—and this
really shocked me—"Faith." You know and I know that we postmodern intellectuals didn't go to these teachers because of faith.
We went because of skepticism and interest and passion for
truth, but not faith. But what she said really resonated. It was
very refreshing, actually. I am still reflecting on that personal
sharing.

The practice of every moment is just precisely what we are
doing every moment. But who has the faith, the conviction, to
wholeheartedly live that insight? Knowing that there is nothing
else at that moment *is* the practice of daily life, in whatever we are
doing in every moment. That takes faith, or at least trust and inner conviction; it is not something easy to fabricate. However, I
think it is important to realize that we can cultivate it. That is the
genius of the Buddhist path, the practice path. We can cultivate
these qualities: what we sow we will reap. We can cultivate faith
also. Not that faith is the goal, except perhaps in some deep
sense, but faith is something that I think would surprise us when
we can get into seeing what it really is. It is really about conviction, about knowing, about clarity, about letting go, trusting, surrendering, allowing, accepting. The faith to know that This is it,
which is quite steep. We usually have to go through many steps,
like guru devotion, reuniting with the guru in the guru yoga
practice, or some other approach that gradually delivers us there.
We have to practice gradually and mature our inner insight, so

we better know ourselves and realize our true nature more deeply. Then we do realize total trust in the Great Perfection, the *isness,* the justness, the perfectness of things just as they are— including ourselves. This reveals pure experience just as it is, without a middleman, without a mediator, without the mediation of thoughts and concepts. I don't just mean without a priest between us and Buddha. I mean without *myself* as a middleman; I am speaking of pure, pristine experience without a middleman. *We* are each the middlemen getting in the way of pure experience, of rigpa, of pure being, the naked immediacy of the natural state. That takes some faith and some trust, doesn't it, not always having to be in the middle trying to work things out with our busy minds and concepts—controlling, manipulating, and keeping score in various ways. Who has that kind of trust, conviction, faith, or wisdom?

Tibetan commentaries say there are three different kinds of faith. At the beginning is longing, aspiration. We're hoping for something good to happen. We have a tiny bit of intuitive knowledge, faith, belief, or something, but it is still unformed. That's the longing phase of faith. Then we get more mature or experienced and we start to experience how things actually are. We start to attain more trust and lucid conviction based on both experience and knowledge; that's the second kind. Finally, we develop unshakable, unswerving faith, trust, and knowledge. Through spiritual prayers and practices we can cultivate this progressive development. That's what we do through the different formal *sadhana* practices, from refuge and foundational practices onward, approaching gradually as well as at the same time maintaining that overview of the Great Perfection. Such a view actually has to be grounded in or based on something: some form of experience, or devotion and trust; some openness, or something interior and non-intellectual, not just a mere abstraction.

In a relationship with a teacher, if we have faith or devotion, or if we have questioning and skepticism—those are two sides to the same thing—if the teacher is actually in our lives and not just in our imagination, he or she can really push our buttons, can really point to our sore spots, can really light a fire under our bottoms and provoke us to get us moving—which we definitely need. If we feel inspired or grateful or devoted to a teacher, that can help cut through discursiveness and selfishness. It can be a very powerful inspiration for our daily practice life and can take us beyond our narrow, egocentric, finite conceptual mind. I personally feel that although we Westerners generally seize on meditation and lift it out of its whole cultural context, there are several other significant aspects of BuddhaDharma besides just meditation and study, which can degenerate into mere mental activities from the eyebrows up. Buddhist tradition around the world, throughout time, is rich with prayers, rituals, devotion, yoga outer and inner, and contemplative arts—all kinds of things we should not too quickly overlook. These can really round out our spiritual life so we don't become just meditation addicts or quietists, like bumps on a log or ice cubes sitting in our little black, square trays in the zendo refrigeration vault.

Living Dharma is like a spiritual flame rather than a frozen, well-behaved, perfectly square ice cube just sitting there in a neat tray. In devotion to the teacher, there are different levels of intensity and different kinds of relationships. For example, who is your parent in this life? Are you devoted to that person? Maybe it's not your biological parent. Perhaps you're devoted to somebody else, the parental person or guardian who raised you, loved you, or nursed you. Does that mean you see them as infallible, perfect, and like God, or just that you are devoted to them? A relationship with a teacher can be very intimate. This depends partly on you. Again, if you want a relationship, for example, with a vajra master or with a Mahayana bodhisattva teacher, who is more like a doctor or an older brother, it's up to you. You decide. Your choice can also evolve over time.

The relationship could be very personal, but it doesn't have to be. Earlier, I described several models of the student-teacher relationship pointing out that there are different ways of tapping into this principle of learning from elders. There are many monks who have an abbot but who don't have a guru or spiritual director because they are not in that kind of tradition. There are different models of teacher-student relationships; not understanding this simple fact gives rise to various misunderstandings. Devotion and gratitude cut through doubt and discursiveness, but if you don't feel it, fine. We can find another Dharma gate. I feel very grateful for all I received from my teachers. They were very kind to me, like parents. Thus, how to pay them back is a question I often have. Gifts are squandered unless shared. I feel it is incumbent on us to share the gifts our teachers have passed on to us in any way we can. I try to contribute to others, not to convert people. Contributing is something the Dalai Lama has exhorted us all to do: sharing the Dharma through altruistic service, love in action; being unselfish and loving in our own life; and integrating Dharma practice and mindfulness into daily life. Is there any other practice? There is no other way except every moment. That's the practice of daily life. Just this, right now. Just this!

Finding What We Need

The big question, then, which comes up at some point for so many of us, is, Do we need a teacher? That's up to each of us. Do we need to be part of a group? That, too, is up to each of us. Check it out. I myself find it is helpful to sit with a group, to be part of a sangha community, to collaborate and work with friends and kindred spirits. It is very supportive. I have also found it extraordinarily helpful and supportive to learn from all kinds of teachers and gurus, although it is a complicated field, perhaps these days more than ever. We need to pay attention as we enter into those relationships. There could be a lot there for us, more than we imagine. But I want to tell you frankly: it's not really such a big deal what I got from my beloved master and teachers. The big deal is that these things are there for the taking. Teacher and author Jack Kornfield, who is a bit of an iconoclast, says, "You have to steal fire from the gods. They will never give it to you!" It's as if you have to accost the teachers. You have to pound on their door and make them teach you. This may sound somewhat outrageous, but it is not far from true. Yet they want to, so don't be shy. These teachers want to pass on their precious heritage.

I personally feel that just going to sangha meditation one night a week is not really enough. It's like a club. Going from there to watch Monday-night football at the sports bar and getting drunk, or whatever, might mitigate what we did at meditation. As you drag yourself back to work the next morning, what is more "with" you, the meditation or the hangover? I have tried to do this Dharma practice full-time in my life, because I think it is vitally important and invaluable. That's what I learned from my teachers through all of their years of practice, retreat, and integrating Buddhist practice in life and in service. I learned that spiritual life cannot be set *apart* from everyday life. It is not just a hobby, a club, a fad. The wise and loving life of Dharma is itself the pearl beyond price, and well worth immersing ourselves in it.

I learned this in great part from my teachers. It's very hard to learn it experientially from abstract theories, from holy historical books and scriptural texts, or from hagiographies and tales about how Christ, St. Francis, Buddha, and others lived a long time ago. By meeting exemplary living embodiments of genuine spiritual values, I took in inspiring lessons on a sort of cellular level, not just an intellectual level. How they lived, how they drank tea, how they talked about or to their parents and siblings, and how they tied their shoes—all was instructional. Living teachers can be helpful and empowering, transmitting a great deal more deeply than the conceptual level of knowledge. Sogyal Rinpoche talks quite a lot about this in *The Tibetan Book of Living and Dying*. Maybe he talks about masters a bit too much, but that is part of our Tibetan Vajrayana tradition. In his book, he sometimes makes it seem that you can't do it without a teacher; which is questionable. Yet that is the teaching in the Tibetan tradition. The tantric traditions say to seek a genuine master, enter into a spiritual apprenticeship, and devote yourself to learning and practicing the teaching. Then you, too, can and will inherit the entire legacy that the teachers themselves have inherited. It is not personal, really, it's *trans*personal. It is a lineage, from the Buddha to now, passed down until today—not unlike when a candle burns down and the living flame is passed directly to the next candle. The living teaching, the truth of enlightenment, burns even here and now today, so let's not overlook it! It warms, illumines, and enlivens our lives.

I have found that meeting live teachers really made the teachings come alive for me. It can sometimes be hard to find an authentic teacher these days. We might ask, How long does it take? Where do I go? How much contact does it take? It's like asking how often do you need to see your wife to really feel married? There is no fixed answer; only you know. Some people live apart but are married. The relationship with a teacher can be very open and fluid, and can take many forms. Some might say that the Dalai Lama is their teacher, and when you ask how often they see him, they say once every few years. Maybe that's enough. That's more often than seeing Jesus, who has been the teacher of many. But I myself sought a more day-to-day learning environment and relationship with my teachers, so I learned their language and lived in their monasteries and ashrams.

There is no particular way to play this game, but it is a very profound practice if one is called to play it. The nonsectarian Tibetan practice lineage definitely emphasizes the value of a teacher; but it's not about the teacher-person per se; it's about engaging in a genuine spiritual relationship with the enlightenment principle. Sometimes it's called in Tibetan Sanskrit *samaya*, meaning tantric bonds or commitments. Samaya includes commitment on both sides, on the part of both master and disciple, the teacher and the student. It is a profoundly meaningful and transformative practice to treasure the spiritual relationship between oneself and the guru, and to keep that pure samaya, that commitment and relationship, alive and well amid all the ups and downs of the path. It should also be said—having stressed the importance of a teacher—that the Buddha himself said, "Don't rely on the teacher-person, but rely on the teachings. Don't rely on the words of the teachings, but on the spirit of the words, their meaning." We shouldn't get hung up on personality cults, imitate outer lifestyles or mere appearances, or slavishly worship charismatic leaders. And if our teacher dies, we don't necessarily have to feel devastated, as if bereft of teachings and inspiration. Our teacher hearkens back to Buddha, and even to enlightenment itself. The Dharma is our teacher. The sangha is our teacher. We can learn a lot from each other and from the truth of every moment, as well as through explicit practices such as meditation and yoga. Everything can function as teacher if we are open to it. My elder teachers may have passed on but I feel them always with me.

So do you need a teacher? Only you can know for sure. As they say, when the student is ready, the teacher appears. (Or, more amusingly, when the teacher is ready, the student appears.) We are also all teachers to one another. So let's be responsible stewards and guardians and engender leadership in others, not just creating Buddhist followers. Let's strive to always bring out the best in others. Only *you* can decide when you know who you feel most connected to, or grateful to, or who you learn from the most. That's a very personal, inner matter. With the teacher, you might feel you want to establish a formal relation and ask them to accept you as a disciple, depending on what tradition you are in; then you might also take vows, precepts, voluntary roles in the community, or whatever. Or you might not. You improvise; you explore. You follow your heart and your nose and see where it leads you. You check it out. How can you not?

I have a lot of faith in this path, and I have a lot of faith and confidence in my teachers. I asked them a lot of questions. Kalu Rinpoche used to call me "the ocean of questions." In the 1970s, when I lived in his Sonada Monastery in Darjeeling, West Bengal, when he would ask after a Dharma talk, "Are there any questions?" he knew where to look first in the crowd. I said one day, "Rinpoche, is it okay to ask so many questions?" He said, "Ask all your questions. Then one day you will *know*." I am still questioning, but am less dependent on mere answers.

One day we ourselves can step up to teaching. That doesn't necessarily mean we have to have a pulpit or be a spiritual teacher. But we could recognize that one of the best ways to keep learning is to teach and to share. There is always somebody above us to learn from (speaking hierarchically, because it is simpler), and there is always somebody below us to teach, to pass it on to. So let's not always be on the receiving end. Let's also be on the giving end. Consumers must eventually become sharers, providers, distributors. I personally found that I grew more and learned more from my first three years of teaching around 1990 than if I had done a third three-year retreat in our cloistered Dzogchen center. Teaching and working with others, both with groups and with individuals, was really demanding. It pulled out the best of me; I learned a lot. I'd guess that the best college professors, just for example, are those who are really lifelong students with undimmed passion for their fields as well as for sharing knowledge with others.

Therefore let's respect the teacher principle in all of us, so we, too, can eventually step up to that. Let's work together and collaborate. The Buddha, Dharma, and sangha are three facets of one single luminous jewel. It is not just that the enlightened one, the Buddha, is our teacher. The enlightened teachings, the

Dharma, is also our teacher. The enlightened community, the sangha, is also our teacher. Truth is our teacher, of course. Reality is our teacher and master. If and when we find it embodied in anyone, let's not overlook the opportunity to apprentice ourselves, for a time at least, to that teacher. It might be a lunatic on the street who might be teaching us something; we could be open to that. The Taoist sage Chuang Tzu said that we can learn as much from the fools as from the wise. From the fools we learn what not to do; from the wise we learn what to do and how to be.

CHAPTER 13

THE LION'S ROAR

THE CHALLENGE OF DHARMA

MAY ALL BEINGS EVERYWHERE WITH WHOM WE ARE INTERCONNECTED,
AND WHO WANT AND NEED THE SAME AS WE DO;
MAY ALL BE AWAKENED, ENLIGHTENED, FULFILLED, AND FREE.
MAY THERE BE PEACE IN THIS WORLD,
AND AN END TO WAR, VIOLENCE, POVERTY, INJUSTICE AND OPPRESSION,
AND MAY WE ALL TOGETHER COMPLETE THE SPIRITUAL JOURNEY.
HOMAGE TO THE GREAT PERFECTION, THE BUDDHA WITHIN EACH OF US.
MAY ALL REALIZE AND ACTUALIZE THAT.
—LAMA SURYA DAS

On this first snowy evening of New England winter, when the trees are still red and gold and while the snow is falling, it is a good opportunity to reflect on the change of seasons; on impermanence; on mortality, death, and rebirth; on loss, change, and the opportunity for learning from difficulty and disappointment. These themes are all part of the Buddha's liberating teaching, the Dharma.

We often begin our meditation sessions by chanting *Om Mani Padme Hung*, the Mantra of Unconditional Love and Compassion, personified as the Buddhist archetype or meditational deity Avalokiteshvara. Avalokita is the personification of love and compassion, truth and love, wisdom and mercy joined as the radiant, splendid, four-armed form of the Buddha of Compassion. Often imaged as a female, he/she actually is beyond gender, and includes male and female both. Loving-kindness, compassion, empathy, tenderheartedness, forgiveness, altruism, warmth—*bodhicitta*, as we say in Sanskrit—awakened heart-mind, unselfish wakefulness, helpfulness are the heart of the living Dharma and of the enlightened life, the high ground, according to enlightened vision. Of course, we ourselves must choose how to be and how to live; the enlightened ones only serve to remind us how loving, how open, how connected and unselfish we actually can be. We could choose to contribute to and serve others, rather than harming or exploiting them. We could help others and bring forth great good in the world. We could be like a light in the world, not a troublemaker.

The meditation of loving-kindness is called Chenrezig's Meditation, in Tibetan; Avalokiteshvara in Sanskrit; Kwan Yin in Chinese; Kannon Bosatsu in Japanese. It is a way of warming up inside, of melting some of our frozen separateness, our hard-heartedness, and selfishness; a means of communing together, of realizing our oneness. And I don't mean oneness in a superficial way, as if we are all one and everything is everything, so nothing matters. That's superficial. However, let's explore how different are we, really? Don't we all want and need more or less the same things? For ourselves, for our loved ones and our neighborhood, too? This kind of practice helps us realize that. Buddhism has a genius for method, for path, for skillful ways to get *there*. Skillful means is Dharma. Not just to believe in something, to accept and follow dogma, but to travel there ourselves and experience it, to confirm it for ourselves. This kind of practice brings us to the place where we can, as it says in the Bible, treat others as we would be treated and love our neighbor as ourselves. This is the way to that great ideal. How to be like that? That's the question. Is it just Jesus and Buddha and a few saints and sages who embody that?

BuddhaDharma is called the Lion's Roar. It is a challenge, a clarion call to awakening. As the lion's roar awakens and even intimidates all the little animals in the jungle, the fearless lion's roar of Dharma awakens and challenges us to be all that we are. Not to become somebody else, not to live somebody else's life, not to imitate somebody else's way of dress or diet or thinking, but to be our true Self. To be genuinely ourSelves. How to become what we *are*? That's the conundrum.

Finding our genuine Selves is not about following the rainbow path until we get to an illusory pot of gold at the end. Practicing Dzogchen, the Natural Great Perfection, we realize that the rainbow is actually a circle, as anybody who has seen a rainbow from a plane can verify, and there's no pot of gold at the end; there *is* no end. Every step of the way is golden. It's *all* one big pot of gold; that's the secret! The pot of gold is our natural Buddha nature, our true nature, who and what we truly are. That's why in Dzogchen, it's recognized that we're all Buddhas by nature, and that all we have to do is recognize that fact. We're all Buddhas— not Buddhists but *Buddhas* by nature. We only have to recognize who and what we are. That's the meaning of awakening. That's the insight in insight. That's what satori breaks through to; that's the introduction to the nature of mind. It's not about a Buddha imitating some other Buddha. That's a fake Buddha, a wooden nickel. Buddhahood is not about trying to imitate some *other* Buddha, but being our true Self, which is not the same thing as being our habitual bent-out-of-shape, addictive, self-loathing self. Buddha's not pretending! The limited mind inhabited by our small, egoic self is a con artist selling us a bag of lies. Buddha is for real. Awakening is recognizing and knowing our true Self, which is much bigger, much more interesting, much more positive, than that. Then wherever we are, we are never lost, are never away from home. A Zen teaching says: "Wherever we go, we meet our true Self." This is the essence of the spiritual life, through direct divine encounter: I-thou relationships with all and everything. Buddha-ness is within everything, deep inside, like the strong hand inside all the different Muppets. This is the animating principle, the inner light, the Buddha or the godhead within.

I have had the good fortune to be able to spend many years in Asia with more than several of the enlightened masters of these last four decades. I know now that I'll never be like them, but I *will* be like myself. That's the path—not just to follow, in an overly literal and unimaginative way, the exact footsteps of someone else, wearing the same clothes, having the same hairstyle and eating habits, using the same lingo they do. Authentically following in their footsteps means to seek what they sought, which is authenticity and genuineness, and to actualize one's own made-in-America, indigenous Buddha nature. What we're talking about here is our own *true* nature—our homegrown, organic, natural Buddha nature. We hear too much about this thing called "Buddha nature" today from the historical and intellectual viewpoint of translators and scholars. Maybe we need to call it "natural Buddha" so we understand that it is Buddha-ness, *natural* Buddha, untrammeled pure and perfect spirit inherent in all of us, and not the same entity or thing.

Dry, old translated scriptures and Buddhist books too often make it sound like there's no way; even if there is, *you* certainly can't do it! There is actually no fixed way, and no way to miss it. If you have a pure heart, no problem. Read *It's Easier Than You Think*, by Sylvia Boorstein, the Jewish grandmother bodhisattva, and cheer up! Or read the *Tao Te Ching* by Lao Tzu. Every step along the way is the Great Way.

This is how the way is taught traditionally by Buddha: we can take the altruistic bodhisattva vow and aspire to alleviate suffering and wise up now, without waiting until after we get enlightened. This vow is for practitioners, who—by definition—have desires and aspirations, and imperfection, too. It is part of the practice of going beyond attachment and too much desire and finding the Middle Way, the way of healthy balance and moderation. There is a brilliant poem by my late friend Rick Fields called "Buddha and the Goddess." You might want to read it. At the end of the poem, it says, "Just remember this. You can't miss." Doesn't this resonate with your heart and soul? That's the Goddess speaking. Be genuine: purity of heart is there already. All karma is workable; it can be purified and transformed. The path of awakening is doable, available, accessible. That's Buddha's teaching, BuddhaDharma.

To do that, we really have to conscientiously observe and get to know ourselves. We have to be more consciously aware of ourselves. We have to be able to see things as they are, not just see everything through our projections and distorted egocentric perceptions. Things are not what they seem to be; we are not exactly who we think we are. These practices are introducing a sane and lovely way of being, a way of clarity, harmony, joy. It will help us to see things as they are, be who we are, and treat others and ourselves accordingly. Not harming others, but helping others. Not exploiting others, but serving others. Being close kin to one and all, in deeds as well as intentions. Loving our way to nirvana.

It is easy to articulate these ideals, but it is a challenge to live in accord with them. Therefore we train ourselves. The path is nothing if it is not training. In Tibetan Buddhism it is called *lojong*, sometimes translated as mind training. But there is too much mind talk and mentation in our Buddhism today. Lojong is really attitude transformation, and spiritual cultivation, not just mind training. We can train the mind, like a dog, but what about the rest of us? What about where we really live: in the body, emotions, feelings, attitude, intention, motivation, highest life-dreams, relationships, and the rest. Buddhist training includes refining ourselves spiritually, on the outer, inner, and subtlest secret levels.

The Buddhist teaching is always taught according to the three main themes, as described earlier: sila, samadhi, and prajna—ethics, virtue, and morality—basically, nonharming; meditation, contemplation, or awareness; and wisdom. This is the way of training *ourselves*, of taking the path of awakening, of enlightenment. That's why the Buddha said, "I only point the way. You have to walk it yourself. Be a light unto yourself." Use the miner's light in your own forehead. Don't just follow my candle, because it will go out soon anyway. Make your own light. For your own benefit, and for the benefit of all.

If we really look inside, I think we'll find there is plenty of light there. We are far more beautiful than we think. We don't need somebody else's light, at least not for long. Maybe another can help jump-start us, but we have to move under our own steam eventually. We should be able to outgrow our parents eventually, and eventually even be able to take care of them. In BuddhaDharma, wisdom and compassion always go together. When we talk about mind training, attitude transformation, or spiritual cultivation, what are we talking about? Just making *ourselves* smarter? Not at all. Rather, transforming our attitude of selfishness, which is like lead, into the gold of altruism, of connectedness, of pure unselfish helpfulness, of bodhicitta, loving-kindness, and compassion. Empathy is very relevant: feeling what others feel, sympathizing with them, so we can treat them accordingly. This is the root of compassion.

Trungpa Rinpoche says that taking refuge in enlightenment is like becoming a refugee. You go forth from your home or rut and let go of everything. That's why Trungpa warned us against blindly joining in. But for some reason, nonetheless, he got thousands of people to do it. Homelessness means nowhere to get stuck and to stand; it introduces the possibility of dancing in openness. It sounds good put that way, but it is very challenging. No props. No promise. It takes a lot of trust, doesn't it, to just *be* without looking forward to anything? Standing firm on the groundless ground of being.

What is all the occult mumbo-jumbo and fuss about? It need not be so complicated, mysterious, or fancy. BuddhaDharma is ordinary life. My own teacher, the head of the Nyingmapa sect of Vajrayana Buddhism, the late Holiness Dudjom Rinpoche—author of twenty books, a teacher of the Dalai Lama—said, "The Dharma is not fancy. It's like blue jeans: good for every occasion, every day. It's good for work. It's good for school. You can wear blue jeans to a wedding, to ride horses, whatever." Dharma is everyday Dharma. That's where it counts. Not mysterious, trippy, weird, or fanciful Dharma, but sane, grounded, wholesome, incisive Dharma.

All experiences are illusory and soon pass away, like the weather. Space never changes, but the weather in space changes all the time. Therefore, to rely on the weather is unreal and illusory. Spiritual experiences can be like drug experiences or alcohol experiences. They're a little more inner, but they still extend to our true nature. Such experiences might have a lot of *shakti*, power, energy, learning content, and thrills; they might overwhelm you and give you a charge, but those experiences are very tricky and unreliable. The values that we have been talking about, like intentionally cultivating virtuous states of mind, helpfulness, and unselfishness, are far more reliable and beneficial.

The problem is that we can get very involved in these things, and even entirely lose our perspective. Then we don't know up from down anymore. We get carried away to where we would not necessarily go if we had the presence of mind to make a conscious choice. That's why Buddhists talk about going for refuge; it's a way of entering the Buddhist teaching. You find a sanctuary in perfect enlightenment—not in people, not in gods, not in shamanism, not in powers, not in bottles, not in pills. Refuge draws us deeper toward finding a real sanctuary or place to be; in integrity, in peace, in harmony, in nonharming (ahimsa), nonviolence, in wisdom, and other unimpeachable values. Going for refuge draws us into the ultimate Dharma teaching. Not just believing in the rituals and dogma, but genuinely discovering the possibility of living the basic principles ourselves. Not trying to get to nirvana through special experiences, but realizing that it is now and that we are simply overlooking it. For we can experience nirvanic peace right now, through sufficient awareness, presence, and clarity. We can experience authentic being, through purifying the veils obscuring the innate inner light of reality.

Spiritual authenticity is a big question these days. We all have to look into it. This is not just a problem surrounding televangelists, hucksters, cult members, cult leaders, and charlatans. But what is genuinely our deepest, truest life? What's real and true for us? Not just seeking truth like an abstraction, but being honest, living in integrity, developing character. Not just getting enlightened, but finding our true vocation and finding our true way in life. Not just imitating a guru, or charismatic teacher. Not just sitting on the floor like a frog all the time. An old Japanese Zen master came to the traditional and formal Cambridge University in England in the early 1970s, in the early days of Zen in the West. He said, "You cannot meditate on a chair. You have to get on the floor." Then he said, "You cannot meditate with pants. You have to take off pants." So what's next? You can't meditate and get enlightened with blue eyes and white skin? Who's directing your life? What about the teachings of *anatta*, the question of self and no-self—ungovernable, impermanent, out of control? Who's directing this show? God? Me? You? The impulse of the moment? Who's in charge? That's the anatta side: the deepest, steepest, most mysterious and selfless side of it. When we can let go a little and realize that we are not in charge and directing, we learn to do the best we can and to trust and let go. Whatever happens, happens.

Self-mastery does not mean becoming the ultimate control freak; it's a little more subtle, spontaneous, and free than that. The Buddha is in the palm of one's hand. It is up to each of us. According to the law of karma, it depends on you. Your karma, your world, how you experience life—it all depends on you. Everything is subjective. Make your karma into your Dharma, but don't forget to use the rudder now and then to skillfully steer yourself along the way.

On one side is the groundless and boundless emptiness. The other side is karma, very meticulously calibrated causes and effects. You reap what you sow. Positive things get positive results, and negative things get negative results. You can choose—it is all in your hands. Responsibility for self and for the world is interconnected. You are responsible for your patch, which is part of the bigger patch. Cultivate yourself—cultivate your private patch—and the entire world is better for it. A Zen poem says, "The Great Way is not difficult for those who have few preferences." That doesn't mean we don't have preferences, but we don't need to have a tantrum if we don't get what we want. A bigger perspective is possible. We have preferences and a personality, but that's not the whole story. Back off a little bit, gain some perspective; widen the scope, broaden the gaze. Then you become less invested in it, not so identified with it, not so burdened by it, and joy blazes forth. It is just part of the whole grand spectacle!

There is another whole side to things besides taking charge, which includes the gentle virtues of softening, trusting, and opening. Do we have to have every day all strategically planned out? Can we just drift a bit? Just sniff the breeze and decide which way to walk? Anything might happen. Of course, anything *does* happen; but we close it off a little by how we hold our experience, how we psychologically organize and frame it with the stories we tell ourselves about life and ourselves. I think we could all go a long way in the direction of trust. Not just to trust someone else, but to trust ourselves, trust our intuition, follow our heart, and be genuinely ourselves. Why are we always looking for the ultimate external authority or teaching to tell us what to do? Perhaps we don't have to do anything special. We can just be, and do whatever we have to do in a beautiful, creative, flowing way. As we get more used to that, we unfold more of our own wisdom, autonomy, completeness, and inner directedness. Not necessarily selfish, nor overreactive. I'll quote our late guru, Dudjom Rinpoche: "May I tie around my own head (he's thinking about oxen; he lives in Tibet) the rope that leads from the tip of my nose." Meaning, I am like an ox, but still may I not give my nose rope to anybody. How much are we like dumb oxen, looking for someone to pull our nose rope? Isn't that interesting? Not to hand over responsibility to somebody else.

Beware of who's doing what to whom around here. Don't pass the buck to others. It just doesn't work that way; it just can't work that way! Look into it—look into the BuddhaDharma and see what you see, what you find, and then look some more and more and even more. The Twelfth Gyalwang Drukpa has said that in Dzogchen, awareness is the Dharma. So Attention! Attention! Pay attention! The Dharma, truth itself, can be found in every moment. And while you're looking, I will make a pronouncement: there is really no such thing as an unmixed good or unmixed bad. Nothing is that simple. Totalizing anything—totally good or bad—is illusory. Turn the stone over and over and over and over. The light is within the dark, and vice versa. Things are not as black and white as they may sometimes seem.

Nyoshul Khenpo taught a four-stage process of applying these vital pith instructions or points of Mahamudra and Dzogchen, in order to realize union or oneness (*yugannadha*, in Sanskrit) with all and everything, with every moment, through mingling emptiness, awareness, and appearances. When we contact or experience anything, it is taught that *first* bring attention to whatever arises and appears (known as an appearance, in technical terms, or an object of attention), by just being present to it in bare attention, which is pure presence of mind combined with choiceless, nonevaluating awareness. *Second*, notice any reactive processes or judgments and responses that might begin to arise in response to the object or appearance experienced. *Third*, penetrate or see through the illusory reality and insubstantial solidity of the object or appearance, through recognizing its true, empty nature. *Fourth*, yield to or appreciate whatever comes next, and leave space for the habitual, reactive stimulus-response process to lose its grip and fall apart while experience proceeds to morph into the next experiential pattern; then start again with stage one, pure attention. This is known in the Dzogchen tradition as "cutting the web of existence"; it is from master Longchenpa's special pith instructions. Sometimes we sum it up by describing it as an attentional and attitudinal process of looking, seeing, penetrating, and releasing; or more simply as seeing, recognizing, and releasing.

Dharma is really about moment-to-moment attention and the clarity and comprehension that come with alert presence of mind. This is the essence of all mindfulness and awareness practices. The contemplative practice of pure presence and nonjudgmental, choiceless awareness dissolves dualism and separation of all kinds and helps us to realize that we *are* what we experience, not separate from it. Thus we can simply sit back and enjoy the view, in our beach chair of life, enjoying whatever momentarily presents itself, either outside or within ourselves. The entire field of experience becomes a marvelous spectacle that we can simply appreciate. Check it out. This is the richness and the unceasing fullness of the Dharma—the lion's roar calling you.

CHAPTER 14

SANGHA MEANS COMMUNITY

There is a lot of talk in the spiritual and New Age ghetto about enlightenment, wisdom, mind training, clarity, mindfulness, awareness, higher consciousness, divine mind, spiritual intelligence, and so on. Now Western meditators are excited about brain research and neuroscience. It always seems to start from the head, and go upward. I think we need to ground this talk in our bodies and in the ground of our total experience, not just intellect. We must bring it down to the ground of being, not just in the skyscrapers of thinking and doing that we are all so high on. I think our own life needs to be more grounded in a softness, a friendliness, a warmth that truly connects with earthiness, not just with the rarefied heights of heavenliness.

In looking for Western ideas that are useful here, I have been thinking a lot lately about friendliness, friendship, and cheerfulness. You don't hear so much about that in the meditation halls, perhaps because it has become so much a cliché that we hesitate to mention it. But without joy and celebration, where would we be? I think that sangha is a significant yoga, an important path of the coming decade and centuries. Sangha requires mutual respect and friendly collaboration, a sense of ourselves as kindred spirits working and exploring and playing together. There is wisdom and higher consciousness in that. There is everything that we talk about built into that, and without that we are dead in the water. All the Buddhist learning, all the scholarship is wasted, is useless without that. If we don't pull together, we'll be pulled apart.

There is a story in the sutras: Ananda, Lord Buddha's long-time personal attendant and monk disciple, asks Buddha: "Lord, is it true what has been said, that good spiritual friends are fully half of the holy life?"

The master replied, "No, Ananda, good spiritual friends are the whole of the holy life. Find refuge in the sangha community."

Lately I have been feeling this more and more. We cannot do it all on our own. Enlightenment needs a minyan! It is a collective endeavor, not an individualistic, selfish pursuit. The Vietnamese Zen master Thich Nhat Hanh—who has written wonderful books and is a fine teacher, peace activist, and living example—says that Maitreya Buddha, the coming Buddha of the future, is the sangha. He means the coming Buddha is the community itself; not an individual, not a seven-foot-tall human man as it says in some scriptural teaching. It is the sangha—something taller in stature than any one of us. That's the meaning of this kind of teaching myth.

I feel it is very important that we work in this spirit in our own lives and feel it in the visceral level, with feelings, emotions, and passions. Viscerally feel and experience intimately the truth that is self-evident, as it were, very true and obvious when we tune in to it, and let go of concepts and fixations, including our preconceived notions and self-centered striving. Then we can be more in touch with the source or center of things, the groundless ground of being, rather than being carried away by all the momentary superficial ripples. The ripples are not a problem, but they are just on the surface; don't overlook the still, clean, infinite depth of the ocean, which we are in the midst of. I think this is really a time for us to do something together. I personally feel very gratified that we *are* doing this together. No one of us can do this alone: it's just too vast, too mysterious and too difficult to go it alone, without friends, family, teachers, and teachings. That's why when we talk Buddhism, we talk about taking refuge—finding a reliable sanctuary—in the Buddha, the Dharma, *and* the sangha, the community of kindred spirits. We have the Buddha—Buddha has been around for twenty-five-hundred years (forever, actually). We have the Dharma—the Dharma teachings and books are everywhere. But do we have a sangha? We need the sangha as well—the sangha jewel, the third facet of the Triple Jewel (the three jewels of Buddha, Dharma, sangha). We must cultivate a sangha community, both lay and monastic sanghas, here in this country, if we want the Dharma to flourish. Sangha is beloved community, spiritual kinship.

The Tibetan teachers always say that it's almost impossible to find a yogi or yogini who is like the snow leopard or snow lion, living alone on a mountaintop, in a cave or forest, alone in the wild. One who can awaken alone is very rare in each generation. Most of us need to be part of and interact with a sangha. Many of us have also benefited greatly from wise teachers. I think this is very important for us these days, especially when many of us have a tendency toward individualism, which we are so good at in America. Individualism is a virtue, but, like everything, it has its shadow. We must grow up and be independent, but we are also interdependent, so let's remember that. Let's not fall into narcissism, falling in love with our own image, as individualists or even anarchists, always being new and better and different. Let's recognize our common ground with all beings. The sangha jewel as a refuge can really help round off our rough edges, these points that are sticking out in all directions like jaggedly broken pieces of ore straight from a gold mine. We need to be refined a little. The gold is there, but it might momentarily be more like a rough, jagged rock. On the other hand, the great bodhisattvas—those wise and compassionate, impeccable masters—are like graceful swans, gliding among all the waterfowl without disturbing anyone or anything. Living with sangha helps round off our rough edges and helps us to learn to accept and even love those we don't happen to like.

I had the privilege and opportunity to live in a formal sangha (in one usage, *sangha* means the monastic community). Usually I only talk about lay Buddhism and American-style Buddhism—Buddhism here in the West, and the things that come more easily to many of us here. But I learned something very interesting when I was privileged for several years to wear the Buddha's robes and shave my head in the three-year retreat cloisters. I learned that you don't always get to pick who you intimately travel the journey with. You might think you do, but don't be deceived. And the corollary of that—and this is the real lesson I want to share—is that you start to realize that you can love anybody—and *must* love anybody. We didn't have the privilege of deciding who we were as if married to for three and a half years in our cloister, from which we never went out and into which no one entered. And we found out that these various people gathered together, of various ages, from different countries, with different expectations and habits, were all on the same team. After living together for three and a half years and never seeing anybody else, you get to know, it seems, every single thought that everybody has there, twenty or twenty-five people, monks and nuns. You find out we all want and need pretty much the same things; that we are vastly more similar than different. This was very enlightening. I didn't always like everybody there, but after three or four years, I found out that I loved everybody there because I started to feel what they feel and where they are coming from. Empathy is a large part of compassion.

We are all on the same side, the same team. To use the terms of the Indian Dharma teaching, we are joined together in battling with the kleshas, in struggling with egotism, suffering, greed, and confusion. We are all aligned in that vital way. I think that working together in our sangha here, and in the broader Buddhist nation that we are a part of, is very helpful. It will prove to be very enlivening, enlightening, and grounding. It will put a little more soul into our dry, soulless (anatta) Buddhist act! We're not just trying to reach the rarefied height of the spiritual mountain, standing on tiptoes and stretching toward the sky alone. Let's also descend into the valleys, the shadowy, smelly darkness of the jungle where life actually transpires, where the food grows, where the water runs. Let's get real.

It's okay if one wants to stand tiptoe on the mountaintop, but somebody else has to be down in the valley bringing the food, farming, and that somebody else is all of us most of the time. Let's not overlook that. We must recognize our responsibility. It *is* there; we just don't always recognize it. Whether you call it sangha making or community service, altruism, social activism, love and friendship, whatever—we are all working together, on the same team. There's no real us and them. The person who cuts you off in traffic is also on your side, hurrying somewhere in a similar direction to try to be happier. He and we are on the same team, even though he happened to cut us off. That sometimes happens, but on the other hand, we might sometimes do the same. We must cooperate and collaborate, not just compete. So let's keep showing up, being engaged with others and with our collective concerns, rather than escaping from our responsibilities.

I feel more and more committed to this sangha practice, this community practice, and the love and genuine human friendliness that we share. It's beautiful. I love collaborating. Moreover, I notice by being with other Western Buddhist teachers and experienced students, scholars, and friends, that they provide a clear mirror for me. Let's not overlook the possibility of really finding our true Self, our true heart, through sangha practice, and living it in our life. Walking our talk. Really embodying a sane life here on this planet. Cultivating friendliness and warmth toward all.

I'm not a particularly apocalyptic person. Joanna Macy, a Buddhist scholar I know in California, is always talking about how we only have twenty or thirty years before everything explodes and implodes. Global warming is a huge problem we must face. I know there is a lot we can do about these global issues, but I think such things have been cycling around for a long time, and will continue to cycle around. Of course, we have to save the tropical rain forests and this planet's flora and fauna. The question is, Where do we find ourselves in that ongoing, universal cycle? Are we merely the victims of circumstances, or can we assume the position of the source, the proactive end, and thus begin to embody true action—proactivity, enlightened action, intelligent responsiveness, and not just conditional *re*action? In such a way we can actualize impeccable activity, true creativity, not just semiconscious reactions. That's the big question of today for many people: How to respond skillfully and not simply react? For this is where freedom lies, in the very art of enlightened living. I think if we can embody that kind of freedom and impeccability, we can really be a true sangha, and like Buddhas, express a living, vital Dharma. We would be guiding lights in the world. I don't think that's too ambitious for us to aspire to. We should go for it, and not squander our lives. It's now or never, as always.

During the holidays I feel a spirit of friendliness and warmth and love all around town. It is also a time when we will be tested with whatever family gatherings or whatever situations we find during the holidays, so it is a good time to see what buttons we have left to be pushed. Ram Dass always used to say that after you have spent your ten or twenty years in India being high as a kite, or several weeks or months on a meditation cushion or yoga mat somewhere, then go home, spend some time with your family, and find out what work you might have left to do. It will all be revealed!

The first virtue of character to be developed, according to Mahayana Buddhist attitude training, is generosity. That doesn't just mean giving money; it means letting go and nonattachment, openness, and being generous, patient, and loving with yourself, too—a certain kind of good-natured ease rather than constriction and tightness. Charity, in the Christian sense: caritas, which also includes love. It is something we can work on and develop in ourselves. Generosity is the first transcendental perfection, or paramita, in the Mahayana scheme of six paramitas. It is called *dana paramita,* and there are different levels of it. Giving material help and sharing our good fortune is one level. Preserving, cherishing, encouraging, and protecting life is another level of dana paramita. Selfless service, *seva,* is another form of dana practice; being helpful and even cheerful. Another level, said to be the highest level, is giving Dharma, which includes wisdom, truth, and love; sharing our most precious gifts, our purity of heart, by sharing the truth in helping people to awaken. Those are all practices of generosity that we can participate in, thus cultivating and enacting perfect giving. Generosity ennobles us. And the more we give, the more we receive, as the saying goes. Trusting is also a way of practicing dana. Dana implies nonattachment, letting go—open hand, open arms, open heart and mind.

Many people have told me their lives have been changed just because, for example, they saw a poster on a telephone pole that somebody took the trouble to post, introducing them to something significant and new in their lives; or they read a book or got a tape in their hands; or heard that there was such a thing as a Dalai Lama they could meet and learn from. My friend in Switzerland said that he's been missing something ever since I completed the three-year Tibetan Vajrayana retreat in France. He said he always felt so happy, thinking of me in the three-year retreat, that it gave him something that helped keep him going.

We can share in many ways. We can be generous with ourselves, generous with our emotions. Why are we so stingy with our emotions? What are we suppressing, hoarding, and saving them for? Why be afraid to experience our own feelings? Let's learn to genuinely experience our experience, just as it is, without restriction or inhibition. Let's share freely with each other, collaborating and networking toward a true sense of community.

Traditionally, Buddhism has been taught mainly by monastics. Throughout the ages, monastics have been its most venerated practitioners, with a few notable exceptions. Monastic training—

including vows and precepts—and contemplative practices such as solitude, silence, meditation, purity, restraint, and renunciation have been emphasized. Family life and intimate relationships have rarely been the focus for spiritual development in the Buddhist countries of Asia (except in the tantric tradition), and for good reason; making family life into a spiritual practice is more difficult, more complicated, more messy, and less institutionally controllable than monastic life, in which monks, nuns, and priests live under the strict rule of church, spiritual leader, group norms, and so forth.

Since most of us here today are laypeople engaged on the spiritual journey, intimacy as a path of awakening could be extraordinarily important. Even to monastics, learning to integrate relationships into the spiritual path could be important; monks and nuns relate to their teachers, to each other, to their families, to many people at different points in their lives. Wherever I teach, whether I'm giving traditional teachings like the Noble Eightfold Path or more interdenominational teachings on contemporary spirituality and integrating Dharma into daily life, the subject of relationships inevitably comes up. When I traveled as a translator for some of my late great Tibetan masters like Kalu Rinpoche, Nyoshul Khenpo Rinpoche, and others, people would inevitably come up one by one after a teaching and try to speak to the great master from Tibet about problems with their personal relationships, children, drugs, drink, mental issues, family life, homosexuality, and work. Once Kalu Rinpoche turned to me and asked, "Aren't there any meditators in America?"

We are all intricately involved in many forms of relationship—with others, with ourselves, with something beyond ourselves. We are engaged in intimate personal relationships; lover relationships; relationships to ourselves: to our body, to our emotions, our thoughts, feelings, perceptions; to our passion, desire, lust, internal energy, and so on. How we relate in the moment of encountering any and all of these important, even if transient, things can prove incredibly important. This is why Martin Buber said, "All life is about encounter." It is at that moment of meeting reality that we encounter truth, encounter ourselves, and encounter the holy Other. Buber said, in *I and Thou:* "It is only by virtue of our ability to relate that we are able to live in the spirit."

Dr. Jonas Salk said: "The meaning of life is felt through relationship. . . . The meaning of life flowers through relationship." At all levels—outer, inner, and mystical—everything is connected; nothing exists in isolation. This has been described variously as interbeing and interconnectedness, Indra's net, earth family, and the web of being in which we are all interconnected relationally. I find it is exciting how we can grow with this kind of holistic or systems understanding.

But maybe you thought Buddhism teaches that we have to get rid of attachments, free ourselves of all relationships, and damp down our passions. Even in relatively enlightened circles, still we hear that we have to get rid of our desires, that life is suffering, and other weak translations of Sanskrit or Tibetan words. We must look more deeply into the words that are being translated or mistranslated as attachment or as desire or passion. The same word can be translated as "fixation"—as "resistance"—as "stuckness"—as "grasping and clinging"—and so on. It is not just that human attachments are the problem: it's a little bit more clingy than that.

When the Dalai Lama spoke recently at Brandeis University in Massachusetts, one of the first things he said to an audience of seven thousand people was that the most important thing in the world is warm human affection. I think that's an excellent theme for today: warm and human and affection. Not just cool, calm, and clear eyes-like-ice meditation. Not just detachment, but also warmth and human affection. The Dalai Lama could speak in much more philosophical and highfalutin terms, but he chose that to express his own values in that way. Isn't it the warm heart, the loving heart, that is at the root of spirit anyway? In Buddhism we might call it bodhicitta, but there are so many ways to describe this warm, loving, altruistic awakened heart, the good-heartedness intrinsic to innate Buddha nature. That's what we are, and that's what we can work with and further develop. It's not just the goal we're heading toward. We are cultivating that ideal, but we also have it in us, don't we? Don't we experience it even a little day-to-day, here and there in our best moments or even by accident, when that breaks through? We can't acquire it, but we can align with and be it, at one with our genuine Selves.

Sangha or community is an essential element of refuge and awakening. We should not forget that when focused on Buddha and the teacher and the Dharma teachings and practice. One of the original meanings of sangha is "contact." It means making warm, meaningful contact. At the beginning, sangha specifically referred to ordained monks and nuns, but the later Mahayana revolution and other developments in Buddhism expanded the meaning of sangha to include practitioners of all kinds, not just monastics. And I think we can take it even more widely into the sangha of all beings—of our community, town, and family. This would inevitably include even our adversaries, if we're deep enough and understand what contact really means.

If and when we look into dissatisfaction and its cause, which is the main thesis of Buddhist practice, don't we find much of our suffering has to do with our relationships? With our passions and craving desires? With our mates? With parents or children or colleagues, bosses, or subordinates? Recently when I talked with therapists at our annual local psychotherapy and meditation conference at Harvard, they all said that most people's problems are about their relationships. It was reported that from the teen years until quite late in life, the majority of people talk most of the time about their fraught relationships or lack of relationships. In order to have a living path today, to live the vital formless flame of Dharma, I think we need to practice wise relationships, cling-free relationships that are honest, balanced, loving, and even impeccable.

This all points to the necessity for opening up our relationships to objective spiritual inquiry and growth. We can practice bringing mindfulness and attention to bear, in order to help us see clearly what's going on, to open our hearts, and to listen better and cultivate a little more generosity, loving-kindness, and empathy—feeling what others feel. Let's strive to see the light, the Buddha, or divine—whatever you call it—in others. It's relational, you see: you need self and other to do that most interesting practice of sacred outlook or pure perception in which we see the inner light of Buddha-ness in everyone. I invite you to try it. When you do, you see immediately all the things that come up beside the light in your field of projections. We can easily glimpse the light in our child or in our pet dog or cat, but what about in our colleagues or the people that scare us on the street, or the kinds of insects we're afraid of? The light, the divine, sacred Buddha nature is all. This is the ultimate sangha.

CHAPTER 15

CHANTING AND SACRED SOUND

IF YOU CANNOT TEACH ME TO FLY, TEACH ME TO SING.
—SIR JAMES BARRIE (AUTHOR OF *PETER PAN*)

Tibet's preeminent yogi and poet, Milarepa (eleventh century), is always portrayed sitting in a white cotton robe outside of his Himalayan cave with his right hand cupped behind his right ear, listening to the cosmic sound of reality. His famous *Hundred Thousand Songs of Enlightenment* were spontaneously composed from what he heard from the songstresses of nature, the dancing wisdom dakinis, by tuning in to the cosmic music of the inner spheres. Sufi master Hazrat Inayat Khan wrote, in his book *The Mysticism of Sound and Music,* "Before the world was, all was in sound. God was in sound, we are made of sound." The Gospel of John says, "In the beginning was the Word, and the Word was with God, and the Word was God." Everything stems from, is interconnected by, and returns to vibration, which is pure energy. Sound is vibration. Sound has tremendous power. A Tibetan tantra (scripture) says, "From within the infinite womb of emptiness arises, like a shooting star, the blazing seed syllable of mantra."

Tibetan Buddhism is renowned for its use of mantras, chants, and esoteric liturgies and rituals as an essential part of its tantric meditation and yoga system. In fact, Tibetan Buddhism is more properly known among its exponents as Secret Mantra Vajrayana, or the Sacred Mantra Diamond Vehicle. Chants and mantra practice are among its most significant disciplines. Research by neuropsychologists has shown how music, chanting, and prayerful intention can help increase our creativity, intelligence, and peace of mind, as well as restructure our brains, help healing to occur, and increase longevity. Perhaps that is why Thomas Carlyle wrote, "Music is well said to be the speech of angels." Opera singer Leontyne Price believes that she is in communion with God when she sings, and that all artists are merely vessels who receive their gifts and guidance from God. Sufi poet-saint Rumi sang that he was like an empty vessel, a flute in God's hands.

Mantras are words of sacred power, pregnant with meaning and resonance. The Buddha himself said, "Better than a meaningless story of a thousand words is a single word of deep meaning that, when heard, produces peace." Mantras are such words of profound meaning, redolent with peace. The mantra *Om* is one such example; when intoned, it naturally lends itself to harmony, oneness and unity. My late friend, Buddhist scholar John Blofeld, wrote in his book *Mantras: Sacred Words of Power:* "Though mantras may be used for a variety of ends, their highest purpose is to assist the mantra-practitioner in coming face-to-face with his own divinity. By comparison, all other ends are trivial."

Mantras can be verbally chanted, intoned, or even sung. Inwardly, they can be repeated mentally to oneself and secretly visualized in the inner chakras and energy channels of the "light body" (subtle body), or simply held in mind in deep samadhi (meditative absorption). Mantra repetition is classically one of the most surefire methods to entrain the attention and learn to concentrate, focus, and calm the mind. According to my late great teacher, the erudite old Tibetan lama Deshung Rinpoche, the word *mantra* literally means "something to lean the mind/consciousness on." He taught me how to use mantras to stabilize and strengthen my inner awareness and mindfulness, and then carry that on into daily activities.

Deepak Chopra said, "Mantras are holograms of information and energy. All over the world, people of all kinds use chants to pray, praise, recite and contemplate God's innumerable names and sublime qualities." Mechtild of Magdeburg, a thirteenth-century Catholic lay sister, wrote: "As the Godhead strikes the note, humanity sings. The Holy Spirit is the harpist, and all the strings must sound which are touched by love." I find that when we chant our hearts open, boundaries blur, and we experience solidarity while losing our finite sense of separate selfhood and encountering our innate Buddha nature.

Meditating with Mantras

Changing Sanskrit mantras and Tibetan invocations is used extensively for purposes of blessing, prayerful worship, communion, and healing, as well as for meditation, concentration, and purification. Regular chant practice helps us accomplish the ulti-

mate goal of inner peace, spiritual realization, and enlightenment. There are numerous kinds of mantras: wisdom mantras,
compassion mantras, healing mantras, peaceful mantras, wrathful
mantras, purifying mantras, magnetizing mantras, transforming
mantras, fire mantras, earth mantras, sky mantras, wind mantras,
deity mantras, spirit mantras, obstacle-removing mantras, ego-
destroying mantras, and so on. Mantra meditation can totally
transform the entire atmosphere and effect swift transformation,
both externally in the world and within ourselves. Chanting
mantras helps us open our throat chakra and heart chakra and access the inexhaustible treasury of awareness, bliss, and wisdom to
be found there, from which poetry, song, and wisdom scripture
naturally flows.

In the preliminary practices of Tibetan Buddhism, we practice no less than five hundred thousand recitations of purifying mantras and aspirational prayers, along with visualizations,
bows, and breathing exercises; notable among these is the
hundred-syllable purification mantra of Vajrasattva, the Buddha
of purity and innate perfection. Such sacred mantras have the
mystical power to transform every atom of our body and our entire being into a pure vessel of spirit, and to integrate our outer
and inner life into one radiant, harmonious whole. The mantra
of unconditional love and compassion, *Om Mani Padme Hung,*
which literally means "the jewel is in the lotus," or the Buddha is
within, is the Dalai Lama's mantra and the national mantra of
Tibet. This blessed six-syllable mantra is the heart and soul
of the grand bodhisattva of loving-kindness and compassion,
Chenrezig.

We don't actually chant mantras for their meaning, but the
Sanskrit words in the traditional Tibetan mantras we chant do
have a meaning. One all-encompassing chant we practice is the
user-friendly, simple *Ah.* The exhaled *Ah* is hard to translate. It's
like *Om,* but it's *Ah.* We'll just leave it like that. Buddha is the doctor; he gives us the medicine that heals all disease, unease, and

suffering. Just think that Buddha is saying *Ah!* and checking to see if anything is wrong, whenever you open your mouth and say "ah" to a physician who is checking you. Saying *Ah* deeply opens one up.

Om Ah Hung Benzar Guru Padme Siddhi Hung is the vajra guru mantra of Padmasambhava, the famous lotus-born guru who brought Buddhism to Tibet in the eighth century. He is called the Second Buddha, the Buddha of Tibet. First there's the three syllable *Om Ah Hung;* then it says *Benzar,* or Vajra, and *Guru Padme.* It's like saying homage to the diamond master, born in the lotus. *Padme* is lotus. *Siddhis* means spiritual powers, like love, wisdom, compassion, forgiveness, enlightenment. The meaning is "Homage to the enlightened powers of the lotus-born guru; may they be transmitted to me/us." It's a way of affirming that the lotus grows and flourishes out of the mud of one's own nature, and that those enlightened powers can grow in the mud of our own base nature. Human nature is like the tip of the vast iceberg of Buddha nature.

Om Tare Tutarre Turiye Soha is the mantra of the female Buddha, Tara. Again, we start with the cosmic sound, *Om. Tare* is her name. It's an invocation and exhortation, affirming that Tara is present and guarding and awakening us. *Tutarre* is her name again, as is *Turiye. Soha* or *swaha* is like amen, hallelujah, or so be it. So it's her name mantra. Chanting it attracts her (our) attention, exhorts her swiftly enlightening activity, and brings down and brings out her bountiful blessings. You can practice chanting this and other chants with my CD, *Chants to Awaken the Buddhist Heart,* which meditation music master Steven Halpern and I made collaboratively as a support for those drawn to such chanting practices.

As I said, we don't really chant these mantras thinking of their meaning. When we chant, we focus on the chanting itself and feel the vibration on an energy level. Something happens, much more than just thinking or saying that the mantra means the jewel in the lotus. You can begin with the meaning, but then you go quickly deeper into it and experience it from the inside out by chanting and meditating on it. It works in your chakras and in your psychic energy channels, and so on, vibrating in different sacred dimensions. There are different uses for all these various kinds of mantras: softening mantras; energetic, generating mantras; peaceful and wrathful mantras; healing mantras; purification mantras; and so on as already mentioned.

These mantras are made up of seed syllables. Each of these syllables is called a seed, a *bija* in Sanskrit. *Om* is such a seed syllable. A mantra is a string of them, like a rosary. The string linking the beads is the breath and the attention. Each seed syllable germinates in a slightly different way. Just look at the different seed syllables. Like *P'et!* That's very sharp and cutting, so we call that a cutting syllable. Then there's *Ah,* a very softening, opening, spacious, relaxing, dissolving seed syllable. So we try to harmoniously balance different aspects. We balance the sharpness, the one-pointedness of the *P'et* with the spacious, expansive softness and energy release of the *Ah.* You can feel the different quality of the sounds. Mantric sounds have a lot of vibrations, and different levels that they vibrate on. These mantras are kind of a technology for awakening different energies and actualizing different qualities. It's not really like asking an external deity named Tara to do something, but more like stimulating and actualizing within ourselves the sacred feminine energy that Tara embodies.

With a mantra like *Om Mani Padme Hung,* some lamas make a vow to do huge numbers of recitation practice, like one hundred million times, which they count with their beads. They are always saying it. They try to say twenty thousand, thirty thousand, or fifty thousand mantras every day. They are always concentrating on compassion and loving-kindness, radiating and warming up and softening, seeing everybody as the Buddha and every place as a sacred Buddha field. They radiate blessings and light rays to all the different kinds of beings with *Om Mani*

Padme Hung. I recall taking Kalu Rinpoche to the aquarium in Boston one winter long ago. There were some huge glass walls thick with little fish there. There were thousands of fish in huge tanks. Rinpoche would go up to the glass and, holding his bodhi-seed mala beads in hand, say *Om Mani Padme Hung* again and again. He went up to each fish and individually touched a finger gently to the window near its little face to get its attention, to make a connection, and said *Om Mani Padme Hung.* We couldn't even walk around the aquarium, because he was busy blessing and teaching the fish. He seemed to connect personally with each one. Nor was he the least bit self-conscious about it. It was truly marvelous.

Returning to the Natural State

Chanting is one of the most transformative and nonsectarian spiritual practices, especially since it almost immediately takes us out of our heads and beyond the mind, into realms of pure spirit and bliss. It helps us discover the spiritual breath and cosmic energy (prana) inside the physical breath. Monks and nuns, shamans, yogis, dervishes, chant masters, healers, pilgrims, cantors, singers, and musicians have long known this universal secret. Don Campbell, music master and author of *The Mozart Effect,* says, "Chant is the music of the cosmic spheres and the natural expression of higher consciousness. Chant is not an obscure ritual—it is the important tool used by people everywhere to heal their bodies, quiet their minds, and bring the sacred into their lives. Chant unifies; it brings people together in thought intention, knowledge, and love."

Chanting is an ancient, timeless, way of meditation, prayer, and contemplation. "Chant is singing our prayers; chant is vocal meditation," writes my friend Robert Gass in his fine book *Chanting: Discovering Spirit in Sound.* Sacred sound transports us beyond ourselves, enchants the heart and mind, connects us with the higher power of the universe—however we may conceive of it—and helps return us to the natural state of wholeness and completeness. Chanting is a body-mind-spirit healing and harmonizing practice that cannot fail to edify and awaken the best in us.

Yoga means union. Chanting helps us to merge, dissolve, and experience divine union. Chanting yoga involves the body, mind, and spirit; it utilizes intention, concentration, the breath, the heartbeat, chest, lungs, voice, tongue, mouth, and our entire being. It is both relaxing and therapeutic, while providing direct access to meditative states and higher realms of subtle spiritual experience. Chanting can awaken our subtle energy and stimulate kundalini arising and other forms of energetic breakthroughs and epiphanies. I have had some of my most moving visions while chanting for hours at a time, especially in Tibetan Buddhist retreats where we chant an average of eight to ten hours a day, and on high holidays as much as twenty-four hours at a time or seven days in a row (and even more) without stopping. If that does not change your consciousness, nothing will!

During my first trip to the Himalayas, in 1971, I received the hundred-syllable purification mantra of the Buddha Vajrasattva from my first Tibetan guru, Lama Thubten Yeshe. He lived with Lama Zopa Rinpoche in his small monastery on a hilltop called Kopan outside Kathmandu. I very much wanted to do a solo meditation retreat, having experienced only group retreats until that time, and the lama obligingly sent me up to a hut on Mount Shivapuri, which towered above the Kathmandu Valley, with the instructions to chant the mantra and listen to the sound of the waterfall. He taught me the famous Hundred-Syllable Mantra of Vajrasattva, the Diamond Being, designed to vibrate in all the hundred states of consciousness. Devout Tibetan Buddhists are expected to chant this long mantra at least one hundred thousand times over the course of their lives.

I had just turned twenty-one and was eager to get started. My few belongings in my backpack, I hiked up to a place called Tat-apani ("hot springs"). Settling into my tiny mud hut with its wood-and-thatched roof, I chanted and chanted, broken only by light meals of tsampa (roasted barley flour) and tea. I was trying for four to five thousand repetitions per day—about twelve hours' worth. I sat by the waterfall, day after day, chanting my brains out. I don't know how many days I had been chanting when I first had this vision of becoming a beautiful crystal chalice that was being filled up with pure light. There was so much energy that I stayed up all night chanting *Om Vajra Sattva Samaya Manu Palaya Vajra Sattva Teno Patisa,* again and again, all hundred syllables of the purification mantra.

As the hours passed, I experienced becoming more and more transparent. Thoughts and perceptions floated across the clear screen of my awareness as if in slow motion. It was as if the crystal chalice were filling up with blissful nectar. The sound of the mantra and the sound of the waterfall were one. I no longer knew whether it was I or the waterfall that was chanting the mantra; whether I was chanting the waterfall, or the waterfall was chanting me. I suppose my lips were still moving, but it was truly something other than me and my finite, egoic self that was chanting.

Every moment seemed like the eternal now—neither long nor short—out of time, totally timeless. I felt clear, vast, and luminous like the sky, like the sun and even beyond the sun, a diamond-light being—luminous consciousness. All my five senses folded in toward the center like an umbrella, withdrawing from this world as through the eye of a needle. I became empty awareness. It was all Vajrasattva, the Diamond Being, reflections of a field of infinite Buddhas. It was me, and not me. I was them. Everything was included.

At a certain point, like all experiences, it was over. The umbrella opened—empty, transparent, radiant awareness unfolded out back into the five senses, and I was in my body again, sitting by the hot springs, back in Nepal, feeling totally purified. One week later, I went back down the mountain to Kopan, and told Lama Yeshe of my electrifying revelation. He just laughed, and said: "American boy's dream. You too much! Have some tea." Then we had tea, and that was that.

By concentrating in a skillful manner on different chakras and internal energy channels (*nadis*), you can unleash the prana (subtle energy, vital force) and vastly open different aspects of yourself, bringing out various enlightened qualities that are inherent in your spiritual being. For example, opening the heart chakra brings out love; opening the throat chakra brings out dynamism, creativity, power, and abilities far beyond those of mortal men. The forehead chakra holds the treasury of clairvoyance and psychic clarity, knowledge of past and future lives, and so on. The crown chakra overflows with bliss; it is seen as a thousand-petaled lotus, like a fountain throwing out millions of radiant drops of bliss. All of this is taught, and a lot more, in the extensive Six Yogas of the Tibetan energy movement system—the Vajra Yogas—which stem from the original Yoga Sutra teachings of ancient India combined with later tantric developments. It is important to remember, I think, that all that joy, bliss, and ecstasy one hears about is within us. That's the amazing part. My old friend Bob Thurman. "Mr. Tibet," says:

> In the Vajrayana yoga system, you learn to enter your own subtle body and subtle nervous system, where each moment contains the universe and all of evolutionary causality. You can unravel the seventy-two-thousand knots of the energy channels and open up the pure flow of bliss. As you feel rigidity and materiality dissolve, and the self-grasping loosens, you begin to realize great relief and even bliss. That is why monks and nuns and yogis in the forests and retreat caves and hermitages are having such a great time. They are opening up the neural, Reichian armoring and feeling the bliss of the freely flowing universal energies.

Making Your Life a Mantra

There are so many different kinds of mantras and chants. We have one-syllable mantras like *Ah* and *Om,* and names of deities like Ram that are repeated as mantra meditations. There are long mantras like the Hundred-Syllable Mantra, the Purification Mantra of Vajrasattva, plus everything in between. There are even longer ones than the Hundred-Syllable Mantra. There are *dharanis,* a type of ritual speech similar to a mantra. There are healing mantras and obstacle-removing mantras. There are wisdom mantras and compassion mantras. There are wrathful mantras and peaceful mantras. One interpretation of the name of Avalokiteshvara is the "Sound That Illumines the World." Thus, when we're talking about chanting, we're talking about not only hearing the outcries of the world, but then compassionately pouring out upon the world that which we have most deeply heard through our listening—pouring out prajna paramita (transcendental wisdom) just as Avalokiteshvara did in the Heart Sutra.

Life is mysterious, and our lives are complex, especially these days. To simplify things, try making your whole life into mantra. I don't mean to say that we have to just repeat *Om Mani Padme Hung* all day long, or whatever our mantra collection may include. What we need is to cultivate that attitude—every breath as mantra, every breath as a prayer; then our entire life becomes grace-full and prayerful. If you're a jogger or marathon runner, you could take every step as like a mantra. Every step can be like a tiny, complete meditation, by placing your full attention on it. Every time you touch the good earth you could be making the spiritual connection, if you consciously hold that sacred intention. The venerable master Thich Nhat Hanh has generated an entire collection of four-line chants called *gathas* (mindfulness practice verses) to be used for each activity of daily life. He says:

"Chants and recitations are very important here at Plum Village, and can be used both in daily life and for special occasions. They help us to strengthen our practice of mindfulness, nourishing the wholesome seeds of love and understanding within us and renewing our determination to be aware and awake to the present moment." For example, when you meet and greet someone, you bow, join your hands palm-to-palm at your heart, and say or think: "A lotus for you, a Buddha-to-be." When you sit down, you can recite, either aloud or to yourself: "Sitting here is like sitting under the Bodhi Tree. My body is mindfulness itself, calm and at ease, free from distraction."

When lighting a candle, chant: "Respectful of countless Buddhas, I calmly light this candle, brightening the face of this earth." When contemplating a plate of food before eating, say: "Beings all over the earth are struggling to live. May we practice so that all may have enough to eat." While drinking tea, remind yourself by intoning: "This cup of tea in my two hands, mindfulness is held uprightly. My body and mind dwell in the very here and now." When washing dishes, chant: "Washing the dishes is like bathing a baby Buddha. The profane is sacred. Everyday mind is Buddha's mind."

My late Tibetan master Drukpa Thuksay Rinpoche had a whole handwritten book of mantras and chants to be used for every activity and every single step of the way along the path of daily life. He had a mantra he'd say when sitting down, and another when standing up; a mantra to cross the threshold, and another when actually entering a room. Needless to say he had plenty of prayers and mantras to chant before and after meals, at dawn and dusk, at midday, on full moons, new moons, solstices and equinoxes, holidays, auspicious places and pilgrimage sites, and so forth. Rinpoche has a special mantra for healing, a mantra for the dead and dying, a mantra for every part of the body, a mantra to bless animals, and prayers and mantras for all and every occasion as well as others for every kind of priestly activity—all doubtless learned by rote one-by-one at the foot of his own master Gyalwang Drukchen Rinpoche XI in Tibet long ago. He even had a mantra for sitting on the pot!

Once when he visited us at our retreat center in the Dordogne Valley of southern France, he was so busy saying his mantras and snapping his fingers after each one while packing and washing in the bathroom, as the cars idled outside in the parking lot, that he and his party missed the train back to Paris and had to delay their departure until the following day. My New York motor-mind wondered if there weren't an American mantra that could speed up Rinpoche, when necessary.

Something sacred happens when we chant, meditate, sing, and even more so when we really let our true music out. We must get our true music out, and in any number of ways. We don't want to die and leave this world with our music locked away inside. Let's not get confused and think our music can only be sacred chants, hymns, liturgies, and prayers like *Om Mani Padme Hung* or *Shma Y'isroal.* Our choice of lyrics might be different. Chanting and prayer provide a deep and rooted, coherent center, buttressing us against feeling harried, fragmented, assaulted on all sides. We can learn to settle down through sacred music and more gracefully handle things, through finding and keeping the harmonious rhythm of our own true inner music. This is where using a mantra regularly, and maybe even adding in the use of handheld mala beads, can help as a centering device. I like to listen to chant tapes of all kinds while driving my car, while the miles fly by.

Buddha said, "Mind comes first. Before deed and words comes thought or intention. So guard carefully your own mind." Mantras have power. Mudras, hand gestures, have power. Yantras, or visualizations, and mandalas have power. Of course, it is the concentrated power of the mind that invests in them such resonance. Chanting is an important part of daily practice; don't leave home without it! Singing is believing.

CHAPTER 16

ALTAR PRACTICE

I love altar practice. My home shrine helps focus my spiritual practice and create sacred space, and my meditation seat in that small room daily invites me to practice. Not that you necessarily need an altar or too many other kinds of props for following the path of awakening, but altars are a beautiful part of spiritual life, like private shrines, sanctuaries, gardens, churches, liturgies, and sacred art. If I don't have time for an hour or thirty minutes of meditation, just bowing and offering candles and incense for a minute or two makes quite a difference to my inner state of mind, and therefore to my entire day. Just entering that sacred space calms and centers me, brings feelings of blessings and spiritual solidarity, and helps to provide the joyous gratitude and clear awareness that I delight in through contemplative practice.

You might like to create a home altar or a shrine room, meditation room, or sanctuary as a support for your daily meditation, chanting, and prayers. What are the essentials in a true Buddhist altar? I would say the only thing you need is one holy image: a statue, picture, or even a natural object like a stone you might happen to love, or a flower, a candle, a crystal. A Buddha statue is the most common. Besides that, there are many additional options.

The late Chinese Buddhist teacher Yogi Chen says, on the many meanings of setting up a Buddhist altar:

- To invoke holy beings to come down and stay so as to enrich the wisdom and compassion of the practitioner and his family daily until perfect enlightenment is achieved.

- All sorts of attendant practices such as prostrations, offerings, praises, and so forth are included in the daily practices before the shrine, which helps develop bodhicitta (altruistic spiritual aspiration) and fulfill the accumulations of merit and wisdom necessary for the ultimate achievement of enlightenment.

- By means of gazing at Buddhas, lighting lamps, burning incense, offering flowers, prostrating, sacred chants and music, and so on, the functions of the five sense organs are completely absorbed in the Buddhist practices and hence the purification of the practitioner's mind is enhanced and accelerated.

- It is easier to form a habit of contemplative practice by performing daily practices at a routine place in the home, as well as at a regular time.

- The elegant simplicity, serenity, and even grandeur of a Buddhist altar evinces the practitioner's faith in Buddha-Dharma-sangha as a refuge and reliance and gives both family members and visitors chances of becoming acquainted with the delight and benefits of such practices.

Altar practice is something children can participate in, even before they're old enough to study sacred texts, meditate, or perform the animal-like yoga stretches that children enjoy so much. The basic altar is a focus of spiritual inspiration and beauty; it could be simply a candle or candelabra, or a flower or flowers, a crystal, a holy icon, a picture of a saint or religious leader, or an object endowed with personal meaning, reverentially placed in a clean and raised place. There are many levels of meaning secreted in these offering traditions; for example, lighting candles—an ancient spiritual custom common to all world religions—can be said to represent the kindling of inner awareness and the development of the wisdom that illuminates the darkness of ignorance. In fact, one of the greatest lamas I ever met, Kunu Rinpoche—the Dalai Lama's revered yoga teacher—

wrote a lovely song of enlightenment about how each of the eight offerings is actually a mystical practice, far beyond the duality of donor and recipient, of self and object of offering. If you think the bowing is anything like idol worship, consider the Buddhist understanding that to grok the fact that there is nothing to bow to and no one bowing is truly an act of reverence.

How to Set Up an Altar

A simple Buddhist altar has a Buddha statue or picture, and a candle, incense, fruit, and/or flowers. Buddhist altars should be set in the east; this is because the Buddha himself sat facing east beneath the Bodhi Tree in Bodh Gaya, when he espied the morning star and experienced great enlightenment. The east is where the sun rises, illumining us all. Of course one could visualize this as being the case, regardless of where the altar is most conveniently placed because of conditions and circumstances.

A traditional Tibetan Buddhist altar has specific elements, on three levels. On the uppermost level is a central Buddha statue, and perhaps subsidiary statues. Other images, such as pictures and statues of lineage masters and gurus, would be arrayed on the second level or tier, along with symbolic elements such as a stupa, a reliquary, holy relics, a Dharma wheel, vital Buddhist texts, a mandala, crystal, conch shell, censer, bell, gong, and peacock feathers. For simplicity's sake, it is taught that you need three things on a Tibetan altar to represent the Three Jewels of refuge—sangha, Dharma, and Buddha—and the Buddha's body, speech, and mind. These are a *rupa* (statue), a Dharma text, and a *stupa* (pagoda-shaped reliquary).

In front of these, often on a lower third tier, are offerings to the above holy objects. These are represented by the eight traditional offering bowls, placed in a straight line, approximately one-eighth inch apart from each other. They are filled with either water or the various individual offerings: water for drinking, water for washing, flowers, incense, light (candles, lamp), perfume, food and music, and something representing clean clothes, such as a piece of silk. These eight traditional offerings represent the things a devoted Buddhist householder in ancient India would offer the living Buddha and his monks and nuns when they came to visit. They are called the eight auspicious or significant offerings because they are associated with the arising of Buddhist teachings in the world. We generally make offerings to practice generosity (dana paramita, the first transcendental virtue of the bodhisattva), and to accumulate merits and good karma so that our practice and wisdom may have the conditions necessary to fully develop.

Another interpretation of the eight offering bowls is according to the seven- or eight-limbed offering *puja* (rite) chanted while performing prostrations and taking refuge. This prayer includes the seven or eight limbs of prayer (for blessings and inspiration); bows (of respect and reverence); offering (generosity); confession (acknowledgment of nonvirtues and defects); rejoicing (in the merits and positive qualities of oneself and others); requesting (the Buddhas to remain in this world); beseeching (the Buddhas to teach); and dedicating (the merits and good karma of the practice) for the benefit of all beings without exception.

In general, offerings can be categorized into four types: outer, inner, secret, and ultimate. These would include outer, material offerings such as those listed above; internally offering up and letting go of our internal experiences, feelings, and so forth; secretly relinquishing attachment to our body, our self-clinging, and our life, not to mention the things of this world; and, ultimately, letting go totally and just being, at one with and dissolved in naked reality itself, as it is.

Tantric altars also call for an offering *torma* (handmade cake) and a *serkyim* (goblet for offering tantric oblations, such as meat and wine, or tea and crackers or cookies). Other wrathful offerings might also be placed here, thought to be pleasing to the fierce guardians of the Dharma: snakeskins, skull cups, and so forth. This is in accord with the tantric principle of transmuting the shadow side into light and, through wisdom, turning afflictions into serumlike protection. Many Tibetan shrines and temples have an entire room or separate, smaller temple dedicated to propitiating these *Dharmapalas,* called the Protectors Temple; alternately, you can place an altar dedicated to the guardian protectors at the rear of your shrine room or temple, using darker motifs than the bright, lovely main Buddha shrine at the head of the room.

Blessings

It is fortunate if you can have your spiritual teacher or a holy man or woman bless your altar, meditation room, Buddha statue, *tangka* scroll, mala beads, and stupa. It is usually taught that Buddha rupas (statues, images) are filled with sacred relics and consecrated in a blessed manner to transform them from mere metal or wood and paint into genuinely potent live representations of the Buddha. However, it is not absolutely necessary, as faith alone can infuse objects with sacred power and blessings, as many religious traditions of the world demonstrate through their veneration of the bones, clothes, and other relics of the saints.

In an amusing traditional Tibetan teaching tale, included in my book *The Snow Lion's Turquoise Mane: Wisdom Tales from Tibet,* an old woman venerates a dog's tooth she misconstrues as a holy tooth relic of the Buddha, brought from India by her son; nonetheless, her constant prayers and sincere devotion actually transform her, and bring meaningful blessings and inspiration to her entire hamlet. Although a dog's tooth usually contains few blessings, the power of unswerving faith and devotion ensured that the blessings of Buddha would, as it were, enter that tooth and help fulfill the pure-hearted devotee's sincere prayers and wishes. In such a way the forms of our own sincere devotional practices can act in a supportive fashion for our own spiritual practices and inner development.

For the sake of simplicity, you could just place a cement garden Buddha in your yard, and sit where you can see it through a window of your home. Or put a single object on a small table, perhaps along with a candle or some flowers; you could also use a picture of your spiritual teacher as the altar's focus, or place it alongside a main Buddha image. In addition to the altar itself, you will need the support of a regularly scheduled time suitable for your practice, and a practice "recipe"—that is, what you will do in the beginning, middle, and end of your practice. Remember and appreciate the benefits of meditation in connecting us to the deepest part of ourSelves, our Buddha nature.

I have tried to have a meditation room since 1971 when I began practicing. When short of space, I have also used a corner of my bedroom, walk-in closet, attic, basement, garage, outdoor tool shed, screened-in porch, tent, yurt, cave, and any number of other quiet nooks and crannies along the way for my meditation seat and shrine. I love to create sacred spaces, temples, and shrines, as well as retreats where people can join in this joyous, timeless path of awakening. Sitting outdoors is also delightful. Regarding this kind of natural, old-time religion, our reclusive Massachusetts mystic Emily Dickinson wrote, in Amherst in 1860:

Some keep the Sabbath going to Church—
I keep it, staying at Home—
With a Bobolink for a Chorister—
And an Orchard, for a Dome—

Some keep the Sabbath in Surplice—
I just wear my Wings—
And instead of tolling the Bell, for Church,
Our little Sexton—sings.

God preaches, a noted Clergyman—
And the sermon is never long,
So instead of getting to Heaven, at last—
I'm going, all along.

I love the great cathedrals of Europe, and the great temples of the world, many of which I have visited on my six around-the-world journeys. I have seen some incredible sacred altars and shrines—indoors and outdoors; gilded and elaborate; simple and made of natural materials; ancient and modern; and of all kinds. However, the truth is that this world itself is the ultimate church, and nature is the greatest altar. The holy *now* is heaven on earth—or at least can be, when we are fully awake to it. To me, a mountain, the ocean and the desert at sunset, a power place where rivers meet, where bubbling waters fall, or an old redwood forest forms a cathedral-like canopy—these are my favorite sanctuaries. This is why many saints and sages have found in the wilderness what they were looking for: Moses, Mohammed, Lao Tzu, St. Francis, Milarepa. Gotama Buddha became enlightened sitting beneath a pilpul tree. One hundred and fifty years ago, the great meditation master Patrul Rinpoche of Tibet renounced worldly life and vowed never to sleep inside. Even Thoreau, who wore a white shirt and frock coat much of the time, said he had to spend at least four hours a day walking outdoors through the woods and fields of his beloved Concord or he became rusty, and his two years living in nature in a hand-hewn cabin at sylvan Walden Pond have become legendary.

There is no need to seek afar and travel overmuch when all that we seek is available within. What we seek, we *are*. All and everything is It. We can appreciate being *there* while getting there, every step of the way. Being *here* while getting there. "This very land is the Pure Land, nirvana; this very body the body of Buddha," as Hakuin Zenji sang. This earth is like an altar, and all beings like gods and goddesses walking on it. Cultivate that sacramental vision, and your perceptions will be purified; heaven will unfold before your eyes. Fully inhabit the holy now. *This* is the ultimate fruit of altar practice.

CHAPTER 17

TIBETAN ENERGY YOGA

I first experienced yoga in college at Buffalo in the late 1960s but couldn't really practice it regularly at that time. It seemed impossible to thoroughly take up the healthy and simplified spiritual lifestyle advocated by yoga philosophy in those turbulent days, good as it may have seemed to me. My first yoga teacher in India was Ed Torop from Connecticut, whom his guru called Tukaram. We used to practice together every day in February of 1972, outside in the sun along the banks of the Ganges. Tukaram taught me Integral Yoga according to the system of Swami Satchidananda. At night we would go to see the radiant, silent Mother Nature–like saint Anandamayi-Ma at her riverside ashram overlooking the stone ghats by the Ganges, and chant *kirtan*—devotional hymns—with her and her followers. After a few months, I went myself to Sivananda's ashram in Rishikish, in the Himalayas at the source of the Ganges, for more serious study and yoga practice.

A thin young boy came every morning to wake me up at 4:45 a.m. He didn't speak English or say much at all, saying only "*Om*" when communication was required—in greeting, thanks, good-bye, whatever. I myself felt like a man of many words. In his hands before dawn each day was a rough clay cup full of hot, sweet Indian chai, which he handed to me with a respectful little bow. He must have been around nine or ten years old. I later found out he was one of several orphan boys the ashram had adopted and educated. After tea, I would go off to the ice-cold river for morning ablutions, sans soap, and then to the outdoor yoga room for ritual chanting, followed by morning hatha instruction from one of the saffron-clad, shaved-pate swamis, which always ended with sitting meditation. Breakfast of yogurt, bananas, fruit, and tea was after 7:30. Sometimes there was morning *darshan—satsang,* spiritual audience—with the ashram's master at that time, Swami Krishnananda or Premananda, I can't remember which. I do remember clearly that eminent swami as a blissful lover of God and unfailingly gracious, patient, and kind to us eager young seekers who sat at his feet. A few days a week he would give us a discourse on Hindu dharma: Patanjali's Yoga Sutras, the Bhagavad Gita, the ancient Upanishads—always something deep and rich. Occasionally he sang the holy Sanskrit verses.

That was the daily routine. It was very peaceful there, a sanctuary of quietude amid the gentle noises of the communal life of Rishikish, the capital of yogis. There was holy chanting and altar rituals, including candles, flowers, incense, sprinkling sacramental substances, and bowing. Small group yoga sessions, meditation, and prayers took place each afternoon and early evening. In between times, left to myself, I would read in the small ashram library, take a siesta, or explore the banks of the Ganges, where wandering sadhus (holy men) lived in thatched or mud huts, damp caves, under embankments, and amid the rocks. One of my favorite jerry-rigged, handmade, lean-to-like shelters was made entirely out of flattened vegetable oil tins that an Indian had hammered together into sheets.

Rishikish is like a mecca for ascetic sadhus. There were holy men, and an occasional holy woman, too, of all sects and descriptions: naked, ash-covered naga babas; matted-hair-to-their-ankles babas, chillum-smoking wild-eyed Siva babas, duni babas who always kept their sacred fire alive and carried a live coal when they traveled; chanting Krishna devotees; all kinds of outlandish ascetics; and meditation yogis who sat for hours without respite upstream from town in the blazing sun or on a flat boulder overhanging the cascading river's torrent. Some practiced easily recognizable contemplative exercises, including prayer, pujas (liturgical rites including chanting), yoga asanas (postures), scriptural recitation, fire offerings, and so on; others were engaged in esoteric practices obscure to me. There were ascetic sadhus who slept on beds of nails or thick thorns; or who stood in place with palms together in a gesture of prayer day and night; or who walked around with a stone attached by a cord to a wizened old phallus that hung long like a pendant, to keep it from desire through suppressing the possibility of erection. One hirsute, photogenic character kept one arm upraised with the fist clenched until the fingernails had grown through the palm and out the other side of his hand. What this had to do with worship or spiritual wisdom was never quite clear to me. Perhaps extreme asceticism cracks the shell of attachment to pleasure and pain; however, the true intent of yoga is to coax the clenched, egoic mind (or small self) into letting go of the perceptions and misconceptions that keep it stuck in unfulfilling, habitual karmic patterns so it can ultimately expand and reveal itself as it really is—light, limitless, peaceful, blissful, and powerful.

I am sure nothing has changed in Rishikish, where *rishis* (savants and seers) gather at the head of the Ganges, a timeless pilgrimage place where these customs have been carried on for millennia. Some of these mendicants were saintly and were reputed to have extraordinary powers and abilities, including healing, clairvoyance, and prognostication, mind reading, living without food or sleep, and other miracles. Others were certainly quite mad. Most, not unlike myself, probably fell somewhere in between. In India, being a homeless sadhu is a respectable lifestyle. Many Hindu men resort to this lifestyle after retirement, when their families are secure, for renunciation and "wandering forth alone" is the traditional fourth and final stage of Hindu sacred life. Every twelve years, tens of millions of these sadhus gather on the full moon at the *sangham* (spiritual confluence) near Allahabad in northern India, at the junction of three holy rivers called the Triuvana, for the week-long full-moon Kumbha Mela, the world's largest religious festival. Last year's festival was shown on the cover of the *New York Times,* with a picture and a caption about the several hundred million pilgrims and holy men in attendance. These large numbers are no exaggeration.

All these sadhus, swamis, and babas practice yoga of one kind or another. There are many pathways to God, or ways to practice and progress in spiritual development. In Eastern thought, *yoga* is a term that can subsume them all. *Yoga* literally means "union," "connection," or "oneness." Today in the West, we typically understand *yoga* to mean a series of gentle stretching exercises, which is basically Hatha Yoga. However, the term *yoga* can and does refer to any of a number of physical and mental disciplines, all of which are designed to reunite us with our sacred energy source: the divine, reality, truth, wisdom, and love—Dharma.

In the second century CE, the Indian yogi Patanjali—who is often referred to as the Father of Yoga—codified the millennia-old yoga tradition in his *Yoga Sutras.* Master Patanjali outlined eight specific principles, each of which can provide an entire practice path intended to reunite the seeker with God or the original, primordial, natural state of inner perfection and divine oneness.

The Eight Yogic Principles or Practices

1. Ethical behavior
2. Self-discipline
3. Bodily postures (asanas)

4. Breath control
5. Turning inward
6. Concentration
7. Meditation
8. Ecstatic absorption

Among the various forms that abide by these principles are physical (*hatha*) yoga, mantra (*japa*) yoga, kundalini yoga, meditation (*raja*) yoga, breath/energy yoga, diet and fasting yoga, chanting yoga, work (*karma*) yoga, devotional (*bhakti*) yoga, knowledge (*jnana*) yoga, and visualization yoga. All these can be practiced alone, in pairs, or with a group.

Yoga practice is based on the ancient adepts' timeless understanding of the threefold nature and sacred inner power of the human body, mind, and spirit. According to this view, all phenomena operate simultaneously at three levels of reality: outer, inner, and secret/innermost. The outer level refers to that which is evident to our ordinary perception. The inner level is the more subtle meaning, where the personal lessons and energies reside. The secret level contains the ultimate teaching—the inner truth that we all seek can be found within. Recognizing the potential for profound and transformative yogic experience, the contemporary meditation master Namkhai Norbu Rinpoche translates the Tibetan word for yoga (*naljyor*) as "primordial knowledge and understanding, through which we discover our authentic condition"—who and what we truly are. My Tibetan teachers say *yoga* in Tibetan language means "reuniting with the innate natural state." In the scheme of the Tibetan tantric tradition, Ati Yoga (Dzogpa Chenpo) is the highest, deepest, primordial yoga, the vajra shortcut, providing immediate access to the enlightened state.

Modern science has found that yoga practitioners enjoy many physical and metaphysical benefits. These include stress reduction, relaxation, enhanced health and well-being, inner calm, improved memory and mental acuity, increased flexibility, vitality, sexual prowess, better sleep, fuller respiration, rejuvenation, and longevity. For these reasons, yoga has been called "the ultimate exercise." In all its forms, it effectively purifies, refines, and revitalizes the body and mind while unblocking the subtle nervous system. (Left untended, blockages in this "energy body" or "light body" can inhibit body and mind, spirit, soul, and psyche, causing imbalances, illnesses mental and physical, karmic disturbances and obstacles, mental and physical illness, and so on.) Long-term yoga practice and inner development can also produce psychic powers and other extraordinary abilities.

Like meditation and prayer, yoga practice represents a daily mental and physical hygiene that opens us to the wisdom and truth within ourselves, lending meaning, clarity, and joy to all the facets of our lives. Yoga is an organic body-mind-spirit healing and wholifying discipline. Yoga is gentle meditation in movement. It helps us reconnect the tangible, material world with the more subtle, invisible spiritual world.

Yoga for Meditation

Buddhism is known for its many schools of spiritual thought and practice. Tibetan Buddhism is unique among Buddhist traditions in presenting a complete yoga system. Tibetan Yoga is designed to support meditation, release our inner energies, and help bring about self-realization and enlightenment.

I learned Tibetan Yoga and the six Vajrayana practices from my first lama, Thubten Yeshe, in Nepal. Later much more came from Lama Kalu Rinpoche, who taught the famous Six Yogas of Naropa to the Fourteenth Dalai Lama, and from my own gurus and instructors in our three-year cloistered Dzogchen retreat: Dudjom Rinpoche, Dilgo Khyentse Rinpoche, and Tulku Pema

Wangyal. We used to practice it in four intensive two-hour sessions each day, which were then reduced to two, two-hour sessions a day after a few months. After about six months, I began doing the Six Yogas outdoors every morning with my personal mentor Nyoshul Khenpo Rinpoche before dawn, even in winter, which we continued for a few years.

Tibetan Yoga derives from the most ancient yogic traditions of India and the Himalayas. It reaches us today through an unbroken lineage of spiritually realized Himalayan yogis. These practices have been passed down over centuries through oral tradition and meditation manuals—handed down directly, teacher to student, all the way to us today. Tibetan Yoga has two main paths: the Path of Mind-Essence Yoga (*drol-lam,* or liberating path), and the Path of Energy Yoga (*tab-lam,* or skillful means). The first is more like meditation, and includes Mahamudra and Dzogchen; the latter is more like what we usually think of as yoga, including postures and movements, intensive breathing exercises, inner energy work, visualization, and so forth.

Tibetan Yoga combines the best of the physical, emotional, psychological, energetic, intuitive, psychic, healing, spiritual, and meditative arts. These come together in an enlightening, balancing, and healing system known as the Six Lightning (Vajrayana) Yogas, or the Six Yogas of Tibet—active and contemplative practices designed to help us reach perfect harmony and full actualization of the marvelous powers inherent in our body, speech (i.e., energy), and heart/mind (the *citta,* or consciousness). There are various forms of the basic Six Yogas, such as the Six Yogas of Naropa, the Six Yogas of Dakini Niguma, the Six Yogas of Padmasambhava, and so forth, according to the different major and minor schools of Buddhism in Tibet. However, the Six Yogas are generally the same in each tradition, regardless of utilizing slightly different liturgical rituals, visualizations, and related appurtenances.

The Six Yogas

1. *Tummo: Inner Heat Yoga,* or mystic incandescence. This is the foundation stone of the skillful path of the Six Yogas.
2. *Gyulu: Illusory Body Yoga.* This is the reliance on the path.
3. *Milam: Dream Yoga.* This is the yardstick on the path.
4. *Osel: Inner Light Yoga,* or luminosity (clear light). This is the essence of the path.
5. *Bardo: Intermediate State Yoga,* or afterlife practice. This is what is encountered on the path.
6. *Phowa: Consciousness Transference Yoga.* This is the core of the path.

In brief, these practices—known generally in Tibetan as *tsa-lung trulkhor,* or yogic energy movements—involve *tsa, lung,* and *tigle:* channels, prana (energy), and sphere of consciousness. These Vajrayana *trulkhor* exercises of the Six Yogas practice bring about the purification, harmonizing, and liberation of all facets of our physical, emotional, energetic, and psychospiritual being through intensive, thoroughgoing, disciplined yoga practice and meditation over a sustained period of time. The Six Yogas practice is based on mantra and tantra, empowerment, visualization, commitment, and other preparations.

The actual practices, empowering initiations, and related liturgies should be learned from a qualified teacher of the lineage. On this particularly profound and powerful path, skilled guidance is indispensable, for there can be pitfalls and dangers involved. Miraculous powers can also be gained through this path, which can prove to be either a distraction or an aid to the ultimate accomplishment of enlightenment. Stories abound concerning those who have fallen off the path by being overly attached to the inconceivable bliss, powers, or other side effects advanced yogis are said to achieve. This is one reason my own teacher Kalu Rinpoche mainly taught the Six Yogas only during long retreats for committed practitioners, such as cloistered three-year retreats, and the esoteric teachings themselves are considered secret. However, my first Tibetan teacher Lama Thubten Yeshe taught the Six Yogas to a few western Dharma students at his little Kopan Monastery in Nepal, starting in the 1970s. Lama Yeshe said that although these tummo practices are part of the most advanced Tibetan tantra teachings, he wanted to give students a taste of the inexhaustible treasure of blissful energy existing within each and every one of us right at the present moment, when time is short, and authentically liberating and transformative BuddhaDharma is dissipating in the world. This pioneering effort was certainly effective for me in studying with him in Katmandu Valley in the early 1970s.

Lama Yeshe in his book *The Bliss of Inner Fire* said: "We really need tantra these days because there is a tremendous explosion of delusion and distraction . . . and we need the atomic energy of inner fire to blast us out of our delusion. . . . The human body is the gold mine of tantra; it is our most precious possession." He believed that mastery of tummo, the inner fire as the first of the Six Yogas, quickly brings the mind to its most refined and penetrating state—the experience of clear light, an extraordinarily powerful state of mind and refined state of subtle consciousness that is unequaled in its ability to directly realize ultimate reality. *The Bliss of Inner Fire* explains this practice and its results.

The Six Yogas were brought to Tibet more than a thousand years ago by Indian Buddhist masters and Tibetan translator/sages, including Vairocana and Marpa, who trekked to India, spent years studying and practicing there, and then brought them back to the Land of Snows. Since that time, this profound and powerful Tibetan Energy Yoga for meditation has remained one of the main practices of esoteric Tibetan Buddhism. The Six Yogas traditionally include 112 exercises and asanas, along with an intense, two-hour physical exercise workout (traditionally called *trulkhor,* or "exercise movements"). Some traditions have even more movements and positions, both major and minor.

The scriptural underpinnings of Tibetan Energy Yoga can be found in the mystical Tibetan tantric text known as *The Union of Sun and Moon,* or *Realizing the Oneness of All Polarities.* This eighth-century Dzogchen teaching stresses the reintegration of all dualities, beginning with the solar/lunar and masculine/feminine energies. Harmonizing these complementary forces within our internal energy system, and bringing them all into the central channel—the main nadi or central energy pathway within the inner light body, analogous to the spiritual spinal column— spontaneously liberates our own inexhaustible inner energy flow and awakens our energy body, blissfully opening all the chakras and channels in ascending order, thus helping us evolve and ultimately realize perfect enlightenment. According to the Dzogchen tradition, Tantric Yoga helps us realize that each of us is like a god or goddess; that our bodies are temples, and that this world is like an altar; that we are nonseparate and interconnected; that we are already innately awake and complete and possessed of pristine awareness; that we can be as wise, liberated, peaceful, loving, and free as an enlightened Buddha; and that each moment and every single contact is sacred, holy, miraculous.

As the ancient Hindu Upanishad scriptures say, "Knowledge comes alive only through practice."

The Role of Breathing in Tibetan Energy Yoga

Breath is the juncture between body, mind, and spirit. Conscious breath training accomplishes self-mastery of mind and energy, leading to limitless benefits.

In Tibetan Energy Yoga, we work with breath on the outer, inner, and secret levels:

- Externally, the air and the mechanics of the breathing process
- Internally, the *prana/qi* (the subtle, psychic, or vital energies that constitute our life force)

- Secretly, pure spirit/awareness, through which we realize and actualize ourselves as luminous beings of pure energy and light

An important element in the practice of Tibetan Energy Yoga is the subtle understanding of intentional, conscious breathing in relation to the inner energy body—specifically, the chakras (energy centers) and nadis (channels). The prana that moves through these subtle pathways animates us on levels beyond the physical and material. Ultimately, prana is the basic energy of which we are all composed. Our well-being depends on its constant, vital, untrammeled flow throughout the entire body and mind.

The practices of Tibetan Energy Yoga are means of manipulating, training, and better regulating this energy. As we do so, we learn to master our outer and inner selves, ultimately realizing harmony with the entire world. We are able to awaken our untrammeled energy/light body, releasing our higher, wise Self; our natural Buddha within; our deepest heart and soul. Rather than feeling ourselves victims of external circumstances and conditions, we realize our own internal spiritual center and become grounded in the eternal present. Having access to the timeless dimension of our primordial being in the present moment, we are liberated from all conditions and circumstances, even as we realize our oneness with them.

Nine Exercises

From the hundred-plus exercises of tsa-lung trulkhor—the Six Yogas practice of Tibet—I have distilled and essentialized a thirty- to forty-five minute daily workout for my students. Tibetan Energy Yoga comprises nine simple, yet exhilarating exercises based on the esoteric yogic breath and energy meditation techniques described above. Each exercise is repeated three times. You may increase your repetitions to as many as nine per exercise, extending your workout to forty-five or sixty minutes.

All of the exercises are done sitting flat on the ground, in a cross-legged position. If your legs are flexible enough, you might want to sit in a full or half-lotus. Take time to find your point of balance, until you feel your body stable, like a pyramid. Remaining erect in this dignified position, allow yourself to relax completely. Always begin with a sense of delight as you anticipate the rejuvenating experience you are about to enjoy.

First: Breathe in and out a few times. Relax, enjoy, smile.

Now, center yourself, concentrate, and focus.

Visualize and imagine your bodily form as a luminous sphere of bright light and energy, a stainless radiant being, rather than as a corporeal mass of flesh and bones with appendages, head, and such. Let this stay with you throughout the entire exercise cycle (trulkhor).

Now begin.

Exercise 1: Three Deep Breaths

In exercise 1, you will practice the breathing technique that accompanies all the subsequent exercises. This is a simple, three-part breath and energy process:

- Inhaling and filling
- Holding
- Releasing/exhaling

Inhale deeply through your nose and into your *hara:* the center of physical and metaphysical gravity located approximately two finger-widths below your navel. Hold the breath there as long as you can. Then release the breath vigorously through your mouth, nose, and every pore in your body. Repeat three times.

Exercise 2: Alternate-Nostril Breathing

Make "vajra fists" with both hands by touching the tip of your thumb to the base of your ring finger and closing the other fingers over the thumb. This mudra (hand gesture) closes the energy circuit, keeping your life force circulating within the body-mind complex. Let your fists rest near your groin, at the point where the thighs meet the hips.

Breathe in deeply. Now hold the breath at your hara. Still maintaining the vajra fist, extend the forefinger of your left hand. Use the left hand and forefinger to close the left nostril, leaving the right nostril open. Exhale through your right nostril, clearing the right (solar, masculine) channel of your body. Inhale again through both nostrils, and hold the breath while you extend the forefinger of your right vajra fist to close your right nostril. Exhale through your left nostril, entirely clearing the left (lunar, feminine) channel. Inhale deeply, and then exhale through both nostrils, totally emptying and releasing the central channel, and all the eighty-four thousand energy channels of your inner light or vajra (adamantine, diamondlike) body.

Repeat this threefold sequence three times.

Exercise 3: Potbellied Stove Breaths (Bum-Chen)

Form both hands into vajra fists and lay them near your groin, as before. Inhale into your hara; then straighten your elbows and raise your shoulders as you hold the breath. When you feel the need to exhale, unfold your fists and place your outstretched hands on your knees. Release your breath completely with a big rush of exhalation, through your mouth, nose, and fingertips—through all the pores of your body. Repeat three times.

Exercise 4: Swishing It Around (Shilwa)
Begin as in the Potbellied Stove Breath, inhaling with vajra fists
in your groin. While holding the breath at your hara—with arms
straight and shoulders raised, as before—rotate your stomach
muscles three times in each direction. Place your outstretched
hands on your knees and release the breath, as in the previous exercise. Repeat three times.

Exercise 5: The Soaring Garuda
Begin with your hands resting on your knees. As you inhale, raise
your hands in a beckoning motion toward your eyes. Without in-
terrupting the fluid motion of your hands, form them into vajra
fists as you bring them back down to lie in your groin. Straighten
your elbows and raise your shoulders as you hold the breath.
When you release the breath, drop your shoulders and throw
your arms up and out in an expansive gesture, hands open. Repeat three times.

Exercise 6: Threefold Sky Breath
Let your hands rest on your knees. Inhale deeply and hold the
breath at the hara. When you can't hold it anymore, release it
with a great and sustained *Ah* that continues until you are completely empty of breath. Repeat this three times, slowly and
mindfully. Ater the third repetition, hold the exhaled breath out
for a few moments of pseudosunyata, imitation emptiness,
turned inside out and utterly dissolved—before breathing in
again. Then relax, inhale, breathe naturally, and, as it were, come
back to yourself—to your habitual frame of reference.

Exercise 7: Small Jumps (Bep-Chung)
Let your vajra fists lie near the groin. As you inhale, bring your
hands up in the same beckoning gesture you used in exercise 5
(Soaring Garuda). Bring them back to the groin and straighten
your arms as you hold the breath. When you can't hold your

breath any longer, jump by pushing yourself off the ground with your lower legs. At the moment you hit the ground, exhale and fling your arms down hard to both sides. Repeat three times.

Exercise 8: The Lion's Roar
When you have completed your Small Jumps, let your head and torso flop forward and your arms fall loosely to your sides. Shake your head and arms vigorously and roar, almost as you might if something were frustrating you. Repeat the Lion's Roar three times.

Exercise 9: The Rocking Garuda
Begin as before, inhaling with vajra fists in the groin and holding the breath with straightened arms and raised shoulders. On the exhalation, raise yourself onto your knees with legs still crossed and bring your fists together in the heart chakra (in the middle of your chest). Fling your arms down and out as you release the breath, letting out a loud *Hah!* as you do so. Repeat three times.

When you have completed your Rocking Garuda repetitions, give yourself a heart chakra massage. Inhale deeply. While holding the breath, extend your arms out to either side and clap your hands to your chest with a resounding sound. Your hands should be placed one above the other, so that both palms are in full contact with your chest. Vigorously massage your chest and heart area with both hands, three times clockwise and three times counterclockwise. Finally, fling your arms downward to each side as you exhale. Repeat three times.

Completing Your Workout

Conclude your Tibetan Energy Yoga workout by simply resting in the incandescent clarity and vastness of pure presence, of being. Allow every part of your experience—body, breath, mind, and spirit—to relax into its own natural state, natural flow. This so-called nonmeditation is the ultimate yoga—the great perfection. As you let go into things just as they are, you will begin to experience your own primordial being in harmony with everything that is. Just as it is.

End your yoga and meditation session with prayers and/or chants. A useful one is *Om gate gate paragate parasamgate bodhi svaha,* a Sanskrit wisdom mantra that can be translated as "Beyond, beyond, beyond even the beyond, beyond the beyond right here, awakening, marvelous!" It sums up the essence of the Buddhist Perfection of Wisdom (Prajnaparamita) literature, composed sometime between 100 BCE and 100 CE. The text urges the practitioner to help relieve the suffering of all sentient beings by aspiring to realize the Buddha within, for the boundless benefit of one and all.

The path to this goal is nonmeditation: the practice of resting simply in present awareness and innate wakefulness, calm and clear, without striving to attain any particular state of mind or experience. Thus the most beneficial way to chant the mantra is by letting all thoughts and feelings go, and relaxing into the boundless wholeness and delight of authentic primordial being. To experience the wisdom chant in this way is, spiritually speaking, to have "arrived." You are now qualified and able to just "be yourSelf," your true Self, your transpersonal, highest Buddha-ness—not merely the bent-out-of-shape, conflicted, neurotic personality we are usually identified with.

By doing these or any other spiritual practices, we accumulate spiritual merit and good karma, and our fortunes improve. We clear up afflicted old karma and take a further step along the path of spiritual aspiration and ultimate accomplishment. Buddhist tradition recognizes the danger of becoming selfish, prideful, and hoarding such merit for ourselves; this is why all Tibetan Buddhist practices end with a formal "dedication of merit," a declaration of our willingness to share and give away any merit and good karma we may have earned, with the intention that it may be dedicated to the enlightenment of all sentient beings without exception.

You can dedicate the merit formally, with a spoken chant or in whatever way holds personal meaning for you. To do so is to acknowledge the profound interconnectedness of all things, and to realize that none of us is truly free until all of us are free.

May all beings everywhere be benefited
by whatever merit has been accumulated here
through our sincere prayers, practice, and aspirations,
and may we all together reach the wisdom and blissful peace of en-
lightenment.

CHAPTER 18

TIBETAN DREAM YOGA

WHEN THE STATE OF DREAMING HAS DAWNED,
DO NOT LIE IN IGNORANCE LIKE A CORPSE.
ENTER THE NATURAL SPHERE OF UNWAVERING ATTENTIVENESS.
RECOGNIZE YOUR DREAMS AND TRANSFORM ILLUSION INTO LUMINOSITY.
DO NOT SLEEP LIKE AN ANIMAL.
DO THE PRACTICE WHICH MIXES SLEEP AND REALITY.
—TIBETAN INSTRUCTION FOR DREAM YOGA PRACTICE

What is a dream, we might ask? The Dalai Lama of Tibet has said that "Tibetan Buddhism considers sleep to be a form of nourishment, like food, that restores and refreshes the body. Another type of nourishment is samadhi, or meditative concentration. If one becomes advanced enough in the practice of meditative concentration, then this itself sustains or nourishes the body." Dreams are a significant part of our life. They are as real and unreal as life itself. Dreams are extremely personal—and transpersonal, too. Moreover, they can be meaningful, portentous, and even spiritually significant. Our dreams are a reflection of ourselves; in dreams, no matter how many characters appear, we meet ourselves. Henry David Thoreau said: "In dreams we see ourselves naked and acting out our real characters, even more clearly than when we see others awake."

Dreams are mirrors to our soul. They can help us to better understand ourselves, our world, and the nature of reality. Dreams introduce us to other dimensions of experience. Here, time and space are much more liquid and plastic; they can be shaped and reshaped almost at will. Dreams hint of other worlds, other lives. They are a glimpse of our afterlife. "Dreams are real as long as they last. Can we say more of life?" wrote British psychologist and writer Henry Havelock Ellis. Everyone dreams, although not all dreams are remembered equally. Fifty-six percent of Americans have had a lucid dream—that is, a dream in which one is aware that one is dreaming. Twenty-one percent say they have a lucid dream once a month or more. Meditators report vividly clear, self-aware dreams weekly and even more often.

How Dreams Can Help Us

Great healers have long recognized the power of dreams to inform and support us. Hippocrates said, "Dreams are one of the most important ways to diagnose a patient's illness." Sigmund Freud, whose seminal work *The Interpretation of Dreams* marked the beginning of the era of modern psychology and psychoanalysis, wrote: "Dreams are the royal road to the subconscious.

Dreams are the guardian of sleep." Contemporary Tibetan author Tarthang Tulku says: "Dreams are a reservoir of knowledge and experience, yet they are often overlooked as a vehicle for exploring reality."

"A dream not interpreted is like a letter unread," says the Talmud. Certain dreams can convey valuable information to the dreamer. A week before the tragic event at Ford's Theatre, Abraham Lincoln dreamt that he would be assassinated. The emperor Constantine dreamt of radiant Greek letters spelling the name of Christ and was thus converted, leading to the dramatic conversion of the entire Byzantine Empire. I, myself, have received messages, teachings, and blessings through my dreams from the spiritual masters I have known and loved in this lifetime. When I reported these to my Buddhist masters in Asia, they customarily said something amounting to "It was just a dream." However, on occasion, something else can come out of these luminous dreams. I remember once or twice having prognostic dreams, or receiving detailed teachings in dreams—like a tantric transmission from Jamgon Kongtrul Rinpoche I got during a long retreat, called "The Twenty-Seven Pith Instructions of the Wisdom Dakinis." Unfortunately, when I woke in the morning, I could remember nothing more of it than the title! When I told my teacher, Nyoshul Khenpo, about it, on the following day, he said: "Guard and cherish it carefully; it must be in your consciousness somewhere." I remember Samuel Taylor Coleridge's famous question: "What if you slept, and what if in your sleep you dreamed, and what if in your dream you went to heaven and that there you plucked a strange and beautiful flower, and what if when you awoke you had the flower in your hand? Ah, what then?"

Some contemporary psychologists consider lucid dreaming a valuable practice for personal growth. We can read about these dreams in books by Stephen LaBerge, such as *Lucid Dreaming*. This psychological model is, however, somewhat different from

Tibetan Dream Yoga. The spiritual practice goes deeper, helping us work with the great passages of life and death. Tibetan Dream Yoga teaches us how to navigate the groundlessness of moment-to-moment existence, which typically makes no rational, intellectual sense. It is at this level that we cut through the illusory nature of mind and truly experience our marvelous human existence.

Tibetan masters teach that progress in the practices of dream yoga and the Dzogchen practice of the innate light allow us to realize enlightenment as we become exceedingly lucid and aware during sleep. Moreover, those who have penetrated the luminous nature of mind can liberate themselves directly into the clear light at the moment of death. One of the best ways to enhance and develop our dream yoga and inner-light practices is through what Tibetans call the dark retreat: spending days or weeks alone doing this meditation practice and associated visualizations in total darkness, unbroken by the intrusion of external light even during mealtimes or any other necessary physical activity. Forty-nine days would be a classical full dark retreat. I remember my own experience of this retreat, and how hard it was to stay awake in the first few days of darkness when one is without clocks or reference points such as day and night, light and dark; and how it eventually smoothed out into a natural cycle of continuous meditational practice regardless of external variables. One of the most amazing things is how one learns to see in the dark, as it were, when there are no external light sources to depend on; the internal brilliance and luminosity of awareness starts to function more expressly as a source of guidance on its own.

Through dream yoga practice, cultivating our innate ability to wake up within the dream, one can:

- Increase clarity and lucidity, both waking and sleeping
- Realize the transparent, dreamlike nature of experience
- Free the mind, dispel confusion

- Prepare (rehearse) for death and the afterlife
- Receive spiritual blessings, visions, and guidance
- Release energy blockages, accumulated tension, and stress, remove obstacles and hindrances
- Open innate psychic capacities
- Expose fantasies and bring repressions and denials into consciousness
- Unleash and mobilize creativity
- Unlock aspirations and potential
- Solve problems
- Reveal the process of death and rebirth

The twelfth-century Tibetan master Khyungpo Naljyor taught: "In approaching illusory phenomena, one practices illusory practice in an illusory way to attain the illusory state of illusory enlightenment. All phenomena only appear to be real, without actually being so. A fool treats them as if they were real and is therefore confused. But to see that things appear to be real without actually being so is completely marvelous."

Awakening Within the Dream

The Taoist philosopher Chuang Tzu of ancient China once dreamt he was a butterfly. Upon awakening, he wondered whether he was a man who had dreamt he was a butterfly, or a butterfly dreaming he was a man. Chuang Tzu's musings underscore a fundamental truth: life is like a dream. Spiritual life is about awakening from the dream of unreality, awakening from the darkness into the light and from confusion and ignorance into wisdom, clarity, and bliss. The word *Buddha* itself is from the word *bodhi*, awakeful. Buddhist wisdom and practice help us to awaken to who and what we truly are, and to recognize the difference between the real and the unreal in our daily life. All our spiritual practices are designed to awaken us from the daydream of illusion and confusion, where we are like sleepwalkers, semi-consciously muddling our way through life. Awakening is the essence of spiritual life, self-realization, and enlightenment.

The self-knowledge gained through spiritual awakening helps us become masters of circumstances and conditions, rather than mere victims. This is why the Greek-Armenian spiritual master Georges Gurdjieff said: "Contemporary man is born asleep, lives asleep, and dies asleep. And what knowledge could a sleeping man have? If you think about it and at the same time remember that sleep is the chief feature of our being, you will soon understand that if man wishes to obtain knowledge, he should first of all think about how to awaken himself, that is about how to change his being."

South American shamans call this awakening from the dream of life *shapeshifting*: entering into a spiritual journey with the explicit purpose of transformation. Shapeshifting and other forms of conscious dreamwork can, through regular practice, help us experience other realms of existence, visit our dear departed, and achieve spiritual mastery. Australian aborigines say we all live in the dreamtime: we are like dream characters, living out real lives beyond our illusory self-consciousness regarding being born and dying. Tibetan masters call this dreamtime the bardo, or intermediate stage. Bardos exist between the ending of one state and the beginning of another, such as birth and death—or death and rebirth. Dreaming, too, is a bardo, marking the seemingly unstructured zone between waking and sleeping.

Tibetan Dream Yoga

Tibetan Buddhism is unique among Buddhist schools in teaching us how to awaken within the dream and how to practice cultivating clear awareness while sleeping. "May I awaken within the dream and vividly know I am dreaming and that all are mere dream phantoms and dreamlike, illusory unreality." This is the essence of Tibetan Dream Yoga, and the focus of all the practices associated with it. A good book on this subject is *Dream Yoga and the Practice of Natural Light,* by contemporary master Namkhai Norbu Rinpoche. *The Doctrine of the Dream State,* an ancient Tibetan manual on the practice of dream yoga and lucid dreaming, teaches that we can learn five spiritually significant wisdom lessons through assiduously practicing this path of awakening:

- Dreams can be altered through will, clear awareness, and intentional attention.
- Dreams are unstable, impermanent, and unreal—much like fantasies, magical illusions, mirages, and hallucinations.
- Daily perceptions in the everyday waking state are also unreal.
- All life is here today and gone tomorrow, like a dream; there is nothing to hold on to.
- Conscious dreamwork can lead us to the realization of wholeness, perfect balance, and unity.

For centuries, Tibetan masters have taught their students how to use dreamtime and dreamspace to further spiritual progress by increasing awareness during the dream state. Tibetan Dream Yoga brings you these same techniques for realizing the five wisdom lessons and reaping the benefits of awakening within the dream. Tibetan Dream Yoga is one of the renowned Six Vajrayana Yogas of Tibet, an ancient Buddhist teaching that originates with the enlightened yogic adepts (siddhas) of ancient India. These yogas (or practices), utilized for a millennium by all four schools of Tibetan Buddhism, help us to utilize the body/mind/spirit as a vehicle for awakening and enlightenment—by day, by night, and in the afterlife (bardo). The Six Yogas tradition was first brought to Tibet thirteen hundred years ago by the Indian tantric master Padmasambhava, founder of the Ancient School (Nyingma) of Tibetan Buddhism. Padmasambhava himself received the teachings he codified as "The Yoga of the Dream State" from a mysterious yogi named Lawapa. In ensuing centuries, as Buddhism grew and flourished in Tibet, Marpa the Translator and other Tibetan sages made the grueling journey on foot to India to study from yogic masters, then brought the teaching back with them. Tibet's greatest saint, Milarepa, became enlightened through assiduously practicing the Six Yogas and Mahamudra.

Through practicing the Six Yogas, we come to realize the infinite emptiness/openness, ungraspability, and luminosity that is the true nature of reality. Dream interpretation, the use of dreams for predictions and healing, and the development of psychic powers and healing abilities can arise naturally from the continuous practice of dream yoga and the related yogas (especially clear light, inner heat, and illusory body). You can read some English translations of the esoteric Tibetan instructional texts on these practices, but it is very difficult to make much progress without an experienced teacher to guide you.

Spiritual Benefits of Dream Yoga

In *Sleeping, Dreaming and Dying: An Exploration of Consciousness with the Dalai Lama,* His Holiness the Fourteenth Dalai Lama has this to say about awakening our dream body and using it for spiritual progress and development:

> There is said to be a relationship between dreaming, on the one hand, and the gross and subtle levels of the body on the other. But it is also said that there is a "special dream state." In that state, the "special dream body" is created from the mind and from vital en-

ergy (*prana*) within the body. This special dream body is able to dissociate entirely form the gross physical body and travel elsewhere. In Tibetan Dream Yoga we can learn to give rise to this dream body and time and space travel, visit those who have passed from this world, receive teachings and *darshan* (divine audience) with the saints and sages of the past, do good works, teach and assist in other ways hosts of beings in need, and so forth.

One way of developing this special dream body is first of all to recognize a dream as a dream when it occurs. Then, you find that the dream is malleable, and you make efforts to gain control over it. Gradually you become very skilled in this, increasing your ability to control the contents of the dream so that it accords to your own desires. Eventually it is possible to dissociate your dream body from your gross physical body. In contrast, in the normal dream state, dreaming occurs within the body. But as a result of specific training, the dream body can go elsewhere.

We need to examine and explore the intersection of sleeping and dreaming to penetrate the mystery and experience the spiritual riches of the dream state. According to sleep researchers, we typically experience four stages of sleep.

1. *Hypnotic/hypnagogic sleep.* This is the state of drowsiness we experience as we begin falling asleep.
2. *Ordinary sleep.* Here we enter a true sleeping state but can still be easily awakened.
3. *Deeper sleep.* Vital functions slow down, and we are more likely to sleep through disturbances.
4. *Deep sleep.* Muscles are totally relaxed, and it would be difficult to wake us up (we only spend about 15 percent of our sleeping hours at this stage).

It takes about an hour to cycle through all four stages; then we go back in reverse order to stage 1. Before beginning the cycle again, however, we experience rapid eye movements under our closed lids. This stage is called REM (rapid eye movement) sleep, and research shows that this is when we dream. We spend 20 to 25 percent of our sleep time in this state.

In order to practice dream yoga, we must introduce awareness during the periods of REM sleep (which last from a few minutes to half an hour). If we can identify that stage while asleep—perhaps with the help of an assistant or a dream light device—we can further incubate, develop, and enhance the awareness practice of becoming conscious and lucid within the dream state. Tibetan Dream Yoga texts teach us that, in general, there are three types of dreams:

1. Ordinary, karmic dreams, arising mostly from the day's activities, and from previous life activities, thoughts, experiences, and contacts
2. "Clear light" dreams: spiritual visions, blessings, and energy openings
3. Lucid dreams, which are characterized by conscious awareness that one is dreaming

Under these three broad divisions, dreams can be divided into a further six categories:

1. Dreams of events that occurred while we were still awake
2. Dreams about other people, alive or dead
3. Forgotten elements emerging from the subconscious
4. Archetypal content, evocative symbols, and so forth
5. Extrasensory perceptions, prognosticatory dreams, and omens
6. Radiant, luminous, spiritual dreams

Recurrent dreams, nightmares, dreams of death, and other kinds of commonly reported dreams all fall within the first four dream categories. In developing deeper awareness of your dreams, you may find it helpful to identify the category that applies whenever you recall a particular dream. It is important to create a spiritual context for the practice of Tibetan Dream Yoga. Lucid dreaming can easily be misused to perpetuate the problems we experience in our waking lives. For example, one might direct one's dream toward a gratifying encounter or a vengeful fantasy. You will find that the Tibetan Dream Yoga techniques don't work as well when used for such purposes.

Daytime, Morning Wake-Up, and Night-Time Practice

Tibetan Dream Yoga practice comprises three parts: daytime practice, designed to help us recognize and master the dreamlike nature of all existence and thereby prepare us to experience our dreams as vividly as we do our waking activities; morning wake-up practices that help us recall our dreams and confirm our determination to recall more of them; and night-time practice, which prepares the ground for lucid dreaming and spiritual experiences while we sleep.

Daytime Practice
During the day, practice these four points:

- Contemplating the body as illusory, ungraspable, momentary, and unreal
- Contemplating the mind and mental activities as similarly hollow and insubstantial
- Regarding the world—all outer phenomena and inner experiences—as dreamlike, insubstantial, impermanent, and unreal
- Recognizing the relativity and ungraspability of intangibles such as time, space, knowledge, and awareness

Reminding ourselves of these four truths throughout our waking hours helps to dissolve the barrier between the dream of life and the sleeping dream. As we become more adept at these practices, we begin to regard our night-time dreams as continuations of our waking dream—and we learn how to bring habitual awareness to both. One specific technique for daytime practice is the mirror practice.

Mirror practice is an effective way of perceiving the dreamlike nature of "reality," and especially of "self." From time to time during the day, take a few minutes to do it.

- Stand in front of a mirror and look into your own eyes.
- Hold up a hand mirror behind your right or left ear and look at its reflection in the larger mirror. Keep angling the hand mirror so as to fragment and multiply your image as much as possible. Let your mind fragment along with the image.
- After a few minutes, angle the hand mirror back until you return to the original, single image in the mirror in front of you.

The analogy of a mirror image is, like dreams, traditionally used to describe the insubstantial nature of our everyday experience. The mirror practice helps bring that teaching to life. The fragmented image is the kind we might see in a dream, yet we are seeing it while we're fully awake—or are we? Allowing your mind to "fall apart" also helps ventilate the solidity we typically attribute to our world, and especially to our self.

Another traditional dream yoga practice is one you can do with a partner. This partner exercise is an immensely useful technique, not only for challenging the distinction between sleeping dreams and the dream of being awake, but also for applying your training to practical, everyday situations.

- Insult, blame, and criticize your partner. Your partner should listen to all of this as echoes, empty sounds.

- Trade places. Now have your partner disparage you while you practice just hearing the sounds and not taking the words to heart.
- Try doing this same exercise using praise and flattery instead of blame. In either case, the listening partner should practice not reacting in any way, recognizing what is being said as a dream.

At first, you may find it difficult to maintain equanimity while you do this practice. Stay with it—you will find that doing so yields rich rewards over time.

Wake-Up Practice

The moments immediately after waking are the most fertile for recalling dreams. The following practices are designed to support and strengthen your recall. They will also facilitate a mindful transition between the sleeping and waking dream states.

Upon waking in the morning, practice:

- The lion's outbreath—forcefully breathing out with the sound *ah*
- The lionlike posture for awakening and purifying—sitting up in bed with raised head and gaze and emphasizing the exhalation, repeating the *ah* outbreath three times
- Raising the energy—standing up, reaching the fingertips to the sky, and repeating the lion's outbreath
- Entering into mindful reflection on the transition between the states of sleep, dreaming, and waking reality—coming into the present moment, recording dreams

You will thus enter the day recognizing that all things are like a dream, illusion, fantasy, or mirage.

Night-Time Practice
After going to bed, practice the following five steps to create the conditions for mindful, lucid dreaming.

1. Chant the following dream yoga prayer three times to remind you of and strengthen your resolve to awaken within the dream, for the benefit of the ultimate awakening of all beings. *May I awaken within this dream and grasp the fact that I am dreaming, so that all dreamlike beings may likewise awaken from the nightmare of suffering and confusion.*

2. Lie on one side with your legs together and knees slightly bent. Let your bent arm take the weight of your torso by resting your head on your open hand. This is the posture of the sleeping Buddha, as he has been traditionally depicted at the moment of passing into nirvana (death).

3. Bringing your attention to your throat chakra, visualize your energy rising up out of your body and shaping up at the throat as glowing red sphere that turns radiantly red and incandescent as you focus and concentrate increasingly upon it and your body sense dissolves into this glowing *tigle* (sphere). Feel it rise up from your heart chakra with your breath and pass into your third eye, or brow chakra: the point between your eyebrows. Visualize it as a luminous, ivory white full moon behind your eyes. Go into this scintillating light, and become the light.

4. Visualize the letter *A* (symbolizing infinite space) on the surface of the moon sphere.

5. Notice whatever images begin to appear on the sphere of light behind your eyes.

Deepening Your Practice

To progress still further in Tibetan Dream Yoga, you may find it beneficial to:

- Pay careful attention to your dreams
- Record your dreams in a dream journal upon waking each morning and make other notes
- Recognize recurrent images, themes, associations, and patterns
- Contemplate the archetypal, symbolic content and meanings of your dreams
- Reflect on the similarities and differences between night dreams, daydreams, fantasies, visions, ideas, and projections
- Wake yourself up during the night to reaffirm your resolve to awaken within the dream and grasp the fact that you are dreaming
- Sit up in meditation posture while sleeping to maintain continuous awareness while inducing and incubating lucid dreaming
- Have a dream assistant at hand to guide you while sleep, helping you learn to retain conscious presence during dreams and whispering instructions and the dream yoga prayer to you
- Meditate alone in darkness to develop the inner clarity of the clear-light mind—the mind unaffected by illusion
- During the day, maintain awareness that everything you experience is like a dream
- Chant the dream yoga prayer by day and by night to help reinforce your intention to awaken within the dream

Tibetan Dream Yoga is best thought of as a lifelong practice. Like any spiritual practice, it will reveal more substantial benefits the longer and more consistently you practice it. In the Buddhist tradition, however, discipline alone is not enough for bringing your practice alive. Motivation—the reason you are practicing in the first place—is considered as crucial as any technique and commitment. You will have noticed that the Tibetan Dream Yoga chant includes an aspiration to help free all beings of their suffering. This intention lies at the root of all Buddhist practice. The underlying teaching is that all living beings are interconnected: none of us can be completely free so long as any of us is still asleep.

As you practice Tibetan Dream Yoga, recognize that the suffering you seek to alleviate through spiritual practice is, in fact, universal. Recognize, too, that the more awake you are, the more helpful you can be to those you care about—in fact, to everyone you come into contact with. Practice with the intention of working with your own, individual part of the whole, in order to bring all of human awareness to a new level. In this way, you will derive the greatest possible benefits from your dream yoga practice. Woodrow Wilson said, "We grow by dreams. All big men are dreamers."

> Row, row, row your boat
> Gently down the stream.
> Merrily, merrily, merrily, merrily
> Life is but a dream.
> —Children's song

CHAPTER 19

DEEPENING PRACTICE
THROUGH RETREAT

In the Buddhist cultures of Southeast Asia, the faithful traditionally mark the days of the full moon, half moon, and new moon by visiting temples, meditating, making generous offerings, and observing the moral precepts. It is believed that one's practices and actions have more results on such pivotal days, and should be conscientiously accomplished to speed one's spiritual progress. In the Jewish, Christian, and Muslim traditions, observing the Sabbath can be a profound weekly practice of letting go of work and other ordinary concerns and turning heart and mind toward spiritual matters. In a kind of extended Sabbath or "holy day," retreats are times for dedicating oneself entirely to spiritual life. Some Christians look for inspiration to Jesus's desert retreat in enacting their own retreat of prayer, contemplation, and renewal. Each year, the monks of Southeast Asia remain in retreat for the rainy season, as monastics have traditionally done, going back to the time of the Buddha. Native American vision quests are a form of solitary retreat. The roots of the tradition of undertaking periods of intensive retreat are ancient and worldwide. Retreats are an extraordinary opportunity to learn more and not just earn more.

Spiritual retreat is not only for the professionals. Anyone can undertake a retreat and reap its healing and transformative benefits. Think of it as a learning, growthful experience, like an intensive workshop, a service to your highest, deepest spiritual Self.

It is a gift to yourSelf and a gift to your loved ones, your colleagues, and all whom you encounter, who will benefit from your increased focus, energy, physical and spiritual health, wisdom, and productivity. Undertaking a period of retreat can be one of the most significant aids to progressing in any spiritual endeavor.

I went on my first retreat one weekend in 1968, while a freshman at the University of Buffalo. I had read some books about meditation, and I had heard about the teacher, Philip Kapleau Roshi, and about Zen in some Gestalt workshops I had attended that year. I was favorably impressed by the depth and clarity of the teachings, and by Kapleau Roshi's wisdom and serene presence. But after the weekend was over, I was not able to keep up the daily meditation practice on my own.

I only learned how to meditate on a regular daily basis a few years later, in 1971, by attending several ten-day Vipassana (insight) meditation courses in India. U Goenka was our teacher, one of the first Buddhist masters in India to teach meditation widely in modern times. He stressed the continuity, purity, and simplicity of practice above all else. At the beginning, it was tough going. The retreats were silent, austere, and physically and psychologically demanding. One had to nakedly confront oneself, without distraction. We slept dormitory-style on mats, and there were no flush toilets, no hot water, no diversions, no news from the outside world, no meals after noon—in accordance with the tradition of monastics since the time of the Buddha. The day began at 4:00 a.m., and we meditated for twelve one-hour periods, in which we determined to sit without movement and observe the breathing, a meditation designed to calm, clear, and focus the mind while sharpening concentration. This was interrupted only occasionally—with some chanting, a private interview with the teacher, an evening Dharma talk, or a meal.

For the first five or six days, I struggled with the discomfort and pain of trying to sit still, cross-legged on the floor, and relax in the midst of mosquitoes and heat. Eventually something seemed to mysteriously change, and I began to experience peace, relaxation, and even bliss. My mind felt as sharply focused as a laser beam, resting wherever I placed it, and my awareness seemed incandescent as never before. When I later told my teacher that, he laughed and said, "Beginner's luck! Don't get too excited, just keep meditating." I had gotten over the hump of struggling to learn to sit and meditate, and was actually meditating. I started to like it. I learned not to be deceived by the momentary thoughts and feelings, or the temporary ups and downs of my practice path, but to just keep practicing steadfastly while observing the fleeting, dreamlike nature of all things. This was one of life's greatest lessons for me, and has stood me in good stead over the years.

Without this valuable experience of actually doing meditation in a protected environment under the guidance of an experienced teacher and supported by a welcoming sangha, I doubt I would have been able to continue with daily practice month in and month out, through whatever doubts, difficulties, challenges, and distractions came along the way. Going to occasional refresher retreats with Goenka-ji and other Vipassana teachers during that decade kept me going. In the late 1970s, Joseph Goldstein, Sharon Salzberg, and Jack Kornfield were very helpful in leading retreats in America that I could participate in and enjoy.

I recommend spiritual retreat both to enter a particular practice path, and also as a way to recharge the inner battery, remain motivated, and overcome the inevitable hindrances and obstacles to going deeper on your spiritual path. Undertaking a personal retreat can benefit one on so many levels. The practice of noble silence and sublime solitude helps to reduce external stimulation, create space for what is within us to be more evident, and helps us to better know ourselves. If you want to experience an authentic Buddhist meditation retreat, try one of the Vipassana

retreats, Zen sesshins, or Dzogchen retreats that you can participate in at a low cost throughout this country, for a period of time
of between a weekend and three months in duration. The tools
and techniques taught in these various traditions can help you
both in the short term and long run. There are also excellent her-
mitages where one can practice spiritually in solitude and nature,
but I recommend that you experience group retreat and learn
from a teacher before going off for too long on your own. When
one peers unflinchingly into the mirror of solitude, one must
own one's own projections and recognize who's on first, as it
were, and realize who is responsible for doing what around here.
There is nowhere to hide.

In Tibetan Buddhism, there is a tradition for committed practitioners to make a three-year, three-month, three-day "Great Retreat" once in a lifetime. In the 1980s, I twice completed this
Great Retreat at the Dzogchen monastery and hermitage of my
teacher Dilgo Kh 'entse Rinpoche. The group of Dharma students retreating there, most of whom were Westerners, did nothing but meditate, pray, chant, study, and practice Tibetan Yoga
and "noble silence," which includes periods with no eye contact,
no reading, no writing. The beauty of noble silence is that it
greatly deepens one's sense of solitude and facility for contemplation. We were ordained as monks or nuns for that period, during which time we took vows of celibacy, poverty, and obedience
to our teachers, shaved our heads, and wore maroon and yellow
Tibetan Buddhist monastic robes. We lived under the direct
guidance of Khyentse Rinpoche and his colleague, the beloved
master Dudjom Rinpoche.

Our lives were ordered by a precise schedule, which broke the
typical day into two- or three-hour periods, beginning with our
4:00 a.m. wake-up gong, during which I, along with the other
students, meditated and practiced alone in our five-by-nine-foot
cells—sparsely furnished with only a bed, an altar, and a stor-
age trunk. Some years, our bed was actually a meditation seat—

historically known in Tibet as "the box"—in which we sat up all night doing Tibetan Dream Yoga and clear-light practice. For some periods of time, we concentrated on Tibetan Tantric Yoga exercises to awaken the energy body, develop inner heat (so-called mystic incandescence), and purify karma. During this time, we sat outside in the garden daily for two hours before dawn, dressed only in shorts, even in the winter. There was also a short work period every day after the lunch hour, during which some of us gardened, cleaned, and did household chores in the cloister while others worked on translations and copied scriptures and study materials.

We had no weekends, days off, or vacations. But we did celebrate Buddhist holidays, visits by grand lamas, initiations and empowerments, and auspicious full-moon days with various extensive rituals, tantric feasts, round-the-clock chanting, and offering ceremonies. The intensive practices, year-in-and-year-out lifestyle of discipline and silent interiority, and the blessed developments I felt on occasion helped keep me motivated to continue in that cloistered retreat for eight fulfilling years.

As severe as all the regulation and structure may sound, retreats are set up this way for a reason, and offer great benefit to the retreatant. Life becomes much simpler when pared down to the most basic routines, such as waking up to a gong, living according to a schedule marked by bells throughout the day, and wearing the same clothes and hairdo year in and year out—not to mention remaining entirely cloistered and focused solely on one's spiritual life. Every day seems the same, and one learns to simply focus on the present moment and give oneself utterly to whatever one is doing. You learn what a Christian monk means when he says, "Let go and let God."

While such retreats are logistically difficult for most people to manage, there are many opportunities at Buddhist centers today to enter deeply into the same practices I learned while on retreat. American practice centers offer an abundance of weekend, week-long, and ten-day meditation retreats. Even one-day "re-treats" are available. I myself lead many each year, through my Dzogchen Center, including our hundred-day experienced-student retreats. I continue to spend at least two or three weeks every year in personal meditation retreat at my hermitage. The seclusion helps me reconnect more deeply with myself, my prayer life, and spiritual practice and keeps me in touch with my teachers and lineage. And just as important, it helps me to inte-grate my spirituality into the path of everyday life throughout the rest of the year.

There are many kinds and styles of retreat. There are medita-tion retreats; yoga retreats; wilderness and travel retreats; prayer retreats; writing retreats; solitary retreats and group retreats; men's retreats and women's retreats and young people's retreats; activists' retreats, businesspeople's retreats, artists' retreats, par-ents' retreats, and family retreats. There are silent retreats, chant-ing retreats, and seminar-like studious retreats. There are prayer vigil retreats and healing retreats and vision quest retreats. There are fasting retreats and special-diet retreats (vegetarian, kosher, fruitarian, etc.). And there are retreats centered on specific sub-jects or practices.

Retreats can be undertaken according to different kinds of guidelines. They can be done by time, such as a one-day or week-end retreat, a week-long retreat, a month retreat, a hundred-day retreat, a one-year or three-year retreat, and so forth. They can be undertaken according to place, limits, subject matter, activity, and so forth. Some retreats provide tightly structured schedules, while others leave retreatants with more free time.

To choose a retreat, you could ask your spiritual friends for suggestions and recommendations, or your spiritual director—if you have one. Or ask yourself questions like, What are my as-pirations for doing retreat? What are my spiritual interests and experience, and what environment would best facilitate their ac-tualization? What are my limitations, physical, mental, financial, time-wise, and so forth? Do I want to be silent and solitary, or am I looking for new like-minded friends? Some retreats are silent, with minimal (overt) interaction with other retreatants, while others facilitate group sharing through discussions, group practices, evening activities, and the like.

For how long should I retreat? This will depend a lot on your prior retreat experience. One can make every Sabbath or half of Sunday a retreat time each week, or once a month. For some people, it may be best to start small—with a half-day, day-long, or weekend retreat—rather than jumping into a week or ten days of silence and/or solitude. What kind of structure would suit me— many scheduled activities, or lots of open time for my own established practices and interests? What kind of surroundings would be most conducive? Workshop center or retreat center? Urban or rural? Basic or luxurious accommodations? Do I need to conduct other activities, such as being in touch electronically, while on retreat, or can I sequester myself entirely from the world during that period of time? What specific practices might I like to engage in? Do I want and need lots or little teaching? How much personal guidance or time with teachers and mentors do I want?

There are various kinds of Buddhist retreats, each stressing different kinds of practices, different schedules and practices. In our seasonal Dzogchen Center intensive retreats, we structure our time, place, activities, and attitude according to what I call the Ten S's of retreat:

1. Silence
2. Solitude, seclusion
3. Self-discipline, morality
4. Slowing down, stillness, and simplicity
5. Softness, gentleness
6. Sati (mindfulness)
7. Self-inquiry

8. Satya (truth)
9. Selflessness, unselfishness
10. Sacred outlook

The first three are mostly outer, the second four are internal, and the last three are innermost guidelines. Using this structure, if you have some self-discipline, you can really do a retreat almost anytime and anywhere you choose, and structure it according to what is most conducive to accomplishing your goals during the period of time you can set aside for this worthwhile pursuit. One could even do this at home, by freeing oneself from all obligations, commitments, and responsibilities; turning off the phone, e-mail, and radio and doing a news fast; and simply turning inward for some period of time. Yet the habitual home environment can prove challenging.

Here are a few more tips and pointers I've learned through many years of retreat practice:

- Never give up or give in to discouragement and despair. Everything changes.
- Continuity is the secret of success.
- You can get used to anything.
- Savor time as precious, and use it meaningfully.
- Keep your eyes peeled.
- Don't look back. Start each day and each session afresh. Let go of the past and future and be totally present.
- Give yourself wholeheartedly to whatever you've chosen to be doing.
- Don't make irrevocable, life-altering decisions while on retreat.
- Nothing is as important as you think it is at the moment.
- Everything is subjective
- Life is mysterious, and the spiritual path even more so.
- Be there while getting there every single step of the Way.

Solitude and loneliness are not necessarily synonymous. Marpa, the great Tibetan master of old, sang: "When I am alone in the mountains, I am never alone. All the Buddha and gurus accompany me. I feel blessed and delighted!"

I love to go on retreat. I think it is one of the greatest spurs to spiritual growth and realization. The secret of spiritual life is actually doing it; this means practice, not mere theory, belief, or membership. Take the opportunity to try it for yourself. I think you'll love it.

PART IV

---

contemporary spiritual expressions

integrating dharma into daily life

CHAPTER 20

SPIRITUAL INTELLIGENCE

for several years, I've taught about the basics of Buddhism at our Cambridge Dzogchen Center. But I'm also thinking about contemporary spirituality all over the world, especially in the West, and how to positively transform the atmosphere of religion and spirituality in our country. What do we really have in common, regardless of our different traditions? What *is* this spiritual gene? What *is* this spiritual hunger that so many have in our Judeo-Christian postmodern society, this hunger that our materialistic culture can neither satisfy nor suppress? Every journalist worth his or her salt knows that the towering question of our time is, What is the human spirit?

I have been thinking about it in terms of spiritual intelligence. My old friend Daniel Goleman wrote a significant book called *Emotional Intelligence.* You might be interested in looking it up. I like to call that kind of teaching "stealth Dharma"—it zeroes in right beneath the culture's usual Judeo-Christian radar and scientific inquiry. Goleman insinuates a lot of Dharma from his own deep background in psychology. He wrote his thesis on the *Visuddhi-magga,* the "way of purity," a complete exposition of the ancient Theravadan teachings by the fifth-century scholar Buddhaghosa, and a seminal text of that school. So "emotional intelligence" is not just a phrase recently coined; it's more than a clever title for a best seller. Goleman is exploring our emotions as intelligence agents that bring us a lot of information, if we are attuned to that channel. Now he's speaking about ecological intelligence.

There are, in fact, many kinds of intelligence. Howard Gardner of Harvard and the Boston University School of Medicine counted eight in his groundbreaking work *Frames of Mind,* including mathematical intelligence, musical intelligence, spatial intelligence, interpersonal intelligence, and physical or bodily intelligence. A decade later, in the 1990s, he added naturalist intelligence, which involves being comfortable with other species and at ease with them; spiritual intelligence; and existential intelligence, which actually is spiritual intelligence narrowed down and is the category in which he places the genius of Einstein. He does not include emotional intelligence in the list, since, as he says, each intelligence has its own emotional facets. The gist of his work is that intelligence is the mind's full potential and cannot be reduced to a mere matter of SAT scores. IQ tests and other such measurements indicate only a very small part of the mind's overall capacity. The mind's potential cannot *be* measured. Intelligence and what we think of as intellect—discursive thinking, logic, reason, and information—are not the same. We can know so much and yet understand so little. "To know the world is knowledge; to know oneself is wisdom," as Lao Tzu said.

Spiritual intelligence—what *is* that common spiritual gene? Though it has been valued and given prominence by every known human culture, beginning with the Paleolithic, it's as mysterious as the DNA sequence itself. And yet, how important it is in all aspects of our life, personal and professional, inner and outer, alone and with others. How important this spiritual intelligence, or let's say SQ, is! Don't we all have questions and issues and feel compelled to address life's big questions at some point? Death, suffering and loss, divinity, an afterlife, meaning and purpose: Who doesn't wonder about these matters? To what extent are we really able to discern the difference between the true and the false, the helpful and harmful? To what extent can we discern between authenticity and genuineness on the one hand, and its opposite—deception, pretense, mere ego—on the other? And can we discern the difference between what we don't really love but sometimes think we do, and what we really love? For spiritual intelligence, with its knack for mysticism and its concern for the cosmic, is that which *can* and does discern the real from the not-real. Nyoshul Khenpo Rinpoche sings in one of his poems about distinguishing mind with a small *m, sem* in Tibetan, from *rigpa* or innate awareness, Buddha mind. It's like knowing the difference between brass and gold. They both shine and have the same color, but there the resemblance ends. This points to how we can discern who and what we genuinely are from what we seem to be, our persona and our role in the world.

We all have this intrinsic spiritual intelligence, of course, just like we always have emotional intelligence within us, whether we use it or not. We all have psychic or intuitive intelligence, spatial intelligence, physical intelligence, and all the other intelligences, to some degree. Spiritual intelligence is not just the realm of professional clerics, or the card-carrying members of churches or of seekers. We all have the "Why?" chromosome. We all have some form of active questioning or at least semiconscious wondering about life, reality, the big picture, the nature of God and things—don't we? We all participate in some form of beliefs, myth making, cosmology (the bigger picture), and personal philosophy—whether or not we conceive of it precisely in that manner. So how can we make the most of it? How can we raise our SQ, our spiritual quotient? How can we become more aware and intelligent, wise, self-realized, and conscious? Sometimes spirituality is thought of in terms of consciousness: higher consciousness, deeper consciousness, radiant consciousness. Spirituality includes self-realization, relationship with a higher power—however it's conceived—and being in touch with the mystery and subtle energies of life. The heart is also an organ of perception. We can develop quite a lot of body wisdom through various techniques.

How possible is it to develop this kind of internal capacity that even a scientific researcher like Professor Howard Gardner has come upon in his research? Will meditating do it? Does meditation make us more spiritually intelligent? Gardner says that meditation mobilizes certain brain centers and neural transmitters that otherwise are activated only on a short-term basis by psychedelic drugs. But if we're just sitting here on a black zafu (meditation cushion) trying not to think, is that really meditation? Is that the meditation he had in mind? Tibetan lamas say this kind of meditation gets us reborn as a cow, dumbly chewing our cud again and again. Perhaps all meditation, all limited mind-made meditation, does *not* make us more spiritually intelligent, does not raise what Teilhard de Chardin referred to as our "cosmic consciousness." Some people would say that bowing or chanting would make us more spiritual. But what's our motivation? What are we bowing to, or for what reason are we chanting? *That* determines the results. It's not just the outer act. Even yoga, a famously spiritual practice, can be merely a physical exercise not unlike calisthenics, depending on the attitudes and mindfulness applied to it. So our Buddhist sitting practice may or may not actually make us wise and more intelligent. It may just make us followers or cult members, brainwashed. Or it may do nothing at all for us. Rocks and frogs just sit, too; what matters is what's going on inside, the states of consciousness.

I think it's important to look into what really *is* intelligent spirituality. What *is* spiritual intelligence, and how can we incorporate it into our lives and thus be more sane and loving? How can we develop this potential and genuinely cultivate this higher, deeper consciousness? We need to look into how making the spiritual connection can help us live in the famous sacred zone—help us live in the Dharma and bring it into most, if not all, aspects of daily life so as not to deviate from the path. Maybe there's even a zone diet for this. The macrobiotics think so. Is there a spiritual zone diet? The vegetarians think it's spiritual to be vegetarian. The kosher people think that it's an absolute spiritual necessity to be kosher. First we might laugh; but then we start to say, "Oh! Actually people *are* living and believing this way." Sixties people think it's spiritual to be stoned . . . and so on. We could, by extension, find spirituality in many areas. We could try to make the sacred connection through other changes, like in the clothes we wear. Some people think the color of their clothes makes them holy—yellow for Buddhists, orange for Hindus, white for yogis, black for Christian priests. Thus the saint Kabir sang, "I don't want to dye my clothes the holy color of saffron, I want to dye my heart that color." In other words, it's a change of heart and not a change of clothes and hairstyle that matters when it comes to raising our spiritual intelligence. Having our head shaved or adorned with dreadlocks makes no essential difference. Imitating a master's lifestyle may or may not help bring about the more subtle, less visible changes and transformation seekers are after.

For Buddhists, enlightenment is the ultimate purpose and value, so living the enlightened life and following the path is the intelligent way to raise our SQ. This is how we strive to grow in wisdom and compassion, love and selflessness. We do that through the three trainings of ethics, meditation, and wisdom, laid out in the Noble Eightfold Path, and through the six paramita virtues of the bodhisattva practice—generosity, ethical morality, patient forbearance, effortful energy, mindful concentration, and discriminating wisdom. That's how we raise our SQ, understand the world and our place in it, and come to live intelligently, wisely, and sanely. Reflecting on universal verities such as mortality and impermanence also helps keep us from investing too much in the fool's gold of things that don't last. Recognizing the omnipresence of death and the fleeting, tenuous nature of life sharpens our spiritual intelligence. Sharpening our attention and awareness of the present moment makes it easier for us to experience the sacred zone in all different areas of our life—personal and professional, at home and at work—not just at church on Sunday and on the high holy days or on our meditation cushion in the morning. In one word, to raise our SQ and realize enlightenment, we practice alert *awareness*. To become more aware is to become more spiritually intelligent. To become more aware is to become more sensitive to what's actually going on, to things as they *is* and not as they "ain't." Seeing things as they are—that's clear seeing, or wisdom, according to Buddha. As a result of clear seeing, we maximize our spiritual intelligence, raise our consciousness through the constant cultivation of lucid awareness, and become more sensitive to things as they actually are.

Converging on Common Ground

Hindus might explain spiritual intelligence a little differently. Even within Hinduism, spiritual intelligence is seen differently within the different schools. In Karma Yoga, for instance, the emphasis is on selfless conduct, and seva—service-oriented activity. In the Bhagavad Gita, the Song of God, Krishna says to Arjuna, "For those of clear mind there is the path of knowledge, for those who work there is the path of selfless action. No one can refuse to act.... Therefore you must perform every action free from all attachment to the result." That's the intelligent way to live, in Karma Yoga: action without overattachment to particular outcomes, as in "Virtue is its own reward." The other yogas most familiar to us are Jnana Yoga and Bhakti Yoga, the paths of knowledge (philosophy) and of love. To seek union with God through the practice of these various yogas, or the different paths that bring us to oneness, would be spiritual intelligence according to Hinduism. Yoga in its broadest sense is not confined to India. All who seek the direct mystical experience of fundamental unity, whether tribal shamans or Christian mystics, can be called yogis, in this sense. Prayer, chanting, and meditation are all effective forms of yoga.

According to the Tao, learning to be one with the flow of

things is the true Way or yoga. This is spiritual intelligence speaking from Stephen Mitchell's rendering of the *Tao Te Ching*:

> True perfection seems imperfect, yet it is perfectly itself. True fullness seems empty, yet it is fully present. True straightness seems crooked. True wisdom seems foolish. True art seems artless. The Master allows things to happen. She shapes events as they come. She steps out of the way and lets the Tao speak for itself.

And again:

> The Master does his job and then stops. He understands that the universe is forever out of control, and that trying to dominate events goes against the current of the Tao.

The *Tao Te Ching* is probably the wisest book in our world. It rewards constant rereading.

Interestingly, if we're talking about "allowing" or "accepting," the word *Islam* literally means surrender or submission. All the Old Testament–based religions have a strong flavor of this, whether they speak of the Ten Commandments or the Koran. Even in the notion of surrendering to God's will there often is a sense of social justice and, as in Karma Yoga, of the necessity to engage with this world, not just focusing exclusively on the other invisible world and afterlife. We Buddhists live for Buddha, Dharma, and sangha; we find refuge in and rely on these. We do Buddha (devotional) practice, we do Dharma (mindfulness) practice, we do sangha (community) practice. Jews are supposed to follow the words of the Hasidic master who said, "I came to this world to serve three things—God, Torah, and community." Buddha, Dharma, sangha. God, Torah, and community. It sounds pretty similar, doesn't it? Trinities are common in this arena of world religion.

There's so much convergence. There is so much common ground here on cultivating spiritual intelligence. And we could speak even more externally, not just of religions but of being humane, sane citizens, and deeply recognizing others—not just our ego selves, but others as also equal and with a right to life and to happiness. Moreover, we could consider not only other humans but also animals, and other living beings as well. We can cultivate spiritual intelligence through practical ways of life, including nonviolence or social service and altruism, unselfishness, environmentalism. Gandhi said: "Those who think religion and politics are different don't understand either religion or politics." One way to cultivate spiritual intelligence is through a sense of social justice or rightness, working to relieve the world, people and nonhumans, of injustice, violence, and unnecessary suffering. Therefore I think, in a broad-minded Dharma sense, that we have to say that spiritual intelligence includes a certain kind of social service or social conscience, although some religionists might disagree. Buddha himself, although a monk and meditation master, was a huge social activist who mediated peace between warring kingdoms, broke the caste system, and was the first leader in history to educate women en masse.

I think this broad concept of spiritual intelligence is also profound. It's not merely a secularization of mysticism, but a practical application of it. This is mysticism in action. To be spiritually intelligent is to manifest discerning wisdom and good judgment, to allow wisdom to embody itself *in* us and *as* us and to be balanced and harmonious. We don't want to be like hot-air balloons, lifting off the earth and having our kids have to hold us down with a ballast of hamburgers. That may seem spiritual, but it is just spaced out. It's actually unbalanced, and neither sane nor spiritual. Maybe it's even flaky. I think what is sane and intelligent is to love ourselves and this life enough to be loving, kind, and helpful, since we all are in this together, all in the same boat in so many ways, rising and falling together.

Therefore no matter how much understanding we think we have of the interconnectedness of all things, the more we cultivate our capacity for spiritual intelligence, the more deeply we can actually realize this underlying interconnectedness. As our mindful awareness becomes sharper, we can *observe* it and apply it in nature, in friendships, in couples, in families, societies, business—in fact, in all the different areas of our life. And being more aware of it, we can intentionally bring it more into different areas; we can mend some of the broken hyperlinks in the web page of our life.

Cultivating Spiritual Intelligence

Sometimes I hear people talking to one another, saying: "Oh you're getting your life together." There's the career, the financial situation, and the relationship or the family, and then there's the emotional dimension. I think that at the crux of any of these personal crises, there's something common to all of them, something fundamental. We find that by asking ourselves, How shall I live, work, and love? What is my true purpose here, my true calling? Where's the authenticity, where's the golden mean, where's the balance or Middle Way in each of those areas for me?" *That* is the spiritual. *That* is spiritual intelligence at work through passionate inquiry into what's true and real. That's the Dharma—how to tell the difference between need and greed and where to draw that line in *your* finances, or *your* sex life, or *your* consumption or *your* renunciation. What is too much or too little? Who shall decide? Someone else, some code, or oneself? That's what we need to apply our intelligence to, spiritually speaking. That is like mysticism in action. Then we can achieve meaning, purpose, clarity, and conviction. Because we are right at the balance point—in the center, always—oneness is always available to us. Even when we're balancing our checkbook or paying taxes, contentment is possible. Doing what needs to be done, and wholeheartedly, could be a far truer activity than just sitting on a black Zen cushion or sitting through some clichéd sermon being bored, disinterested, and perhaps even letting negative thoughts proliferate.

When we exercise spiritual intelligence, ethical behavior becomes a *natural* morality rather than a legislated one. It simply makes sense to treat others like yourself when you come to recognize that they want and need the same as you do. When we empathize and can feel the pain of others, we instinctively wish to protect them, not having any impulse to exploit or harm them. Often the quickest way to get to this noble-hearted stage is by connecting directly with people in such a way that we see intimately how "the other half lives," as they say—not just *thinking* about world hunger, but going through the soup line ourselves or handing groceries or clothing out to someone at a shelter or volunteering in the Third World or on the other side of the tracks. All the while noticing and asking yourself, Who is serving? Who is receiving? while watching the artificially constructed lines of separation turning gray. Crossing the line and participating in others' lives in such a way can be a broadening and transformative experience. It's spiritually intelligent to become sensitive to others' needs and feelings rather than being insulated and insensitive in an effort to protect ourselves. In Zen they say, "If you kick an iron kettle and you don't feel its pain, you're not practicing." If we become more conscious and lucidly aware, then we become more sensitive, feel the pain and joy of others, and spontaneously start to treat others more like ourselves, as the Good Book teaches.

Working at the same time inwardly, we could cultivate our spiritual intelligence by becoming sensitive to more subtle phenomena. For example, in the shamanistic way, we could tune in to the signs, omens, dreams, and portents that reveal the movements of the inner mind as well as the minds and bodies and emotions of others—thus cultivating not just our spiritual intelligence, but the psychic, intuitive, and physical intelligence that we all have the potential for, regardless of how rational we appear to be. We were all children once, even though we hate to admit it—little Buddhas before we became big egos. This is not to idealize children, because they have selfish egos, too, but notice that innate sense of wonder, delight, and awe that children have regarding even the smallest things. They remind us of that potential and reconnect us to that in ourselves. This is also a kind of spiritual intelligence, and we can cultivate it to become like little children again, in that sense as Jesus taught.

We could afford to simplify our lives and become more simple. Not simpletons—but we can become more clear, more un-neurotic and uncomplicated, more direct and straightforward even in the midst of complexity. Just practicing doing what we're doing one hundred percent, and being entirely in *that* nanosecond, gets us to the ultimate simplicity. Then there is no complexity. No matter how many billions of connections there are, we're only in *one* nanosecond, one mind moment. The whole and the infinitesimally small fraction are not two. And anyway, there is no such thing as complexity, really. There's only the single moment of *is-ness*. Present time and eternity, the finite and the infinite—these are simply binary. We can be more spiritually intelligent at a more inner level through intentionally cultivating and developing that kind of clarity and simplicity.

Sometimes we can have that moment of total clarity, relaxation, and relief in meditation, before we even realize it's there. We might have spent days, years, or hours meditating—and then all of a sudden, something unhooks. Things fall into place for a moment, and we sort of laugh, if only to ourselves. We have that little smile, a joyful inner lift, yet we haven't even thought mentally about it yet and have thus lost it. *That's* when spiritual intelligence operates. We know, we recognize it—*that* is spiritual intelligence. Nobody has to confirm it for us; we just know it.

What a relief, when things suddenly fall into place! Even if we don't necessarily know how. Perhaps we didn't do anything to put them all into place, but for just a moment they seem to all fall into place—wherever they fall. And it's our spiritual intelligence, our innate spiritual intelligence, that recognizes it. The experience is self-authenticating.

We can rely on that inner intuition of well-being, if we give it room to operate, if we don't overwhelm ourselves with all the input we have going all the time in this overinformation age where we seem to be plugged in at every orifice, as my late teacher Nyoshul Khenpo used to say. You know how it goes: headphones and cell phones, radios and TVs, laptops, beepers and Black-Berries—always plugged in. It's like one nipple at a time isn't enough. He also used to say, jokingly: "Don't you Westerners have your own batteries? Do you always need to be plugged in to the wall? Don't you have anything inside?" You know, Easterners are no better, but he was talking to us. Spiritual intelligence is your own innate natural resource. I'm sure we could all cultivate ourselves more intelligently.

Cultivating spiritual intelligence helps refine our senses, including common sense and sound judgment. It boosts energy and helps us to be more conscious, sensitive, and *true,* in any number of ways. The most important way to walk in this world is the way that works for us. Of course, we can try to do it through the time-tested and tried-and-true ways, such as *telling* the truth and, in our effort to do so, getting closer and closer to *discerning* the truth. Truth telling is a practice. Clear seeing is a practice. Meditating or intentionally focusing, calming, and clearing our minds and vision is a practice. We can sharpen our SQ through yoga, breathing exercises, and all the spiritual regimens, including fasting and other disciplines. Western religions have similar traditions, such as Yom Kippur, Lenten fasts, and Native American sweat lodges and vision quests, in which participants went out alone to solitary places, fasted, and refrained from sleep so that their true name, or higher Self, would be revealed to them.

Self-discipline is actually extraordinarily useful for straightening us out, because we're a little bent out of shape. Actually our innate selfless Self is always straight, erect, untrammeled, and incorruptible. We just need to come back to that, to relax into internal well-being—not unlike what horseback riders call finding one's true seat. That would be the ultimate spiritual intelligence, to be smart enough to just come home and stay home, at least once in a while—home to ourSelves, where heart and hearth and mental health are united as one. I think that today we have many opportunities to become more intelligent. We're so learned—perhaps more learned than people ever were. We can find out about anything we want by logging onto the Internet—"Google and ye shall find." But how can we find, access, and log on to what we really seek, want, and need—to meaningfully connect, to make the spiritual connection in finding ourSelves, awaken the ultimate spiritual intelligence, the cosmic intelligence, the Buddha mind within—whatever you like to call it? That's the big question. What is the nature of our invisible spirit, and what is transformative spirituality today?

Again, I think there is only one way, although we've mentioned many ways. And that is the way that works for *you*. Therefore we each have to find that way, those particular portals or access points and doorways that allow us entry into deeper mysteries, including the nature of God and ourSelves. We have to find those practices, or those prayers, affirmations, spiritual readings, groups, spiritual friends, mentors, or mirrors—those true vocations that simultaneously call us and open direct access to our true way, to our true Dharma. Otherwise it's not very intelligent, it's just religious joining, like blind faith or belief. It's just outer. You can go to all the great temples or holy places and not find anything, if you're not open to it. And you can find it *anywhere*, when you are. We need to find what opens to us, and open to that. What calls us is also what drives us toward it.

Finding the way to spiritual intelligence could require a combination of openness and critical awareness, involving some surrender, if not complete submission. *Submission* is not my favorite word, but surrender is good. Think of it as yielding, as letting go a little. Think of it as letting be. Yes, you could call it submission or surrender to God's will, as the Muslims call it, but how about letting go, letting come and go, as the Buddhists think of it? How about just going with the flow, as the Tao calls it? How about just doing your duty, doing what needs to be done, and practicing Karma Yoga, as the Hindus call it? That's spiritual intelligence. That's the way, and that's also the goal itself. Then we don't have to worry, because then we're there. We're all the way there, right here, every single step of the way.

Knowledge, Confusion, and Wisdom

Spiritual intelligence doesn't depend only on the discursive intellect, knowledge, or literacy or education. Some of the most spiritually intelligent people in the world have been illiterate. There are many stories about that. One that comes to mind is the old lady who shames a proud and erudite Zen monk into throwing away the hundred pounds of commentarial texts he's carrying on his back. In this story, he's a renowned scholar who has written this exhaustive treatise on the Diamond of Wisdom Sutra and is arrogantly confident of his understanding—until one day the shabby old proprietress at the roadside tea shack asks him a question that he can't answer, stripping away his excess baggage and haughtiness. There are so many stories one could recount. They all make a point: none of the stories is precisely historically true, yet all of them have happened at some level! They could have or should have happened, because the *point* is true. The vital point of these teaching tales is that we don't necessarily have to find what we seek in the conventional way, and that we may even encounter it in some very unexpected places. Master Naropa, a leading Buddhist pandit of ancient India, encountered highest truth in the form of a leperous old hag by the roadside with whom he consorted.

The good news is we can actually use the energy of confusion to become more intelligent. In the four Dharmas of Gampopa and Longchenpa, we read: "Bless and empower us that confusion itself may dawn as primordial wisdom." How is wisdom disguised as confusion? In the same way that light comes in the form of shadow. What is shadow made of? Are some shadows darker than others? A little more light makes a lighter shadow. Shadow is a phenomenon of light. Shadow *is* light, there's nothing else! There's no such thing as cold; there's just heat or its absence, depending on how much the energy molecules are moving. It's the same with wisdom and confusion. In confusion, there is just some degree of ignorance or *not* knowing, where as in wisdom there is clear seeing, or *knowing*. Vision ranges from the darkness of a cave, where only a little light—but still *some* light—penetrates, to full sun or en-*light*-enment, where everything is illumined. Confusion and wisdom are not the same thing, yet they are not entirely unrelated.

When you awaken, you don't see different things; you see things differently. You're not *confused* by the mud that's spattering from life's fan all the time; spattering may continue, but whether it's mud or whether it's art depends on who's looking. Whether the mandala is the universal hologram in your vision or just a chaos of fractals—like sharp bits of glass in a broken kaleidoscope that you're trying not to step on—depends on your karmic experience and vision. It's like the Magic Eye.

Are these the best of times or the worst of times? Is it the dark age or the golden age? So many people say it's the dark age, but according to Zen, the golden age is every moment. This is like enlightened vision. Confusion is probably a good thing, because the energy of confusion can facilitate the truth seeking and inquiry that brings emergence of wisdom. There are certain practices that are specifically related to the utilization of the power of darkness and confusion. This is why iconoclastic masters of crazy wisdom like Trungpa Rinpoche are always stirring the pot. Why always try to make things easier? Make things harder. Some gurus engage in this kind of rough trade—like punching your hot buttons rather than just always being gentle and nice to you. A pressure cooker makes the rice cook faster. In Buddhist terms, it's always said that the gods—perhaps like people who live in Hawaii—don't suffer enough, so that they're not *compelled* to seek liberation. The gods are too complacently sated with pleasure to move. The Buddha himself was only stimulated to seek the end of suffering by leaving his palace and experiencing somebody who was sick, somebody who was dying, and other shocking sights he never saw in his godlike palatial abode.

Confusion and suffering has that positive quality of being like a thorn in the side that one has to extract to get comfortable. It's like the pearl principle. It's the irritant in the oyster that helps produce the glowing pearl. If there's no irritant, all you have is a clammy bivalve. But with a tiny irritant inside, the oyster as a defense mechanism lays down layers that eventually form a pearl. The pearl never comes from outside. Similarly, this whole constellation of confusion, irritation, and suffering has that positive potential quality, that pearl-forming capacity. That's why the more we run from it, the more we fall into delusion. The more we can be aware of it, or work with it, or feel it, the more the luminous pearl of wisdom emerges from it. We could learn to lean into all of life rather than pulling back and contracting.

Again, we do have specific wisdom practices. In the path of transformation, you would turn even feces into gold. But that's transformation, common to the Diamond Path of Vajrayana. This last line of the four Dharmas of Gampopa, "Bless and empower us that confusion itself may dawn as primordial wisdom," refers to nondualistic Dzogchen. Each of the four lines represents one of the four turnings of the wheel. And in the non-dual cycle of teachings, where you're not purifying, dispelling, or transforming, you just see the coal as if it's diamond already. You're not waiting and pressuring to transform the coal into diamond, but recognizing coal as a mine of wealth itself. In the Natural Great Perfection teachings of Dzogchen, the main practice for that would be *trekchod*, or "seeing through," recognizing thoughts and feelings as awareness, as innate Buddha mind itself—not trying to get rid of them or transform them into "better" ones, but just recognizing them as display of Dharmakaya (ultimate reality).

The nondual practices see everything as *it*—not just the light or positive things as it, but also the shadows as *it*. The nondual practices are the practices that help us awaken to everything as wisdom, and to every aspect of life as sacred and wholly complete. Because we tend to get caught on things, we think of wisdom a little bit in the wrong way usually, as some kind of *thing* like knowledge or learning. Wisdom, however, is quite different. It's more like common sense. It's realizing how things work. So when we become clearer about things—that's wisdom. Seeing things objectively, just as they are, and intuitively understanding how they form and function.

The practice of pure perception, of seeing everything as *It*, gives us instant access to things as they are. It's like the Zen practice of saying thank-you for whatever comes—because whatever comes *is* it, if we look closely. This is the direct route, the most advanced exercise of spiritual intelligence, which allows us to really awaken in every moment and to smell the coffee cooking and hear the flowers blooming.

The Tao teaches, "Accept the world as it is. If you accept the world, the Tao will be luminous inside you, and you will return to your primal self." This is spiritual intelligence, this is pure perception. This is it.

CHAPTER 21

CREATIVITY AND SPIRITUALITY

FIRST THOUGHT IS BEST IN ART, SECOND IN OTHER MATTERS.
—WILLIAM BLAKE

What *is* creativity, and how *does* it relate to spirituality? How is the creative spark akin to the divine spark that animates us all and suffuses all and everything? What role does the imagination play along the spiritual path? These are rich questions, a compelling and interesting subject close to my heart. Sometimes people feel that contemplation slows, thwarts, or even stifles their creative processes, but this is not at all my own personal experience.

I think that the major art form, actually, is not painting or poetry, music or sculpture, but the fine art of living. What is the creative genie like? I think it is the natural mind open to itself, capable of vivid present awareness and spontaneous expression without constraint or expectation, in a state of childlike grace, wonder, and delight. Theologian Karen Armstrong in her bestselling book *Buddha,* a fine study in biographical history and significance, says:

> Nibbana is found within oneself, in the very heart of each person's being. It is an entirely natural state; it is not bestowed by grace or achieved for us by a supernatural savior; it can be reached by anybody who cultivates the path to enlightenment as assiduously as Gotama did. Nibbana is a still center; it gives

meaning to life. People who lose touch with this quiet place and do not orient their lives toward it can fall apart. Artists, poets, and musicians can only become fully creative if they work from this inner core of peace and integrity. . . . An enlightened or awakened human being has discovered a strength within that comes from being correctly centered, beyond the reach of self-ishness.

In my own experience, what we generally refer to as "life" can seem like a mere abstraction. But *living* day to day and moment to moment is the most authentic art medium that we have, and is how we can actually let the creative genie out of being bottled up inside us. If we really think about it, what *is* art? When we create ourselves and our experience every day, every moment, and create freely according to the view we have of the universe—isn't that art? I think that is how God creates the universe, daily. For the divine power of creation is greater than any of us, yet immanent in each of us.

Musician and friend Robert Gass, author of *Chanting: Discovering Spirit in Sound,* has written:

The Persian Sufi poet Hafiz tells us how God originally made a statue out of clay in His own image. He asked the soul to enter into the body. But the soul didn't like the idea of being so limited, so captive in this form. The soul preferred to fly about freely. God then asked the angels to play music, and as they did, the soul was so moved to ecstasy that it willingly entered the body in order to fully experience the music. Hafiz says, "Many say that life entered the human body by the help of music, but the truth is that life itself is music.

Who hasn't been inspired by the sheer poetry of sacred texts? That is why the fine arts have always been connected to inspiration, mysticism; prayer and contemplation have always entered into it. The early American Transcendentalists of Concord, Massachusetts, understood these secrets. Reclaiming the sacred in our daily lives naturally brings us closer to the wellspring of creativity, spirituality, and nature. That is one reason many American churches today hold open-mike poetry readings, often outside, recognizing the unity of refined culture and faith.

Let's not think creativity is just something restricted to the professionals—that creativity is only splashing paint on canvas, composing a symphony, or choreographing a ballet. We're all artists; we're all dancers; we're all creative spirits in life. Philip Whalen said: "My writing is a picture of my mind moving." Author Kate Wheeler says that we are all fiction writers, especially when it comes to the story of our lives. I think it's very important to recognize and take responsibility for this fact, that we ourselves are creating all the time, not only every day, but every moment of every day. We're not just puppets. Nobody else is pulling the strings behind the curtain. It's called *our* life experience because *we* create it, and we are creating ourselves even now. We may be like robots, programmed and conditioned by what went before us, karmically speaking; we may be like finger puppets or Muppets, whose existence depends on what is inside. Still, we have to stand up and take responsibility for ourselves.

I know we might feel under the thrall of others, but I assure you that this is not the case. We might blame society for our problems, or big bosses somewhere; but if they obstruct us, it's because we empower them and allow them to do so. There have been realized beings who've found freedom even in prison, like Mahatma Gandhi and Sri Aurobindo, who said, "The British can imprison my body, but they can't imprison my mind." The spirit is always free, inherently pure, perfect, and untrammeled; it is through this attitude of inner freedom and autonomy that everything comes. Perhaps that's what Shelley meant when he said: "Poets are the unacknowledged legislators of the world."

Authentic Creativity

We may go through life with a victimlike mentality. However, it's really a matter of following or *not* following our own destiny creatively in accepting responsibility for our karma, character, and experience, without fooling ourselves about this. We do not benefit by editing out this or that memory, denying the truth, telling ourselves stories and pretending; we must at some point recognize that even if this life *is* theater and we *are* pretending, it can still be an *authentic* pretense. We can be authentic pretenders: pretending to be ourself, pretending to be a human being, pretending to be an expert standing up here and lecturing you now. What an act! And, yet, it's an authentic act—there's no hesitation or deceit involved. What you see is what you get—garbage in, garbage out, as it were. It's an authentic act, our own act, isn't it? Strutting about on stage for a moment, as Shakespeare said, before moving.

Authentic creativity is the art of freedom and autonomy. It is proactivity, like Buddha activity, which simply selflessly and spontaneously occurs according to needs, conditions, and circumstances. This is called *wu-wei* in Chinese and expresses the Taoist notion of nonstriving, going with the flow, oneness, and effortless being rather than overdoing everything. How different from our ordinary, conditioned reactivity, the totally predictable and highly conditioned stimulus-response reactivity that is known in Asia as karma. Creativity is proactivity. It comes forth freely and fearlessly, impeccably even—not always in reaction to what others think and do, or what the circumstances around us seem to call for, but *freely,* as we must respond. There can be a difference between simply reacting and intelligently responding. Enlightenment embodied means unobstructed, uninhibited, spontaneous Buddha activity—the ultimate creativity.

Trungpa Rinpoche titled his book of poetry *First Thought, Best Thought,* a Mahamudra slogan embodying the notion that raw unedited "isness" is the stuff that real poetry is made of. In his *Mind Writing Slogans,* Allen Ginsberg said that "Ordinary Mind includes eternal perceptions." The unedited expression of what emerges before we have a chance to edit and alter it is the primal stuff that art is made of. This is where unleashing the creative imagination comes in; the more that comes up out of our unconscious and subconscious mind, the better we get to know ourselves, and the more primal stuff there is, the more raw material there is for the artist to work with—just as in yogic breath energy work and in mindful meditation. It is not a matter of suppressing or repressing anything—thoughts, emotion, sensations, perception—but of becoming more aware of all that is within us. This is how we directly experience reality, as it is, and not as we would like it to be. Buddhism calls it clear seeing, which is one form of wisdom—seeing things objectively, just as they are, stripped of the tinted glasses that usually distort our perception. Proactivity is not relational; it is nonreactive. It's like unconditional love and openness. It's not relational; rather, it's free, unconditional—like dancing when no one is looking, or singing in the shower. More than simply creative, it is *creating.* The process itself, spontaneous, uninhibited, is what comes out of it. It takes time and practice to get oneself out of the way enough to enter into the state from which such true art emerges.

Writing teacher Natalie Goldberg was told by her Zen master, Katagiri Roshi, that since she was having so much trouble sitting in meditation, she would do better just doing her writing, for her own well-developed creative process freed her from constraint and self-consciousness; this is what I call a natural meditation. This is the point of the training in the Zen arts, where one learns the meaning of the old adage "To forget yourself and find your true self." My favorite book by an artist of self-mastery is the classic *The Book of the Five Rings,* by Miyamoto Musashi, who has the status of a saint in Japan and is the hero of filmmaker Kurosawa's renowned *Samurai Trilogy.* When Americans, trying to glean nuggets of worldly wise wisdom, talk about Sun Tzu's *The Art of War* and the Bhagavad Gita today, I ask if they have read Musashi's *Five Rings,* a little jewel of a treatise on self-mastery and authenticity. Musashi actually wrote it in seclusion in a cave after retiring as the undefeated heavyweight samurai champion of his world, in order to find peace of mind.

Perhaps surprisingly, the best-selling poet in America today is Rumi, the great thirteenth-century Sufi saint and mystic. What *is* creativity, and how *does* it relate to spirituality? What role does the imagination play? I get the impression that trying not to think does not help but can even stifle and thwart my creative process. I think this really points to the intimate way creativity and spirituality are related. In fact, saints have always loomed large among the giants of literature and mysticism. St. John of the Cross, St. Francis, Hildegard of Bingen, Tolstoy, William Blake, Wordsworth—not to mention ancient China's great Buddhist artist, the hermit Wang Wei, poet, painter, and musician; Milarepa, Tibet's greatest poet and saint; and Basho, Japan's greatest poet—have expressed their spirituality through art and their art through their spirituality.

I have found personally that meditation helps clear my mind and open my heart in a way that is very conducive to creative expression. I am not alone in this. That is why there is such a large amount of religious art, and spiritual practices including the creative arts, such as in the Zen Buddhist tradition, but also in other spiritual and religious disciplines. Zen poetry (haiku), painting (*sumi-e*), the tea ceremony, gardening, and other Zen arts are considered ways to meditate in action, bringing the same kind of results as zazen (sitting meditation).

Unleashing the Genius

Divine creativity flows through us amid the innate creative process that we can tap into, if and when we learn to better exploit our own inner natural resources. That is why it can be extraordinarily helpful and inspiring to find our own natural meditative state through that which most passionately enlivens us, whatever it may be. This is congruent with the principles of tantra, which teach us that every aspect of life is and can be sacred, providing direct access to the innate awakened state. It is difficult to predict when and where such grace may happen, for it's almost like an accident when that state of creative grace descends on us; but practicing our craft definitely makes us more accident prone, in this sense. This is the place where creativity and spirituality overlap—in getting ourself out of the way, so the inner light show may proceed, unhindered, unedited, unaltered. The struggle to open these inner doors and windows often precipitates psychological breakdown as well as breakthrough; this is why artists and mystics are often akin to madmen. Psychosis such as Van Gogh's can give birth to the most beauteous forms, feelings, and perceptions, as for any mystic who plumbs the source of vision through endeavoring to tear off his or her inner blinders and open to the infinite effulgence of being. Spiritual madmen and holy fools—such as Kabir and Mirabai, Surdas, St. Francis, Han Shan, Mulla Nasruddin—exemplify that kind of sublime craziness. Milarepa himself sang: "My lineage is crazy, I am crazy—crazy for dharma, for enlightenment!"

If what today's world thinks is real is sanity, may we all be blessed with at least a little craziness. It is difficult to stretch that far and unleash the inner genies if one is too well adjusted and fits precisely into society too well. If we want to think of ourselves as imprisoned, as enslaved, helpless—we are free to do that. However, I promise you that the door of one's interior prison is always open, and God's playing field awaits fearless exploration and discovery. Are we ready to step out, or have we gotten too used to cowering in our own cozy and secure little corner? I've read that when prisoners stay in prison for ten or twenty years, they're afraid to come out afterward. They feel at a loss; the big, wide, unstructured, and unregulated world seems too free and wide open for them to cope with. Almost inevitably, they end up back inside.

The true artist is never really lost, however it might sometimes seem. Every moment, there are infinite possibilities. The muse finds him, and dallies with him—waiting in ambush, if not actively sought after and pursued. The artist says in Henry James's story "The Middle Years": "We work in the dark—we do what we can—we give what we have. Our doubt is our passion and our passion is our task." The artist is always searching, like the spiritual seeker, but is never really lost, no matter how he or she may occasionally feel. And it's not simply a matter of choosing the right muse or art form; whichever one you choose can be the right one. Creative people find every opportunity to step out via creativity, and enjoy exploiting their own innate natural resources in the most unexpected ways. There is no such thing as art except what we invent. Who said that a Campbell's soup can was art until Andy Warhol saw it afresh and placed it up on a wall in the form of an oversized painting? That's called fresh *seeing*. If we see freshly every moment, *that* is art; that is creating life anew. Reinventing ourselves every moment, rather than being *caught* by our conditioning, by our illusion of limited and finite self. True art introduces a new way of seeing and *being*. Art awakens us.

If we are involved in a self-concept like "I'm an artist" or, for that matter, "I am a lover," we are not really an artist, we are not really in love. There is not unconditional selfless love there; it's still self-conscious, a sort of narcissism. It is the same with art. When we learn how to get out of our own way, then art—like love—flows unimpededly. It's quite transpersonal. We must step out of our own way to let the larger Self, the greater vision, come through. When we do that, that's genuine creativity, proactivity, and freedom. Stating "I'm an artist" is mental fixation, reification. When we step aside, creative energy can really flow. Think of it as channeling: get out of the way and let the muse speak. What we're talking about is dancing freely, free-style. We can't always request the tunes, but whatever tune comes, we can dance to it. *That's* choreography in the fine art of living.

When we formally practice meditation and other time-honored contemplative practices, our practice helps us be like a monk in robes. The robes, the shaven head, the mala beads remind that monk within us that all we have to do is sit it through, weather the storm and be aware. Because we create a sacred space, we can go through the chaos without fleeing. We might even welcome it, eventually, as more grist for the mill of spiritual awareness. If we cut off the chaos too soon, or if we're unwilling to really *hang* in the void and dance in the openness of craziness before contracting back into being socialized again—back into the gilded cage of egotism and normality—we will limit the breakthroughs we might have had. We could go further.

Many have evolved greatly by integrating the complementary insights coming from the irrational, intuitive, right side of the brain. That's the "Far Side," as cartoonist Gary Larson would call it, but it's actually not so far from the truth. These insights can truly set us *free*. Of course, we're not just talking about the mind; we're discussing the heart-mind, the emotions, the total embodiment of conscious being on all levels—not just mental, intellectual, psychological, but deeper than psychology and personality, beyond person and individual to the deeper level, the *be-ing* level. All of these comments are addressed to the heart-mind.

We have a lot of self-concepts, embedded in limitations we have constructed around us. My elementary-school music teacher told me not to sing. "When everybody else sings, just mouth the words, don't ruin the harmony." But eventually I realized that I could sing, chant, and play music well enough for my own purposes. Making music is not just for musicians. Arlo Guthrie asks, "Since when did music become a spectator sport?"

Who can keep us from re-creating our life as we would like it to be—as it could and should be? Nothing can keep us from being artists, rather than marching forward like mere consumers, corporate robots, or sheep. From *dancing* with life, instead of goose-stepping? Maybe not putting ink on rice paper, but every moment recognizing our own creative imagination, seeing the living pictures that we continuously paint on the canvas of our lives.

How we interpret things does paint this picture in front of us, doesn't it? These pictures determine the quality of our experience, for it is not what happens to us as much as how we respond to it that determines the quality of our lives. Right now, some people think it's hot in here, and some people think it's cold in here. That's like a visualization, a painting, a concept. *Everything* is subjective, a matter of conditioning, interpretation, and imagination. Imagination can be freedom, as well as bondage and conditioning. I was fortunate to train in the Zen arts. It's so unlike how we were taught creative writing in the hallowed halls of American academia, and even in the streets of Greenwich Village and San Francisco.

In Japan, the first thing you had to do in my calligraphy class in Kyoto was to spend an hour rubbing the ink stone in the water to make the ink before even making a single stroke with the brush. To prepare that ink, you had to sit on your knees in a meditative posture, relax and breathe; it was really a form of meditation. Only then did you have the honor of making the stroke of the letter for "one." You know, big deal—one single stroke . . . blop! After about three hours of practicing "one," you were allowed to do "two." Blop, blop! You have to slow down so much that after a while, something truly inconceivable begins to happen. You begin to realize that art doesn't happen just how you thought it did, and it has nothing to do with imitation.

We are creating every moment. We create the self, reifying the notion of self every moment, and reify our entire world. We create by how we see things, how we hold them, how we conceive of them. Zen and the art of calligraphy, Zen and the art of tea ceremony, Zen and the art of archery, Zen haiku—these are total trainings in focused attention combined with spontaneous expression. We are all spontaneous, naturally, all the time, whether or not we know it. We simply have to recover that faculty so we can better recognize it and actualize it in our own life. Have you ever seen the famous Zen painting with one swordlike stroke? Five hundred years later, people are still *oh*-ing and *ah*-ing over that one single stroke. It has so much chi in it—so much energy, so much nonconceptual directness—that nobody knows what to do with it, or how to interpret or imitate it; it simply boggles the mind. *That's* art—a new and fresh way of being and seeing. Art is not just dabbing expensive watercolors or handmade ink on expensive paper. *This* is the most precious and expensive thing, right here right now—this moment that we create and live. Let's not ruin it, crumple it up, and throw it away too quickly while always seeking something elsewhere. Far better to sink our roots deep into the present moment, and thrive on the rich nutrients found there.

The art of living demands a certain degree of freedom from conditioning. Even being *one* with conditioning is freedom, for not trying to get away is freedom. Not having to deny or suppress is freedom. Freedom is keeping the dance alive, not trying to find the right place and be stuck there forever. I think in the coming times, as things are getting pretty dicey in the great big wide world, it behooves us to know how to dance joyously with life, not just how to march to the tune of preplanned retirement benefits. The global situation is a little more overarching than that. It may or may not take into account our retirement plans. Let's face it: we don't know what's going to happen. Let's not just fiddle while Rome burns.

Are we living in a way that is conducive to dancing with whatever tune the band is playing? Or do we only know one or two little stutter steps—the cha-cha, the lindy, the twist, or whatever. Are we afraid to get out there on the dance floor and just freestyle? Do we want to be wallflowers our whole life, rather than enjoying the bash, as it were? What are we *afraid* of? That's the joy of creativity—there are no standards to worry about, except to excel ourselves by acting impeccably. No one is watching the dance; no one can realistically tell us we may or may not dance that way. However, fear and hesitation is a huge hang-up of ours, and it does tend to inhibit us. That's where inner courage, confidence, and even fearlessness comes in. We can't pretend to be fearless, but we can notice how fear holds us back—fear and doubt, hesitation, anxiety. Noticing that, and coming to better understand ourselves, we can let go a little. We can walk through our wall of fears, dance through it—just by *seeing* through it.

Are we afraid to make mistakes? When I first started teaching Dharma, I was talking to the Dalai Lama of Tibet, a significant mentor and inspiration to me. He said, "Don't be afraid to make mistakes—otherwise you'll never do anything." That simple advice was very helpful. Afterward, it reminded me of that creativity that I'm often, for some reason, trying to squelch, as if the spontaneous imagination is nothing but a distraction. This is the kind of dualistic thinking that inexperienced meditators can fall prey to, who too often try not to think and feel anything in their simplistic pursuit of limited concepts of inner peace and serenity. Sometimes before I even write down a poem, I edit it in my mind, ruling out large areas of fertile, preconscious material before it ever sees the light of day; then the original poem can never unfurl itself. How about trying to just write, write, write, write— keep the hand moving; and then tomorrow or the next day, revise, revise, and edit? If we are not careful, the internal editor can be too much like an inner tyrant, ruling us with a strong fist while preventing us from finding our own voice and freely expressing ourselves.

Let's reflect on whether we live our lives the way we dance or make love, freely and totally, as if no one is watching. Or do we instead live our lives and decide everything like actuaries, calculating the entire possibility curve, increment by increment, before we make the slightest move or investment. If you're an actuary, it might be appropriate; but as an ordinary person simply living our own life, muddling along, do we have to be that fanatically cautious and calculating? Do we have to take everything so goddamned seriously? Let's face it, if we can't laugh at ourselves, it's pretty absurd. We *must* have a sense of humor. Otherwise, it just ain't funny.

Open yourself, awaken your energy body, and see what can come from the other side of the brain. Breathing exercises are very good at opening the psychic channels and undoing the knots in our psyche that keep an incredible nuclear energy tied up in us. Nature walks and still, silent listening can be one of the best tonics for our agitated, febrile brains—as well as our weary bodies—and a most creative, natural, organic meditation. When we ease into the realm of nondoing—*wu-wei*—there is more room for our unknown, mysterious, unfabricated inner Self to emerge. We can try simply looking up at the sky like a child lying back in the grass, or looking into the fire in the fireplace, meanwhile opening up to tuning in to, listening to, what's coming from the other side of the brain. Not just to what's useful and productive, but to what's useless and unproductive, yet deliciously delightful. *Don't miss that!* That's where art comes from. Chuang Tzu said something like, "I'm just a plagiarizer. I never had an original idea in my life, I assure you." And he was one of the seminal founders of Taoist philosophy. What Chuang Tzu observed about his contemporaries twenty-three-hundred years ago rings true in our modern times:

"Everybody today knows the use of usefulness. Who remembers the use of uselessness?"

Do we ever leave a gap in our life, in our day, in our work week, when we don't have something "productive" to fill it—where things can just come up that are not part of our calculated tactics, not part of our overall strategy and war plan? The things that suddenly spring up, weedlike, may then surprise us. Weeds, too, can be useful, medicinal, edible even.

I used to think I needed to meditate more and write less, and wanted and needed to undertake more silent intensive retreats. I misconstrued the Buddhist teachings on nonattachment and equanimity as a call to suppressing and repressing thoughts and feelings, avoiding complications, and suppressing my own innate creativity. After decades on that track, I now find that being receptive, sensitive, and listening to what's being called for loosens and releases more attachments and preoccupations—while revealing more natural freedom and creativity—rather than imposing a cookie-cutter-like model on the rising internal dough of mind. I feel that, in the times to come, it is not only incumbent on us, but that we actually have no *choice* other than to be extraordinarily flexible and creative in learning an intelligent and skillful approach to sane living.

Are we willing to be the right person in the right place at the right time? Carl Jung said that the most terrifying thing in the world is to accept oneself totally. *Why* is that frightening? What are we afraid of? We fear we're not the perfect person, not good enough; isn't that how we often feel? Have we done something infinitely wrong? What are we guilty about? Carrying around that kind of stale old psychological baggage is not very original or creative. Maybe it's too late, we might think; maybe we'll get on with conscious evolution and personal transformation in the next life. Nonsense! This *is* the next life, anyway. Tomorrow is the next life; the next moment is the next life. This moment is the next life. Let's not wait. If we're killing time, we're just deadening ourselves. Why do that! Don't squander this precious life.

How do we really find our true vocation; follow our highest imagination or calling, thus making a life and not just a living—what Buddhists call right livelihood? How do we live creatively and proactively and passionately, not just getting through the workday like a chore and marking time until we die? What criteria do we need to go by? There are no easy answers here. I do have a few ideas that might have something to do with it—with the feeling of aliveness and completeness we might experience and feel through the creative process, in contrast to the deadening effect we get from other, less salutary processes. This presents us with a choice. As poet Robert Frost wrote: "Two roads diverged in a yellow wood, . . . and I—I took the road less traveled by, and that has made all the difference." I don't know why I took it. But it was less traveled, less advertised, and deeper, I have found. I sat out the seventies and eighties, but I did not miss much.

If we tune into ourSelves, we can find out our own true motivation. It can be very helpful when you see what's driving *you;* then you can choose to be driven in that way or not. Just because the wind is blowing from a certain direction doesn't mean all sailboats have to go that way if there are skillful, experienced sailors. That's freedom. Goethe said: "Whatever you can dream, imagine, or aspire toward, begin it. Boldness has beauty, power, and magic in it." Go forward. If not you, who? If not now, when? Are you waiting for the kingdom of heaven? Why not usher it in yourself? Let's usher it in, right here in this world. Let's create a new sublime vision of heaven on earth. That would be the ultimate creative art form, not just hanging some old, square religious pictures on museum and church walls.

There are many ways to trace back the source of all this creative radiance and to directly encounter the original creator, the innate creativity naturally within us. There within your primordial nature you may find the divine creator we've all heard so much about. We are continuously creating and re-creating our world, every moment. Through wisdom awareness—through meditation and self-inquiry, with clarity and honesty, we can be much more free of our creation, rather than being like a spider caught in a sticky web of its own making. We can be like a soaring garuda effortlessly enjoying the firmament, like the phoenix, rising from the ashes. The whole teaching of the innate perfection and wholeness of Dzogchen is about this natural ease and inherent freedom of being, which is the joy of creativity, of proactivity—the joy of total radiant meditative awareness, not just formal, quietistic meditative activity. The joy of contemplative sweetness and inner peace reaches its wings beyond duality, beyond the dichotomy of noise and silence, movement and stillness. The peace and stillness at our inner center is great peace, not mere quietude or slowness. In that light, every moment shines anew, like fresh morning dew on a blade of grass. When you notice that things have stopped shining for you, breathe deeply and start anew. Begin again.

One of my favorite poets is the eccentric Zen sage Ryokan, who lived alone in a mountain hut in Japan about a hundred years ago. However, Ryokan didn't just stay there all day and all night, looking at the moon and meditating like an ordinary Buddhist hermit. He loved children, and would come out almost every day to play with them. Zen master, poet, calligrapher, scholar, priest, Ryokan would walk down to the neighboring village in his flapping, ragged black robes, looking like an eccentric crow, and play ball with the children. When he went out, he always kept a rubber ball in his capacious robes so if he ever met any children, he could get up a game with them. In one of my favorite poems of his, he says something like "This old sponge ball in my pocket which I've bounced with children every day is more priceless than the golden Buddha in Daitoko-ji temple." This is why Ryokan's poems and hermitage are a national treasure of

Japan—in memory of a humble man whose little ball is far more precious to him than the golden Buddha of Daitoku-ji, an antique national treasure. The little ball, or the little child, the little pencil, or whatever it is in our lives that releases our creativity, our joyous spontaneity, is more precious than the golden Buddha in the national treasure house. This is wisdom; this is creativity.

CHAPTER 22

LIVING UP TO DEATH

The Sufis say: "Die before you die, and you shall never die." They are talking about ego death, which is the "big death," the real one. I want to talk about how to live up to our own deaths, as well as how to be with the dying.

The topic of death is absolutely relevant to our living. It is, in fact, a matter of life and death for us. We should attend to this very carefully. There are so many different ways to die, and so many things that can kill us every day. Life is so fraught, tenuous, and fleeting. The Buddhist philosopher Nagarjuna said long ago: It's not really amazing that we die, it's amazing that we're alive. It's amazing that we wake up in the morning. The *tenuousness*, the uncertainty, the insecurity of life, faces us every day. When we drive, how close we pass to that oncoming traffic! We could have a head-on collision any second. Each time we cross the street, we face danger. Our lives are potentially threatened hundreds of times every day, and we so take for granted the very functioning of the body and all the finely syncopated physical systems. A tiny bubble of air in our bloodstream can intrude on the heart or brain and kill us. During a meal, a bone could lodge in our windpipe. It's a miracle that we even draw our next breath, nor are there any guarantees that we will.

The teachings on death and mortality are among the most profound teachings of Buddhism. There are many sutras about impermanence discussed extensively in such writings as the Abhidharma. But the actual business of mindful living and conscious dying has been most lucidly explained in Tibetan Buddhism, the Vajrayana or Tantrayana, in the thorough explication of the *Bardo Thödol* or "liberation through hearing," the so-called *Tibetan Book of the Dead*. The Bardo Thödol is so named because it is a guide that is read to a dying person, to instruct them on their spirit's journey through the bardo (transition stage) after death. It is an eighth-century *terma*, a treasure revelation, from Padmasambhava, which explains what Zen calls "this great matter."

In the Bardo Thödol we find the teachings about clear light and the six bardos, literally "intermediate stages," "transitions," or "passages." What we usually think of as the bardo is the passage or transition between the moment of physical death and rebirth. There is also the bardo of dream, between falling asleep and waking up in the morning. There is the bardo of meditation. There is also the intermediate state after birth and before death, and there is the bardo of clear light. These are the four main bardos. The teachings clearly explain how we go through the very same phases in all of them—this is due to the fact that we are always in transition.

Training in Tibetan Buddhism is based on the teachings no-solid-separate-self, or the *openness* of being, as opposed to ego contraction, informed by a deep understanding of the imminence of death and impermanence of all conditioned things. It teaches how we can awaken in the present moment, now, while we're dying, or after death and before rebirth. This is precisely where meditation and awareness come in. Awareness is curative; meditation is like Buddha in the palm of our hands, for our use.

Buddha said that Yama Raja, the Lord of Death, was his greatest teacher, inspiring him to seek liberation and transcendence from suffering. My late teacher Kalu Rinpoche, the great Kagyu meditation master, said, "Awareness of death is the greatest teacher." When I was twenty years old, at his monastery in Darjeeling, Kalu Rinpoche instructed me, "You should always prepare yourself for death, for the moment of death." I thought, "This is just old monks' talk. I'm young like Zorba the Buddha—I want to live, I don't want to die, I don't want to think about death. I wanted to follow my bliss, as Joseph Campbell says. Kalu Rinpoche helped me realize that I, too, could one day become old and die; that suffering, illness, and death are inevitable. This realization still helps me to be more present in my life and to prioritize my activities in the light of the uncertainty and tenuousness of life and the imminence of death. It has freed me from a lot of attachments, from investing too much in sand castles that will be soon washed away with the changing tides of time. It has helped me to seek timeless truth amid the flotsam and jetsam of experience. It has helped me to find truth and inner conviction amid the vagaries of this world.

Venerable Kalu Rinpoche himself died in Darjeeling in the late 1980s; the Buddha died, too. We all die. Everything that's created, compounded, or fabricated dies. There's a fact of life—everything that is born dies. All those who come together are separated. Everything that is built falls apart. Kalu Rinpoche taught us how to meditate at the time of death—how to breathe out in the great skylike breath and dissolve all the elements into mind, and the mind into infinite space. When he died in his monastery in Darjeeling in spring of 1989, Kalu Rinpoche breathed out one great breath and dissolved into the skylike Dharmakaya awareness of Mahamudra, and he sat upright in that luminous state for three days. His great Dharma friend, Chatrul Rinpoche, who is still alive, was talking with him and guiding him all the way through that, reminding him of the pith instructions, of Mahamudra and Dzogchen. Kalu Rinpoche sat and meditated for three days after his heart and breath stopped, until he slumped over. This is possible—having this great out-breath at the time of death and dissolving into the clear light, the open space of Dharmakaya. A year or so later, he was reborn in that same monastery as the son of his translator-attendant.

I happened to be there with Kalu Rinpoche during that time, working as part of his monastery's translation committee. The thing I particularly remember is that when Rinpoche died, everything seemed to stop during the time he was sitting in his *tukdam* (death meditation); it was as if the entire universe were in suspended animation. It was a very unusual feeling, in teeming, cacophonous India, in a busy refugee center and thriving monastery. I felt that it was if Rinpoche were holding his breath, and his mind, and everything else in the entire surrounding environment was pacified, abated in perfect harmony.

Don't think that only a realized master can do that. This is the true power of awakened mind at its most consciously aware. We all have our share of the innate dharmakaya, and we can realize those transcendent states, too; however, it does require the kind of diligent, continuous spiritual practice that these masters have undertaken in their lives. It takes tremendous presence of mind. It takes tremendous levels of consciousness and awareness, and detachment from the body and the emotions, to be able to allow the fire and the heat and the solidity of the earth element to dissolve without struggle, without resistance, when you die and must relinquish the ties of this earth and this body. Then the water, air, fire, and space elements go, too, and the consciousness principle, which is like a light-body, moves on into the bardo transition after death and eventually toward the next life—within about seven weeks, the Bardo Thödol tells us.

Self-attachment, clinging, and *resistance* limit us and bind us incessantly to suffering and dissatisfactoriness—not outer things or experiences in themselves. We ourselves are essentially far more boundless than we might believe and than we generally experience. Within our own habitual conceptual framework, *we* project the suffering onto experiences and consider them positive or negative, good or bad, when all things are subjective and are therefore merely wanted and unwanted, neither more nor less. Nothing else and no one else is the source of our problems and dissatisfaction. Nothing else—no material object, no other person—is the source of our delight or fulfillment, either. Holding on to that which is in any case forever passing through our fingers just brings irritation, conflict, and anguish, just as holding too tightly on to a moving rope produces the pain of rope burn. It is in our higher self-interest to be able to loosen our tight grip on things and let go a little. After all, we are hardly in control here, are we? This is where letting go and letting things come and go—letting be—comes in handy.

My guru Dudjom Rinpoche, the late head of the Nyingmapa school, sat up meditating in tukdam or clear-light samadhi for nine days after he breathed his last in 1987. His skin was pink and translucent, and some heat still stayed around his heart, although he was clinically dead. Rather than going uncontrolled into the bardo passage after death, he died consciously, and he remained in meditation for nine days. One of my close friends, a British doctor who had trained as a lama, checked him daily; he could find no pulse, and yet there was heat around his heart, and it seemed as if the master was meditating. His skin was translucent and shining, and there was none of the physical deterioration of death until after nine days, when the meditation was over. Then he slumped over from his sitting position and started to show the signs of death and the body deterioration.

Among spiritual masters, death is often an extraordinary event. In an excellent book called *Japanese Death Poems,* one master said: "For eighty years, the clouds have gathered. Today the clouds part. The full moon sails on." He was joyful while the clouds of his evanescent human body-mind were dissolving in the full moon of his immutable Buddha nature. Another Zen master shouted, *"Ha!"* and then died. Another died standing up, gaze upraised, breathing in and out with the sky, and remained standing as if in meditative equipoise.

In August 1999, my beloved Dzogchen master Nyoshul Khenpo Rinpoche died at our Nyingmapa retreat center in Dordogne, France. I was fortunate to be able to visit with him a few days before he left this world. He was suffering from a tumor in the brain and was often only semiconscious, yet he could still speak on occasion and give blessings and instructions. I shall never forget the last time I saw him on his deathbed, shortly before he passed away. It was late summer in the forest. Rinpoche was near an open window, with birds filling the air with song; he was very frail, and comatose. I knelt alongside him and chanted one of our favorite lineage prayers and offering rites, and presented him with a white offering scarf. He perked up, used his good hand to take the silk offering scarf and place it next to his heart, and turned one eye toward me and smiled good-bye. As my wife, Kathy, who was also there, later said: "He still had one very good eye."

We are all going to die. Can we really face that fact? Our whole culture is in denial of death, and we hide the old and the dying from the young. Our cemeteries are like lovely, peaceful parks. But as we become adults, we have to face the fact of our own mortality, don't we? People we know start dying more often. We must seize the moment, take charge of our energy, be the guardians of this precious existence, and use it for the highest good, not just squander it in extremely momentary pursuits like investing in fool's gold. As Tolkien's saying goes, all that glitters is not gold, and all who wander are not lost. Let's not be deceived.

People die as they live. Living a good and true life does not mean that one will escape the pain of sickness and dying, but it does mean that one will pass on with less doubt, fear, guilt, and regret. A genuine recognition of death and impermanence, coupled with gratitude for the life we have been given, urges us to undertake what will make us and those around us truly happy. We don't have to speak so loftily about becoming enlightened: forget about that! The question is, Can we live sanely and gracefully today, and go through the passages of *this* life consciously and impeccably, until completing our work here and graciously taking our leave? When it comes time to die, nobody says, "I wish I had spent more time in the office." It's extremely important to prioritize our life now, and utilize our time wisely now, in the light of death, so we don't leave this world with regrets and an unfinished mess behind us.

If we practice meditation and awareness techniques, self-inquiry, and purification practices, we will diminish our selfishness, live more lovingly, and be fulfilled. There is great peace and serene joy within. There's great fulfillment, even if we don't die sitting up in the lotus position like a perfect Buddha. One Zen master died standing on his head. Another one died saying, "I don't want to die." And the students said, "Master, give us your final wisdom." And he said, "I *really* don't want to die." He simply spoke the truth. And then he died. This reminds me that even in death we can and must be authentic, not try to pretty it up with any kind of whitewash or superficial New Age veneer. Who has time to be inauthentic, anyway; life is too short, and every moment counts.

My dad left this world several years ago, after a brief illness. He was seventy-six. I was fortunate to be there with him when he died, at a New York hospital at seven o'clock on a summer morning. I was staying nearby at a hotel, and happened to be alone with Dad at that time. The rest of our family had, the night before, returned to their homes on Long Island and elsewhere, planning to return again the next day. I was sitting with Dad while he slept, my chair pulled up alongside his bed and near his shoulder, when I noticed that he had stopped breathing while he slept. He was so peaceful. I just sat with him for about forty-five minutes;

it was some of the best times we have ever spent together. Eventually a nurse came along to check on Dad. She took his blood pressure, seemed to start, and looked at me. "He is gone," she said. "Don't you know?" I said nothing. I knew. We knew.

Self-Inquiry

If we ask exactly *who* dies, this could be very liberating. Self-inquiry is one way to plumb the depths of our unborn and undying, fundamental nature. It's said that at the time of death, the clear light of reality dawns. However, the truth is that it dawns every moment, even now. If we don't recognize it now, how will we be able to recognize it at that chaotic moment of death when the whole physical system falls apart? The bardos are all passages, full of phantasmagorical, dreamlike images—phantoms, mirages, echoes passing through the stream of consciousness. Bardo consciousness also is unreal and dreamlike. All that occurs in the body-mind continuum is just a momentary occurrence and a mere appearance that we label, reify, and then get all hung up with concepts about—including strong concepts of how things are, how we are, and what things mean and signify.

What dies? Who dies? Who is reborn? Who *lives*? Who is it, exactly, experiencing your experience right now? It's the same *who*, the same identity. I know it's not a very satisfying answer for the rational mind, but you can find satisfying answers if you look into yourself in that way. There's a fine book by Stephen Levine called *Who Dies?* that looks deeply into these very questions. If I'm not exactly who I think I am, who are you? Are you who you think you are? Look into that. I found out that I wasn't who I thought I was, but even now I'm still not who I think I am. There are no limits to this not-knowing, this mystery, this dream, inconceivable and beyond the finite mind. We're so limited by our self-concepts and our self-representations. They must go. They *are* going to go—so might as well let them go gracefully and *be* reborn into a greater existence even *now*, thus living up to death. Can we live up to death, live up to the facticity of death? Can we also live until the *moment* we die? Not avoiding or denying fact of our own mortality. What does it *profit* us, to kill time just to get by, to wait for the weekend or next summer vacation—and overlook the possibilities of the present moment, the miracle of being alive right now? One of my students, Brian Maguire, had a heart attack in his mid-fifties. Afterward, he said it was the best thing that had ever happened to him, for it completely changed his life and helped him to stop taking everything for granted, to begin life anew in an entirely different spirit of appreciation, gratitude, and awe.

Perhaps we don't believe in rebirth; we could at least consider then, that in this life, we're reborn every moment. Every single moment is a passageway and a rebirth, a re-creating of ourselves and our self-concepts. Even if we're not sure about the time after death, this is something we can experience even now. It's like the amusing movie *Groundhog Day* with Bill Murray. Every day we wake up, it's the same day, in a way. We *re-create* it according to our karma, our projections, how we interpret things. We are continually being reborn. We can't graduate until we learn the lessons. This kind of unsatisfying pattern of frustration and incomprehensibility continues in a vicious cycle until we can break it and evolve further; this is called the endless wheel of samsara (conditoned existence). This continuation—what goes around, comes around—is the law of karma.

Have you ever noticed how we are *continually* re-creating ourselves? We're the artists painting the canvas of our life, again and again, as we are karmically predisposed to do so. Poets and artists tell me that every poem they write and every painting is a new version of the same one, trying to work itself out for the final, ultimate transcendent "perfect version." That is how I sometimes feel; this year I have become Surya Das version 5.7; next year it might be 5.8, or I might even evolve faster than my physical age. Ultimately, it'd be SD version ∞ (infinity). We would do well to more consciously create our new versions of our so-called self.

It works just the same as when we find our next rebirth according to our karmic predispositions or imprints, our *bakshak,* in Tibetan. Bakshak are the imprints or seedlike impressions in the subtlest form of our consciousness—which condition us like karmic software. *That's* what's reborn, according to tantric teachings—the subtlest form of consciousness, the clear-light aspect of being or consciousness—the habitual bent or patterning in our light body. This is what continues on according to the karmic flow (cause and effect, conditioning) from lifetime to lifetime, according to Buddhist thought. Bakshak are not particularly individual consciousness, but that's where the imprints occur and go and proceed toward rebirth when the body, memory, and personality are left behind. The being's consciousness is blown about by the winds of karma, gusting through the difficult passages of rebirth before rebirth is found in any of the different realms of existence, animal or insect or god or goddess or hungry ghost, according to one's karma. It is not so unlike how water flows toward the sea, finding its way amid all the various inclines and defiles and sideslips along the way, always according to the law of gravity.

This brings us to the *joyous* teaching of the opportunity to awaken every moment. It's not just a depressing teaching ("Oh my God, no! We're all going to die!") where we grimly sit around with long faces. We can awaken through these teachings to that in us which is *beyond* birth and death. We can awaken to our own reality, which is our own immutable nature—Buddha nature. It's open and luminous, like *sunlit* space, not empty like a vacuum chamber. This innate Buddha nature is ever accessible, all pervasive, not a thing yet, ever animated and ever animating us. When we awaken to it, we are like Buddhas, regardless of previous beliefs or knowledge.

If we practice deeply now, we still may not want to die, but at least we won't be so *afraid* of death. If we can acknowledge and face our fear, we will elicit the courage that is within us, and our lives will be energized and feel much more alive now. If we're just killing time—if we're avoiding, if we're in denial, if we're waiting for something to happen—we're just *deadening* ourselves. Life is now or never, as always. It's in *being,* not just in doing and achieving and gathering. It's in the quality of our authentic presence. It's in simplicity and in genuinely being ourselves, if that's not too facile a statement. It's extremely important to have faith and conviction in our true nature, not just in our incessant projects; not just in our actions, but also in our inner being. We need not lose our essential beingness amid all the doing, achieving, and becoming.

If we could let go now and pass more gracefully through our life, and be *ready* for death, that would be the ultimate. Then we could go gracefully through death, too. Stephen Levine, whose main service has been to the dying, has pointed out that death can be particularly difficult for New Agers and new meditators, because we all want to die in a way that's special and without struggle. It's very difficult for us to die in simple struggle and suffering. As long as we're not *masters* of our own energy and minds, we are not prepared for death; when everything breaks down and the blood stops going to the brain, and oxygen doesn't reach vital organs, we're going to struggle. This is difficult; so we must train and prepare for consciously letting go and letting be, at that crucial moment.

It's usually not as easy as just hearing about that and releasing everything. Maybe we need to live and experience a little bit more. World-weariness and renunciation take time and are a process; in Tibetan we call this the "arising of certainty," a synonym for renunciation and letting go. I think the truth is that we have to live a little first; we can't just throw away or renounce what we haven't experienced. So I would not say to anyone who is unhappy, who is bereaved or anxious, "Just let go." Everybody in the Buddhist ghetto says, "Let go, let go, let go." It's not always working! How about trying to hang on as much as you can? See where *that* leads you. See if you can hang on to this body, to this world, to your relationships, to everything—and see what *that* brings you. Just hang on, hold on as much as you can. Hang on until you're tired. And then, things will slip away on their own, and you'll be glad to let go. It'll be a *relief,* not a sacrifice or a strain. So I say—let come and go. That is my meditation instruction, and also my advice for ordinary, everyday life. Let come and let go, learning to let be.

One method for cultivating this ability to let things come and go is the practice of visualization. In tantric visualization practice, one generates a whole universe or Buddhaverse, and oneself as a deity, and then dissolves the visualization. With the proper guidance, this can be a powerful method for realizing the play, the charade, of all the self-representations, including self-identification and self-concepts, and how we live and act, governed as we are by so many causes and conditions. The idea is to see through this illusion of always wanting more, always needing more, which is a big fabrication and can go on forever, without ultimate satisfaction.

The practices for preparing for conscious death are also the right ones to prepare for life, so that we can begin *living*—living more fully, genuinely, truly, living with integrity—so that we tend toward sanity rather than insanity, dysfunction, conflict, and confusion. *Sanity* is the touchstone here. Sound sense, not nonsense. Preparing to die is preparing to live. We can't wait any longer to do that, because we *are* already living. And then when we die, we won't just be subject to the vagaries of our own physical body and outer circumstances but will have more inner mastery and realization, wisdom and *freedom.* This is a practice and art of freedom.

Clear Light

As we're preparing ourselves for death through living fully and well, we can also specifically begin to prepare ourselves for the moment of death. The moment of death is very important in the Tibetan Buddhist tradition, and there is a great deal of wisdom passed down to us about that moment and the time right after, and how to be with and assist those in those transitional passages. It's very difficult to know what actually happens after the moment of death. Reports from there are rare, although there are some people who have had near-death experiences. We also have reports from some reincarnate lamas, and from clairvoyants and different kinds of psychics. Yet it remains quite difficult for us to assert with certainty what exactly happens after death.

What we do know is that the moment of death is a very crucial turning point and significant moment of passage. All we have at that moment is our inner truth, spiritual realization, and wisdom, not our possessions. If we really want to move along the path, the time to prepare is now, not the moment of death. If we're not aware now, why would we suddenly become aware then? We'll simply continue to overlook and miss the luminous moment, just like now.

In Tibetan teaching, it says the clear light dawns at the moment of death. But the clear light dawns every moment. Don't miss it—awaken into that! Missing it now means we'll miss it then, unless we train and evolve more consciously into total self-recognition of this so-called clear light, which is not an optical light, but the inner luminosity or radiant clarity of nondual awareness. It's awakening itself, bodhicitta, enlightened heart-mind. It's what the Buddha himself recognized and realized— enlightenment. It's about awakening from this vicious cycle of endless rebirth and becoming. Dissolving into the clear light, one is spiritually reborn, even in this very life.

The clear light is the clarity of mind when the fog clears. It's the *inner* luminosity, not just the brilliant mind. Luminous, joyful, abundant effulgence—it's the clear light of reality. *That's* illumination, enlightenment. It's the vivid presence you might experience when you're with a true master, whose face is shining with it most of the time. *That's* the clear light, the inner light shining.

Many people—not just people from Eastern religions—say that this light is actually there. People who have had near-death experiences have talked about dissolving into the light. There is the story of Moses looking into the burning bush, an embodiment of that which "no man can see and live." I believe these are all experiences of something similar. Christ said: "Let your eye be single and your whole body will be full of light. That is, be wholehearted, collected, fully concentrated. Be totally present, and your whole body will be full of light. Your whole being will be illumined. The clear light dawns when you're totally present, and that *is* the kingdom within. That is freedom, nirvana. "This very land is the Pure Land, nirvana; this very body, the body of Buddha," as Zen master Hakuin proclaimed in the "Song of Zazen." He didn't just mean himself. He was pointing directly at *you*, at each of you. Don't just look at the masters. Don't just look at the teacher. Don't just look at *me;* this is all about *you.* Don't miss it! *That's* where it's pointing. See the clear light shining in everyone, even now. See Buddha shining out of everyone's eyes—humans, pets, everybody—and find the kingdom of heaven even now.

In the bardo after death, there are said to be all kinds of roaring sounds along with flashing lights and colors, as the karmic knots in the subtle inner energy channels unravel in the process of dying, and one is cast adrift and begins to create, from many circumstances, the next birth according to karmic conditioning. Traditionally, one's lama would guide one through each stage of this difficult passage, leading one to recognize the clear light by chanting *The Tibetan Book of the Dead,* thus pointing out the way into the light.

At the moment of death, the clear light dawns particularly brightly, as everything else falls away. The lama says, "Now the clear light of reality is dawning, so recognize that, as your guru has taught you. Recognize that and dissolve in that, rather than being attracted toward the darkness and the lower realms of re-birth. Recognize the empty translucence of awareness, and rest in that, rather than being blown about by the winds of karma, by the blowing waves of conditioning."

The important thing is this guidance, more than the Tibetan chanting. When my own dear friend Monk Martin, who had been on eight years of retreat with me, died during an epileptic seizure at about age forty-five, our teacher, the remarkable lama Tulku Pema Wangyal Rinpoche sat next to Martin and straight-forwardly guided him in English. He didn't read *The Tibetan Book of the Dead* but just sat there and guided him from his own experience. After Martin died, he sat there with him for twenty-four hours or so, and then he and another lama continued over the next few days to guide the consciousness, which is said to stay near the body in that time. Meanwhile, we held prayerful chants, liturgies, and meditative rituals in our center's Tibetan temple nearby.

It is important when with the dying to give them space to experience it in their own way, without imposing one's own agenda on them. Let them go into that light, into that gentleness, *peacefully,* cultivating a really sacred space and a holy atmosphere. Keep it very simple. Don't make a big trip out of it. Don't let there be a lot of wailing and gnashing of teeth. Just meditate together, or do whatever fits for them. Just be present with them and for them, not for yourself. They can read your heart.

The outer death, according to Tibetan medicine and tantric evolution theory, is when we breathe our last, but the conscious-ness and the inner energies continue to circulate and remain around the body for some days before they are totally separated and move on. Therefore, it's extraordinarily important that we treat the body respectfully, carefully, and gently. Guidance can be given then, just as while the person is still alive. It's said that the subtle consciousness can still hear the instructions and see those who are there, not through the ear and eye organs of the corpse, but through the clairvoyance of the subtle consciousness that hovers about the body in that place.

It's very important then how we treat the body. I advise people to remain compassionately with the body for however long they can after death. There are some places where we can actually do this on a regular basis, such as in the hospice wing of a general hospital in San Francisco, the Zen Buddhist Hospice Project run by the San Francisco Zen Center. After the medical people have ascertained that the person has breathed his or her last, they leave and let the hospice workers sit with the deceased for an hour or two afterward, meditating and continuing to be with the deceased in a reverent way, cherishing and witnessing the person's passage.

According to Tibetan Buddhist tradition, the subtle consciousness of the departed experiences some degree of turmoil, because it is still attached to that body, and so it's important to maintain a reverent and peaceful atmosphere around the body for as long as possible. It's said to be very distressful for the deceased if the relatives are bickering, dividing up the inheritance, and fighting. Buddhists want to try to facilitate a very sacred space during that time and not just abandon the deceased when their last breath is gone. If we find a dead creature of any kind, we try not to disturb it but protect the sanctity of its body space for a day or two prior to cremating the body or disposing of it in other organic, environmentally sound ways.

There are many traditional Buddhist ways of being with the dead and dying. If you really have experience in meditation, such as a profound experience of not-self, of things as they are; if you realize your total interbeing with that person, you can rest in the openness of this clear-light awareness and actually dissolve your heart-mind in theirs, and *carry* them into a deeper place for their meditation. If you do this, you'll be very helpful to them.

If you happen to be an experienced yogi or yogini, a powerful lama, you can perform phowa, the consciousness transference practice. If you are the guru of the deceased, and that person has faith in you, and the karmic connections are there, then you can help transfer the consciousness of that person to a higher rebirth from which she or he can continue to evolve on the path to enlightenment, such as rebirth in the so-called Pure Land, or in the gods' realm, or in a good family, with all the advantages, where he or she will have the leisure and opportunities and endowments in the human realm to meet the Dharma and to continue on the path of enlightenment in the next life.

Even if you can't perform this consciousness transference practice, you can do the more subtle awareness phowa where you transfer, as it were, *your* consciousness into the enlightened state of rigpa, and you share that with the deceased through meditating with them. You can do that also for an unconscious person. My brother is a scientist with expertise in neuroscience and artificial intelligence, and he has pointed me to some very interesting professional articles. Results have come back recently related to making contact with people in comas through breath work. Even though the people in comas are unconscious, if you *breathe* with them, they start to breathe in the same rhythm as you do, resonate with you. You can feel you're making some contact. Sometimes it helps them come out of the coma. At the least, it shows there's some responsiveness there. And this is very interesting, because if you consider, when you *breathe* meditatively with the deceased, even though the outer consciousness is no longer there, you are connecting with them on some level.

If you meditate with them and if you have bodhicitta—altruistic intention to awaken them, to liberate them and all beings—you can dissolve your heart-mind with theirs and really *effect* a significant, conscious transference or higher evolution for them. I really believe this and know this to be true. I do this with dying people, and lamas do this, and I've seen this happen.

In being with the dying and in preparing for your own death—which also means preparing for your own *life*—I advise you to really *be* present. Help sanctify and sacralize this profound process for those who are going through it. Remember, we will all go through this process, and *are* going through now anyway. We're always with the dying anyway, since we're all dying, so let's proceed with conscious care.

There are many passages to go through in life and in death, and every one provides us with ways to fulfill our karma and to awaken. They allow us to use every stumbling block, every experience, as a stepping stone along the path—including illness, suffering, and death—and to awaken through every experience. Tantra says *everything* is part of the path, part of the mandala of being. Since everything, this very moment, shines with the radiant clear light of reality, awakening is now or never. Realization is now or never, as always.

Can we create those moments in our own life, small intermissions when we recognize this inner luminosity? We don't need to wait until we're falling asleep, or dying, or, for that matter, having an orgasm. We don't need to wait until the next retreat, or our morning or evening hour-long meditation practice. Let's bring it into our day, with many short moments of just breaking through to recognize this, of turning awareness upon itself with this laserlike question—Who or what is aware? Who or what is experiencing our experience? Then let go into *that*. Dissolve the solidity of our self-concepts thus, and realize this undying innate nature, our own true nature, the Buddha nature within. It's one's *own* true nature. There's sublime peace there. *That* is reality. That is the divine. That is Dharmakaya, absolute truth.

Remember the tenuousness of life and the imminence and inevitability of death. Carlos Castaneda's mentor, the Yaqui Indian sage Don Juan, instructed him that "a warrior always keeps death on his shoulder." In other words, she always remembers death is looking over her shoulder. This means, remember the tenuousness of existence, and gratefully appreciate what is given, reprioritize actions, look into what we're doing and how and why, and refine our own life. A "warrior" is an impeccable, awakening spiritual warrior, a peaceful warrior, a bodhisattva-like spiritual aspirant. Life *is* spiritual. We're all living spirits. These are the basic facts of life, according to the truth of reality, and we need to refine ourselves more in accord with them. This is a teaching about life, about living up to death.

May your way through all the bardos of becoming be beautiful and *adorned* with harmony. And may we all together complete the spiritual journey.

CHAPTER 23

OPENING THE THIRD EAR
THE ART OF TRUE LISTENING

Everyone has heard about the third eye—the eye of inner vision and psychic perception, located in the center of the forehead near the pineal gland. Lobsang Rampa's book *The Third Eye* helped introduce the mysteries of Tibet to us in the West about sixty years ago; it included a fictional account of the Dalai Lama's getting his third eye opened with a corkscrew operation, in a cellar deep in the bowels of his towering Potala Palace in

Lhasa. I have been in the basement of the Potala, have studied history, and can assure you that that no such operation took place. There are, however, mortuary monuments (stupas) containing the embalmed remains of several Dalai Lamas in a sanctuary; the lamas preserved inside the gilt stupas are sitting upright in meditation posture. The first book published in English by the present Fourteenth Dalai Lama is called *The Opening of the Wisdom-Eye*. Published in Bangkok in the 1960s, it concerns Buddhist wisdom. Here, I want to talk about what I like to call the "third ear," and opening the ear of true listening. For truly listening is the secret of genuine communication. Listen, and ye shall understand. Hear, and ye shall be heard.

David Wagoner writes in his poem "Lost":

Stand still. The trees ahead and the bushes beside you
Are not lost. Wherever you are is called Here,
And you must treat it as a powerful stranger,
must ask permission to know it and be known.
The forest breathes. Listen. It answers,
I have made this place around you.
If you leave it, you may come back again, saying Here.
No two trees are the same to Raven.
No two branches are the same to Wren.
If what a tree or a branch does is lost on you,
You are surely lost. Stand still. The forest knows
Where you are. You must let it find you.

Let's begin by meditating on sound, wherever you are, right now. Who or what is listening to the sound? Contemplate this conundrum. Is the sound outside or within? Do the ears hear? (Corpses have ears, but they don't hear much, I hear.) What does the hearing? Who or what hears sounds? And who is aware of and interprets sounds when they are heard? This kind of self-inquiry helps us plumb the nature of knowledge, perception, and consciousness, and gain insight and wisdom regarding the nature of self. We could apply this technique to any of the six senses. For example: Who sees forms and colors? Who feels tactile sensations, smells odors, and so forth? Who is thinking our thoughts? Who is on first? Rabindranath Tagore said that within the question "Who am I?" all things concerning God and man could be revealed.

Where do thoughts come from? Where are they when we experience them? And where do they go when they dissolve? Can we trace back the source of all this inner effulgence, this cognitive radiance? Plumb into this bottomless abyss of groundless and boundless, centerless openness; the lights are on, but is anyone home? Through this kind of inquiry, which is part of the subtle discernment *rushen* practice of Dzogchen, we learn to trace back the source of all arisings within our mind—all appearances, all phenomena and noumena—and plumb the bottomless, groundless, and boundless well of emptiness—the luminous womb of sunyata, voidness—and reach the groundless ground of being. This is a Buddhist way of exploring what modern physics has been calling the event horizon. It is a window into our own nature and the nature of consciousness and identity.

There is the hearing itself, the process, and there is the hearer. To move into that contemplative space with it, we trace everything back to the real hearer, who or what is hearing the sounds we hear—and sense it directly, not theorizing. If you read this sentence aloud, you're hearing these words. Where are they resonating? Who is hearing them? Is it the ear that hears, or is it the consciousness? Corpses have ears, but they don't hear very well. So what's missing there? Remember, we're tracing back to the source of all our experience, our consciousness. That's how the practice gets deeper. That's where you start to find you can awaken through this practice of opening the third ear, or really, truly hearing: hearing sounds, all sounds, whatever sounds, in the context of pure perception and clear comprehension.

Listening like this can help us a lot in our everyday life. We can hear where people are coming from, not just hear the words. We can hear what is between the lines, under the words. We learn to really communicate by listening better, not just by talking and broadcasting our message and, if people still don't understand, just shouting louder, like tourists in a foreign land. So listening and hearing, I think, are very important for today, on many levels—externally, in day-to-day situations and in our relationships, as well as in regard to the inner spiritual realm. To still and silence ourselves within will help us to hear our inner voice, hear our own needs and wishes, and find inner guidance, inner truth that is usually lost in the general cacophony. We could learn, like Rilke, to "see more seeingly" and to hear more hearingly and feel more feelingly.

Hearing Truth Beyond the Stories

I have noticed that, even while meditating, I'm constantly telling myself stories and listening to them! We're always telling ourselves a story. That's the autobiography of samsara, the merry-go-round of confused existence. Telling ourselves a story: where I've been and where I'm going and what it means and what I'm getting out of it, and every variation on that theme, especially regarding how it all affects the precious ego self. Even when we're sitting in meditation, we're telling ourselves some story: "Oh, this is a good one." Or, more often, "This is not a good one!" They're equal, those two stories, regardless of the content. Or, "This would be a good one if the person in front of me would stop moving or if my knee didn't hurt." Or whatever it is during this hour. Always telling ourselves a story. And believing it—thus being caught like a spider in its own sticky web.

Awareness is curative. The more we become aware of it, the more likely that we might get tired of the storytelling. It can be amusing, and we can even enjoy it, but we don't have to be so invested in it—as if without the story nothing would be real. Actually, it's quite the opposite: With the story, we lose the actual reality. Our inner story obscures it. We're all telling ourselves the story of who and what we are, and wondering "What about me?" Every moment, if we check, we are always telling a story through our subconscious and unexamined concepts, which are not the reality itself, but just overlaid on reality, like maps that outline the territory yet are not the real territory. Endlessly telling ourselves stories. I think it would be interesting to look into the practice of everyday life, into what story we're telling ourselves now. Like, "Oh, I've come a long way so I can just indulge in this now," as if there is some real meaning in that. If you want to indulge, go ahead—no need to fabricate an entire rationalization. That's just extra energy wasted, when you could just be indulging straight ahead!

We're telling our story and then inevitably telling others' stories, and if they don't buy into our stories, having disagreements, conflicts, and even ending up with wars about them. Let's look into what we are really getting out of all this storytelling. See if it isn't just as rewarding, or even more so, just to tune in and listen to the real story being broadcast, as it were, every moment. In Buddhism generally, we emphasize the dreamlike nature of things and unreality because it's a deconstructive approach that loosens clinging and reification. The positive side is freedom, openness, loving-kindness, altruism, mastery, impeccability, authenticity, and joyous living. That's the reality. Too often we're missing that story because we're telling and listening to our own story constantly and then trying to pass it on to others, reinforcing our own storytelling. In fact, our entire self-story and personal history is more like a long, vestigial tale we can leave behind like outdated excess baggage rather than indispensable functional appendages.

Meditation mindfulness is something we can really use to

learn to listen better, to tune in, to be receptive. Not just to try to control or understand or get somewhere necessarily. This present-awareness practice prepares us to simply be and deeply live ordinary moments with no fuss, without having to overdo or polish up everything. Organic naturalness is really the practice of every moment. Not to make every moment into some kind of pious, Buddhist thing, but to realize the Buddha nature in every moment, the light shining as every moment. It is the practice of every moment in a very naked form. Not having to add on any of these mantras and Buddha fields. Nothing supernatural about it, simply supremely natural.

This openness and natural awareness practice of Dzogchen really attunes us to an authentic receptivity and transparent openness, a way of being that is both practically and radically transformative. We can tune in to things as they actually are. We can listen better, rather than story-telling and talking so much. Receive what is happening and surrender selfishness in giving ourselves up to the process.

Hearing the Cries of the World

Sound is a good object of perception for beginning awareness practice. Avalokiteshvara Bodhisattva, the spiritual hero of the Heart Sutra—who is practicing the highest transcendental wisdom, according to the beginning of the sutra, and from his own intuitive realization speaks it forth—actually became enlightened through hearing and sound. His biography says that he got enlightened by hearing—by hearing all the sounds there are, excluding none. He awoke from delusion's sleep by hearing—tracing back to where all sounds come from. Has anybody heard this? Avalokiteshvara: he who hears the outcries of the world. That's what his divine name means; that's one of the meanings of the name. Avalokiteshvara is the word in Sanskrit; in Tibetan, it's

Chenrezig, but Avalokiteshvara arises there also as Tara. This deity is actually androgynous because Buddha nature has no gender. In China, Korea, and Japan, Avalokita is seen as the beauteous form of Kuan-yin, Kanzeon, or Kannon, among her many mellifluous names. Guardian of the high ground, goddess of the awakened heart—the noble soul of selfless virtue and caring at the very heart of us all.

She heard the outcries, or the sounds, of the world, and because she had heard them in her heart-mind, she awoke, and organically responded in the form of loving, liberating action. Isn't that interesting! How can we, too, awaken by hearing? How can we awaken through the ear door, through the aural (ear) or auditory consciousness? How can we awaken through hearing the sounds and the cries of the world? Do we even hear these cries, or are we almost desensitized by the entire cacophony of worldly stimulation?

Many people say Avalokita's great spiritual awakening happened because she was compassionate. She heard the cries of the world, which opened her heart to even deeper compassion, and she became enlightened as an exalted *mahasattva bodhisattva*. This may be a good explanation in a relative sense, since she does personify and embody profound compassion and unconditional love. Yet the matter goes much deeper than that.

A man told me recently that even though he was quite happy and fulfilled with his life, he could see that there were other people around him who were suffering. He asked how to deal with that. I pointed out to him what he already knew—that his perfect life was perhaps not entirely so perfect. That is why we say, in Mahayana Buddhism—the universal vehicle of deliverance—that there is no individual freedom and liberation from suffering until all together are delivered and free, since we are all inseparably bound up with each other and interconnected. This is where the bodhisattva's great ideal comes in—to forgo personal peace and liberation until all are likewise liberated. The tantric twist is that by doing so, we feel more peaceful and free, having diminished a great deal of the self-clinging and preoccupation that lies at the heart of our own angst.

If we feel and hear other people's suffering, it's not so very different from feeling our own suffering. This is why empathy is the root of compassion. When there is suffering—any suffering—somehow we feel moved, and it is incumbent on us to see if we can do anything about it. We need to be careful though; it can get complicated trying to fix or save people, or tell them what to do, or to get them to do what we're doing. So it's good to look into our own heart and mind, our own motivation, being very clear and honest with ourselves about what we are doing and why.

I find it's very hard to say that I'm really happy and content when there are other people suffering nearby, for then there's some suffering in my life, too—some disturbance some unease or dis-ease, something wrong. We instinctively feel moved to do something about that, which is only natural. Not to mention the fact that when I see myself in others and others as myself, who could I harm, who would I be capable of manipulating, using, or exploiting? Empathy and compassion are at the root of nonviolence, altruism, selfless generosity, and service. Through it we come to be a great deal less concerned about mere happiness and pleasure and can get on with a life truly worth living.

However, misery, suffering, and dissatisfaction are not so simple. Obviously, we all have difficulties and troubles; life is difficult. This is Buddha's first noble truth. But suffering is also a very deep and subtle matter, not easily assuaged. If and when we experience real inner peace and freedom—nirvanic peace, divine oneness—it's so different from what we usually call happiness that we start to realize we didn't notice how dissatisfied we were much of the time. We could go more and more deeply into the suffering we perceive and feel around us, and within us, and delve more deeply into where ultimate fulfillment lies, rather than just settling for the cheap thrills, sensual gratification, temporary relief, and other stopgap measures.

In a relative sense, Avalokiteshvara does embody this compassionate response to the cries of beings, a sane and beautiful, loving response. And yet, in a deeper sense—and this also addresses the deeper roots of suffering—the reason or the way she awoke to prajna paramita was by finally understanding—by awakening to—the truth of the emptiness of hearing and the absence of a hearer listening. Remember, her name means "hearing the sounds." This means hearing the true sounds. Hearing from that place where they come from, which is truth, or sunyata; this is where the sounds come from. So as an exercise, let's try to hear where the sounds actually come from. When I strike a gong, do you think the sound comes from there? Isn't that what we think, generally? That the sound comes from the gong, from the bronze ritual instrument? Yes, generally we do think like that. Yet sound is not just what we usually think it is. If we trace the sound, the source of sound, we might trace it all the way back to where everything comes from.

That's what Avalokita, the exalted bodhisattva, did. That's how she awoke—through the spiritual practice of listening closely and becoming intimately engaged with the entire process of sound—subject, object, and interaction/perception—until reaching that oneness and luminous openness, sunyata, emptiness, the great void that is really the fertile womb of voidness, where everything comes from and to which everything returns. We can practice that, too. Just follow the sound. Go where it goes. Follow it to the vanishing point, and let your mind see if it can vanish or dissolve there, too. You can similarly follow thoughts or physical sensations back to the vanishing point. That's an experience we can actually have. That's the experience of arising and dissolving that they talk about in the mindfulness sutras, where we realize the inseparable reality of impermanence and no-solid-separate-self or thing. That's also the experience of Dzogchen, of the three vital points in the Tsiksum Nedek: going all the way to the vanishing point, the event horizon—the far reach of our experience, from which things arise and back to which they dissolve . . . simultaneously, coemergent, even.

Therefore, if we listen deeply to the sound and look into—and not just think, but directly sense and intuit—who or what is hearing, we can get closer to the source of everything, which is where we come from and where we return. It is also actually where we are. Let's really open this inner ear of hearing, this third ear. In this case, we're talking about the third ear, the heart of the "inner ear"—not just the little bones that make up biology's internal physical ear structure, the eardrum and the stirrup and all the little bones. I am talking about the real inner ear, where we're really listening, where we're really receiving and receptive, sensitive, resonating because we are being touched. That's Avalokita— being touched. Not just filling up our mental space with the flotsam and jetsam of our projections, wants, and needs, but leaving it spacious and open in order to be still and silent enough to receive the direct, unmediated communication and let ourselves be truly touched. Then we can expand and develop that in a deeper sense, and start hearing through all the senses, even hearing through our eyes and hearing the stars twinkle, as Saint-Exupéry's Little Prince called it. Are you listening? Do you read me?

Meditating Through Music

Deep listening is a beautiful practice, something we could really get into and greatly profit from—anywhere, anytime. We might not yet know how to just sit still in silence for a long time, but that's not the only way to meditate. We can learn and train ourselves to just listen—to start listening—through intentionally, consciously, tuning in to music. My own teacher in Vermont, Harinam Das, uses music as a tool for awakening to the fresh immediacy of experience through self-inquiry combined with sound. Our music sits are extremely refreshing. Many people think of meditation as being silent, but this is not always the case. There is chanting meditation, and the use of ritual instruments for offering sound is also popular in various spiritual traditions of the world. The late Indian master Sri Aurobindo taught disciples in his ashrams around the world not to meditate silently; instead, they listened to certain kinds of music. Aurobindo ashrams around the globe now always meditate while listening to music; they say it awakens the inner soul. Sri Chinmoy, who consecrated the meditation room in the United Nations building in New York, taught likewise. Steven Halpern, aka "Dr. Music"— with whom I collaborated on the CD *Chants to Awaken the Buddhist Heart*—is the founder of music for relaxation and meditation. I like to listen to certain kinds of music for this purpose, such as Eric Satie's marvelous piano music, some compositions by Bach and Mozart, and Chick Corea's surprising piano improvs. It is easy for some people with so-called musical intelligence to enter into deep contemplation that way, just as some Tibetan chant masters, Hindu yogis, and Christian mystics do through chant; Jewish mystics through their continuous rhythmic davenning, which is chanting and swaying at the same time; and Sufis through spiritual song, whirling, and dancing. If you try meditating this way, don't use music you're familiar with. That brings up too many associations with yourself and who you think you are, what you think you're doing in life. Find music that's not what you listen to every day, music that's not from your favorite band. Let the music soothe, calm, and caress you, transporting you far from your ordinary everyday concerns and preoccupations. Dissolve with it and into it, like listening to the waves while sitting on the sand near the sea—letting yourself be carried away. Thus contemplate. This is music meditation.

I have learned from my Tibetan lamas and ritual teachers as well as poets and bards like Allen Ginsberg; Ysaye Barnwell, a singer in Sweet Honey and the Rock who gives fine workshops; Krishna Das, my favorite Hindu chanter; Robert Gass, author of the book *Chanting;* Bhagvan Das; and others how to unfold the glory of spiritual voice. When I chant, it feels as if my own guru is right before me. Mysteriously, I find that the same one who learned the birds to sing learns me, as long as I keep writing poetry and songs, chanting and singing. Singing is believing.

The sound we use to meditate on and to trace the source of hearing does not have to be music, of course. Whatever it may be, there is the sound that is heard; it could just as well be the music of a waterfall, a stream, or the ocean waves that help wash your ordinary preoccupations and emotions away, leading into a naturally organic meditative state. One could listen to the sighing of wind, birdsong, or even the sound of silence, and thus access the contemplative state of mind. For this purpose, white noise, even if artificial, is better than more complex types of sound. The point is to use the gateway of hearing to access the deeper realms of consciousness and awareness, beyond consciousness into the unconscious and beyond.

When we chant, part of the chanting is dealing with this dimension of sacred sound, of hearing, of the mind's "ear" consciousness. We have six consciousnesses, according to Buddhist psychology. The first five correspond to the eye, ear, nose, tongue, and body perceptions and sensations. The sixth is mind—thoughts and feelings. Each of these depends on consciousness, not just the physical organ. If we trace back, deeply within, we start to find that actually we're not just who we think we are, and that sounds really aren't just outside or inside. In fact, we ourselves are not just inside or outside. And the other people aren't just outside or inside, as they seem to be. Then things start to get a little more interesting, or even scary. Concepts start to erode. Reality becomes more fluid, malleable, transparent even. You don't know exactly where you are. That can be very revealing, very liberating, even.

When we practice mindful chanting, we're working with this dimension of third ear practice. Third ear practice involves the ear and the ear consciousness. It involves the level of looking into who or what is hearing, and what the relation is between outer and inner in regard to ourselves; and moreover, how we interpret and create things out of these bare vibrations. Vibrations come to our ear, and we call it "music" or we call it "noise." Actually it's just waves and vibrations. That's where our consciousness enters into experience—interpreting our experience for us. Otherwise it's just sound vibrations. It's not noise or music. It's simply the energy vibration in the moment, resonating on our inner ear bones, and us knowing it, receiving it. We can start to strip away our interpretations and projections and know the bare experience of reality, without liking and disliking, without judging. Then we're in that place where we just feel the vibrations internally in our different chakras, or externally in our different senses, which can be very liberating. Then we can nakedly meet life along the entire length of her body. Not just bump heads or shake hands with life, but meet life along the entire length of her body, as the fifteenth-century Hindu mystic and poet Mirabai said.

If you like chanting, chant. Practice chanting meditation through *shabda,* sacred sound. You can definitely learn the chants we do together, and do them yourself. Don't feel shy or self-conscious. Don't worry! When I was young, the music teacher at school used to tell me to just stand in the back and mouth the words, because I couldn't sing—or so it seemed. I don't hear music very well. But somehow when I was in India and trained in chanting, I felt that it opened my throat chakra and accessed certain inner natural resources I had been totally unaware of. And no longer was I so hesitant and concerned how it sounded to others. I didn't care what it sounded like, because it was my spiritual practice. Then it all started to unfold. It was like opening a chakra, opening the heart, opening other dimensions—it just all started to happen. I don't want to make sacred sound seem too mysterious or airy-fairy. I simply wasn't self-conscious anymore, because we were just chanting, just practicing; I could let myself go, and put myself into it, heart and soul. And then within a year, some years later, I ended up being one of the two chant masters of our retreat center. Now people say, "Oh, Surya, you chant so beautifully. How did you learn? I myself can't chant at all." And they don't believe me when I tell them I used to sound like Bob Dylan or Leonard Cohen with a cold. . . . Maybe I still do!

It's very simple. When I think I am who I think I am, then I feel like I can't sing, because my personality is conditioned by the early authoritarian voice informing me that I can't. Where I grew up, people generally thought that girls could sing better than boys. When you reflect on and question the basis of this assumption, you see how limited it is, yet such limiting beliefs are often deeply ingrained. I can hit baseballs and shoot basketballs and ride horses, but I can't sing—or so I got used to thinking. But when you're in a different mind-set and relating to a different self-concept, like being a wandering vagabond pilgrim in the Himalayas stopping for a while at a monastery in Nepal where the chanting and liturgical rituals go on day in and day out, sometimes day and night, you start to forget who you are, who you thought you were, and then it can just happen. As I said, it's as if my throat chakra opened through chanting mantras and learning how to do so unself-consciously without worrying too much about what it sounded or looked like and who might be listening. (These were Buddhist prayers being chanted after all, so that means no one was up there listening!) It was as if something vibrant and outrageous suddenly began to unroll and unfurl within me, like a musical gene that had been smothered and constricted throughout my upbringing. The point to this story is this: what I am saying here goes far beyond just singing, doesn't it? It's a live demonstration of our mind-forged manacles, our self-imposed limitations, and how we hold ourselves down by how we think about ourselves and our possibilities. This story is really about deep listening—listening to the inner music of our true, untrammeled Selves. So I'm sure you can chant, too, and really enjoy it; then all the angels and deities will dance to your tune.

Sometimes as we chant, we might visualize our heart opening like a sun or a sunflower, or visualize the various chakras with their different-colored petals and radiant Sanskrit letters in them and other such esoteric details. These samadhis (concentrative absorptions) can help you focus and concentrate deeply, becoming totally absorbed in the visualization process to the exclusion of all else, and stretch even further beyond who you thought you were. Instead of hearing in the mind's ear a voice from the past, exclaiming, "Don't sing, Jeffrey!" you might feel more like a star, an inexhaustible sun radiating in all directions at once. You have long forgotten the nasal schoolteacher voice in your head that said, Don't-Sing-Jeffrey, and you're just radiating. Nobody's saying to the sun, "Don't shine, sun, you're not radiating at the right pitch." Through the various kinds and levels of samadhis, we can learn how to meditate with chant and visualization, eventually penetrating deeper into these heart-opening, transformative practices. Anyone can.

If we would open our third ear, the inner organ of true listening, we could discern four different planes or levels of sacred sound (shabda, in Sanskrit). First, there is the ordinary level of external noise, speech, mantra chanting, hearing, and auditory consciousness. Going deeper, there is the more subtle energetic component of sound and vibration, such as imagined sounds and music, inner music (such as composers sand musicians hear and can arrange and orchestrate), and visualized mantric seed syllables (bija) seen in our radiant inner channels and chakras, the root of external sound and expression. Thirdly, going even deeper, there is the divine ear, clairaudience, and sacred sound— like the so-called music of the celestial spheres—that can neither be heard nor imagined, but which can be tuned in to through subtle yogic states of consciousness. And, finally, there is the ultimate realm of shabda, truly sacred sound, the unborn and undying realm of deathless reality—in which form and emptiness are inseparable—the most subtle, ineffable dimension of the dance of being itself.

Chanting helps attune us to hearing those deeper planes of experience and pure being, awakening the little Buddha within us all. I find chanting prayers and meditative liturgies to be one of the most beautiful of the contemplative arts and practices. Sacred sound uplifts us all, nurtures the soul, illumines the spirit, and emanates outward throughout untold universes in effulgent waves of light and delight. That is why most if not all the world's religious and spiritual traditions utilize it as part of their spiritual discipline.

If you do this kind of loving practice, it comes out naturally in many ways. Lama Kalu Rinpoche used to say the compassion mantra *Om Mani Padme Hung* over bowls of rice or sand every morning. Then he'd throw the grains out the window or spread them as he walked so all the ants and dogs and snakes around his hillside monastery would eat the rice or touch the sand and make a spiritual connection, thus being blessed and benefited. He did that every day of his life. He even suggested to us, his students, that we do the same. I must admit to not living up to his standard.

Converging in the Heart of Wisdom

Ultimately, all authentic spiritual practices converge in the heart of wisdom, in the luminous heart of Dharma, in the true nature of reality. That's why it's so important, I think, to look now and then into the who or what is chanting—not only and always just while chanting. Look into who or what is hearing—not just hearing. The Buddha said, "In hearing, there is just hearing. Nothing outside to hear and no one hearing it." We would do well look into that; it's a very fruitful area for exploration and self-inquiry. We could extend that to seeing, smelling, tasting, feeling; for example, investigating and noticing that there's just feeling—no real lasting feelings, and no separate individual feeling them. In thinking, there's just thinking—nothing thought, and no one thinking it. There are no concrete, "real" thoughts. There are just mind moments that we string together with the crazy glue of our own concepts into "Oh, my funny mind!" or "Oh, my angry mind!" Or whatever other kind of label we habitually like to lay on ourselves. But actually, in thinking there is just thinking, and no one thinking it. It's just mind moments bubbling up.

For homework, I hope you'll feel inspired to look into who or what is hearing, and trace back to the source of what is heard. Are the sounds outside? Are they within? That's a good kind of koan or conundrum for purposes of self-inquiry, an excellent practice for inquiring deeply about the nature of identity and the self. The sound doesn't have to be the striking of an Asian meditation gong; it could be the sound of the traffic or a siren. It could be the delivery person ringing the doorbell, or a dog barking. It could be whatever the third ear happens to pick up. Stop for a moment, as if it is a mindfulness bell ringing to call the community to prayer and meditation. Pay attention—it pays off.

You don't need an operation to open your third ear, the inner ear of true listening. This spiritual organ is already within you, readily being developed. Thich Nhat Hanh says, "Listen, listen, this wonderful sound brings me back to my true home."

CHAPTER 24

BEING PEACE, DISARMING THE HEART
ANGER AND NONVIOLENCE

On the eve of war in Iraq, when the sweet scent of peace was in the air along with autumn's leaves, I kept thinking that we must look into our hearts and minds and see what we may be doing to contribute to these problems, and how we might become part of their eventual solution. Aren't religions supposed to further peace, unity, and harmony, rather than contribute to prejudice, bigotry, and violence? Nonviolence is the first precept of Buddhism, and a fundamental tenet of many world religions, yet look what actually happens in the world, recently in the Middle East and Bosnia and Sri Lanka as well as throughout history, and even here at home in proudly Christian America, where guns in the schools and at home continue to harm us. Violence has come to the fore in our time as a major focus of concern, but we have not made much progress in averting or dealing with it. We all need to learn how to intelligently confront and deal with the anger and hatred at the root of violence. The heart-mind is mightier than the sword.

Martin Luther King Jr. said that we have two choices: to peacefully coexist or to destroy ourselves. Do you know how many countries in the world are experiencing war right now? Dozens! Yet here in America we don't feel as much evidence of it as we did during the several wars of the twentieth century. War does not begin outside somewhere, on a battlefield, along some disputed border, or in a diplomatic conference room or economic summit meeting. War begins with the cupidity, hatred, prejudice, racism, ignorance, and cruelty in the human heart. This is because the true battlefield is the heart of man, as Dostoevsky says. If we want peace in the world—and I firmly believe that we all do—we need to face this fact and learn how to soften up and disarm our own hearts, gaining some degree of control over our anger, as well as working toward nuclear disarmament and peace in our time. We need to think globally and act locally, beginning with ourselves and each other—at home and in the family, as well as outside at work and in the community, reaching out more and more in broad, all-embracing circles of collective caring and responsibility.

In Buddhism, Avalokiteshvara is the embodiment of the Buddhist heart of unconditional love and compassion, loving-kindness, mercy, forgiveness, acceptance, and joy. He/she is the spiritual archetype personifying those qualities that are latent in all of us, only waiting to be developed, cultivated, and actualized. That's what it means to become enlightened and to be a Buddha, which anyone can do if they follow the spiritual path to the end. Becoming enlightened means to realize and actualize all that is already in us. That is our Buddha nature, or the innate Buddha within—not the historical teacher from India, but the actual awakening of the god or goddess, the wisdom and compassion that is in all of our hearts and minds. Being Buddha means awakening to our wisdom and compassion, actualizing that through and through, and embodying it in the world by sacralizing our entire life. We chant the Tibetan mantra of love and compassion, the mantra of Avalokiteshvara *Om Mani Padme Hung,* the Dalai Lama's mantra, while visualizing infinite light rays radiating out from our heart chakra and reaching out to touch and awaken all beings, illumining them all with healing love and blessings. We cultivate the four boundless states of mind: compassion, loving-kindness, joy, and equanimity/forgiveness. This meditation on love and compassion is one of the most important Buddhist meditations and is common to all the various schools of Buddhism.

Key elements of spiritual awakening through most traditional paths are the practices of nonviolence, forgiveness, altruism, and compassion—which necessarily include learning to deal with anger and hatred by purifying ourselves and rooting out anger from our hearts and minds. One of the principle tenets of Buddhism, as of all deep spirituality, is nonviolence, nonharming—and, even more radically, to be helpful and altruistic. But I don't want to ask too much on the first attempt! At least let's start with nonviolence, nonharming, and living lightly on this planet rather than destroying it and ourselves. That's the minimum, I think. And this is a *practice,* not just an ideal; these virtuous principles of nonviolence and nonharming are not just something the Dalai Lama or Mahatma Gandhi, Albert Schweitzer, Mother Teresa, Jesus, and Buddha could do, but something we can each practice in our own lives, in countless ways great and small. We all care about, and perhaps even work for, peace in the world and in our communities and homes, and for inner peace, too, in ourselves and in our relations with others. But the war, violence, and aggression we struggle with on so many levels all come from the anger, hatred, greed, and ignorance in our own minds. That is the root, and the only root, of these evils.

Therefore, let's zero in on the negative emotions, which so often lead us into undesirable behaviors and results. *Klesha* is the technical Buddhist term for them. *Klesha* is sometimes translated as "afflictive passions" or "obscuring emotions." These translations are not totally accurate. They easily lead us to misunderstand, to judge too quickly, and perhaps to think we have to get rid of all of our feelings, emotions, and sensitivity in the name of some kind of idealized equanimity and spiritual detachment. For our purposes here, kleshas are disturbing, egocentric habits of thought and conflicting feelings that drive us into unconscious reactions and unskillful, nonvirtuous actions. The kleshas we are discussing here are the selfish, overwhelming, destructive emotions such as anger, hatred, jealousy, overweening desire and lust, avarice, and the like. We are not considering here the positive or healthy emotions such as love, tenderness, and compassion. In dealing with the difficult negative emotions, anger is a particularly crucial one to talk about right now. How do we assert some self-control in dealing intelligently with that intense energy?

Dealing with Anger

Buddhist teachings say that at the heart of the vicious cycle of samsara, the wheel of becoming, are the three poisons, the three root kleshas: greed, hatred, and ignorant confusion. The main klesha that fuels this whole dualism of attachment and aversion that drives us is ignorance, or delusion and confusion. From ignorance comes greed, avarice, desire, lust, attachment, and all the rest. Also from ignorance comes anger, aggression, cruelty, and violence. These two poisons—attachment and aversion—are the basic conflicting forces within us. They come from ignorance, and they're really not that different: "Get away" and "I want" are very similar, just like pushing away and pulling toward. Both cause anger to arise.

Anger is often singled out as the most destructive of the kleshas, because of how easily it degenerates into aggression and violence. However, anger is easily misunderstood. It is often misunderstood in our Buddhist practice, causing us to suppress it and make ourselves more ill, uneasy, and off-balance. I think it's worth thinking about this. Psychotherapy can be helpful as well. Learning to understand the causal chain of anger's arising as well as the undesirable, destructive outflows of anger and its malicious cousin hatred can help strengthen our will to intelligently control it. Moreover, recognizing the positive sides of anger—

such as its pointed ability to perceive what is wrong in situations, including injustice and unfairness—helps to moderate our blind reactivity to it and to generate constructive responses. As the Dalai Lama says, "Violence is old-fashioned. Anger doesn't get you anywhere. If you can calm your mind and be patient, you will be a wonderful example to those around you."

It can sometimes feel that the most frightening thing in the world is to honestly face ourselves. How do we deal with difficult emotions such as fear and rage when they arise like a tsunami or a volcano? It is good to start by examining ourselves in a some-what less stressful situation, starting first with the little forms in which the difficult emotions arise, like during meditation. When we are alone in daily practice, or maybe in a Dharma center, yoga studio, or meditation retreat—where everything's perfectly arranged for our protection, comfort, and security—it's hard to get too overwhelmed by anger. But still there are the little irrita-tions, like mosquitoes buzzing around the ears or traffic sounds from outside. Perhaps somebody inadvertently steps on your toe in the lunch line, or the person sitting next to you keeps cough-ing and shifting around; or maybe the teacher says the wrong thing for your hypersensitive ears. How do we deal with that anger, aversion, and judgment when it flares up? Do we just keep a stiff upper lip and suppress it, mistaking this stony pseu-doserenity for calmness, detachment, and equanimity, when it's actually violence against our own nature—violence in the form of suppression, repression, and avoidance? This kind of avoid-ance and repression is similar to more blatant forms of aversion, such as in the gesture that pushes undesirables away. Some peo-ple can seem very cool, calm, and collected, yet they may be seething inside—and some of us may be those very people! Maybe our fangs and claws are not out, visibly pointed toward others, as in the case of some short-tempered individuals; but those jagged weapons may be pointed inward toward ourselves, as in the case of low self-esteem, self-loathing, and self-hatred, which are all common strands of depression. Denial is one of the largest rivers running through our heartland. We would do well to consider our little subterranean upsurges of anger and hatred along with the occasional larger outbursts, and not pretend they're not there, if we want to be in a better position to deal with them. The seeds of anger are in all of us. There's no shame in that.

Shantideva, the gentle master who wrote the classic book *Entering the Bodhisattva Path* (*Bodhicharyavatara*) twelve hundred years ago, said: "Anger is the greatest evil; patient forbearance is the greatest austerity." Isn't that interesting? Anger is thought to be the greatest negativity, just as killing is the greatest sin. Patience and forgiveness are said to be the greatest virtue, the hardest practice or austerity. Usually we think of austerities as fasting or vigils; staying up all night in prayer; pilgrimages; or as fakirs in India sleeping on beds of nails or never sitting or lying down. Yet Shantideva said that patient forbearance is the greatest austerity, rather than mere physical vicissitudes. Isn't that amazing?

Why is anger the greatest evil? This is because a small amount of anger can in an instant burn down a whole forest of merits and good karma. For example, you might become blind with rage and do something that you regret for the rest of your life. In a moment of blind rage, or being drunk one night, you could ruin the rest of your life if you get in the driver's seat. The car could become a deadly weapon in just one moment. That's why we have to be careful, attentive, and mindful rather than mindless. That's why Shantideva warns about how destructive anger can be, just as a mindless moment of carelessness in throwing a cigarette butt out the window of a car can burn down an entire national park. Even the acid-tongued eighteenth-century poet and social critic Alexander Pope recognized that, in his own words, "to err is human, to forgive divine." We can access our inner divinity by practicing forgiveness, which is within our heart's capacity. Shall we choose to exercise that innate capacity, or not? We all know life is not always simple, and that it really *is* hard to practice patient forbearance and forgiveness in the face of injustice and in the face of harm. And yet we must, if we're going to walk the radical path of nonviolence, as Gandhi, the Dalai Lama, Aung San Suu Kyi, and others have shown. I think it *is* possible, once we commit ourselves to it.

Working from the Inside Out

We can work on ourselves from the outside in as well as from the inside out, in order to be better people and cultivate our noble heart. Certainly we need to work externally for peace in the world, for disarmament among nations, and against injustice and oppression, racism and genocide; for "The gift of justice surpasses all gifts," according to Lord Buddha in the ancient Dhammapada. But we also have to work from the inside out, disarming our hearts, softening up, unveiling the tender caring heart in our breast. The good heart, the little Buddha, is in each of us, underneath all those intractable defense mechanisms, underneath that socialization we were put through—the hard carapace of a spic-and-span persona we've developed like armor to cope with the exigencies of life. This basically means finding our tender heart, letting down our defenses, loosening up the impacted persona, and cracking the hardened shell that we formed around ourselves to protect our vulnerable, defenseless selves when we were growing up. Disarmament is not just about war and weapons. It's about fear, survival, and vulnerability. The more secure we become interiorly, the less threatened, fearful, and aggressive we'll be in life.

A great deal of aggression comes from fear, from egotism, and from perceived danger. When I feel angry, I find it personally useful to look at what am I afraid of. I ask myself, "Where and how do I hurt?" This instantly helps me better get in touch with what's going on, rather than just blaming somebody else or reacting in kind. After calming down, to get some higher guidance, I like to ask myself: "What would Buddha do in this situation? What would Love do here and now?" This helps me cool my passions; be more creative and proactive, rather than simply reactive; feel fearless, yet gentle, and more comfortable; and transcend blame, resentment, and bitterness. Here are a few clues about anger: a lot of it stems from fear and fright, and in the primitive fight or flight response. Peace comes about from working with our own mind, disarming our heart, not just passing gun control legislation or cease-fire treaties. It's people that kill other people, not guns per se. In Buddhist training, there's a great deal of emphasis on cultivating loving-kindness and compassion, forgiveness, acceptance, and mercy, as well as the nonattachment and desirelessness that uproot greed and cupidity and that have an incredibly soothing effect on our troubled, dissatisfied minds.

My own teacher, His Holiness Dilgo Khyentse Rinpoche, wrote a wonderful book on bodhicitta, the awakened Buddhist heart and enlightened mind, called *The Heart Treasure of the Enlightened Ones*. Khyentse Rinpoche was the Dalai Lama's Dzogchen teacher and the lama of many other lamas, including Chogyam Trungpa Rinpoche, Sogyal Rinpoche, and Tsoknyi Rinpoche. There is much for us to learn here. We should not be paranoid, despondent or hopeless, because we all have anger in us; it is part of human nature. The Dalai Lama has written *Healing Anger: The Power of Patience from a Buddhist Perspective*. The Dalai Lama himself admits that he gets angry; he knows what to do with it, however. Thich Nhat Hanh gets angry, too, as does Aung San Suu Kyi and other pacifist Buddhist leaders. These Buddhist activists have plenty to be angry about, considering what they have experienced in their lifetime and what they have seen happen to their countrymen and their homelands of Tibet, Vietnam, and Burma in recent decades. Yet their anger doesn't destroy their peace of mind and serenity, because they have purified and transformed their interior selves and can constructively channel that hot emotional energy. They've learned how to do that, through Mahayana attitude transformation practices (lojong) and mind training.

Buddhist author Ani Thubten Chodron in "Mind and Life 2000: Destructive Emotions" wrote:

> Science says that all emotions are natural and okay, and that emotions become destructive only when they are expressed in an inappropriate way or time or to an inappropriate person or degree. . . . Therapy is aimed more at changing the external expression of the emotions than the internal experience of them. Buddhism, on the other hand, believes that destructive emotions themselves are obstacles and need to be eliminated to have happiness.

In the moment of anger's arising in our body-mind complex, at first there is just an energy, a feeling, the merest glimmer of an experience; it has not yet devolved into violence and aggression. We can learn to deal with it, through mindful awareness coupled with patience, self-observation, and introspection. Afflictive, destructive or negative emotions can be skillfully antidoted by cultivating positive emotions, such as patience, compassion, loving-kindness, and so forth. When feeling hatred, cultivate forgiveness and equanimity, trying to empathize with others and see where they are coming from—see things through their eyes for a moment, if you can. If moved toward aggression, try to breathe, relax, quiet and calm the agitated mind, and strive for restraint and moderation, remembering that others are just like yourself in wanting and needing happiness and avoiding pain, harm, and suffering. Regarding violence and rage—the ultimate external extreme of the internal emotion of anger—redirection and psychological reconditioning are absolutely necessary.

One very simple practice to apply in the moment that anger arises is:

1. *Say:* "I know that I'm angry now." (Or fill in the blank: afraid . . . sad . . . lustful . . .)
2. *Breathe deeply:* While breathing out, with the exhalation, say, "I send compassion toward that particular emotion/energy." Doing that mantra, or some variation of it, will magically interrupt the general pattern of unskillful, thoughtless reactivity. This on-the-spot practice can instantly provide a moment of mindfulness and sanity. It helps you take better care of yourself, rather than putting yourself down; and it heads off negative behaviors that we realize we don't want to do, because such reactions have not really helped us in the past.
3. *Remember:* This, too, shall pass.
4. *BREATHE IN, BREATHE OUT:* Then consider how and if to respond, and not simply react.

Through these four remembrances we can learn experientially not to identify so completely with whatever arises in our mind, and to recognize that it's not just *my* anger—thus keeping from getting even more angry about it, just adding fuel to the flames (as when we say to ourselves, "I'm an angry person, goddamn it; when is this anger going to stop!"). By simply feeling anger or any strong emotion arise and directly experiencing the heat of it, or the earthquake or volcano of it, perhaps experiencing it in our stomach as heat, or as vibration, energy, and maybe shaking a little with it—by being aware and balanced enough to just mindfully, consciously feel that experience—it need not immediately drive undesirable behavior. Just because you have a sharp feeling doesn't mean you have to bite and get hooked, like a fish smelling the bait. Therefore, I think what we have to do with anger in the present moment is to see it simply as an energy, just like any other klesha or emotion that arises. It's nothing but a momentary surge of energy. We don't have to judge it harshly, suppress it, or repress it. Repression and denial also have negative, unskillful, and unwholesome effects on our physical and mental health. Emotional energy such as anger is just like a swollen balloon; if you push it down somewhere, it bulges out somewhere else. That pressure has nowhere to go unless we know how to discharge and release it; perhaps channeling it creatively, productively, rather than destructively. So when we press down on or repress the anger, it makes us sick. Maybe it bulges out into our organs, gives us ulcers, migraine headaches, hypertension, cancer, or kidney stones. That is why it's important not to suppress it when it comes up, but to be wise and aware enough to lighten up about these things by taking yourself and everything that happens just a wee bit less seriously.

When we look at anger closely, and search for clues in dealing with it, we find a whole spectrum there—anger itself, and then all the different levels of feeling it can degenerate into. There's a difference between mere irritation and anger, hatred, aggression, violence, and rage. Let's consider the first band of the spectrum, anger itself. "When people get angry," says the Dalai Lama, "they lose all sight of peace and happiness. Even if they are good-looking when normally peaceful [he's so practical—he knows what we care about!], their faces turn livid and ugly." You don't want to get angry, do you? Tibetans say that when you get angry, your face shrivels up like a roasted shrimp! It says in the Buddha's loving-kindness teachings that if you practice loving-kindness, you'll be less angry, your face will shine, you'll be more cheerful, you'll have fewer wrinkles, more friends, more happiness, and so on. Loving-kindness can help protect us from the destructive aspects of anger; loving-kindness is the greatest protection.

Going to the next more intense band of the spectrum, there's hatred. Hatred is a little more developed and lasting—it's when unchecked anger becomes more like a grudge or vendetta, something that you intensely feel in an ongoing manner about an object of dislike. Anger settles in and hardens in place, spawning seething hatred. The antidote for that is forgiveness, tolerance, nonattachment, and equanimity; it is in our own higher self-interest to learn how to let go a little. In the third band, the inner feelings of anger and hatred degenerate even further, into aggression. Notice we haven't even gotten to actual physical violence yet! Anger is not the same as aggression and violence. We need to renounce violence and the aggression that leads to it—not necessarily to entirely renounce anger itself, which just begins as a natural feeling. Violence is an action, a problem, and destructive. From anger comes hatred and meanness, and from that comes aggression. From there, aggression devolves into the fourth band of the spectrum, violence. The extreme and fifth band, I think, is rage. What is the antidote for that? I don't know. Enlightenment, perhaps. Or at least some form of professional help, such as therapy or anger management techniques and training.

Those are the five bands in the spectrum of this troublesome klesha. The best place to get a grip is when we're in the first band, simple anger. In the Buddhist practice path, there are five steps we go through in dealing with a klesha or difficult emotion. The same five steps work for all of the kleshas; right now we're talking about anger, before it devolves into violence. After much trial and error, I have come up with my own practice for dealing with strong emotions through mindful anger management. I call it the five mindful steps to dealing with anger in the present moment.

Five Mindful Steps to Dealing with Anger in the Present Moment

1. *Notice and recognize what you are feeling,* and where that feeling is in the body. Notice it with equanimity, recognizing the stimulus that pushes your hot buttons. Step 1 is to actually acknowledge your anger rather than suppressing or ignoring it. Just being able and willing to say that it's there, aware that it's coming up for you. This does take some mindfulness, some significant attention in the present moment. I'm not talking about a theory

or an ideal—I'm talking about the application in practice. Experience the anger and feel it. Feel what it is, where it is in the body. Maybe you feel it as heat; maybe your heart is pounding or your pulse is racing; maybe you're trembling a little. Whatever is happening in you, you want to know about it; this is the essence of self-knowledge and self-observation. This continuous practice of being mindful—this awareness of how it is—gives us some space for just experiencing anger as an energy that has not yet become destructive or aggressive or violent. For anger, on arising, *is* just an experience, just a momentary energy. Our ego hasn't yet seized on it and reacted. There is no violence and aggression directed outwardly or inwardly yet. I'm talking about in the present moment, just being *with it.*

2.   *Embrace it with awareness,* remembering the downside to returning anger with anger, harm with harm. Embrace the anger; cradle it like a child having a tantrum. We don't throw the child out of the house. We don't *like* the tantrum, but we still love the child. There's a bigger perspective, a bigger container, a bigger heart to embrace that child having the tantrum. We cradle it, as Thich Nhat Hanh expresses it, like a baby. In other words, not throwing it out, not rejecting it out of hand, not just labeling it as "bad," any more than you can tell your child he's a bad child. He may be acting badly, or have acted badly, but he's not a bad child. Gandhi said we don't judge the person, we judge the action—a big difference. That way we can learn to love even what we don't like, even those we don't like. There's a difference between "love," which is of the heart-mind, and "like," which is merely of the egocentric personality and of our own particular circumstances and psychological conditioning. Try to let go and let be. Acceptance helps bring transformation. Everything changes.

3.   *Create space for your habitual negative reaction and try to examine it and see how it works,* what it does to you, and where it's coming from. Investigate it inwardly and examine it outwardly and try to determine the *real* reason for your anger. Ob-

serve it in relation to what you're disturbed or irritated about, what your likes and dislikes are, what attachments or aversions are driving it—"I want; I don't want." Simply observe it, get to know it, apply mindfulness to it. Pay attention, because mindful attention pays off. Pay attention, and see what gifts this anger may have to bring. Cultivate feelings of compassion for those who anger you. Maybe the child's having a tantrum for some reason. Maybe there's something wrong with her that we don't know about, that we would *want* her to cry about. Maybe her tooth is disturbing her, or one of her little bones is fractured. She shouldn't necessarily stop crying. Maybe she should cry until we take her to get x-rayed. There is a lot of learning possible here in seeing what the message is. Maybe there's a good reason for that anger.

4. *Give up the habituated reactivity* and accept the fact that such urges arise. Here we either release the energy of our anger, or we transform that energy so that it is constructive rather than destructive. We have two alternatives. One is the Dzogchen way of natural spontaneous release, which frees the pent-up emotional energy. It feels kind of like when a soap bubble bursts; we just stretch our awareness and relax, and release the energy— though that's easier said than done. Rather than dumping on somebody, or returning harsh words with more vitriol, we could just burst the bubble. Maybe we learn how to let the energy dissolve into the twelve Vajra laughs, or we shout *P'et* into the void, instead of shouting back at someone. Releasing emotional energy immediately on its arising is the Dzogchen style of practice. To do this, you must be clear enough to just experience things as they are and see through them as they momentarily appear, recognize their dreamlike emptiness and impermanence. But this is advanced practice and can prove tricky.

The second alternative is to transform and recondition the anger. One way of doing that is to recognize the bad karma somebody's getting by harming you. Recognizing the negative karma being generated by the harmful acts done by another, you feel the way you do when you see children doing something silly that will hurt them. In the Buddha's own words, hatred is never overcome by hatred; it's only overcome by love and patience. I think that's an injunction to all of us, to try to learn how to forbear and to return harsh treatment with tenderness, with understanding and compassion, recognizing who is *really* being harmed when somebody harms us. Those who harm us are really harming themselves; it's their bad karma.

5.   Lastly, while refraining from reactivity, *reflect on how little this will matter* in a few years or months or days, and choose other, more desirable ways of responding—appropriately, intelligently, creatively, and proactively. Remember, this, too, shall pass. The *Tao Te Ching*, in Stephen Mitchell's wonderful rendering of it, says: "Patient with both friends and enemies, you accord with the way things are. Compassionate toward yourself, you reconcile all beings in the world."

The awareness that we gain in these steps gives us more space and time to decide whether we are acting intentionally from our higher principles, or just reacting from the reptile brain or the flight-or-fight instinct. This is all part of growing up spiritually and maturing our inner wisdom by dealing skillfully with our combativeness and our reflexive reactiveness. That's why we have practices like attitude transformation, mind training—*lojong* in Tibetan. That's why we have behavioral vows in the outer level of training precepts, so we start to learn how to restrain ourselves. Until we've retooled our inner workings and reconditioned our conditioning, the vows and precepts can help prevent us from devolving into aggression and violence. It's like holding on to an external barrier—our vows—so we don't get blown away by the wind, until our interior energies are more refined and harmonized, and more wise and loving attitudes are developed.

The Vietnamese Zen master, poet, and activist Thich Nhat Hanh says: "Our attitude is to take care of anger. We don't suppress it or hate it, or run away from it. We just breathe gently and cradle our anger in our arms with the utmost tenderness." In his book *The Path to Tranquility*, the Dalai Lama writes:

> When people get angry they lose all sense of happiness. Anger upsets their physical well-being and disturbs their rest; it destroys their appetites and makes them age prematurely. Happiness, peace and sleep evade them, and they no longer appreciate people who have helped them and deserve their trust and gratitude.

Recently I was reading sermons given by Desmond Tutu, whom I consider an exemplar of moral leadership in this world. During the lengthy apartheid crimes tribunal in which he participated in South Africa, despite all the cruel and horrible acts of violence perpetrated against his own people that came to light, he came to the incredible conclusion that, ultimately, "people are beautiful." When I read this, I instinctively felt that this Christian bodhisattva had really taken Jesus's message to heart in order to transcend bitterness and arise with such a radiant spiritual realization, like a phoenix out of the ashes. Holy people such as Archbishop Tutu, the Dalai Lama, Thich Nhat Hanh, and Aung San Suu Kyi have learned how to manage and deal with anger, and all the many difficult feelings, emotions, and mental states that inevitably arise in human beings. In the world but not entirely of it, they do so through opening the heart to the difficult sides of life—not suppressing anger or moral indignation, but fully experiencing it and then knowing how to either use it, or to channel it creatively to release it through the strength of their inner spirit.

Disarming the Heart

Buddhist wisdom teaches us how to find inner serenity, harmony, and freedom from conflicting emotions by practicing meditation and intentionally cultivating mindfulness. We use pure attention and awareness to experience emotionality and delusions directly, in the present moment. This kind of contemplative practice helps further mental clarity and balance while insightfully recognizing the transitory, dreamlike, insubstantial nature of all such mind moments, seeing through them to their essential emptiness. In this way we see more clearly the inner light, not just the lampshade around it, and become more aware and transparent to ourselves. This is self-knowledge and spiritual realization.

Emotions occur quickly; moods may linger longer. These temporary states of mind are conditioned and can therefore be reconditioned; all are workable. Through self-discipline, attitude transformation, and internal practice, negativity can be transformed into positivity and freedom and self-mastery achieved. The Buddha said: "See yourself in others, and others in yourself; then whom can you harm, whom can you exploit?" One of the best practices to disarm the heart is to try to meaningfully connect, to see others in ourselves and ourselves in others, and recognize the interwovenness, and the interbeingness of us all. We practice seeing others in ourselves and ourselves in others, finding the common ground, and connecting heartfully through all our different relationships, all our daily contacts.

That can make a tremendous difference in our lives. This kind of practice can transform our days and all of our lives: seeing others in ourselves and ourselves in others through our intimate relationships, our family and friends, our colleagues and acquaintances and pets, too; finding the common ground, how we're much the same and all want and need the same. In our neighborhood, we can include the people that we pass on the street—the bus driver, the mailperson, the dry-cleaning people, everyone we meet. And the animals, too, not just the pets we love so much—what about the other animals and creatures? When we recognize the light shining in one and all, then who can we harm, who can we exploit? Therefore we are instinctively impelled toward nonviolent practices such as vegetarianism, conscious eating, animal rights, living lightly on the planet, not using up all the resources, and treating others as we would be treated—not to mention not littering and not polluting. All these beautiful practices come naturally when we make that spiritual connection and genuinely perceive how others, beyond just the people we love, are just like us. Even the ones we don't like are also just like us; and we can learn to love them in a bigger way, even if we disagree with them, or don't like what they do. Even if they don't look like us, and even if they are the "them" to us. The other color, the other gender, the other age group, the other social class. Or the other race, the other side of the world, the other religion. Yet they are us. That's the secret—the secret of spiritual love or compassion—realizing they are us. And realizing that we are "them" in their world, to them.

In disarming the heart—in practicing empathy, in cultivating nonviolence in ourselves—*ahimsa,* as Gandhi called it—it's important to remember again and again that violence and war don't come from guns, war doesn't come from outside, and the soul and spirit are far mightier and longer lasting than the sword. Morihei Ueshiba, founder of aikido, wrote:

> The Way of the Warrior has been misunderstood as a means to kill and destroy others. Those who seek competition are making a grave mistake. To smash, injure, or destroy is the worst sin a human being can commit. The real Way of a Warrior is to prevent slaughter—it is the Art of Peace, the power of love.

War comes from our hearts, from the anger, fear, and greed in the human heart and mind. This concerns me, especially because our lives seem to be getting increasingly stressful and frazzled. With the lack of security and the erosion of family and community life; the increased pace of life and the number of interruptions in our days; all the portable technology beeping and buzzing all the time, and the speed of things in the information age; with the lack of privacy, the widening gap between the rich and poor, and the materialism rampant in our materialistic, corporate-led society, it should come as no surprise that we have a lot of depression in our society today, and a lot of hyperactive kids, plus road rage and people going postal, not to mention kids with automatic weapons at school and at home. The problem is systemic, not just individual. There is a huge amount of anger and frustration, dislocation and alienation. We need to look seriously at the anger in ourselves first, and then we can be clearer about it and see what's happening outside of ourselves, and how to address these personal and societal problems. I think it's very important to recognize that today there's a great deal of violence in the world, and that we must become part of the solution, by becoming peace. I no longer want to be fighting for peace and kicking ass for peace, as we did in the sixties. Fighting and waging war for peace is an enormous contradiction in terms. We should *become* peace. *Be* the changes we want to see in the world.

We need more connectedness and grounding in fundamental universal verities and humanistic values to feel more balanced, secure, comfortable, and at ease. There's a tremendous power in nonviolence. Gandhi freed India through nonviolence, the great power of nonviolence, coupled with the power of truth. In his essay "Peace Is More Persuasive," the Thai Buddhist activist, Sulak Sivaraksa, known as father of the International Network of Engaged Buddhists, wrote:

> It is very important to understand that nonviolence is an effective and very powerful response to conflict. It does not mean doing nothing. It is actually a powerful force that can be acted upon. Peace is not merely the absence of war. Peace is a proac-

tive, comprehensive process of finding ground through open communication and putting into practice a philosophy of non-harm and sharing resources. Creating a culture of peace is an active process.

The Hindu classic the Bhagavad Gita tells us not to be attached to our actions. You do what has to be done, and try to be less attached to the outcome. It doesn't mean we don't care, but that we know we can't control everything. We do the best we can, and then we let go; there's a joyous certainty in that kind of trust in the universe and its lawful working. We spiritual activists today try to be engaged Buddhists rather than enraged Buddhists. Karmically speaking, we understand that like produces like, and what goes around comes around. Therefore, we try to cultivate compassion in action, altruism, empathy, and a peaceful heart, and to act from that state of mind. Only skillful means motivated by compassion ca be the truly Buddhist intention driving forceful actions.

In the Metta Sutra (loving-kindness scripture), Buddha said that loving-kindness is the greatest protection. At a private meeting, the Dalai Lama advised President Bill Clinton: "You are the most powerful man in the world. Every decision you make should be motivated by compassion." I think we can learn to live in this sacred way, with our hearts as wide as the world. Each of us is the most powerful person in our own world.

CHAPTER 25

OPENING THE BOOK OF NATURE

NATURE IS THE ONLY BOOK I NEED TO READ.
—TIBETAN YOGI MILAREPA, ELEVENTH CENTURY CE

natural spirituality is all around us. We can hardly escape from it, although we do often tend to overlook it. I rarely feel more at home and in the spirit than when I am outside, any-where. I love to ride bikes, ski, sail, and swim; walk, hike, and mountain climb; play ball, explore beaches, parks, and wild forests; and so forth. Perhaps this green gene of mine comes from all the green beer I've imbibed in Boston. My next-door neighbor here near Spy Pond near Cambridge, who happens to be a lapsed Catholic, says she never feels closer to heaven than when she is kneeling in her garden. Cardinal Newman wrote: "By a garden is meant mystically a place of spiritual repose, stillness, peace, re-freshment and delight." When I hug my dog, it is like being encompassed by a beautiful, fragrant, living garden. At my best moments, this world is the Garden, and all are its pure Edenic inhabitants.

Nature worship is probably the oldest and original form of sa-cred spirituality, reaching into the furthest antiquity. Walking, sitting, or lying down outside is a beautiful way to connect with Mother Nature and join the lineage of nature mystics; even look-ing out a window or staring up at the night sky can put one in touch with life's greater mysteries. Like contemplating a flower or a bouquet or blazing fireplace in the hearth; walking in a forest, garden, or cemetery in an attentive, contemplative, silent-ish fashion; or listening to a waterfall, stream, or ocean waves—natural meditations spontaneously present themselves all around us. The Buddha meditated almost entirely in forests and on mountain peaks, and realized enlightenment while sitting beneath a tree. Nature also exists, more discreetly, in cities, too. Meditating outside is a wonderful way to reconnect with our true nature, and find our place in the bigger picture. My nineteenth-century-Concord neighbor Henry David Thoreau said that if he didn't walk four hours a day outside among the hills and forests, he got rusty; his mentor and Transcendentalist friend Ralph Waldo Emerson—author of the classic essay "On Nature," along with countless books, philosophical essays, and poems—wrote: "Man is a spring whose source is hidden."

Walking helps me tread the spiritual path toward that source. In fact, when I speak in public, people often ask me for a simple spiritual practice they can learn and do anytime, anywhere, and I always say, "Just take a walk outside, the longer the better. Let what you seek come to you." Shakespeare said: "One touch of nature makes the whole world kin." In 1918, the tough-minded pioneering American labor leader Eugene V. Debs intuited life's wisdom lessons of interconnectedness and universal responsibility through close kinship and said one day when arraigned in court for labor union activities: "Your Honor, years ago I recognized my kinship with all beings and that I am not one bit better than the meanest on earth. While there is a lower class, I am in it, and while there is a criminal element I am of it, and while there is a single soul in prison, I am not free." Here in his statement of universal responsibility and oneness is the essence of global citizenry, authentic environmentalism, and the altruistic bodhisattva's compassionate and selfless activism.

Many mystics have said and sung that all of creation is holy, sacred, divine, both within and beyond pantheism. Today we as a race are slowly growing into a new and engaged appreciation of our environment and humankind's participatory responsibility concerning its condition, maintenance, and potential future. According to the tantric or all-inclusive, nondualistic view of Tibetan Buddhism, everything is sacred, all is holy, all are equal—human and animal. All creatures and all living things seen and unseen are manifestations embodying pure and untrammeled Buddha nature. This sacred outlook or spiritual sight helps us reenchant our everyday human lives. Like children, we all are naturally endowed with luminous spirit or radiant heart; we need only to reconnect with what is already there within us and bring it more and more into our daily lives. This is where transformative personal spiritual practices come in—yoga, meditation, chanting, prayer, self-inquiry, introspection, and the like. Yet just sitting in meditation is not enough; we also must take positive action in this world, develop a social conscience, make a contribution. No one person can do it, yet no one is exempt from participating. A Buddhist wise guy, turning conventional wisdom around, has joked: "Don't just do something, sit there." However, man cannot live by meditation alone. Take my word for it—I've tried. "Even if you're on the right track, you'll get run over if you just sit there."—Will Rogers

Spiritual Tropism

As spiritual seekers—fellow travelers on this sacred journey—we all have innate in us a spiritual tropism or natural seeking of the light, not unlike flowers, a leaning toward and attraction to the higher and deeper meaning of things, however we conceive of the religious life and truth quest. One of my learned Tibetan lama friends in Colorado says, "We all have a primordial instinct for happiness. This instinct moves us toward enlightenment." We can, and I believe *must*, practice awakening to this immanent reality: the "beyondness" in the most ordinary daily things, the deeper spirit between the lines and at the very heart of all things. Through the practice of "pure perceptions" or sacred outlook, we learn to see the infinite in the finite and the timeless and eternal in the most fleeting of moments. This trenchant Vajrayana (Diamond Path) Buddhist approach helps us transcend our ordinary, limited, dualistic perceptions and egocentric judgments and enter directly into the profound magic of everyday reality, wherever we are. We simply have to make consistent efforts to look a little more deeply, to learn and integrate life's lessons; reflect upon our experiences rather than just rushing blindly from one to the next, carried unthinkingly forward by the momentum of events and habitual conditioning; and strive to recognize the divine or Buddha light shining in everyone and in every thing. This is a daily meditation practice you can do at home, at work, alone or with others, with or without sitting down—a meditation that depends more on your view or outlook than on your posture, beliefs, mantras, or breathing. Just cultivate this higher view, recognizing that "This very land is the Pure Land, nirvana; this very body the body of Buddha," as Japanese Zen master Hakuin once sang.

Tibetan lamas teach us that each of the five basic elements—earth, water, fire, air, and space—are worth revering like goddesses. In connecting deeply with nature's elements, we can both learn to and actually experience transcending ourselves while being transported into a more splendidly divine reality through the Dharma gate or spiritual access portal offered by the naturally moving beauty and grandness of nature, as well as through prayer, bowing, sacred music chant, yoga, or contemplation in any great cathedral, temple, or mosque. Is there a loftier, more uplifting cathedral than a redwood forest or massive mountains, or any shrine or sanctuary more soulful than a vast, shimmering desert or a sunset over the ocean? Isn't being genuinely moved and transported beyond oneself and one's ordinary habitual preoccupations the very essence of most transformative spiritual disciplines? Thus, exactly *what* moves us is secondary. Being transported is the point.

I myself take a walk outside almost first thing every morning; if I catch dawn crowning the world, so much the better. This is how I open the book of nature and reconnect naturally with spirit. Sometimes I take a walk alone with God or Buddha, my "eternal companion" as it were, other days with my dog, depending on whether I am at home or abroad. Either way, paradise is where I am. I seem to need this sacred time outside in nature—rain or shine, even in the snow, in a city or at home in the country—to grow my inner garden and stay healthy, sane, and awake. Before, I related to my genetic confrere Woody Allen's curmudgeonly New York City–dweller statement, "I am at two with nature;" but I wanted to do something about it, and now I can.

I like to recall Rabbi Nachman of Bratzlav's prayer:

> *Lord, grant me the ability to be alone;*
> *May it be my custom to go outdoors each day*
> *Among the trees and grasses, among all growing things,*
> *And there may I be alone and enter into prayer*
> *To talk with the one that I belong to.*

Nature is the original fountain of knowledge, beauty, sustenance, and inspiration for all people around the globe. Mother Nature or Goddess Gaia is the fertile and effulgent motherlike womb to all of us. She belongs to no one, and she belongs to us all. We could and should cherish her, love and protect her, just as she always and unfailingly embraces and holds us. We are the stewards of this good earth and cannot afford to take it for granted or run it into the ground.

Magic All Around

In Tibetan we think about the *drala* principle, referring to the intrinsic magic and sublimity of reality itself, visibly manifest in the form of the actual, nitty-gritty world all around us. The drala refers not to nature sprites, angels, or gods and goddesses per se, but to the "beyondness" or intrinsic magic, energy, blessings and delight that is available and ever-accessible through each moment to those with eyes to see, ears to hear, noses to smell, and so forth. Drala represents the facticity or actuality of the principle of all-goodness, primordial perfection: everything as right and just and a lawful karmic unfolding just as it is, beyond mortal mental constructs and interpretations or value judgments and other forms of conceptual evaluation. It lends credence to the Mahamudra dictum that ordinariness and naturalness is the Way, and to appreciate and savor everything as it is. For example, even feces and rectums have their invaluable role in our wondrous and mysterious existence; where would we be without them?

We can call upon the drala as an ally, as a way to reach beyond ourselves, when we need to take refuge from confusion and distress and find a safe harbor for respite from the stormy emotions and travails of daily life. We also can simply recognize the drala through those moments of what I call "natural meditation" or "spontaneous meditation," with or without the tangible actuality of external "green" nature, when we are moved and pulled out of ourselves almost accidentally, by whatever most transports us and reconnects us to that which is beyond, yet simultaneously within, each of us. For example, we all used to lie in the grass or sand on our back as kids and stare up at the clouds and into the vast sky, losing ourselves, forgetting ourselves while simultaneously absorbing and learning many things—whether or not we were conscious of it. Looking at the ocean waves, listening to a waterfall, staring at a candle flame, a blazing hearth, or a bonfire—dissolving in the natural elemental energy of fire, water, and wind and being washed or burnt away while being transported far beyond our limited selves—this is natural meditation. It is not at all foreign to us. These are the simple, practical essentials of nature mysticism. This is why and how "everything must be meditated," to quote the great contemporary meditation yogi and master Twelfth Drukpa Lama.

Nature is our treasure; this world is our home and our garden, to love and to cherish and protect, in sickness and in health, till death do us part. And what about future generations who will inherit what we leave behind? What kind of world and environment will that be? Bill Moyers once asked his friend on Wall Street, "What do you think of the market?" "I'm optimistic," the financial man answered. "Then why do you look so worried?" And he answered: "Because I am not sure my optimism is justified." I think this sums up how I feel about the environmental crisis we face today.

Buddha was one of the first ecologists; he exhorted his followers to protect the purity of the waters and to plant one tree each year to repay the earth for resources used. St. Francis of Assisi used to live outside and took the animals and birds as companions, talking to and embracing them. St. Patrick of Ireland sang:

> I arise today through the strength of heaven;
> Light of the sun, radiance of the moon,
> Splendour of fire, speed of lightning,
> Swiftness of wind, depth of sea,
> Stability of earth, firmness of rock.
> I arise today through a mighty strength,
> The invocation of the Trinity,
> Through belief in the threeness,

Through confession of the oneness
Of the Creator of Creation.

The earth is like an altar, and we are all the gods and goddesses, Buddhas and bodhisattvas on that sacred ground. In that light, reverence for all forms of life comes naturally. In this sacramental vision or Buddha vision, a pure outlook that clearly perceives things just as they are, we recognize the great perfection and boundless wholeness and completeness—the justness, the rightness, the very *isness* and immediacy—of it all. We grok the fact that we are not merely human beings trying to live a more spiritual life, but spiritual beings learning how to live a human one here on planet earth. We are part of nature, and nature courses through every atom of us. Human nature, Buddha nature, Mother Nature—three in one.

As Emerson wrote in 1836:

> But if a man would be alone, let him look at the stars. . . . If the stars should appear (only) one night in a thousand years, how would men believe and adore; and preserve for many generations the remembrance of the city of God which had been shown! But every night come out these envoys of beauty, and light the universe with their admonishing smile. The stars awaken a certain reverence, because though always present, they are inaccessible; but all natural objects make a kindred impression, when the mind is open to their influence. . . . The wisest man does not try to extort her secret, and lose his curiosity. . . . Nature always wears the colors of the spirit. To speak truly, few adult persons can see nature.

The book of nature is our operating manual; try to open it and take in a small chapter daily. I think you'll love it.

The Five Natural Elements

This is the timeless principle of natural meditation, a very organ-ically practical form of everyday contemplation we all can and do participate in, whether we always know it or not. Why do so many people visit the Grand Canyon out west in Arizona? There's nothing in it, just a yawning chasm; yet the greater the void, the more awesome the spectacle. The nature element of earth is nakedly revealed at its most vast and profound, trans-porting us beyond ourselves and into the maw of the infinite and timeless. You can find this spontaneous natural contemplation taught in the Semde section of Dzogchen teachings about the na-ture of mind, in the nature mysticism practices called the five nails or rivets, which directly relates to utilizing the five natural elements. There we learn how each of the five elements could provide us with support for the riveting, intense contemplative absorption that characterizes natural meditation, where we con-template, concentrate on, and gradually become absorbed into a tree, flower, blazing hearth, bonfire, waterfall, mountain, canyon, rushing wind, or musical notes so totally that we forget ourselves and our habitual dualistic framework (of separateness), becom-ing totally one with that object of meditation, and thus with everything. It is all about working with the earth element, the wa-ter element, the fire element, the wind element, and the space el-ement—the five natural elements. According to the mandala principle as well as Hermes Trismegistus, the microcosm encom-passes and reflects the macrocosm—as above, so below. The holographic mandala principle teaches us in an inner way that the five elements, the five skandhas (components of individual-ity), the five bodily limbs, and so forth, are all the five meditation Buddhas or cosmic archetypes within the holistic mandala prin-ciple of totality—leading to the realization that the universe is our body and all beings our minds, along with other profound insights and ineffable experiences. We learn to work with these five elements, utilizing the water—the "goddess of water," as the Tibetans call it—to carry us away; the goddess of fire to carry us away; the goddess of wind to carry us away; the goddess of earth to carry us away. For example, I love the ocean: just being near it, watching the waves, listening to it naturally expands my vision and imagination. For me this is natural meditation, through the blessings and resonance of the water goddess, delivering the immediacy and isness of pure being.

How to meditate on earth? Try lying down on the grass; relax, let go, breathe, and be patient; relax and breathe some more; let come and go, let be, and gradually dissolve into the grass, into the good earth's accepting, supportive embrace. You could try to do this through skygazing, ocean gazing, or waterfall listening, or offer yourself into the sacred fire of pure unadulterated spirit while being consumed in fireplace gazing. You can also connect with and be carried away by the awesome earth element by, for example, looking over the rim at the Grand Canyon or up at some vast, snow-capped mountains. It doesn't only have to be big things; it could be small ones, too. A rock, a fossil in a rock, and the intuitive experience of the entire unfathomable mystery of infinite time and limitless space, when attentively contemplated can completely blow away your mind and ravish the heart. We can naturally feel connected to and humbly venerate before the glorious goddess of the earth element, who unstintingly provides us with all we need, including food and nourishment, shelter, source, and home.

Encompassed in this is what Tibetans call the drala principle, which refers to the beyondness in nature, the sacredness and extraordinary secret magic of ordinary reality that remains hidden there for those with insight to see—where it can utterly transport us, carrying us far beyond ourselves. The drala is not really a goddess or deity but is similar to our term *Mother Earth*, personifying nature as Mother Earth although we know it is not an external goddess or like the wife of some ancient and eternal white-bearded one sitting up above the clouds. Not unlike Mother Earth, the drala personifies and embodies the natural animating principle, the beyondness that transports and carries us away from separateness of egoic identity. The sublime animating principle is encountered when we are so inspired that we're suddenly, spontaneously, unthinkingly transported beyond dualism, over and beyond the dichotomy of self and other, the border of *otherness*. For example, you might meet the drala through solitude. Does anybody here like and love to be alone in nature, as I myself do, or in sanctuaries and houses of worship? Do you go to the woods or parks, lakes and rivers when you feel troubled, perhaps, or treasure a room of your own? What do you meet there when you're alone? What exactly is it in solitude that you go to find, meet, reconnect to? That's the drala, within one's intrinsic true nature. They are there to meet you. So it's the beyondness, or what carries you beyond, which remains somewhat indefinable while being totally experienceable. It is not something separate from yourself, or that isn't always there and accessible; it's more like taking a walk or sitting down in your room and going into solitude to reconnect with your muse or your true transpersonal Self, beyond your ordinary, quotidian, egoic workaday identity. This is related to principles of natural meditation, spontaneous meditation, connecting with the goddess or the transcendent and immanence of spirit or of Buddha nature, of *isness*, through finding organically fitting ways to return to yourSelf, through more fully inhabiting the present moment in all its delectable richness and possibilities. The immanence of isness is accessible in ordinary moments, such as this one right now. It doesn't have to be shaped like a holy Buddha statue or garden angel. It could be a piece of tree bark, the perfect orb of an eggshell, or even dog turd, richly brown, with warm odiferous steam rising from it. That's also a goddess right there, a goddess dancing in the steam, and in your nostrils. Don't overlook her.

CHAPTER 26

DANCING WITH LIFE

An elderly nun named Gelongma Palmo told us the story of her younger days as an assistant to the Sixteenth Karmapa, venerable lama, in a monastery in Sikkhim:

> More than anything, I looked forward each day to my own quiet time to sit quietly on my zafu. I would get all of my chores done and, just as I would sit, someone would beckon me, "Rinpoche needs you right now." Day after day the same thing would happen. Try as I would to just sit a little, as soon as I sat, I would be called to come. Finally, I realized I must make everything I do my meditation. And so I did. With a twinkle in his eye, Rinpoche said that from now on, he would probably not be needing me so often—especially when I was sitting! That's how Karmapa Rinpoche trained me.

I'd like to talk about dancing with life, integrating the Dzogchen view and meditation into the actions and conduct of our daily life—where it really counts, after all. Enlightenment should show up in behavior, don't you think? Everyday life can actually help enhance our meditative awareness, when we understand the secret of integration.

First, how to practice in daily life and bring our awareness practice into life. Second, how—from awareness practice—enlightened behavior, impeccable conduct, can occur. Not just trying to be religious, to conform to any particular ideal or style, but how enlightened behavior and unselfish compassion naturally proceed from cultivating self-awareness along with mindfulness in action. We need not let preconceived notions about what spiritual life should look like tarnish and impede the freshness and spontaneity of our own untrammeled purity of heart and true nature. The true path is that from which one can never stray. Everything is part of it.

When I think about dancing with life, I think about fear and doubt, withdrawal—our hang-ups and behavioral armor, as Wilhelm Reich called it. The armor that we put on when we were young, probably very young, to protect us ourselves; our persona, our personality and defense mechanisms; our way of managing feelings and coping with things to make them less painful. Of course, it is very easy to be externally spiritual, quiet, peaceful, and lovely when we're together on retreat in the woods—lovely flowers growing on their little, square seats, in their little pots, and everybody just doing what they're told. You ring the bell, and everybody salivates and goes to the kitchen like Pavlov's well-trained dogs! The volume control is down very low, and the speed is slow. But when we leave retreat—or even our daily meditation practice—the volume goes up a little, the fast-forward button engages, and things start to move faster. All the pots start bumping against each other like bumper cars at the amusement park. Horns blare and drivers start cursing—then where are you? How are you amid all of that? What happens to your calm serenity then? That's life testing us.

Can we handle that? Are we afraid we're going to lose something when we leave the nice oasis of a peaceful week-long, protected meditation retreat? Can we dance with life, or do we need to stay on our meditation cushion all the time, surrounded by other people who are like us and agree with us on almost everything? So do we wish to walk cautiously through life, like a waiter bearing a brimming bowl of hot soup? Are we willing to go forward, to grow and change, or are we just trying to find the right place to stay, like a peg in a hole, and just remain there, like a safe harbor where we can anchor our boat in snugly without being troubled by the wind or the waves? For me, the point of life is not to find a safe little harbor, to anchor where the waves and the wind can't get us. That's a very temporary situation, not a real refuge. We can't just stick our head in the sand like ostriches and wait for the big storm to blow over. We are great vehicles meant to enjoy freely the vast sea of life, not little tipsy canoes in constant danger of being swamped. We're not just to find safe corners to sit in like a bronze Buddha statue in a niche, or a dog that's been kicked too often. As long as we stay in the corner like a wallflower, we're safe, but what kind of way of life is that? Is that why we meditate? Is that how we want to carry on in life, as avoiders, thinking we just have to put in our earplugs, eyeplugs, and mindplugs and get home as soon as possible to our meditation room and yoga mat, where it is safe? Enough retreat already. Let's advance, and raise our gaze, elevating our angle of attack.

Opening Up

Can we open up a little, let go of our resistances, face our fears and anxieties, and have some tolerance and acceptance of uncomfortable feelings? Can we really inhabit and fully experience them fully for once, not just try to protect our illusory selves from any uncomfortable feelings, doubts, and anxiety? We always hear about greed, hatred, and delusion—all termed bad! Yes, they're problematic. But what about the things we don't hear so much about in Buddhist scriptures? Does anyone here ever feel lonely, anxious, nervous, insecure, hesitant, doubtful, shy, inadequate, depressed, alienated? Where does it say in Buddhist scriptures about feeling inadequate and having low self-esteem? Sutras usually say you have no self; that could too easily become self-denial and self-deprecation.

The notion that we are not who we think we are—that we're not an independent, concrete, solid self—doesn't mean low self-esteem. We might realize very high self-esteem when we realize what our true Self is, our transpersonal, luminous, loving, infinite Self nature. That's your true Self. Selflessness is not synonymous with low self-esteem. You might say it's *no* self-esteem. It's like not esteeming your ego, but esteeming that interconnected higher nature in all. Low self-esteem is actually an ego problem, in which the alienated and separate, clinging, individual ego is strongly attached to its view of itself, its story. "I am no good. I'm pathetic and can't do anything. I had a miserable childhood," and so on. That's low self-esteem, as well as an inverted form of egotism. Anatta, not-self, is beyond egotism. It's *unselfish*. If you have low self-esteem, it's very hard to be unselfish, isn't it? You are always fighting to survive, to hold on to your tiny bit of turf. Ego is constantly fighting to shore up its tenuous, illusory domain.

Bodhicitta is the opposite of that. There's no struggle for ego to survive. It has infinite possibilities. One problem afflicting many of us is that we bring our low self-esteem to our spiritual practice and we wonder, "How can I do it? I'm not good enough." Or, "I'm not doing it right." You look around the room out of the corner of your eye, and everybody else seems to be sitting like a Buddha, but you're sitting there feeling like the famous fan that the shit always hits. But everybody is really the same. There is nobody sitting there like a Buddha any more than anyone else. We are all equal in the eyes of Buddha; in Buddha vision, no one is closer than anyone else. We're all struggling with karma and kleshas—condition and emotional obscurations.

One of my teachers, Tulku Jigme Khyentse, said to me once, "Surya, it's good to be confident, but you should be confident in the right thing." He was talking about self-confidence. He was saying don't be confident in *your* self; be confident in your true Self, in your Buddha nature. Be confident in your awakened nature, not in your ego self. That's the difference between your low self-esteem, which holds desperately on to its ego dummy, and true realization of the liberating possibilities of Buddha nature. That's bodhicitta. That's awakened spiritual heart and mind.

It's really just a slight shift in perspective, and yet it makes all the difference in the world. It's like that Gestalt image that can be seen either as a goblet in the center or two faces on the sides. When you look at it the first time, you see it one way, but then there's a shift and you see it the other. So how do you intentionally shift from one view to the other, from egotism to true authenticity and genuine presence? This can be challenging. It's like with form and emptiness, or self and other. The more aware we become, the more transparently open and less rigid we are the easier it is to shift from one to the other. From the figure (the goblet) to the ground (two faces). We can see that we are different, and yet we're the same. We can see that we're bound, and yet we are also free. We're a self, an individual conventional person, an ego, walking around with an identity card and all the rest. That's the goblet. On the other hand, we simultaneously are the ground of being, Buddha nature. We're not just an identity card–carrying, conventional person. Consider the waves in the sea as a simple example. Should we say there are no waves because we're just looking at the larger sea? Which part do we pick out? If you have bigger perspective, bigger view, more wisdom, you see there are waves in the sea. The waves are made of the sea; the sea has waves. They're not so separate, and they can also be distinguished. There's a wave, there's a trough, there's a wave, but it's all the sea. It's like the figure and ground shift at the same time, form and emptiness. Sunyata on one hand and bodhicitta, compassion, on the other hand. Egotism is just a ripple in the divine Buddha nature. Why identify with our narrowest small self and lose touch with Buddha vision?

It just takes a little shift, but it's a very profound one. It's not a small thing. It is really a very radical shift, to be able to have sort of double vision. On the one hand, we know rationally who we are and where we live, where we work, and all that, in the conventional sense; meanwhile, on the other hand, we can also remember and know intuitively who we are and where we live and how things work in the ultimate sense. That's the Middle Way of Buddhism, a balance including both the conventional and the absolute levels of reality, at one and the same time. Two levels of truth. You need both: separate, independent, individuated, grown-up, healthy ego and at the same time realizing the transpersonal and higher true nature. Then you can have real self-confidence: confidence in your true nature, not just your nature, but the true nature of all. Not just confident in one's self and not in others, but real confidence in Buddha nature. Discovering it shining through all and everything.

The Dalai Lama, in a conference with Westerners a few years ago, was explaining how easy it was to just rest meditatively in your Buddha nature, even if you didn't believe in God or in any other religious dogma. Some of the Western psychologists present pointed out that that was also a belief. He replied, "No, that's not a belief in Buddha. It's just your own basic goodness that everybody feels." The psychologists tried to explain to him that Westerners have a problem with low self-esteem, which he said he had never heard of. They explained that they didn't believe that they were basically good and that there was no problem in their essence. Western cultural assumptions and Christian doctrines, including original sin, need to be considered in dealing with our particular conditioning.

This is a subtle point here. We assume a lot, perhaps too much, when we use traditional ways of explaining Dharma. The Dharma teaching is that everybody can do it themselves. "Be a lamp unto yourself," Buddha said. "Work out your own salvation with diligence." But many of us come from an upbringing that tells us that, no matter what we do, we're not good enough. It is very difficult to overcome that conditioning, with all its self-doubt and hesitations, feelings of inadequacy and low self-esteem. No wonder we are afraid to just jump into naturalness and noncontrivance, as Dzogchen teachings suggest. It is much safer to sit in our little flowerpot here, on a nice square meditation cushion, than to jump onto the dance floor and dance with life, where anything might happen unexpectedly. As long as we stay here in our little pot, like a little stunted bonsai, we are safe. But is that the kind of spiritual life we want to lead? Aren't we stunting our growth by staying in a very small mold, like the square cubes in ice cube trays? Everybody gets a square maroon meditation cushion, and every Buddhist fits. Or you get a little round black zafu imported from Japan. If your roots grow even a little bit, protrude in any way, somebody comes around and goes, "*Whap!* Get back in the ice cube tray." Is that what we are doing with our development? Trying to be good little boys and girls? Keep trimming off every surprise growth branching out, cracking the mold, reaching for the light or the nourishing water in all directions, like growing shoots and roots? Is there no room for creativity and imagination in this growth process?

What are we afraid of? Afraid of making mistakes, of absolutely fucking up? We've already made so many mistakes and messed up so many times, why be afraid of making a couple more? Can't we try to be just a little more playful about this? We're not born to be wallflowers at life's dance hall and just sit on the side and watch, where it's safe and we won't sweat in our new clothes, our party clothes. What kind of life is that? Yet we all do that, in different ways. Maybe we're out-to-lunch and not really inhabiting fully our being and existence. Admittedly, it could be painful and confusing to become more aware, which can also mean more sensitive. You might feel some feelings, you men! That's scary. I can't talk to you women, but the men at least know this problem: fear of feelings. They are so messy, unmanageable, unexpected.

An American Zen master, George Bowman Roshi, said to me when we were joking around one evening, "You don't seem to get angry very often, Surya." And I said, "No. I'm proud that I haven't been angry in at least five years." He said, "Oh, yeah. I was really angry once. It was in 1974!" It was all a good joke. Like the ice cubes in the tray: well placed, seemingly very imperturbable, but totally frozen. Of course, we get angry every day. But do we allow ourselves to feel it, acknowledge it? No. Never! We just keep it in and hide it. Blazing anger is like the fires of hell, but cold anger is like cold hell. It makes us crazy if we keep it inside, brooding over it and becoming ever more hardened and solidified.

Surfing and Sailing

Can we dance with life? We *are* the dance. Let's not be too dualistic here. We can use all kinds of metaphorical images, but we *are* the dance. Can we be the dance, or do we always have to contract and constrict, take ourselves out of the dance and be the observer, the wallflower, the detached meditator, the dispassionate philosopher, the lover of truth? Not true and authentic, yet claiming to be lovers of truth. "Truth is over there, and I love it. I study it all the time. I talk about it, write about it. Put it on the shrine." *Philosopher* means lover of truth, and yet how dualistic putting it out there is! Do we seekers have to contract and pull out of the dance in order to stand back and appreciate the dance? That's what we usually do, because we're afraid of getting carried way. But maybe we have to renounce that holding back sometimes and let ourselves be carried away. That's the tantric flip: use the force of the opponent, as in aikido or jujitsu, to flip it over. Don't try to resist and push back the enemies, the klesha negativities—just stick out your foot and trip them. They flip over under their own momentum.

You can't control these energies, these karmic winds, but you can learn how to sail them more skillfully. We can surf on the waves, and even seek bigger waves when we know how to surf.

Then we have more fun dancing with the waves of life. Of course, when we surf, we get knocked over, we get soaking wet. That's part of the fun. We have to get wet. Or do we just want to be wading in the shallows of life? Just get our toes wet, never make the plunge, because it's too dangerous and we might drown? If we are not willing to drown in something, we can't really experience it fully. Whether it is making a commitment to a relationship, a commitment to a practice or to your vocation, or taking a risk to go beyond your self-imposed limits, it is risky, it is challenging, but it is worth it. This outrageous tantric approach called Dzogchen really opens up all the possibilities—not just the pious, religious possibilities, but all the possibilities—of freedom and proactivity, unrestricted creativity, outrageous spontaneity. It can inspire us to experiment in our own life. Not just to meditate here in the hall and stay quiet and walk slowly. You can also do fast walking meditation, by the way. You can also run! In the Rinzai Zen tradition, they practically run around the hall. One of my friends in Korea told me that in her monastery every morning for a half an hour the master would come out and jog with all the monks *backward*. Just imagine how much attention you have to pay to jog backward in line for a half an hour. Attention is the entire point. Try it. Jogging backward requires full presence of mind, total attention—meditative training.

Let's not be too square about what is meditation, what is awareness, what is cultivating mindfulness. Try jogging backward in the morning or just walking backward; notice the natural vigilance and focused attention it brings forth. That'll wake you up. You might also feel less driven, less compulsive to get somewhere. It can reverse the tendency to drive and strive forward. We're always trying to get somewhere, driving forward. Let's hurry backward for once. Maybe that'll be a good deconditioning of our achievement orientation, our Buddhist bulldozer mind. Forget about Enlightenment or Bust. Buddha Here Now!

Let's not be afraid that we are going to lose something, or lose what we gained in our meditation retreat or daily morning practice. Anything we are going to lose, we should lose; it's not the real thing. It's just temporary: our peace, our concentration, the reassuring little routines such as our little flower pot meditation cushions that we find to sit in—that's not home, not our true home. That's just a good little test tube. Let's come home to our-Selves and to our being and to our own organic way, wherever we are. To our true life. Reclaiming our true Selves, our Buddha nature; being the host in this life's temple, not just guests.

Of course, when we go into the world from our meditation cushions, we are going to have less precise concentration. The mind starts going faster, the decibel level increases dramatically, there are other demands on us—family and work and all sorts of things. Even if you do a three-year retreat, three years also pass by and then you're out pounding the streets, a pedestrian again. It is what we learn, it is what we *are,* that counts—not merely what we do. Whatever we learn here or in Buddhist practice—it is the wisdom, the insight, the clarity, the heart opening, the change of heart that counts. Not just the state of mind, which is what passes. Therefore, let's not be so concerned that we are going to lose something. In fact, let's consider that we've been out to lunch and it's time to really get on with it and get back to where spiritual life really matters: in our own life, where we are fully responsible for our lives.

Sometimes it's easy to meditate with a group, with a teacher. That is all well and good and even significant. It's important to recharge our batteries sometimes this way. But in another way, it also makes it too easy. You can just be on retreat and Surya Das shouts at you or makes you laugh, and you temporarily forget all your problems. But the problems don't magically go away, do they? The problems remain, to be worked out day by day, don't they? One's path remains to be worked out. This Dzogchen *view* of everything, complete and perfect as it is, recognizes everything that happens as perfect, even if it seems unwanted; it is all lawful karmic unfolding. Dzogchen *meditation* allows us to better accept everything as it is, seeing through everything and remaining free and unconditioned. The *action* of Dzogchen—spontaneous, unpremeditated—blossoms as appropriate, impeccable behavior. Whatever form it takes, it is just an expression of our innate Buddha nature, our true, original nature; we don't need it to fit into any special form or explicitly religious, pious practice. Water can take any form; that's its genius. The Great Way, the Tao, truth, reality can take any form. Our being can take any form and fit in anywhere. When we're not too fixed, square or rigid, we can fit in anywhere. Whatever music the bands of this universe play, we can dance with it. Whatever waves come, we can surf on them. Whatever winds come, we can sail with them. We are masters rather than victims of our fate.

This brings up fearless courage, even in the face of adversity, fear, illness, and death. This is also a good preparation for death and dying. Let's face it, we're all dying. We're all getting older. We don't know how long we'll be alive, so it's good to prepare for that vital event now. At the last minute, it's too late, when the body, energy, and mind get out of control. This is the time to begin the practice of conscious dying, by facing our fears, doubts, and questions. This is the time to prioritize what we want and need to do in our lives and to do it in order to find our true purpose and complete our karma here. Not to procrastinate and vacillate, thinking we'll have time later. The time is now or never, as always.

Let's not waste time. How long does it take to wake up and be responsible, and to really let go? How long does it take to become yourself? How far do we have to go to become *That,* what we are? How to become what we are? I hope that you'll find it possible to use some of the tools in this book—whether it is the specific meditative practices, the Dzogchen view or just the lightness and cosmic humor at the absurdity of things. Dharma should lighten your load, help you throw off some of the extra baggage, to be honest with yourself and others—lightening up while enlightening up. Not just nostalgically remembering how great your meditation was here today and thinking, "I can't wait for the next retreat," always looking forward to the next thing, the next place, and avoiding the simple here and now. Let's start really digging into our true life, wherever we are. This is the right time, the right place, and we are the right people.

It is helpful to have some regular formal daily meditation, yoga, or prayer practice. I hope you will do some formal meditation, some chanting, some breathing and relaxation exercises at least every morning or night. We are soulful, hearty, passionate people, why not just chant for a whole hour every morning if you like it, and forget about silent meditation for a while. Or chant when you are driving around or jogging around. It's hard when you're driving your car to just close your eyes and meditate. But you can always chant. Or listen to Dharma talks in the car. Driving around New England to these meditation retreats is one of my best private, personal times. If you don't like what the teacher of the recording is telling you to do, you can always push the fast-forward button and get onto the advanced teachings! (Just joking!) Or replace Dharma drivel with some good music. Man cannot live by Dharma alone, you know! I've tried.

Practicing Creative Dharming

It is very helpful and even necessary to be creative about bringing the Dharma into our life. I call this creative Dharming. It's not just Dharma Lite or Dharma for Dummies. It is smart to uncover and find Dharma—the light of spiritual life, living spirit—in every situation, each and every moment. In the Mahamudra/Dzogchen tradition, we discuss *bokden,* enhancement or integrative advancement. I was really happy to learn about this advanced practice of stepping up the current of practice. I always felt after silent intensive retreats that I should really hold on to my practice, as if I had made a few more steps and must hold on to the progress a little harder and not lose it. Then I'd become gradually discouraged as the days and weeks went by, back at work, feeling like my practice was slipping, and that my intensity and focus were fading. But the practice of bokden, advanced enhancement, is like taking your practice on to the next step, stepping up the electric current, making a leap.

The oft-given example of bokden is Naropa. He was the abbot of Nalanda University and a great pundit, scholar, master, and monk in ancient India. After doing that for thirty or forty years, he had a vision of an old witchlike woman who told him: "Naropa, you're just dancing on books. You know the words but not the inner meaning. You're missing the whole point. Go and find your destined guru, Tilopa." Tilopa was a crazy yogi, like a feral dog living by a river. Naropa gave up his position as august abbot and went wandering in search of that crazy yogi by the Bengal River. Then once more this witch—who was actually Vajrayogini, the feminine wisdom deity incarnate—appeared, in the form of a leprous, untouchable beggar by the roadside, and the hag seduced him. Suddenly, Naropa found himself rolling around in the mud with this old untouchable! Making love to any woman was bad enough for a chaste monk-abbot from the Brahman caste, but a leprous untouchable! And yet, there he was experiencing more delicious bliss than he had ever had in his yogic samadhis, kundalini openings, and enlightenment experiences. He realized that he was no longer just a monk, that he had become a tantric yogi. This is advanced enhancement, bokden.

It is always said that in the Mahamudra lineage from then on, Pandit Naropa no longer had dualistic ideas of clean and unclean, pure and impure, leprous and beautiful, untouchables and Brahmans, and so on. He gave up being a restrained, celibate monk and became a blissful crazy yogi like Tilopa, through the blessings of this leprous beggar dakini woman. Of course, she was an incarnation of the ruby-red, sow-headed chow-hound Vajrayogini, the dakini whose head was like a pig's head. (Why is her head like a pig's head? Because she doesn't discriminate between clean and dirty; just like a pig she eats anything, goes anywhere, does anything. That's an example of freedom.)

The peerless Saraha, the fletcher, once sang: "Who can blame me for just rolling around in the mud? What's wrong with the mud? It's just earth and water." Brahman priestly rules were very strict about wearing clean white clothes, avoiding the caste of untouchables, and many other prejudices and discriminations. We look down on and judge harshly such prejudices; and yet, don't we, too, have our own puritanical New Age prejudices or liberal conditioning? "Oh, I want it to be quiet, not noisy." Or, "I should be with spiritual people like the vegetarians and pacifists who do yoga every day, not the hunters, rednecks, and beer-drinking rowdies at our local Oktoberfest."

Enhancement practice could include going right from a silent meditation retreat to the Oktoberfest pavilion, having a drink, and dancing, while noticing how you handle it and if those activities are intrinsically any better or worse than any others. In Kyoto, Japan, in the Zen temple of Antaiji where I studied in the early seventies, at the end of every five-day meditation sesshin there was a big sake party in the monastery, which the Zen master led. I used to hate that. I had been living in India at my teacher's monastery in Darjeeling, and I thought, "Five days of intense meditation. I don't want to just waste it getting drunk, feeling hung over the next day." But aged Uchiyama Roshi—an authentic Zen master—demanded it, and led the way. I never could understand it then, in 1973 and 1974; I didn't get the point. But as I grew up more, I gradually got the point: I was holding on to my small comfort zone of temporary peace and concentration and afraid of entering into the mansion of spontaneous expression, letting go of the past, trusting in innate Buddha nature, and entering the fertile groundlessness of the wholly now. Spic-and-span Naropa had to enter into the greater Way, to get in the sloppy mud to get real and live like everyone else—not just as a precious monk in a protected monastic sanctuary where everything was under control, like an anal-retentive bachelor controlling his own life and environment. He had to let go and let things be as out of control as they actually are. That's called enhancement, or stepping out. This is how true tantric practitioners iron out and even out the difference between the holy Dharma and gritty, daily life. Eventually one's practice goes beyond any separation between meditation sessions and breaks, and one enters the freedom beyond meditation.

To end the story, Naropa found Tilopa by the river near Calcutta. Tilopa's eyes were staring, bloodshot, and yellowed. He was wearing rags and living under a bridge, subsisting on what the fishermen threw away, the entrails of fish. This yogi Tilopa, by the way, is the patriarch of the Mahamudra lineage, the Holy Tilopa. You can read about him. Even now, a thousand years later, people are still singing and teaching spontaneous songs of that crazy yogi who blew Naropa's mind, made him a mensch, kicked him in the head, and made him an enlightened siddha.

Let's practice enhancement by taking our formal sitting practice to the next stage, bringing it into our life, whatever it is that we're doing. Dance with life fearlessly. Take this great vehicle out on this vast sea where it belongs, and enjoy it, cruising around; that's what vehicles are for. We don't have to hide in a cozy, snug, safe harbor. This great vehicle of spontaneous expressions is unsinkable, like the waves. There's nothing to fear from the waves of change when we are inseparable from all that is. I personally found that the many years of trying to protect whatever I gained in the spiritual life was one of the biggest hang-ups of all. The tantric pioneer Chogyam Trungpa Rinpoche used to rag us mercilessly about this feebleness of spirit. Personally, I have found that this sort of tantric enhancement is very helpful in balancing out all the general Buddhist discipline and controlling and purifying. The five days in Zen sesshin drinking green tea and eating brown rice purified our bodies, but my mind felt very attached to that noble silence, meditative equipoise, purity, and tranquility. The sake made me forget about that. Zen-crazed Japanese monks would smoke unfiltered cigarettes and stay up all night drinking coffee, Coca-Cola, and sake and then wrestle. Fortunately, I didn't have to do that. I think they were afraid of me; I was too big. (I was afraid of them.) Imagine if instead of having a lovely circle-sharing group process at the end of retreat, as we do here at Dzogchen Center, we'd all wrestle on the floor together, just rolling around like kids at a pajama party or in a pillow fight. If I said we were going to do that tomorrow, before we go home, I bet half of you wouldn't come. But why not? What's the big deal? Is it too unspiritual?

This tantric teaching of enhancement is truly marvelous. Last month on my European teaching tour, I went to hot baths in Bavaria and was there for many hours. I was looking into combining relaxing, meditating, and sky gazing, just dissolving in the natural state, floating in the mineral water, and so on. It was like rebirthing, resting in nondual rigpa, primordial awareness. How naturally it came to me there! Much easier than sitting in a funny cross-legged position with my body hurting. That bathtub experience became an enhancement. This is the secret, finding out how to practice anywhere, through improvisation. Even though there were a hundred old spa-goers lolling around and making a racket, it didn't matter—not at all. I was truly there.

You don't have to be alone to meditate. You can be doing it on the highway or at the beach or anywhere at all. I think it is very important to be creative with taking what we have learned in our practice—for example, letting go, sky gazing, or cutting through—and find moments during the day to apply it. Of course, every moment is the best moment, but maybe we can't remember every single moment. Let's just try our best to use it during the day and not just during one hour of meditation in the morning. Even one moment in the middle of the day, or once in a while, can make a difference. Break up the day by just stopping what you're doing and saying *Ahhh*. It stops everything. It stops the world. Five times a day Muslims stop their work and bow to Mecca. It punctuates the day, makes the whole day sacred. Why don't we Buddhist meditators do it five times a day or ten times a day? Just for one moment would be enough. Not just waiting for our hour on the meditation cushion, or waiting for next Sunday, or waiting for the next ten-day meditation retreat with a teacher from afar. Let's bring it into our life, those moments that cut through the solidity, the claustrophobia, the veils of illusion; let's perforate the solidity, make little holes in all the solidity of all our concepts in our daily life and let the fresh air blow through. It is a lovely way to live.

Each moment can be a little awakening, a little prayer. Or use nature. Go out in a garden or look at the sky. Relax, let go totally, and dissolve into it. We become one with it, but actually we *are* one with it, even pre-merging. Just stop withdrawing and pulling out of it. Stop constricting and contracting out of it; just *be* it for one moment. *Be* the breath. Pure, pristine awareness, unmanipulated presence of awareness. Stop doing for a moment, and just be. You don't have to *be* anything. You don't have to *be* anyone. Just be. That's before we've even been constructed as someone, as a separate, suffering self. Pure being.

Living Like Zorba the Buddha

I hope you can find creative ways to celebrate every moment, gratefully taking joy in the smallest things. Appreciate every moment, whether it's wanted or unwanted, positive or negative in appearance; it can all be assimilated into the path. Even shit can become manure, fertilizer, and help flowers grow. Let's work on becoming more calm, clear, objective, spiritually detached, and equanimous. And enjoy the roller coaster, surf the waves. Not just trying to flatten everything out and make it all boring and say, "Oh yeah, I haven't been mad since 1974." That's denial. That's pathological almost. Does the ocean improve when the waves die down? I don't think so. We don't have to try to iron out all of life's waves and flatline our emotions.

Let's keep up-to-date with things. Rather than storing all our anger for twenty years until we explode one day, let's just release it little by little every moment. Let the energy, the bubbles, release. One of my friends teaches a kind of Tantric Yoga. She says to release these bubbles, these energy knots, into your aura, into your energy field every moment. Don't store them up. Don't hold on to them and suppress them. Just keep releasing them every moment, like bubbles arising from the depths and popping as they rise to the surface. Can you feel what that would do? Rather than holding it in so you get neckaches and headaches and backaches, release it every moment. Don't tense up and tighten up around these ephemeral energies. If your partner does something you don't like, just say "I don't like that." Don't close it off and hoard it and keep it for ten years until you have ten thousand of these energies built up and you explode and dump all over your mate. Better to stay emotionally up-to-date, every moment. Be honest. Release it, release it, release it. "I don't like that. I wish you wouldn't do that." You can say that. Not, "Don't do that. You shouldn't do that." That's different. Use "I" statements. Simply acknowledge the emotion; don't suppress it. That's how we can integrate clarity into every moment in our life. Just as when we are meditating: allowing things to happen and then pass by, effortlessly doing and undoing themselves so they don't pile up like a big snowdrift. This is the practice of freedom through nonreaction. The more awareness we have, the more we can acknowledge these things rather than just cut them off. Too often, before we even feel an emotion, we cut it off, push it down, suppress it. We make ourselves crazy that way. The internal pressure builds up:

tension, stress, high blood pressure, ulcers, bitterness, resentment. Who needs it?! Release it. It is a great relief not to carry all that shit around. Learn to die a little by releasing each moment, and to be born afresh each moment, too. That's how we can let go of our vestigial tail, our personal story, like so much excess baggage.

The whole sea is in the bubble of the ego. The bubble is transparent and contains the whole sea. You don't have to get rid of your ego; just see through it. You don't have to fight with it. The bubble is the sea, and it is dancing in, and as, the sea already. We don't have to figure it out: yes or no, right or wrong, smaller or bigger, or many or one. These are all just intellectual concepts. Life's a paradox, but only to the mind. Can we tolerate the paradox of yes and no, of will on one hand and allowing on the other? Of course, you can give your opinion and do your best, but you also have to be able to let go, maintaining the bigger perspective. It's a challenge and there's no easy answer. Better to keep the question alive than to come up with some quick, superficial answer. Every moment try to investigate: where is the Middle Way, the golden mean, between the two sides of everything? Concepts are quite limiting. You are not just *that*. This is the view. Concepts are not really a limitation; they are just a momentary form of emptiness. Don't identify with and get stuck in that construct. You can momentarily experience feelings, thoughts, and sensations, but they are not really yours. Just because you feel sharp feelings and have vivid thoughts doesn't mean that you have to bite the bait and get hooked.

The practice of everyday life *is* everyday life. Just doing what needs to be done, no more and no less—neither compulsively overdoing, nor avoiding through quietism and underdoing. Of course, what we bring to everyday life determines whether it is really practice or not; let's not pretend otherwise. It doesn't say in the Bible to be little children; it says to become again *like* little children. Of course, everybody is living everyday life—is actually living spirit—but spiritual practice is to intentionally come back to it again, with conscious awareness, in order to know clearly what's what, which end is up, and who's on first—as Abbott and Costello repeatedly inquired. To be fully aware of that. Then it is true that all beings are Buddhas, in the light of pristine realization. Awakened Buddhas recognize them as Buddhas, but sleeping Buddhas don't; that's the crucial difference. It all depends on the scope and depth of our realization, or awareness wisdom.

In daily life, no fuss. That is very ordinary, but also most extraordinary. Bokden helps us to be supremely natural rather than supernatural. Who can be that simple, rich, and content? The seminal Buddhist philosopher of ancient India, Nagarjuna, said, "Contentment is true wealth." Who can be content to just be with whatever is, and just to do whatever we're doing? Who can just do what we have to do, without resistance, comparing, doubting, or complaining? If not complaining, then crowing about it, being proud of it, making a big deal of it; making it into a story. Telling ourselves stories. Dressing emptiness up in drag simply to suit our own needs and fancies. As a master once told his dog: I told you to fetch, not kvetch! Just doing what has to be done is our true work, with little or no need to be attached to the outcome.

Contentment and acceptance has its own transformative magic. Such spiritual detachment and objective equanimity is not the same as uncaring complacence and indifference. If we care enough, we must learn to accept things as they are even as we feel the desire to improve and change things. Change happens anyway, and we need to accept the flowing, growing, and fleeting nature of things, including ourselves. We can also accept the heartfelt wish arising within us to change things for the better, and act intelligently—after due consideration—on those impulses. Sometimes I feel as if we meditators and yogis in the West are too often just sitting around, sewing our silk robes and building gilded statues and monuments, fiddling with our brocade-covered altars and Oriental antiques while Rome is burning—not to mention the pressing environmental issues, political hypocrisy, spiritual vacuity, social miseries, and the injustices and inequalities of our time. Even if we're on the right path, if we just sit there we'll get run over.

Bokden implies a willingness to step up, break out, live outrageously, and risk being spiritually incorrect. Just as our world's major problems cry out for radical solutions and not just temporary, cosmetic solutions; the prisons of our inner world require total transformation rather than mere interior decoration. I fear that yoga and meditation in this country are becoming mere health hobbies for members of the liberally minded leisure class on the Upper Middle Path, just one more way to pour icing over our cozy little ruts rather than enduring any of the challenges, sacrifices, and anxieties necessary for actually getting out of ingrained ruts and leaving them behind in order to find a new life. The eccentricities and outrageous behavior of the iconoclastic masters of the crazy wisdom lineage are examples of how we might break down our self-imposed limitations and puritanical attachments to divisions between the sacred and the mundane to find the natural state of freedom through fearless authenticity. We sincere seekers are too often rather grim in some way, like Calvinists or fanatic true believers; the idea of enjoying and celebrating life may seem a little frightening to our rather dainty and timid sense of spirituality. The idea of dancing with life might seem frivolous, but we could choose to live like Zorba the Buddha. We don't always have to conform to any model, such as being the perfectly charitable world-saver, or achieve any kind of spiritual success, which is just a more subtle form of ambition. The joy of life is much more simple and surprisingly joyful than that. Like love, authenticity is not necessarily a big achievement. You can't really brag about it, and everyone can realize it. Even though it may actually turn out to be quite a big deal, in the long run, you can't boast about it; nor do you have to do it better than anyone else. You and I are nothing, in the light of sunyata, of wisdom. Yet, mysteriously enough, one is everything: one with everyone and everything, in the light of unconditional love and interbeing. And in the creative tension between these two sides we find the Middle Way, the golden mean, that is our true life.

That's why dancing is so great. I think dancing with life is a good image of how we can go along. Thomas Merton, a truly erudite and serious seeker, said, "God prays by dancing." Did you ever practice dancing until you drop? It's a great practice. In Dzogchen we do that sometimes. In some kinds of unconventional practices such as rushen (subtle discernment), you strive to exhaust yourself through energetic movements until you just collapse; then, in that moment, when you can't even remember who you are anymore, pop the question: Who am I? What is this right now? That's the moment to turn the mind on itself. When you can't even move, when you can't even be yourself anymore—then what? Who are you? What is the animating principle, ultimately, the hand inside this Muppet?

Let's take this principle out into life, and not hold back, shield, barricade, and protect ourselves, like we're saving ourselves for the real job or hoarding our energy for later. This is the real work. Let's renounce holding back. It is now or never, as always. American Buddhas, awaken—take back your authentic life.

WHAT I TEACH AND WHY

I was on *The Colbert Report* comedy TV show recently, and when host Stephen Colbert asked me what I teach, I replied, "Sanity." This got me to thinking.

It's too simple to take the easy way out and say I teach Buddhism, or Dharma, as we like to call it, and particularly Tibetan Buddhism—especially the profound direct-access Dzogchen meditation and nondual outlook—and that I lead meditation retreats and workshops, give classes and lectures, write, translate texts, and introduce Tibetan masters to America. Generally speaking, all Buddhist teachers teach what Buddha taught as the way to realize enlightened wisdom akin to his own, for this remains his ultimate intention, gift, and raison d'être. As Dharma teachers, we base our work on the Buddhist teachings of the Four Noble Truths, the Eightfold Path, and the panacean paramita virtues. And we cover discerning wisdom, loving actions, altruism, unconditional compassion and kindness, ethical self-discipline, mindfulness, nonattachment, contentment, serenity, and nonviolence. Specifically, we teach the way of awakening from confusion and delusion through the enlightening middle path of awareness cultivation, which helps us to develop objective clarity and balance, inner freedom naturalness, happiness, and authenticity. This awakening brings the realization of ultimate reality, complete peace, and the blissful harmony known as nirvana.

Like many of my Western Dharma teacher colleagues, I am more interested in teaching the transformative principles and enlightening practices of Dharma wisdom as they relate to universal concerns on the inner quest, and how to understand and adapt, integrate, and realize timeless wisdom and love, rather than teaching the historical and cosmological background of Buddhism from which our ancient practice lineage has emerged.

Like my own Asian masters, elucidating and transmitting the essence of Dharma itself seems more important to me than just teaching about Buddhism as an academic, theological, historical, cultural, and political phenomenon, or about the sociology of its development in the modern world. Nor am I satisfied to see Buddhism become just one more form of self-help or coping therapy, just a healing modality or mere relaxation technique—although Dharma does cure our deepest afflictions and has proved conducive to both physical and mental health. In Dharma talks, I strive to cover the many Buddhist topics one by one, emphasizing how they can be practiced and understood, then applied and integrated for the betterment of all. I try to teach only what I practice and know from personal experience.

People today generally are not very interested in studying cosmology, belief systems, ontology, and philosophy; performing rituals; memorizing and reciting texts; or praying for better rebirths. They seem more interested in attaining the practical and reasonably immediate benefits of practicing yoga, meditation, and prayerful chants; finding health and healing through right living and right livelihood; simplifying their busy lives; learning to manage difficult emotions; cultivating gratitude; and developing the inner wisdom, joy, compassion, and love that is at the heart of us all. For these practical and achievable goals, the Buddhist practice of mindful living is remarkably well suited. Comparatively new on these shores, Buddhism seems to be refreshingly insightful, instructive, useful, relevant, and even scientific in an interior way. Buddhism and neuroscience, for example, have lately found a marvelous intermarriage that is bringing forth a plethora of new discoveries and benefits. This relatively recent opening to Eastern wisdom provides us with a historical, teachable moment in which to take full advantage of what Buddhism has to offer before it becomes overly institutionalized, commoditized, and even taken for granted. Buddhist practice is good in both this life and the next, and has both temporal and ultimate benefits. Moreover, I believe that what we do with it now will help determine the course of Buddhism in the West, and will help us attain what Keats termed "knowledge enormous." Just knowing about the Dharma is insufficient; we must become what we seek. The secret is daily practice.

We need to transform the atmosphere of religion in our country today, with its spiritual vacuity and patriarchies; intolerance and prejudice; insularity and even cultism; and the yawning partisan chasm between the dogmatic true believers on the one hand and the disenfranchised masses of disillusioned, free-thinking individuals—many in recovery from disappointing early religious instruction—on the other. I sense that the hopeful new Obama era augurs well for more tolerance and diversity in religious as well as cultural and political matters, although age-old animosities and strife cannot be easily ignored in the larger global picture. In both my personal practice and teachings, I emphasize nonsectarian, humanistic, psychologically astute and practical ways of working consciously on oneself and together, including relational mindfulness and group and community practice. This includes meditation and self-inquiry, yoga, breath and energy work, ethical self-discipline, unselfishness and generosity, nonviolence, healthy living, and universal responsibility. We begin with ourselves and each other, loving our way to enlightenment. For we need each other to develop the warmhearted compassion, unselfish altruism, and discriminating wisdom that comprise enlightenment. I try to promote critical thinking and spiritual intelligence among my students, along with the spirit of free inquiry, while inculcating joyful, service-oriented leadership rather than mere followership, so we all progress together.

Dharma means wisdom, reality, spirituality—that subtle elixir of truth and selfless love that heals what divides us. We need to import the Noble Dharma (*Su-Dharma*) and not just culture, which would be merely more exotic, foreign forms of creed and doctrine, of which there is already no shortage in our diverse society. Nor is there a shortage of ancient foreign artifacts and Oriental antiques. What do seem to be in short supply are the actual wisdom techniques and profound and efficacious practices that the yogic and meditative traditions of Asia— especially from the great Indian subcontinent and the Himalayan region—offer intact and in abundance. This is the inexhaustible mine of sublime Dharma that I daily endeavor to further learn, teach, preserve, apply, translate, and share with those who are interested. Natural meditation, emphasizing the naked-awareness practices of Dzogchen, the innate Great Perfection teachings of Tibet, provides direct access to the enlightened aspect of our true nature and does not necessarily require a great deal of theory, ritual, or other complicated preparations. Here we find the nondual, direct-access teachings that *we are all Buddhas by nature* in the holy now. We only have to awaken to who and what we truly are. This leads us directly to living an enlightened life here and now.

All the sutra teachings spoken by the enlightened Buddha are available for us to study and learn—the fruit of his enlightenment as expressed during his forty-five-year-long teaching career in this world—as are the numerous texts, commentaries, tantras, sacred art and music, meditation manuals, and whispered oral pith instructions. We also have the inexhaustible oral lore of the lineage saints and masters handed down through the centuries to inspire and guide us, recounting in fabulous detail how they lived, became enlightened, taught, and transmitted the vital essence of inner realization while continuing to practice spiritual living. This is the living flame of enlightenment that has been passed from teacher to student since the time of Buddha until today.

All the schools, traditions, and lineages of BuddhaDharma

are included in this landscape of Buddhism in the many countries where it has flourished for twenty-five hundred years, regardless of the color of the robes, the language of the chants, or the emphasis of the teachings. The voluminous Buddhist tradition contains a wealth of tools and techniques useful for those of us who seek freedom from confusion, negativity, and conditioning; the attainment of profound wisdom and inner peace; and inner illumination through self-knowledge and spiritual realization. Buddhism is an inner science of mind and genuine higher education as well as a guide to the enlightened life, a truing device for the heart, and a touchstone for the soul of those who don't know the unmistaken causes of happiness and unhappiness or where they are to be found. In other words, that what we seek and need is not necessarily to be found outside, but can be found within—by looking deeper. For as Buddha taught and demonstrated, the mind and body are workable, malleable, changing; no situation is completely hopeless; and happiness and fulfillment are learnable skills and achievable goals, requiring only understanding, effort, perseverance, and patient cultivation. We can fulfill our own humanity's great promise and potential, heart and soul, if only we know how to do so and are willing and able to proceed.

To help bring the ancient yet timeless wisdom of the enlightened ones down from the roof of the world, as the Himalayas are known, and into our lives, we must consider not just what has been taught and transmitted through the ages, but also how to teach and authentically transmit the liberating essence of Dharma here and now. In creating a future for Buddhism in the West, we need to improvise and experiment, imaginatively adapting timeless Dharma principles through skillful means to enable these contemplative practices to lead us to engaged wisdom and selfless activism. With this in mind, I strive to translate not only the words but also the concepts of Eastern thought and philosophy in a manner conducive to daily practice and understanding by modern Western seekers. This is my attempt to further spiritual literacy and to demystify the insider language of esoteric Vajrayana Buddhism, making it accessible so that we may bring the mystic fire down from the high Himalayas and onto our own paths, igniting our internal lamps and warming our hearts so that we may—to shift metaphors—assume the authentic high ground ourselves. For it is the lofty and noble inner Himalayas that we most need to keep alive, beyond any external borders or nationalities. Like the lineage masters before us, we can emerge into and occupy the splendid mansion of transpersonal, transcendent yet imminent divine spirit, innate Buddha nature.

When it comes to our ancient yet timeless wisdom tradition, most contemporary Dharma teachers are aware of the challenges involved in preserving and maintaining while simultaneously interpreting and adapting the unchanging pure essence of Dharma amid a multiplicity of places and circumstances, changing forms and appearances, languages and modes of communication, as Buddhist ethics and insight are transmitted, practiced, and applied in new worlds and new times. Historians say that one of the most important events of the twentieth century was the fruitful encounter between Buddhism and the West. At this tipping point in the movement of transformative Dharma from East to West, it appears crucial that teachers and students, translators, interpreters, facilitators, and patrons alike serve as accessible bridges between East and West without losing the bigger picture, remaining well aware of roots and origins, being Buddha's own intent and purposes—where it all comes from—as well as where it is now, how it's developing and why, and the most fruitful direction for American Dharma traditions. With one foot firmly planted in the venerable tradition and the other in the present, we can serve the spiritual thirst of many by providing the elixir of BuddhaDharma like fine old wine in new bottles with appropriate labels.

In striving to maintain a presence online and in teleteaching, media, bookstores, and on college campuses, the speaking circuit—as well as in meditation halls, temples, ashrams, seminaries, churches, and spiritual centers everywhere—I aim to present living Buddhism as it authentically was, is, and can be. Perhaps this combination of venues can help to redress some of the misconceptions that exist about Buddhism in our Western world today, where it is fairly new and unknown compared with the three Abrahamic faiths: Judaism, Christianity, and Islam. In actual fact, Buddhism has been in the West for more than a hundred and fifty years, with some popularity and significant depth for fifty or sixty years. It seems vitally important to emphasize transformative teachings and skillful practices in order to lay the groundwork for fully enlightened teachers to arise on these shores, rather than indulging in proselytizing, empire building, or religious politics. So, future Buddhas of America, awaken! Throw off your chains—your illusions, concepts, and hang-ups. Help usher in the peacedom of Buddha. You are the ones!

I believe that the radiant essence of Dharma is daily spiritual life itself. Our lives must become mingled with and eventually realized as one with Dharma for us to find what we seek and long for, however unconsciously, to be and become what we are and can be. Like suitable clothes, Dharma must *fit*; otherwise, what good is it? Dharma teachings must remain alive, adaptive, and applicable, integrated with modern life, not ossified or preserved like ancient dried-out relics or museum pieces. If Dharma practice doesn't fit, we won't be able to practice it regularly, thoroughly, continuously—as needed to edify and transform our lives. The best spiritual practice is the one we do regularly and that ultimately *does* us. Dharma is an inside job, and continuity is the secret of success.

Experienced spiritual teachers and suitably fitting teachings are essential. The presence, personal guidance, and experiential instructions of a living master is one key that unlocks our growth potential. A good relationship with a living master who embodies the teachings and walks the talk can model how it works here and now; answer our questions; and provide regular spiritual tune-ups year after year, while suitably tailoring the practices in accordance with our capacities, aspirations, interests, obstacles, and possibilities. In India, it is said that the guru is the doorway to God, truth, and reality. The Buddha, guru, and oneself are actually, mystically, one and inseparable from the very first. A wise guru is like a mirror, reflecting our highest, truest, most authentic self and interior being. A spiritual teacher is like a caring, truth-telling, unselfish mate. There is nowhere to hide from the unflinching, benevolent gaze, however discomfiting it may sometimes feel. A guru has been likened to a bonfire; those who fear the heat of transformation should not stay too close.

There are many maps and frameworks for spiritual life and development. My own Six Building Blocks of Spiritual Practice is a nonsectarian, postdenominational framework that forms a firm foundation for an authentic, beautiful, wise, and liberating spiritual life. These practices will help bring spirituality down from the mountaintop and out beyond the monastery walls in assimilating the liberating Dharma into our daily lives. These practices can easily be integrated into life today with its complex challenges, changes, and uncertainties—without renouncing the world and withdrawing to a cave, desert, monastery, nunnery, or ashram. Integration is the way now, not seclusion and asceticism. What we do need to renounce is self-centeredness, selfishness, ignorance, deception, and violence, not necessarily external possessions and relationships. It is not outer things but inner ignorance and attachments that entangle us, as the masters agree.

These six building blocks of a personal practice can help create a spiritual life from scratch and more fully develop the foundation of a well-rounded, doable, meaningful, and effective spiritual practice. They are:

1. Daily-ish formal personal practice, such as meditation, yoga, chanting, and prayer
2. Spiritual study, introspective self-scrutiny, and opening the book of nature and/or the book of significant relationships
3. Inner growth work, self-inquiry, journaling, creative work, psychotherapy, and support groups
4. Group practice, relationship mindfulness, parenting, and community life
5. Learning from teachers and wise elders
6. Altruistic service and spiritual activism, community making, mentoring, volunteerism, and environmental responsibility

The first triad of the six building blocks is more alone-ish, and the second triad is more related to others, although these are not hard-and-fast categories. I believe that anyone can positively transform his or her life by taking on one or more of these building blocks, regardless of religious affiliation or spiritual orientation. Continuity is the secret of success, as my first meditation teacher always used to say. Conscientiousness and sincerity of intention and purpose also help. Most of us will recognize these things as part of the lives we already lead and be encouraged. For we are spiritual beings living meaningful lives rather than mere lost souls struggling to survive. The hidden river of spiritual energy and blessings already runs right through us and our lives, whether we always recognize it or not. Signs of it are abundant. We may feel far from the light of truth and reality, or even divinity, but I assure you that it is never far from us.

There are many extraordinary teachers and teachings available today, and countless spiritual gatherings and events we can attend. At some point, commitment becomes important. We may have spiritual experiences, breakthroughs, insights, epiphanies, glimpses of reality, or satoris. But a single experience or uplifting weekend, however genuine, does not an enlightened *life* make. To develop a transformative and meaningful spiritual life, we need to follow up on and develop these breakthroughs, glimpses, and epiphanies, ironing out each peak experience into the valleys, depths, wrinkles, and ruts in the plains of daily life. It seems today it's easier to get enlightened than to stay enlightened—in that sense of the word *enlightenment*. Many claim to have had the experience, but few demonstrate the enlightened qualities and lead enlightened lives as exemplified by authentically enlightened beings past and present. We, too, can evolve from our initial enlightenment experiences into an unshakably principled and spontaneous spiritual life, as an enlightened embodiment illumining this ephemeral world for the betterment of all.

In a vivid dream one night, the Dalai Lama handed me a burgundy lama robe and said: "I only wish to lift everyone up." It is my hope that this collection of new Dharma talks will help us continue to benefit from the profound wisdom, liberating practices, and ethical training of the ancient yet timeless Buddhist Dharma tradition; assist us to become wiser, kinder, happier, and more sane people, and to pass it on to the younger generations; and help us co-create a better, more beautiful, safe, and peaceful world. Please join me in these prayerful aspirations.

Dzogchen Osel Ling Retreat Center
Austin, Texas
Easter 2009

INDEX

To Contact Lama Surya Das, go to:

Dzogchen Center
www.dzogchen.org
www.surya.org

P.O. Box 340459, Austin, Texas 78734

DZOGCHEN
FOUNDATION